INTERNATIONAL WILDLIFE LAW

An analysis of international treaties concerned
with the conservation of wildlife

INTERNATIONAL WILDLIFE LAW

An analysis of international treaties concerned
with the conservation of wildlife

by
SIMON LYSTER

A PUBLICATION OF
THE RESEARCH CENTRE FOR INTERNATIONAL LAW,
UNIVERSITY OF CAMBRIDGE
in association with
THE INTERNATIONAL UNION FOR CONSERVATION OF NATURE
AND NATURAL RESOURCES

CAMBRIDGE

GROTIUS PUBLICATIONS LIMITED
1985

SALES: GROTIUS PUBLICATIONS LTD.
LLANDYSUL, DYFED SA44 4BQ, UK
ADMINISTRATION: GROTIUS PUBLICATIONS LTD.
PO BOX 115, CAMBRIDGE CB3 9BP, UK

©

GROTIUS PUBLICATIONS LIMITED
1985

International Standard Book Number: 0 906496 22 5

Typeset by Afal, Cardiff

Printed in Great Britain by
Gomer Press, Llandysul, Dyfed

Cover Image supplied by National Remote Sensing Centre, Farnborough

CONTENTS

PART II

PART III

Appendix: Texts of Conventions

Many people seem to think that the conservation of nature is simply a matter of being kind to animals and enjoying walks in the countryside. Sadly, perhaps, it is a great deal more complicated than that. For one thing nature consists of both plants and animals as well as the places and environment in which they struggle to survive. Furthermore every animal and some plants only survive at the expense of other animals or plants and mankind has gradually become the most significant exploiter of nature of them all.

The most urgent problem of the conservation of nature is to control this exploitation and to modify the consequences of the massive increase in the world's human population.

Part of the solution lies in specific projects designed to directly protect the most endangered species and their habitats but these can only be last ditch attempts to save species from almost immediate extinction. In the long term effective conservation of the multitude of species in the plant and animal worlds depends upon acceptance and conscientious application of specific obligations under national and international law.

In this book Simon Lyster has rendered a most valuable service to the cause of conservation of nature worldwide by setting out in detail the purposes and provisions of the major international treaties and conventions designed to give the remaining wild places and populations of our world a reasonable chance of survival. I am glad that this is a subject with which the Research Centre for International Law in Cambridge University is now closely concerned.

Much more needs to be done in the fields of national legislation and international conventions but the existing conventions provide a solid base. As usual with all legal systems, the crucial requirement.is for the terms of the conventions to be widely accepted and rapidly implemented. Regretfully progress in this direction is proving disastrously slow. I hope very much that this book will help to speed things up before it is too late.

1984.

ACKNOWLEDGEMENTS

First and foremost I would like to thank William B. Roe without whose support this book would never have been possible. I would also like to thank Jocelyn Alexander and Harry Tarak for their very generous help. The Center for Environmental Education, the New York Zoological Society, the Fauna and Flora Preservation Society, Defenders of Wildlife, the Society for Animal Protective Legislation, Fund for Animals (Australia), World Wildlife Fund — India, World Wildlife Fund — U.K. and the Research Centre for International Law, University of Cambridge have all given assistance in one form or another, and I am extremely grateful to these organisations.

Hilary Carrington, Maria Dennard and Bixie Nash all put in long hours of typing (and re-typing!). Jenelle Arnold had the invidious task of checking and revising my references in order to ensure they were correctly cited. Robin Pirrie and Marty Devine have each devoted many hours to seeing the work through the press. Many people were kind enough to read drafts of the book as it emerged and to make helpful and constructive criticisms. They are too numerous to list, but I would like to express special gratitude to Jane Thornback and my father, John Lyster, who both gave up enormous amounts of their precious free time to help in the seemingly never-ending process of re-drafting and editing.

Simon Lyster
31 December 1984

ABBREVIATIONS

A.T.S.	Australian Treaty Series
B.F.S.P.	British and Foreign State Papers
CCAMLR	Convention on the Conservation of Antarctic Marine Living Resources
C.F.R.	Code of Federal Regulations (United States of America)
CITES	Convention on International Trade in Endangered Species of Wild Fauna and Flora
EEC	European Economic Community
Europ. T.S.	European Treaty Series
FAO	Food and Agriculture Organization of the United Nations
GATT	General Agreement on Tariffs and Trade
I.C.J. Reports	International Court of Justice Reports
I.L.M.	International Legal Materials
I.L.R.	International Law Reports
IUCN	International Union for Conservation of Nature and Natural Resources
IWC	International Whaling Commission
IWRB	International Waterfowl Research Bureau
L.N.T.S.	League of Nations Treaty Series
NGO	Non-governmental Organisation
OAS	Organization of American States
OAU	Organization of African Unity
O.J. Eur. Comm.	Official Journal of the European Communities
SCAR	Scientific Committee on Antarctic Research
SCOR	Scientific Committee on Oceanic Research
SSSI	Site of Special Scientific Interest
Stat.	Statutes at Large (before 31 Dec. 1949, United States of America)

TAC	Total Allowable Catch Limit
T.I.A.S.	Treaties and Other International Acts Series
Treaty Series	United States Treaty Series (before 1945)
U.K.T.S.	United Kingdom Treaty Series
UNEP	United Nations Environment Programme
UNESCO	United Nations Educational, Scientific and Cultural Organization
U.N.T.S.	United Nations Treaty Series
U.S.C.	United States Code
U.S.T.	United States Treaties and Other International Agreements
WWF	World Wildlife Fund

INTRODUCTION

The use of law to protect wildlife has existed for centuries. Forestry conservation laws in Babylon date back to 1900 BC. Akhenaten, King of Egypt, set aside land as a nature reserve in 1370 BC. Emperor Ashoka of India issued a decree in the third century BC which has a particularly contemporary ring about it. Towards the end of his reign, he wrote:

> Twenty six years after my coronation, I declared that the following animals were not to be killed: parrots, mynas, the aruna, ruddy geese, wild geese, the nandimukha, cranes, bats, queen ants, terrapins, boneless fish, rhinoceroses. . .and all quadrupeds which are not useful or edible. . .Forests must not be burned.

However, the use of international treaties to protect wildlife is a more recent development. The first such treaty, the Treaty Concerning the Regulation of Salmon Fishing in the Rhine River Basin, was signed by Germany, Luxembourg, the Netherlands and Switzerland in 1886. Several more wildlife treaties were concluded in the first half of this century, but it is only in the last twenty five years that there has been a dramatic increase both in their number and in their importance as a force for conservation.

In one sense it is surprising that wildlife treaties have taken so long to develop. The need for international cooperation to protect species which migrate from one country to another, which are in demand for their skins in foreign markets or which live on the high seas, has existed for a long time. However, it is only recently that conservation problems have become so grave and the need for international cooperation has become so compelling that governments have felt bound to act. International trade in ivory and other wildlife products goes back for centuries, but in the last twenty five years it has become a multi-million dollar business threatening the very survival of many animals and plants. Animals in territory belonging to nobody, such as the high seas or Antarctica, have always been vulnerable because they are open to exploitation by everybody, but only recently has man developed catching techniques capable of wiping out entire stocks and freezing techniques making large-scale fishing trips to distant oceans commercially viable. Migratory species have long been subjected to shooting and trapping on their migratory routes, but it is in the last two or three decades that the more invidious threats of pesticide use and habitat degradation have become so serious as to make international cooperation to protect migratory species a vital necessity.

This book is the first comprehensive analysis of international wildlife law. It describes twenty seven treaties in detail and many others in brief. It is divided into four parts. Part I is a brief description of basic principles of international law and how they relate to wildlife treaties. Part II looks at treaties designed to protect either a single species or a group of species. In the former category treaties have been specially concluded for polar bears, (*Ursus maritimus*), vicuna (*Vicugna vicugna*) and northern fur seals (*Callorhinus ursinus*), while in the latter category there are treaties for whales, migratory birds, Antarctic seals and North Atlantic seals. These species or groups of species have been made the subject of separate treaties because they are particularly vulnerable to human exploitation, and many of them have been heavily over-exploited in the past. With a few exceptions, these treaties concentrate on restricting the killing or trading of animals rather than dealing with other threats such as loss of habitat.

Part III examines four regional nature conservation treaties affecting the Americas, Africa, Europe and Antarctica. In contrast to the treaties in Part II, the main emphasis of the first three of these treaties is on habitat protection, while the fourth is primarily designed to limit fishing in Antarctic waters to a level which will not damage the Antarctic marine ecosystem. The Parties to this latter treaty were particularly concerned that the development of a krill fishery in Antarctica should not impede the recovery of depleted populations of baleen whales which depend upon krill for food.

Part IV covers the 'big four' wildlife treaties, which were all concluded in the 1970s and are open to almost any country wishing to join them. They cover wetlands, habitats of outstanding universal value, international trade in wildlife and migratory species. They form the centrepiece of international wildlife law, and are by far the most important treaties discussed in this book.

Two final introductory comments need to be made. Firstly, this book is limited to treaties directly concerned with wildlife conservation. As a result, it does not describe the many treaties on pollution and other factors affecting wildlife. They are ignored solely for reasons of manageability to prevent the book from running into several volumes, and not out of any belittlement of their importance to a healthy natural environment. Secondly, fisheries treaties are excluded — except for the treaty regulating fishing in Antarctic waters, mentioned above, which covers more than just fish. There are more than fifty bilateral and multilateral fisheries treaties, and to have examined them all in detail would have added enormously to the length of the book. In addition, international fisheries law has been covered by other writers, and it seems more sensible to limit this book to subject matter which has not been described elsewhere.

PART I

CHAPTER 1

BASIC PRINCIPLES OF INTERNATIONAL WILDLIFE LAW

"We must indeed all hang together, or most assuredly we shall all hang separately."
(Benjamin Franklin, at the signing of the Declaration of Independence)

1. *Introduction*

There are two kinds of international law: private and public. Private international law is concerned, primarily on the plane of relations between individuals, with the resolution of conflicts between the laws of different States. It is not relevant for the purposes of this book and will not be considered any further. Public international law is the system governing relations between States and covers every aspect of inter-State relations such as jurisdiction, claims to territory, use of the sea and State responsibility, to name but a few. Public international law can be subdivided into treaty law — in which the obligations of States are enshrined in and derived from a written agreement, usually known as a treaty or convention — and customary law, which embraces all international law not specifically included in treaties. Since this book is concerned exclusively with treaties and conventions which protect wildlife, this chapter is limited to a description of some of the principal aspects of the law relating to treaties.

2. *Nature of treaties*

Most States have a supreme law-making body — a Parliament, a Soviet, a National Assembly or similar organisation — to adopt laws for their citizens. The international community, however, has no legislature capable of formulating laws binding on individual States or their peoples without their individual consent. Consequently, treaties and conventions have developed as a means by which States wishing to cooperate on a certain course of action can establish mutual legal obligations to pursue that end. Since there are more and more activities in the modern world which require international cooperation and agreement if they are to be efficiently carried out, treaties and conventions have proliferated in recent years. More treaties are now concluded in one average year than were concluded in the first two decades of the twentieth century. They cover subjects as diverse as the international mail, nuclear non-proliferation and wildlife conservation, and they range from bilateral arrangements to large multilateral agreements by which as many as 130 States may be bound.

Whereas national legislation can be strong because the will of the majority in a State's law-making body is normally sufficient to override the opposition of the minority, treaties are often (although not invariably) weaker because no State can be bound without its consent. The greater the number of participants in the formulation of a treaty, the weaker or more ambiguous its provisions are likely to be since they have to reflect compromises making them acceptable to every State involved. Wildlife treaties, which are often intended to attract a large number of Parties, are especially exposed to this risk.

3. *Formation of treaties*

There is no uniform procedure for the conclusion of a treaty. The process of elaboration may begin in a committee consisting of representatives of a small group of States or within an international organisation. In the case of general "law making" treaties, the International Law Commission of the United Nations plays a special role.

Wildlife treaties have generated from a variety of different sources. International organisations such as the Pan American Union (now the Organization of American States), the United Nations Educational, Scientific and Cultural Organization and the Organization of African Unity have all been responsible for the formulation of important wildlife treaties. Another significant driving force has been the International Union for Conservation of Nature and Natural Resources ("IUCN"). Formed in 1948 as an independent international organisation with the objective of promoting wise use of the earth's natural resources, IUCN has a membership consisting of governments, government agencies and non-governmental organisations from 111 countries. It played a major role in the formulation of the African Convention on the Conservation of Nature and Natural Resources, the Convention on International Trade in Endangered Species of Wild Fauna and Flora, the Agreement on the Conservation of Polar Bears and the Convention on the Conservation of Migratory Species of Wild Animals. IUCN also contributed, although to a lesser extent, to the conclusion of the Convention on Wetlands of International Importance Especially as Waterfowl Habitat and the Convention Concerning the Protection of the World Cultural and Natural Heritage.

Special interest groups have also stimulated the conclusion of wildlife treaties. Hunters anxious to maintain a healthy supply of their prey species have pressed for migratory bird treaties, and so have farmers who were worried about declining populations of insect eating birds. Whalers concerned about decreasing whale stocks were the main proponents of an international system to regulate whaling, and the same can be said for sealers and sealing treaties.

Generally speaking, the last stage in the formulation of a treaty is the holding of a conference at which plenipotentiaries — duly authorised representatives of participating States — sign the agreed text. However, signature alone is generally insufficient for a State to become a Party to a treaty and thereby legally bound by its terms. To become a Party, the signature must be confirmed by a process known as ratification. A treaty will only enter into force when a certain number of signatories — usually specified in the text of the treaty — have deposited instruments of ratification. Although ratification is the most commonly used term, some treaties use the words "acceptance" or "approval" as well. For example, Article XVI of the Convention on the Conservation of Migratory Species of Wild Animals states that the Convention "shall be subject to ratification, acceptance or approval."

States which are not among the original signatories to a treaty are often allowed to become Parties at a later stage by a process known as "accession".

a) *Signature*

The fact that a State has signed a treaty does not impose a legal obligation on it to ratify at a later stage. Brierly, a leading international lawyer, stated that "there is no legal nor even moral duty on a State to ratify a treaty signed by its own plenipotentiaries; it can only be said that refusal is a serious step which ought not to be taken lightly."[1]

Although signature does not alone impose a legal obligation to abide by the terms of a treaty, the Vienna Convention on the Law of Treaties,[2] which codifies rules of international law on the subject of treaties, stipulates that signature creates an obligation of good faith to refrain from acts calculated to frustrate the objects of the treaty until the signatory State makes it clear that it does not intend to become a Party.[3]

[1] Brierly, *The Law of Nations* (6th ed., 1963), p. 320.
[2] U.N. Doc. A/CONF.39/27; 8 *I.L.M.* 679; *U.K.T.S.* no. 58 (1980), Cmd. 7964. The Convention came into force on 27 January 1980.
[3] Vienna Convention, Article 18.

b) *Ratification*

The idea of ratification developed because it was thought reasonable that, after a treaty had been signed, States should have a further opportunity to consider the often complex and important issues involved before finally becoming legally bound by them. Signatories may also need time to enact any necessary national implementing legislation. In addition, the power to bind a State to a treaty is often vested in an organ of government which cannot itself conduct negotiations with other States. The Constitution of the United States of America, for example, grants the President the authority to negotiate and sign treaties, but ratification requires the advice and consent of the U.S. Senate. The actual act of ratification consists of deposit of a formal written instrument with the depositary government or organisation.

c) *Accession*

It is common practice for treaties to specify a certain time limit within which they may be signed and to allow States which do not sign within that limit to become Parties at a later date by the single step of depositing an instrument of "accession". The Convention on International Trade in Endangered Species of Wild Flora and Fauna ("CITES"),[4] for example, was concluded on 6 March 1973 and was signed by 21 States on that date. The text of the Convention specifies that any other State wishing to sign had until 31 December 1974 to do so.[5] However, it allows States failing to meet the signature deadline to become Parties at any time thereafter simply by depositing an instrument of accession with the depositary government.[6] At the time of writing 87 States are Parties to CITES, and the vast majority have become Parties since 1974 by means of the accession procedure.

d) *Entry into force*

A bilateral treaty obviously needs to be signed and, if ratification is required, ratified by both signatories in order to enter into force. However in the case of multilateral treaties, where the requirement of ratification is more general, the number of ratifications required for entry into force varies considerably. For example, Article XXII(1) of CITES states that the Convention "shall enter into force 90 days after the date of deposit of the tenth instrument of

---

[4] 12 *I.L.M.* 1085; *T.I.A.S.* no. 8249; *U.K.T.S.* no. 101 (1976) Cmd. 6647; 27 *U.S.T.* 1087.
[5] CITES, Article XIX.
[6] CITES, Article XXI. For a detailed discussion of the Convention, see Chapter 12 below.

ratification, acceptance, approval or accession with the Depositary Government." This did not occur until 1 July 1975, more than two years after the Convention was signed. The Law of the Sea Convention (1982), which has been signed by 134 States, will not come into force until one year after 60 States have deposited instruments of ratification, acceptance, approval or accession. Since just nine signatories have ratified the Convention at the time of writing, its entry into force is bound to take considerably longer than CITES.

4. *Participation in treaties*

Treaties vary considerably as to which States they allow to become Parties to them. It is a matter for express provision in each case. The Convention on International Trade in Endangered Species of Wild Fauna and Flora, for example, has no restrictions on participation other than that Parties must either be sovereign States or, under an amendment to the Convention which is not yet in force, "regional economic integration organisations". This amendment was adopted in order to allow the European Economic Community to become a Party to the Convention. Other treaties are more limited as to which States may participate in them. The Agreement on the Conservation of Polar Bears, for example, is open only to the five circumpolar States; the Convention on Nature Protection and Wildlife Preservation in the Western Hemisphere is restricted to member States of the Organization of American States; the Convention Concerning the Protection of the World Cultural and Natural Heritage is open to member States of the United Nations Educational, Scientific and Cultural Organization ("UNESCO") and to non-members specially invited to accede by the General Conference of UNESCO.

5. *Interpretation of treaties*

Article 31(1) of the Vienna Convention on the Law of Treaties states that:

> A treaty shall be interpreted in good faith in accordance with the ordinary meaning to be given to the terms of the treaty in their context and in the light of its object and purpose.

Article 32 permits recourse to supplementary means of interpretation such as the use of the preparatory work leading to a treaty and consideration of the circumstances of its negotiation. But this is allowed only when the ordinary meaning of the text is ambiguous or obscure or when the ordinary meaning of the text leads to a result "which is manifestly absurd or unreasonable". It is important to remember the dominant role attributed to the textual approach to interpretation by Article 31(1) of the Vienna Convention — i.e. the text of a treaty is the best guide to the most recent common intention of its Parties — when considering the meaning of the treaties examined in this book. Unless there is an ambiguity or evident absurdity, a treaty should always be interpreted strictly in accordance with the ordinary meaning of the words it uses in the light of its object and purpose. An interpretation which fulfils, rather than frustrates, the objectives of the treaty should be preferred if there is any ambiguity.

Preambles, which set out in general terms the purposes of a treaty and the principles behind its adoption, also have a role in interpretation. The International Court of Justice has used preambles to elucidate the meaning of clauses in a treaty[7] and to indicate the climate in which they should be read.[8] There have even been instances in which the International Court of Justice has suggested that the provisions of a preamble are as binding as the main text of a treaty. In the *Rights of Nationals of the U.S.A. in Morocco* case, speaking of the "principle of economic liberty without any inequality ...inserted in the Preamble of the Act of [Algeciras]", the International Court of Justice stated:

> It seems clear that the principle was intended to be of a binding character and not merely an empty phrase.[9]

The preambles to several wildlife treaties bind their Parties to very strong conservation principles. "Wishing to protect and preserve in their natural habitat representatives of all species and genera of their native flora and fauna, including migratory birds, in sufficient numbers and over areas extensive enough to assure them from becoming extinct through any agency within man's control..." (preamble to the Convention on Nature Protection and Wildlife Preservation in the Western Hemisphere); "recognising the importance of safeguarding the environment and protecting the integrity of the ecosystem of the seas surrounding Antarctica" (preamble to the Convention on the Conservation of Antarctic Marine Living Resources); and "recognising that wild animals in their innumerable forms are an irreplaceable part of the earth's natural system which must be conserved for the good of mankind"

---

[7] See the *Asylum* case, *I.C.J. Reports* 1950 at p. 282.
[8] See the *Rights of Nationals of the U.S.A. in Morocco* case, *I.C.J. Reports* 1952 at p. 196.
[9] *Ibid.* at p. 148.

(preamble to the Convention on the Conservation of Migratory Species of Wild Animals) provide just a few examples.

6.   *Reservations*

Multilateral treaties frequently contain provisions allowing Parties, if they wish, to release themselves from certain aspects of the treaty. The exercise of this right is generally known as making a "reservation".

There are two types of reservations, and they need to be carefully distinguished. The first type is a reservation to a substantive article of a treaty made at the time a State becomes a Party to the treaty. For example, the International Convention for the Regulation of Whaling applies to "all waters",[10] yet Peru and Chile both made reservations on ratifying the Convention in 1979 to the effect that none of the provisions of the Convention diminished their sovereign rights up to 200 miles from their respective coastlines. The second type of reservation is, strictly speaking, not a reservation at all although, confusingly, it is often hailed as such. It occurs when a Party registers a declaration that it does not accept a regulation adopted under convention procedures. For instance, the International Whaling Commission meets annually and has the authority to amend the Schedule to the International Convention for the Regulation of Whaling. The Schedule contains details of whale quotas, permissible hunting methods etc. In 1982 the International Whaling Commission decided to impose zero quotas on commercially exploited whales from 1986. Japan, Norway and the U.S.S.R. each registered an objection to this decision, and their objection is an example of this second type of reservation.[11]

Reservations — in whichever sense the word is used — are useful because they encourage States to join, and to continue to participate in, a treaty in circumstances where they are prepared to accept most but not all of its provisions. However, reservations also provide a loophole enabling a State to defend its vested interests which conflict with the spirit of the treaty. For example, the Convention on International Trade in Endangered Species of Wild Fauna and Flora regulates international trade in specimens of species listed in three Appendices to the treaty, but it has a reservations clause allowing Parties to exempt themselves from trade controls on any species listed in the Appendices which they specify at the time they become Parties. They may also make reservations with respect to any changes to the Appendices made at a later date and thereby

[10] See p. 21 below.
[11] See p. 27 below.

exempt themselves from the impact of those changes. Fifteen of the 87 Parties to the Convention currently have such reservations in effect. Japan heads the list with reservations on 13 threatened species of mammals and reptiles. This means that Japanese dealers can, and do, continue to trade in these 13 species notwithstanding that some of them are under serious threat of extinction.[12] Reservations made by a few Parties to a treaty can also totally undermine the effect of a decision approved by the vast majority. The objections by Japan, Norway and the U.S.S.R. to the zero quotas agreed by the International Whaling Commission as from 1986 provide a good example of this since they are the only major whaling nations left and are therefore the only ones seriously affected by the decision.

Some treaties specifically prohibit their Parties from making reservations. When a treaty is silent on the matter, Parties are allowed to make reservations unless they are incompatible with the object and purpose of the treaty.[13]

7.   *"Hard" and "soft" law*

It is helpful to bear in mind the distinction between "hard" and "soft" law.

"Hard" law refers to firm and binding rules of law. The content of treaties — as well as the provisions of customary international law — are by definition "hard" law, and the relevant States are bound by them as a matter of legal obligation. Some treaties provide that the obligations of the Parties may be varied in certain circumstances by a majority vote of the Parties. Such variations, unless the terms of the principal treaty permit objections or reservations, are as binding and "hard" as the terms of the treaty itself. For example, the Schedule to the International Convention for the Regulation of Whaling is "hard" law because the Convention expressly provides that the Schedule shall be part of the Convention itself.[14] However, the Schedule may be amended by a three quarters majority vote of the International Whaling Commission.[15] An amendment to the Schedule is therefore legally binding on all Parties to the Convention — even those which voted against it — unless they register an objection.

"Soft" law refers to a type of regulatory conduct which, because not expressly provided for in the treaty, is not binding in the same sense as "hard" law. It ·consists primarily of recommendations or

[12] See pp. 262-264 below.
[13] Vienna Convention on the Law of Treaties, Article 19(c).
[14] See p. 18 below.
[15] See p. 24 below.

declarations made by international conferences or inter-governmental organisations and has been described by one international legal commentator as "rules which have to be considered as law insofar as they fix norms with which States should comply, but which cannot be enforced in the traditional meaning of the term".[16]

Soft law is particularly relevant in the context of international wildlife law because it is common for a wildlife treaty to require its Parties to hold regular meetings at which recommendations to improve implementation of the treaty are made. Recommendations made in these circumstances are classic "soft law". They do not have the same legal force as the text of the treaty, but they are regarded as rules with which Parties should, and usually do, comply. They have, therefore, a considerable practical significance.

8. *Compliance*

International law cannot be enforced in the same sense as domestic law. Only rarely can States be compelled to perform their legal obligations — and even then only by means not involving the use of force. There is a procedure for "going to court" in international law, but because it is seldom satisfactory greater attention has been given to developing non-forcible techniques which, in practice, can be more effective as means of persuading States to comply with their international legal obligations.

a) *Judicial and arbitral procedures*

Once negotiation has failed to resolve a dispute, the international equivalent of "going to court" within a State is recourse to international arbitration or to the International Court of Justice at the Hague. In either event — and in contrast with national legal systems — proceedings cannot take place without the consent of the prospective defendant. This consent may be given in advance in, for example, the text of the treaty over which the dispute has occurred or by special agreement after the problem has arisen. Arbitration cases as well as cases before the International Court of Justice are rare. The Court has heard less than fifty contentious cases since its establishment in 1946 as the principal judicial organ of the United Nations. States are reluctant to take each other to the International Court, partly because it is seen as a politically unfriendly act to be avoided if possible and partly because it is often difficult to achieve a satisfactory remedy by this means. In the first case ever brought

---

[16] A.C. Kiss, *Survey of Current Developments in International Environmental Law*, IUCN Environmental Policy and Law Paper, No. 10 (1976).

before the Court, the *Corfu Channel* case of 1948,[17] damages of £843,947 were awarded to the U.K. against Albania, but not a penny has ever been paid.

The International Court of Justice has only heard two cases even remotely connected with wildlife, and both were disputes over fishing zones. The first was the *Fisheries* case,[18] which concerned a dispute between the U.K. and Norway over Norway's system of baselines for measurement of its fisheries zone. The Court upheld the Norwegian system. The second was the *Fisheries Jurisdiction* case[19] in which the Court held that the concept of "preferential rights", i.e. preferential rights of coastal States to fisheries in waters adjacent to them but beyond their territorial waters, had crystallised as customary law. The Court also held that the interests of States which had fished in the area for a long time should be taken into account.

b)   *Other compliance techniques*

The various administrative or non-judicial mechanisms available under treaties are much more effective for securing compliance with their provisions than reference to the International Court of Justice.

For example, simply by requiring its Parties to meet regularly to review its implementation, a treaty can ensure that it stays at the forefront of its Parties' attention. It may sound trite, but this is extremely important since treaties can very easily turn into "sleeping treaties" of little practical value unless their Parties are constantly reminded of their treaty obligations. Regular meetings also enable Parties to take appropriate action as circumstances change — to revise fishing or hunting quotas, to amend lists of protected species, to recommend specific habitat protection measures etc. In addition, the knowledge that recommendations made at these meetings will be the subject of international scrutiny at another meeting in one or two year's time greatly increases the likelihood of the recommendations being implemented.

The establishment of an administrative body to oversee and assist in the implementation of a treaty is also important. The Convention on International Trade in Endangered Species of Wild Fauna and Flora, for example, has a Secretariat which monitors enforcement on an international level and provides technical assistance to Parties experiencing enforcement problems. The Convention also requires each of its Parties to set up a national authority specifically to enforce

---

[17]   *I.C.J. Reports* 1949, p. 10.
[18]   *I.C.J. Reports* 1951, p. 116.
[19]   *I.C.J. Reports* 1974, p. 3.

the permit system established by the treaty — another very perceptive move since a body which has been set up for a specific purpose is likely at least to try to carry out its duties, if only to justify its existence.

Reporting requirements are also useful. If Parties have to submit regular reports on what they have done to enforce a treaty, they may prefer to comply with the treaty rather than have to report that they have done nothing. Reporting requirements work especially well if reports have to be submitted to a formal meeting of the Parties — and are even more effective if that meeting is open to non-governmental conservation organisations which are quick to publicise poor enforcement and to bring the weight of public opinion to bear on transgressor States. In addition, reports provide valuable information which can greatly assist enforcement in other ways. Discrepancies in reports submitted by Parties to the Convention on International Trade in Endangered Species of Wild Fauna and Flora, for example, have frequently helped identify sources of illegal trade.[20]

Other measures which can help enforcement include observer schemes, systems of inspection, financial sanctions,[21] ascribing trading disadvantages to States which do not comply with a treaty's terms[22] and offering financial lures for those which do.[23]

c) *National legislation*

Treaties are normally implemented by national legislation, and national law is much easier to enforce than international law. A wildlife conservation organisation has no standing in the International Court of Justice but may, if the national laws concerned permit it, be able to force its government to comply with an international treaty by bringing an action in its national courts pursuant to the law implementing the treaty in the country concerned. In *Defenders of Wildlife, Inc. v. Endangered Species Scientific Authority*,[24] for example, a U.S. conservation organisation obtained a ruling from the U.S. courts prohibiting the U.S. government from exporting bobcat (*Lynx rufus*) skins pending proper compliance by the U.S. government with its obligations under the Convention on International Trade in Endangered Species of Wild Fauna and Flora. Defenders of Wildlife brought the action pursuant to the

---

[20] See p. 269 below.

[21] All of these are used to help enforce rules promulgated by the International Whaling Commission. See Chapter 2 below.

[22] See Chapter 12 at p. 256 below.

[23] See Chapter 11 below.

[24] 659 F.2d 168, (D.C. Cir.), *cert. denied*, 454 U.S. 963 (1981).

Endangered Species Act of 1973, as amended, which implements the Convention in the U.S.A.[25]

d)   *Conclusion*

International law inevitably presents serious enforcement problems, simply because there is no international police force and the International Court of Justice is far weaker than any national judicial system. In practice, however, treaties are better enforced than is often realised. The adoption of administrative measures and use of national legislation, in the ways described above, have contributed substantially to this. But there is another overriding factor which ensures that, by and large, States make every effort to enforce a treaty once they have become a Party to it: it is in the interests of almost every State that order, and not chaos, should be a governing principle of human life, and if treaties were made and freely ignored chaos would soon result. This is nowhere more true than in relation to wildlife treaties, where a collapse in the systems carefully devised to protect species of concern to more than one State might lead to a few short term gains but would ultimately be everyone's loss.

---

[25]   16 U.S.C. §§1531-1543 (1976 & Supp. V 1981). See p. 252 below for further discussion of the case.

PART II

   Part II includes treaties which are concerned either with a single species or with groups of related species. In the former category, there are treaties governing the conservation and exploitation of northern fur seals (*Callorhinus ursinus*), polar bears (*Ursus maritimus*) and vicuna (*Vicugna vicugna*) — indeed three treaties dealing exclusively with the conservation and exploitation of vicuna have been signed in the last fifteen years. In the latter category, there are treaties covering whales, birds, Antarctic seals and North Atlantic seals.

   There are two common factors applicable to most of the treaties in Part II. The first is that nearly all of them are concerned with economically valuable animals which have been subjected to significant exploitation by man. Whales, seals, polar bears, birds and vicuna have all been killed in large numbers at one time or another for their meat, oil, skins, feathers or cloth. Consequently, the primary objective of almost every treaty in Part II is either to provide strict protection for species which have been seriously depleted in the past or to regulate exploitation of species which could become depleted in the future unless controls are imposed. Most of these treaties therefore place their greatest emphasis on regulating exploitation. With a few exceptions, other threats such as habitat loss and pollution, which could prove just as damaging in the long term, either receive lesser attention or are not covered at all.

   The second common factor is that species covered by these treaties almost all occur either in areas outside national jurisdiction or within the jurisdiction of more than one State. International cooperation in the protection of these species is therefore especially important. Whales and seals are particularly vulnerable because, occurring on the high seas or in areas such as Antarctica which are outside national jurisdiction, they would be open to exploitation by anyone if there was no international agreement on controls. Migratory species which cross international borders during the course of their migration are also vulnerable because heavy exploitation at just one stage of their migratory route can undermine the most stringent protective measures at all other stages. Recognition of the need for international cooperation in conservation endeavours was the foremost stimulant to the conclusion of every treaty examined in Part II.

CHAPTER 2

THE INTERNATIONAL CONVENTION FOR THE REGULATION OF WHALING ("THE WHALING CONVENTION")

"The moot point is, whether Leviathan can long endure so wide a chase, and so remorseless a havoc; whether he must not at last be exterminated from the waters, and the last whale, like the last man, smoke his last pipe, and then himself evaporate in the final puff."
(Herman Melville, *Moby Dick*)

1. *Background*

The history of man's depletion of one species of great whale after another is perhaps the most infamous example of human mismanagement of the earth's natural resources. As early as the thirteenth century, Basque whalers had so over-exploited right whales (*Balaena glacialis*) in the Bay of Biscay that they were forced to look further afield for their prey. Since then, the whaling industry has proceeded in a series of booms and slumps as the discovery of new whaling techniques and new whaling grounds has been invariably followed by rapid depletion of one population after another. Great whales and whalers now survive in numbers which are a small fraction of their former abundance, and the commercial whaling industry, which once employed over 70,000 people in the U.S.A. alone, is almost dead.[1]

Since so many whales occur beyond the boundaries of national jurisdiction, the need for international cooperation in preventing their over-exploitation is self-evident. Rather surprisingly, it was not until 1931 that the first whaling treaty, the Convention for the Regulation of Whaling,[2] was concluded. The 1931 Convention went some way towards controlling the worst whaling practices, but it only scratched the surface of the real problem. It prohibited commercial hunting of two particularly depleted species — right whales and bowhead whales (*Balaena mysticetus*)[3] and tried to

[1] For a more comprehensive analysis of the history of whaling and its early regulation, see J. Scarff, "The International Management of Whales, Dolphins, and Porpoises: An Interdisciplinary Assessment", *Ecology Law Quarterly*, Vol. 6 no. 2 (1977), pp. 343-352. See also J. Jenkins, *A History of the Whale Fisheries* (1921).

[2] 155 *L.N.T.S.* 349. The Convention came into force on 16 January 1935.

[3] However, Article 3 of the Convention exempted aboriginal whaling of right whales and bowhead whales, provided that native craft propelled by oars or sails were used, no firearms were carried, aboriginal people only were involved and they were not under contract to deliver the products of their whaling to a third person.

prevent excessive wastage of other species by requiring whalers to make full use of all carcasses and by banning the killing of calves or suckling whales, immatures and female whales which were accompanied by calves or sucklings.[4] However, it made no attempt to restrict the numbers of whales killed, except for right whales and bowhead whales, and it had limited practical value because five whaling States — Japan, Germany, Chile, Argentina and the U.S.S.R. — refused to accede to it. Neither did it establish a Commission with powers to amend whaling regulations, with the consequence that any changes in regulations required the negotiation of a separate protocol. Two such protocols were concluded later in the 1930s.[5] They prohibited the taking of whales below certain minimum lengths, set closed seasons for humpback whales (*Megaptera novaeangliae*) in the Antarctic and required every factory ship to have at least one inspector on board. However, they were also of limited value because neither was ratified by all the major whaling States.

These agreements were soon superceded by the International Convention for the Regulation of Whaling (the "Whaling Convention"),[6] which was signed in Washington, D.C. on 2 December 1946 and came into force on 10 November 1948. Originally signed by most of the major whaling States, the Convention has since been left by some and joined by others, but it has overseen most of the world's whaling activities from its entry into force to the present day.[7] The Whaling Convention established the International Whaling Commission ("IWC"),[8] which meets annually and adopts regulations on catch quotas, protected species, whaling methods etc. These regulations are contained in a Schedule. The IWC has the power to amend the Schedule, although the latter is an integral part of the Whaling Convention.[9] For the first fifteen years of the Convention's existence the Schedule

---

[4]   See Articles 5 and 6 of the Convention.

[5]   The International Agreement for the Regulation of Whaling (190 *L.N.T.S.* 79) was signed in London on 8 June 1937 and entered into force on 7 May 1938; the Protocol Amending the International Agreement of 8 June 1937 for the Regulation of Whaling (196 *L.N.T.S.* 131) was signed in London and came into force on 30 December 1938.

[6]   161 *U.N.T.S.* 72; *T.I.A.S.* no. 1849; *U.K.T.S.* no. 5 (1949), Cmd. 7604; and *U.K.T.S.* no. 68 (1959), Cmd. 849.

[7]   Japan, for example, did not become a Party until 1951. Peru and Chile were among the original signatories to the Whaling Convention but in 1952, together with Ecuador, they established their own Permanent Commission for the Exploitation and Conservation of the Marine Resources of the South Pacific which regulated whaling in waters within 200 miles of their respective coastlines. Peru and Chile finally ratified the Whaling Convention in 1979. Ecuador is not a Party but no longer takes whales.

[8]   Whaling Convention, Article 3(1).

[9]   *Ibid.*, Article 1(1).

imposed few restrictions on whaling. An unprecedented number of whales were killed during that time, reaching a peak of approximately 64,000 in the 1960/61 season.[10] Since then, faced with grossly depleted stocks of several species of whales and an increasingly powerful anti-whaling lobby, the IWC has adopted a more conservationist approach. Catch quotas have declined steadily, and in 1982 the IWC agreed to the following historic amendment to the Schedule:

> Notwithstanding the other provisions of paragraph 10, catch limits for the killing for commercial purposes of whales from all stocks for the 1986 coastal and the 1985/86 pelagic seasons and thereafter shall be zero. This provision will be kept under review, based upon the best scientific advice, and by 1990 at the latest the Commission will undertake a comprehensive assessment of the effects of this decision on whale stocks and consider modification of this provision and the establishment of other catch limits.

The effect of this amendment is to prohibit commercial whaling from 1985/6 in Antarctica and from 1986 elsewhere until the IWC decides otherwise, with a mandatory review of the situation in 1990 at the latest. However, like many wildlife treaties, the Whaling Convention contains an objections procedure, and the three major whaling States — Japan, Norway and the U.S.S.R — have registered objections to the amendment. It is still uncertain at the time of writing, therefore, whether or not commercial whaling will actually stop in 1986.

This chapter looks first at the objectives and scope of the Whaling Convention, it then examines the structure and functions of the IWC, the objections procedure, the circumstances in which special permits for scientific research are allowed, the methods used to enforce the Convention and its relationship with other treaties.

2. Objectives

The Whaling Convention has mixed objectives. On the one hand it aims to protect whales from over-exploitation. The preamble to the Convention recognises that "the history of whaling has seen over-fishing of one area after another and of one species of whale after another to such a degree that it is essential to protect all species of whales from further over-fishing." It goes on to state that the Parties desire to "establish a system of international regulation

[10] See *International Whaling Commission, 13th Report* (1963), pp. 4-5. Copies of the International Whaling Commission annual reports may be obtained from IWC Headquarters at the Red House, Station Road, Histon, Cambridge, England.

for the whale fisheries to ensure proper and effective conservation and development of whale stocks."

On the other hand the Convention is by no means a protectionist treaty. Its preamble also says that it is in the common interest to achieve the optimum level of whale stocks "without causing widespread economic and nutritional distress" and that the Parties have "decided to conclude a convention to provide for the proper conservation of whale stocks and thus make possible the orderly development of the whaling industry." The Convention clearly wants to achieve a situation where stocks have recovered sufficiently to be able to sustain controlled exploitation. However, the phrase "...and thus make possible the orderly development of the whaling industry" makes it quite clear that the primary purpose of the Convention is conservation of whale stocks for the secondary objective of enabling the whaling industry to develop in an orderly fashion. Conservation is the top priority; development of the whaling industry comes next.

3. *Scope of the Whaling Convention*

a) *Parties*

At the time of writing 39 States are Parties to the Whaling Convention.[11] Any State which did not originally sign the Convention, whether or not it is involved in whaling, may become a Party simply by notifying the depositary government in writing.[12] The vast majority of Parties are not whaling States. The fifteen original signatories all had interests in whaling, but of the eighteen States which have ratified or acceded to the Convention since March 1979 only two had whaling fleets. Indeed voting records at IWC meetings suggest that most of these eighteen States joined the Convention with the express object of bringing commercial whaling to an end.[13] A moratorium on commercial whaling was considered and rejected by several IWC meetings prior to 1982, and the fact that the 1982 meeting finally agreed to halt commercial whaling, at

[11] They are: Antigua and Barbuda, Argentina, Australia, Belize, Brazil, Chile, The People's Republic of China, Costa Rica, Denmark, Egypt, Finland, France, Federal Republic of Germany, Iceland, India, Japan, Kenya, the Republic of Korea, Mauritius, Mexico, Monaco, Netherlands, New Zealand, Norway, Oman, Peru, Philippines, St. Lucia, St. Vincent and the Grenadines, Senegal, Seychelles, South Africa, Spain, Sweden, Switzerland, U.K., Uruguay, U.S.A. and U.S.S.R.

[12] Whaling Convention, Article 10(2). The U.S. government is the depositary government.

[13] The Verbatim Record is the official source of voting records at International Whaling Commission meetings but is not published. However, voting records are sometimes reported in ECO, a paper which is published daily during meetings of the IWC by Friends of the Earth. Copies may be obtained from Friends of the Earth, 377 City Road, London N.1.

least temporarily, from 1986 is as much an indication of the voting power of these new Parties as of any change of heart by the whaling States.[14]

b) *Types of whaling covered by the Whaling Convention*

The Whaling Convention applies to "factory ships, land stations and whale catchers" under the jurisdiction of Parties to the Convention.[15] A factory ship is defined as "a ship in which or on which whales are treated whether wholly or in part", a land station means "a factory on the land at which whales are treated wholly or in part" and a whale catcher is defined as "a ship used for the purpose of hunting, taking, towing, holding on to or scouting for whales."[16] By a protocol to the Whaling Convention adopted in 1956, the definition of whale catcher was extended to include helicopters and other aircraft.[17]

The Convention cannot, of course, apply to whaling ships operating under the jurisdiction of non-Parties. This has resulted in periodic upsurges of "pirate" whaling — whaling by vessels, often manned by nationals of Party States which fly the flag of a non-Party as a flag of convenience in order to escape IWC controls. Although both the IWC and individual Parties have taken measures to thwart "pirate" whaling, which are described later in this chapter and have enjoyed at least temporary success,[18] it poses a serious obstacle to the ability of the IWC to supervise all whaling operations.

c) *Waters covered by the Whaling Convention*

The Whaling Convention applies to "all waters" in which whaling is carried on by factory ships, land stations or whale catchers.[19] By extending inside States' 200 mile coastal zones and even into their territorial seas and inland waterways, the treaty applies to a much wider geographical area than most international fisheries agreements. However, in view of the provisions of the Law

[14] The vote for zero catch limits for commercial whaling for the 1985/6 pelagic and 1986 coastal seasons and thereafter was 25 in favour, 7 against and 5 abstentions. 15 of the Parties who voted in favour were non-whaling States which have acceded to the Whaling Convention since March 1979.

[15] Whaling Convention, Article 1(2).

[16] *Ibid.*, Article 2(1)-(3).

[17] Protocol to the International Convention for the Regulation of Whaling, 1956, 338 *U.N.T.S.* 366; in force 4 May 1959.

[18] See pp. 29 and 33 below. Not one instance of "pirate" whaling has come to the attention of the International Whaling Commission since 1979 when measures were first taken to combat it (comment made to the author by R. Gambell, Secretary to the IWC).

[19] Whaling Convention, Article 1(2).

of the Sea Convention (1982) with respect to 200 mile "exclusive economic zones", the question has been raised as to whether "all waters" should in fact be limited to the high seas beyond these zones.[20]

d) *Whales covered by the Whaling Convention*

The main text of the Convention refers only to "whales" without defining what it means by the word "whales". Since the distinction between "whales", "small whales" and "dolphins and porpoises" is ambiguous from a taxonomic viewpoint, the jurisdiction of the IWC over smaller cetaceans is unclear. The question of jurisdiction is particularly important because large numbers of small cetaceans are killed each year either as a result of direct exploitation or incidentally to other fishing operations. In the early 1970s, for example, it is estimated that as many as 250,000 porpoises may have been killed annually in the course of fishing for tuna.[21] For reasons not fully understood, yellow-fin tuna tend to swim beneath large schools of porpoises, and fishermen have adopted the practice of encircling large schools of porpoises with nets in order to catch the tuna underneath. Some porpoises inevitably become entangled and drown.[22]

The IWC has traditionally limited the scope of its regulations, with a few exceptions, to the larger baleen and toothed whales. In 1976, however, the IWC agreed that Parties should submit data on their "small-type whaling" operations.[23] Small-type whaling is defined as "catching operations using powered vessels with mounted harpoon guns hunting exclusively for minke, bottlenose, beaked, pilot or killer whales."[24] Requiring data on these species is a long way from regulating the direct and indirect taking of all small cetaceans, but it is a cautious step forward by the IWC towards extending its jurisdiction beyond traditional limits.

[20] See P. Birnie, *The Development of the International Regulation of Whaling: Its Relation to the Emerging Law of Conservation of Marine Mammals* (Ph.D. thesis, University of Edinburgh, 1979), pp. 176 and 520-581.

[21] See Scarff, note 1 above, p. 379; see also E. Mitchell, *Porpoises, Dolphins and Small Whale Fisheries of the World,* IUCN Monograph No. 3 (1973), pp. 87-9, obtainable from IUCN, 1196 Gland, Switzerland.

[22] In recent years, the numbers of porpoises killed incidentally to fishing operations in U.S. coastal waters have decreased considerably due to the requirements of the Marine Mammal Protection Act of 1972 as amended (16 U.S.C. §§1361-2, 1371-84 and 1401-07) and improvements in the nets used. In 1981, the total allowable take of marine mammals under U.S. domestic and foreign commercial fishing permits was 29,474 animals compared to 78,000 in 1976.

[23] Whaling Convention, Schedule, para. 26(b). The Schedule is published by the International Whaling Commission and may be obtained from the Commission headquarters at the Red House, Station Road, Histon, Cambridge, England.

[24] Whaling Convention, Schedule, para. 1(c).

4. The International Whaling Commission

The IWC meets annually and is composed of one voting representative of each Party who may be accompanied by experts and advisers.[25] The Whaling Convention makes no provision for the admission of observers to IWC meetings, but the IWC's Rules of Procedure allow non-Parties and intergovernmental organisations to be represented by observers if they have previously attended meetings or if they submit a written request to the Secretary 30 days prior to the meeting.[26] Non-governmental international organisations with offices in more than three countries may also attend.[27]

Most wildlife treaties contain a clause authorising the Parties to deny access to observers to any meeting of the Parties if a two thirds majority so wish, but there is nothing in the Convention or in the IWC's Rules of Procedure authorising the Parties to deny access to observers who satisfy the above conditions. The large numbers of observers, comprising representatives of both the whaling industry and conservation organisations, who have attended IWC meetings in recent years in order to lobby for the positions they espouse, demonstrates the widespread public interest in the work of the Commission.

The IWC is serviced by a staff of a Secretary, together with twelve full time and various part time assistants. It has an annual budget of about £370,000 for administrative purposes and £50,000 for scientific research.[28]

a) Research

The Whaling Convention authorises the IWC to:

(a) encourage, recommend, or if necessary, organise studies and investigations relating to whales and whaling;
(b) collect and analyse statistical information concerning the current condition and trend of the whale stocks and the effects of whaling activities thereon;
(c) study, appraise, and disseminate information concerning methods of maintaining and increasing the populations of whale stocks.[29]

---

[25] Whaling Convention, Article 3(1).
[26] Rules of Procedure of the International Whaling Commission, para. B(2)(a). These Rules, together with the Financial Regulations, the Rules of Debate and the Rules of Procedure of the Scientific Committee and the Technical Committee are reprinted in *Rules of Procedure and Financial Regulations* (International Whaling Commission, July 1983).
[27] *Ibid.*, para. B(2)(b).
[28] The staff are based at Commission headquarters (see note 23 above).
[29] Whaling Convention, Article 4(1).

The Convention encourages the IWC to publish reports and other information relevant to whales and whaling.[30]

Although knowledge of the population levels and conservation requirements of many whale stocks is far from satisfactory, substantial research has been done and continues to be carried out. The 32nd annual report of the IWC (1982), for example, published progress reports on cetacean research from Australia, Brazil, Canada, Chile, Denmark (Greenland), France, Iceland, Japan, Republic of Korea, Mexico, New Zealand, Norway, Peru, Seychelles, South Africa, Spain, the U.K., the U.S.A. and the U.S.S.R. and published an additional fifty scientific papers on whales and whaling. Unlike some international fisheries commissions, the IWC does not employ its own research scientists but relies on individual Parties to undertake research themselves.

b)   *The Schedule*

The Schedule contains the detailed regulations governing the protection and exploitation of whales. The IWC has the power to amend the Schedule in order to fix:

(a) protected and unprotected species;
(b) open and closed seasons;
(c) open and closed waters, including the designation of sanctuary areas;
(d) size limits for each species;
(e) time, methods and intensity of whaling (including the maximum catch of whales to be taken in any one season);
(f) types and specifications of gear and apparatus and appliances which may be used;
(g) methods of measurement; and
(h) catch returns and other statistical and biological records.[31]

The Whaling Convention stipulates that amendments to the Schedule shall be based on scientific findings, that amendments shall only be made when "necessary to carry out the objectives and purposes of this Convention" and that "the interests of the consumers of whale products and the whaling industry" shall be considered.[32] To be adopted, amendments must be approved by a three quarters majority of Parties voting.[33] The Convention prohibits the IWC from allocating catch quotas among the Parties

---

[30]   *Ibid.*, Article 4(2).
[31]   *Ibid.*, Article 5(1).
[32]   *Ibid.*, Article 5(2).
[33]   *Ibid.*, Article 3(2).

or from restricting the number or nationality of factory ships or land stations.[34]

c) *Major changes to the Schedule since 1949*

It is beyond the scope of this analysis to describe every amendment to the Schedule which has ever been made. Amendments of one kind or another have been agreed at each of the thirty six annual meetings of the IWC.[35] However, examples of some of the most significant amendments will be considered in order to illustrate the development of the Commission since its first meeting in 1949.

For over twenty years, the IWC used the "blue whale unit" as its yardstick for annual catch limits. This device regulated the total amount of whales that could be taken in a given year but did not control the harvest of individual species. One blue whale unit was considered to be either one blue whale (*Balaenoptera musculus*) or two fin whales (*Balaenoptera physalus*) or two and a half humpbacks (*Megaptera novaeangliae*) or six sei whales (*Balaenoptera borealis*) or an appropriate combination.[36] Until the mid-1960s, when the most important whaling produce changed from oil to meat, the system of blue whale units hastened the decline of blue and fin whales because whalers preferred to hunt these two oil-rich species notwithstanding that they could catch larger numbers of smaller whales.[37] The system was abandoned in 1972 in favour of quotas on a species by species basis. The latter gave way in 1976 to the "New Management Procedure" which pinpoints quotas still further and is still in operation today. Under the New Management Procedure each species is divided into anything up to twenty different stocks, and quotas are set on a stock by stock basis. Each stock is classified as an "initial management stock" or a "sustained management stock" or a "protection stock" depending upon the relationship between the population level of the stock and the level of its

---

[34] *Ibid.*, Article 5(2). Since 1962 various agreements have been concluded by the whaling nations themselves in order to allocate national quotas as percentages of the total quotas set by the International Whaling Commission. They are published in the annual reports of the Commission.

[35] The best sources of information on the history of the International Whaling Commission and the amendments to the Schedule are the annual reports of the IWC. See also Scarff, note 1 above, pp. 358-372; and McHugh, "The Role and History of the International Whaling Commission", published in *The Whale Problem* (W. Schevill, ed., 1974). An updated version of the Schedule is published each year by the International Whaling Commission.

[36] See para. 8(b) of the Schedule as it was in 1949, published in *International Whaling Commission, 1st report* (1950).

[37] See Scarff, note 1 above, p. 352.

"maximum sustainable yield".[38] Commercial harvesting of protection stocks is prohibited,[39] and exploitation of stocks in the other two categories must be sustainable.[40] Classification frequently varies for different stocks of the same species. The fin whale, for example, has stocks in all three categories. The Newfoundland Labrador stock of fin whales has been declared an initial management stock, four other stocks of fin whale have been designated sustained management stocks, and all remaining stocks are classified as protection stocks.[41]

In 1949 the Schedule protected only grey whales (*Eschrichtius robustus*) and right whales — and it even allowed these two species to be taken provided that their meat and other products were used exclusively for local consumption by aboriginal peoples.[42] The Schedule set an overall quota of 16,000 "blue whale units",[43] and there were no restrictions on the methods of killing whales. By 1985 the Schedule had undergone radical changes. Blue, right, humpback, bowhead and grey whales are now protected from commercial whaling,[44] although aboriginal/subsistence whaling is still permitted, subject to strict catch limits, for grey whales of the North Pacific eastern stocks (off Siberia), for humpback whales of the North Atlantic Stock (off Greenland) and for bowhead whales of the Bering Sea stock (off Alaska).[45] The Indian Ocean has been declared a sanctuary from commercial whaling,[46] and commercial whalers are prohibited from using the particularly cruel non-explosive "cold grenade" harpoon.[47] Quotas for fin, sei, sperm (*Physeter macrocephalus*), Bryde's (*Balaenoptera edeni*), minke (*Balaenoptera acutorostrata*) and bottlenose whales (*Berardius* spp and *Hyperoodon* spp) are a small fraction of the quotas permitted three

---

[38] Whaling Convention, Schedule, paragraph 10. For a detailed explanation of the New Management Procedures, see P. Birnie, *Legal Measures for the Prevention of "Pirate" Whaling*, IUCN Environmental Policy and Law Paper No. 19 (1982), pp. 13-14; see also Scarff, note 1 above, pp. 369-372. For an explanation of "maximum sustainable yield", see J.A. Gulland, *The Concept of the Maximum Sustainable Yield and Fishery Management*, FAO Fisheries Technical Paper No. 70 (1968); see also M. Bean, *The Evolution of National Wildlife Law* (Praeger, 1983), p. 264.
[39] Whaling Convention, Schedule, para. 10(c).
[40] *Ibid.*, para. 10(a)-(b).
[41] *Ibid.*, Table 1.
[42] See para. 2 of the Schedule as it was in 1949, published in *International Whaling Commission, 1st report* (1950), p. 15.
[43] See para. 8(a) of the Schedule as it was in 1949.
[44] Whaling Convention, Schedule, Table 1.
[45] Whaling Convention, Schedule, para. 13. These whales must be used for local consumption and cannot be sold for commercial gain.
[46] Whaling Convention, Schedule, para. 7.
[47] *Ibid.*, para. 6. Explosive harpoons cause a quicker death than the non-explosive variety. Whalers tend to prefer the latter, particularly when catching smaller whales, because they destroy less meat.

decades earlier.[48] And, of course, the Schedule prohibits all commercial whaling from 1986 until the IWC decides otherwise.[49]

d) *Objection procedure*

Any Party may avoid being bound by an amendment to the Schedule by registering an objection within 90 days of notification of its adoption.[50] If a Party registers an objection within the prescribed 90 day period, an additional period of up to 120 days is allowed for other Parties to withdraw their previously registered approval of the amendment. Once these periods have lapsed, a Party may not subsequently register an objection.

Use of the objection procedure has undermined decisions of the International Whaling Commission on a number of occasions. As early as 1954, Canada, Japan, the U.S.A. and the U.S.S.R. objected to a prohibition on the taking of blue whales in the North Pacific — one of the IWC's first real conservationist initiatives. Since these four were the only States hunting blue whales in the North Pacific, their objection rendered the IWC action totally ineffective.[51] In 1981 Brazil, Iceland, Japan, Norway, and the U.S.S.R. objected to the decision of the Commission to ban the "cold grenade" harpoon as a means of killing of minke whales for commercial purposes.[52] Again, as they were the only States catching minke whales, their action rendered the ban meaningless. In 1982 Peru objected to the IWC quota for the Peruvian stock of Bryde's whales (164 animals) and Chile objected to the zero quota set for the Eastern South Pacific stock of Bryde's whales — again rendering the quotas ineffectual since they were the States directly affected.

The IWC decision to bring at least a temporary halt to commercial whaling from 1986 is also seriously jeopardised by the fact that Japan, Norway and the U.S.S.R. have registered objections to it. These three States catch by far the largest number of whales, although it should be pointed out that Brazil, Iceland, the Republic of Korea, Peru[53] and Spain are all whaling nations which have accepted the IWC decision. The latter will therefore have at least some beneficial impact even if Japan, Norway and the U.S.S.R. do carry on whaling. It should also be said that Japan,

[48] Whaling Convention, Schedule, Tables 1-3.
[49] Whaling Convention, Schedule, para. 10(e).
[50] Whaling Convention, Article 5(3).
[51] See *International Whaling Commission, 6th Report* (1955), p. 5.
[52] See para. 6 of the Schedule to the Whaling Convention and accompanying footnote. Japan and Norway are currently researching into alternatives to the "cold grenade" harpoon which do not destroy an excessive amount of meat (see note 47 above) and may withdraw their reservations if experiments with newly developed devices prove successful.
[53] Peru initially registered an objection but subsequently withdrew it.

Norway and the U.S.S.R. could withdraw their objections at any time, and their decisions to register objections may reflect nothing more than a political decision to keep their options open until 1986.

e) Committees

The International Whaling Commission is authorised to establish "such committees as it considers desirable to perform such functions as it may authorise."[54] To date, three permanent committees — Finance and Administration, Scientific, Technical — and numerous short-lived *ad hoc* committees have been set up. The Finance and Administration Committee consists of representatives from five Party governments and is responsible for budget, expenditure and personnel.[55] The Scientific Committee, on which all Parties have the right to be represented, is responsible for studying available information with respect to whale stocks and whaling and for making appropriate recommendations to the IWC.[56] One of its most important tasks is to advise on the appropriate classification for whale stocks under the New Management Procedure and on the size of quotas to be set.

The Technical Committee, on which all Parties also have the right to be represented, acts as a balance to the Scientific Committee, advising the IWC on non-scientific matters such as aboriginal whaling, humane killing or whaling outside the jurisdiction of the IWC.[57] For example, while the Scientific Committee has consistently recommended that no animals should be taken from the Bering Sea stock of bowhead whales, the Technical Committee has frequently reminded the IWC of the importance of the annual bowhead hunt to the culture of Alaskan Eskimos, and the Commission has consequently allowed a limited number of whales to be taken each year. In addition to its conventional role, the Technical Committee is also used as a convenient forum in which the Parties sit temporarily at IWC meetings in order to conduct a kind of dress rehearsal of voting on crucial scientific issues such as catch quotas before these issues come to a vote in full plenary session.[58] A proposed amendment to the Schedule needs only a simple majority to be approved by the Technical Committee, and its consideration in Committee enables the proponent government to test the proposal's prospects of

[54] Whaling Convention, Article 3(4).
[55] Rules of Procedure of the International Whaling Commission, note 26 above, paras. J(1) and J(7).
[56] *Ibid.*, paras. J(1) and J(3).
[57] *Ibid.*, paras. J(1) and J(6).
[58] Personal observation of the author.

ultimate success in plenary session where it will require a three quarters majority to be adopted.[59] It also enables the proponent and other interested parties to identify their supporters and opponents before the decisive vote and then to conduct an intensive lobbying campaign in the time between Technical Committee and plenary sessions.

f) *Recommendations*

Finally, the IWC is authorised to "...make recommendations to any or all contracting Governments on any matters which relate to whales or whaling and to the objectives and purposes of this Convention."[60] Pursuant to this authority, the IWC has made recommendations on a number of different issues.

In 1979, for example, alarmed by the amount of "pirate" whaling outside its jurisdiction, the IWC recommended each Party to "...cease immediately any importation of whale meat and products from, and the export of whaling vessels and equipment to, non-member countries and operations" and to consider prohibiting "...whaling by non-member States within their fishery conservation zones."[61] Taking the case against "pirate" whaling one step further in 1980, the IWC recommended each Party to

...prevent the transfer of whaling vessels and equipment and, as far as possible, the dissemination of whaling information and expertise, or the provision of any other type of assistance specifically designed for and likely to be used for whaling, to any nation or entity under the jurisdiction of such a nation which is not a member of the IWC

and to take

...all practicable steps within their jurisdiction to prohibit their nationals from offering services or expertise directly relevant to whaling to any vessel belonging to any nation, or entity under the jurisdiction of any nation, which is not a member of the IWC.[62]

The IWC has made dozens of other recommendations over the years. They have varied from urging Denmark to encourage aboriginal whalers off the coast of Greenland to substitute fin whales for humpback whales as the target of their subsistence hunting,[63] to urging Alaskan Eskimos to reduce to zero the number

[59] See p. 24 above.
[60] Whaling Convention, Article 6.
[61] *International Whaling Commission, 30th Report* (1980), Appendix 9, p. 38.
[62] *IWC, 31st Report* (1981), Appendix 1.
[63] *IWC, 29th Report* (1979), Appendix 3, p. 32.

of bowhead whales struck but not landed,[64] to urging Party governments to conduct research into the effects of shipping and off-shore mining and drilling activities on whale stocks.[65]

These recommendations do not, of course, have the same legal force as amendments to the Schedule, and they require only a simple majority of Parties voting to be adopted. However, they are "soft law" and have some legal standing.[66] In addition, the fact that no instances of "pirate" whaling have been reported to the IWC since 1979 indicates that its recommendations can have a significant practical impact, although much of the credit may also belong to the virulent anti-pirate whaling activities of non-governmental conservation organisations such as Greenpeace.

5. *Special permits for scientific research*

Notwithstanding any of its other provisions, including the Schedule, the Whaling Convention allows Party governments to grant special permits authorising their nationals to kill whales for the purposes of scientific research.[67] Under its Rules of Procedure, however, the Scientific Committee is responsible for reviewing proposed special permits before they are issued.[68] Each government must report to the IWC all such authorisations that it makes, together with the results of the research.[69]

The recommendations of the Scientific Committee with respect to special permits have generally been followed. For example, a Japanese proposal to take 120 Bryde's whales in 1977/78 for research purposes was modified by the Scientific Committee and carried out by Japan on the basis of the recommended modifications. After the Scientific Committee had rejected an application by Peru to take a blue whale for the purposes of displaying its skeleton, the Peruvian government refused to grant a special permit.[70] However, the Faroe Islands Authority (which is under the jurisdiction of Denmark — a Party to the Convention) had its application for a special permit to take nine fin whales rejected by the Scientific Committee in 1982 but awarded itself a permit to take three anyway.[71]

---

[64]   *IWC, 32nd Report* (1982), Appendix 4, p. 36.
[65]   *Ibid.*, Appendix 7, p. 37.
[66]   For a discussion of "soft law" see pp. 10-11 above.
[67]   Whaling Convention, Article 8(1).
[68]   Rules of Procedure of the Scientific Committee, note 26 above, para. F.
[69]   Whaling Convention, Articles 8(1) and 8(3).
[70]   *IWC, 29th Report* (1979), p. 8.
[71]   See *Report of the Infractions Sub-Committee*, IWC/34/8, submitted to the thirty fourth meeting of the IWC in 1982.

6. Enforcement

The enforcement provisions of the Whaling Convention and the Schedule, together with the domestic measures which Party governments have taken to implement them, are particularly interesting for three reasons. Firstly, the Convention and the Schedule have established a system of national enforcement with international supervision which is unique in international wildlife law. Secondly, some Parties have gone to unusual lengths to ensure that their nationals neither participate in nor assist whaling operations anywhere in the world. Thirdly, U.S. law authorises sanctions to be taken against States whose activities diminish the effectiveness of the IWC.

a) Inspectors

Since 1949 the Schedule has stipulated that at least two inspectors shall be maintained on each factory ship "for the purpose of maintaining twenty four hour inspection provided that at least one such inspector shall be maintained on each catcher functioning as a factory ship." In addition, the Schedule requires that "adequate inspection shall be maintained at each land station".[72] Inspectors are appointed and paid by the government with jurisdiction over the factory ship or land station concerned.[73] Inspectors are, therefore, national enforcement officers responsible to their own governments and, in addition to recording information required by the Schedule such as the size and sex of whales, they are often required to perform additional functions by their employers.

b) International observer scheme

The establishment of an international observer scheme was first considered seriously in the 1960s but was not agreed by the IWC until 1971. The scheme was set up because the similarity in appearance between the products of different species of whales and the capacity of factory ships to process carcasses at sea makes it relatively easy for a whaling company to cover up illegal catches by falsely representing them as legal catches of other species.[74] In the 1960s, populations of certain stocks of humpback whales in the southern hemisphere showed declines of a magnitude not readily explicable by reported catches, suggesting that humpbacks had

---

[72] Whaling Convention, Schedule, para. 21. Inspectors need not be appointed to "ships which, apart from the storage of products, are used during the season solely for freezing or salting the meat and entrails of whales intended for human food or feeding animals."

[73] Ibid.

[74] See Scarff, note 1 above, p. 606.

been illegally taken and reported as other species.[75] In addition, there was some concern that nationally appointed and controlled inspectors might not be totally impartial.[76]

In contrast to the nationally appointed inspectors, observers are appointed by and responsible to the IWC, although they are paid by the government which nominates them.[77] The Schedule makes no provision for the number of observers to be placed on the ships and land stations of whaling nations, and in practice there are very few — four or five in total in recent years. The observer scheme is implemented by bilateral or trilateral arrangements between the States concerned. For example, the U.S.S.R. and Japan make mutual arrangements for observers in the Antarctic and Iceland, and Spain and Norway do the same in the North Atlantic.[78] The Republic of Korea, Brazil, Chile and Peru have all indicated their willingness to receive international observers, but other States have not been prepared to pay the costs involved in sending an observer.[79]

The observer scheme, as it presently operates, cannot possibly provide a comprehensive check on the work of the inspectors, but it does give at least some international oversight of whaling operations and some degree of confidence in the accuracy of reports submitted by the whaling States.[80] In recent years, the reports submitted by international observers have generally tallied with the reports of infractions submitted by the whaling States, suggesting that the latter have usually recorded infractions accurately.[81]

c) *Infractions*

Each Party is responsible for punishing infractions against provisions of the Whaling Convention which occur in the course of operations carried out by persons or vessels under its jurisdiction.[82] Each Party must also submit an annual report of such infractions to the IWC and of measures taken to prosecute them.[83] These reports are considered by the Infractions Committee, which is a permanent sub-committee of the Technical Committee. The killing of undersized or lactating whales is the most common type of infraction. Several prosecutions for these offences are reported each

---

[75] *IWC, 14th Report* (1964), pp. 73 and 82.

[76] See Scarff, note 1 above, pp. 606-7.

[77] Whaling Convention, Schedule, para. 21(c).

[78] The number and area of operation of observers is recorded in each of the annual reports of the IWC.

[79] Comment made to the author by R. Gambell, Secretary to the IWC.

[80] *Ibid.*

[81] *IWC, 29th Report* (1979), p. 7.

[82] Whaling Convention, Article 9(1).

[83] *Ibid.*, Article 9(4).

year, and the normal punishment is a fine of U.S.$1,000 — 2,000 together with a loss of any bonus due to the whaler concerned.[84]

d) *Register of whaling vessels*

In 1979 the IWC requested its Secretary to compile a register of whaling vessels subject to IWC quotas and regulations. The intention was to make it easier for States, whether Parties to the Whaling Convention or not, to detect and take measures against whaling vessels flying flags of convenience and operating outside the jurisdiction of the Convention. In 1980 the Schedule was amended to require Parties to supply certain statistical information on all factory ships and catcher ships.[85]

e) *National controls of citizens and vessels*

Article 9(1) of the Convention requires each Party to take "appropriate measures" to enforce the terms of the Convention, a loosely defined obligation which gives each Party broad discretion as to the action it chooses to take.

Most Parties have limited the scope of their regulations to whaling by vessels, whether domestic or foreign, within their coastal waters and to whaling by vessels flying their national flag even if outside their coastal waters. However, some have gone further. The U.S.A.'s Marine Mammal Protection Act, 1972, prohibits U.S. citizens or U.S. registered vessels from engaging in whaling on the high seas.[86] New Zealand's Marine Mammal Protection Act of 1978 goes further still. It prohibits New Zealand citizens from taking whales wherever they may be, even if within the coastal waters of another State and even if the taking is legal under local law.[87] Australia's Whale Protection Act of 1980 contains similar provisions to the New Zealand legislation.[88] In order to deter "pirate" whaling, South Africa has prohibited persons under South African jurisdiction from supplying stores or offering services or expertise to foreign whalers.[89]

---

[84] See, for example, the *Summary of Infractions Reports Received by the Commission, Antarctic Season 1981/2, Outside Antarctic 1981*, Doc. no. IWC/34/6 presented to the 1982 meeting of the IWC.

[85] Whaling Convention, Schedule, para. 28.

[86] Marine Mammal Protection Act of 1972 as amended (16 U.S.C. §§1361-2, 1371-84 and 1401-07).

[87] Marine Mammal Protection Act of 1978 (Act No. 80), section 1.

[88] See sections 3(1), 6(2), and 9(1) of Australia's Whale Protection Act of 1980 (No. 92). For a good comparative analysis of national legislation on the protection of whales, see Birnie, note 20 above, pp. 88-101.

[89] Regulation 89 (15 June 1979), Government Gazette No. 6497, promulgated under sections 10 and 13 of the Sea Fisheries Act, 1973 (Act 58 of 1973).

f) Sanctions

Two U.S. laws, known as the "Pelly Amendment" to the Fisherman's Protective Act of 1967[90] and the "Packwood-Magnuson Amendment" to the Fishery Conservation and Management Act of 1976,[91] authorise the U.S. government to take economic sanctions against any State whose activities diminish the effectiveness of the conservation measures of the IWC. The threat of sanctions is undoubtedly a much greater incentive for the whaling States to comply with IWC decisions than the other enforcement mechanisms established by the Whaling Convention because the U.S. government has the power, if it chooses to exercise it, to inflict serious economic losses on States which flout IWC decisions.

If the U.S. Secretary of Commerce determines that foreign nationals are "conducting fishing operations in a manner or under circumstances which diminish the effectiveness of an international fishery conservation program"[92] or "directly or indirectly, are engaging in trade or taking which diminishes the effectiveness of any international program for endangered or threatened species", the Pelly Amendment authorises the U.S. President to prohibit the import of fish products from the offending State "for such duration as he deems appropriate and to the extent that such prohibition is sanctioned by the General Agreement on Tariffs and Trade."[93] If the President does not impose import restrictions following such a determination by the Secretary of Commerce, he must give his reasons to the U.S. Congress.[94] Under the Packwood-Magnuson Amendment, if the Secretary of Commerce determines that foreign nationals "directly or indirectly, are conducting fishing operations or engaging in trade or taking which diminishes the effectiveness of" the Whaling Convention, the State concerned will automatically lose 50% of its allocation of fish products taken within the U.S.A.'s "fishery conservation zone" which extends 200 miles from U.S. coastlines.[95] If the State refuses to rectify its conduct within a year, its entire allocation will be terminated and its nationals will be

---

[90]   22 U.S.C. §§1978 (Supp. V 1981).

[91]   16 U.S.C. §§1821(e)(2) (Supp. V 1981).

[92]   An "international fishery conservation program" is defined to include "any ban, restriction, regulation or other measure in effect pursuant to a multilateral agreement which is in force with respect to the United States, the purpose of which is to conserve or protect the living resources of the sea" (22 U.S.C. §§1978(g)(3)). This definition clearly includes measures taken by the IWC to protect whales.

[93]   22 U.S.C. §§1978(a). Article XX(g) of the General Agreement on Tariffs and Trade recognises the validity, under certain circumstances, of trade restrictions relating to "exhaustible natural resources".

[94]   22 U.S.C. §§1978(b).

[95]   16 U.S.C. §§1821(e)(2)(B).

unable to fish at all in U.S. coastal waters.[96] In contrast to the Pelly Amendment which gives the President discretion as to whether he actually embargoes fish imports, there is no discretion under the Packwood-Magnuson Amendment. Sanctions *must* be imposed.

The threat of these sanctions may have been an important factor in persuading whaling States to abide by the lower quotas set by the IWC in recent years, but the real test of their importance is likely to occur in relation to the IWC decision to halt commercial whaling from 1986. If Japan, for example, maintains its objection to that decision and continues to take whales for commercial purposes after 1986, it stands the risk of suffering considerable economic loss. The wholesale value of fish caught by Japanese fleets in U.S. coastal waters in 1981 is reported to have been over U.S.$425 million and the value of 1981 Japanese fish exports to the U.S.A. has been reported at approximately U.S.$320 million. The value of Japan's annual whale catch is estimated to be below U.S.$50 million.[97]

In the mid-1970s there was some doubt as to whether the U.S. government had the political will to impose economic sanctions on a foreign country such as Japan, with whom its general trading relations are so important, merely for the sake of whales. The Secretary of Commerce made the appropriate determination under the Pelly Amendment against Japan and the U.S.S.R. in 1974 after both countries had objected to IWC quotas for the harvest of minke whales in the Antarctic and had set their own higher quotas. But the President refused to exercise his option to impose sanctions on the grounds that he expected Japan and the U.S.S.R. to abide by future quotas and that domestic economic disruption would follow.[98] On the first point history proved him right, but on the second point there will always be some adverse internal economic effect whenever sanctions are applied. Recent events, however, indicate that the U.S. government may now be prepared to adopt a tougher line. In 1983 it withheld 171,000 tonnes from Japan's fish allocations within the U.S.A.'s 200 mile coastal zone (worth approximately U.S.$55 million) in retaliation for Japan's objection to the IWC decision to halt commercial whaling in 1986.[99] And further cuts in Japanese fish allocations may follow unless the objection is withdrawn.

---

[96] 16 U.S.C. §§1821(e)(2)(D).

[97] See ECO, note 13 above, Vol. XXI, No. 3, July 21, 1982, pp. 1 and 4.

[98] See Bean, note 38 above, p. 266; see also "Not Saving Whales: President Ford Refuses to Ban Fish Imports From Nations Which Have Violated International Whaling Quotas", 5 *Environmental Law Reporter* 10044 (1975).

[99] See *IWC Commissioners Briefing*, No. 1, (January 1984).

7. *Relationship to other international treaties and organisations*

a) *The Law of the Sea Convention (1982)*

The Law of the Sea Convention (1982), which has been signed by 134 States but is not yet in force, has implications for the IWC. In particular, Article 65 of this Convention requires that its Parties shall co-operate "...with a view to the conservation of marine mammals and in case of cetaceans shall in particular work through the appropriate international organisations for their conservation, management and study."

Article 65 also states that nothing contained therein restricts the right of coastal States or international organisations from prohibiting, limiting or regulating the exploitation of marine mammals more strictly than is provided by the rest of Part V of the Law of the Sea Convention. The implication of Article 65, although some States dispute this, is that States must abide by the regulations of the IWC, whether or not they are Parties to the Whaling Convention, except where they adopt stricter domestic measures for the conservation of whales. This is particularly significant for States which ratify the Law of the Sea Convention, but are not Parties to the Whaling Convention, and have allowed their national flag to be flown by "pirate" whalers in order to escape IWC restrictions. Article 65 appears to require them to halt this practice.

b) *The Convention on International Trade in Endangered Species of Wild Fauna and Flora ("CITES")*

CITES regulates international trade in species which are listed in one of the three Appendices to the Convention. The "introduction from the sea" of species in the Appendices — i.e. bringing specimens taken on the high seas into a State which is a Party to the Convention — is deemed to be international trade and requires a CITES permit. The introduction from the sea of species in Appendix I of the Convention is prohibited if it is for commercial purposes. Sperm, fin, sei, blue, humpback, bowhead, right, Bryde's, grey and bottlenose whales are all currently in Appendix I. From 1 January 1986 all cetaceans whose catch is regulated by the IWC will be added to Appendix I. This was agreed by the fourth meeting of the Parties to CITES, held in April 1983, in order to bring the Convention into line with the IWC decision to halt commercial whaling from 1986. However, Japan and the U.S.S.R. have both entered "reservations" under CITES with respect to the listing of sperm, fin, sei, bottlenose and Bryde's whales in Appendix I and with respect to the CITES decision to put all whales, whose taking is regulated by the IWC, in

Appendix I with effect from 1 January 1986. The "reservations" procedure under CITES is similar to the objection procedure under the Whaling Convention and has the same effect of exempting the reserving Party from the provisions concerned.[100]

All whales not in Appendix I of CITES are in Appendix II, although from 1 January 1986 this will have little importance from an IWC viewpoint since all whales with which the Commission is currently concerned will be in Appendix I. The Parties to CITES have recommended that "the Scientific Committee of the International Whaling Commission together with other sources" should be consulted whenever they are considering a proposal to add a species of whale to Appendix I or II.[101]

c) *European Economic Community*

In 1981 the European Economic Community adopted a Regulation prohibiting the import for commercial purposes of whale products that are listed in an Annex to the Regulation. The Regulation requires an import license for any non-commercial imports.[102] EEC Regulations are directly binding on all Member States of the EEC and do not require implementing legislation in order to enter into force in the Member States.

d) *The Convention on the Conservation of Antarctic Marine Living Resources*

This Convention, which came into force in April 1982, has potentially significant implications for whales in that it regulates the exploitation of marine living resources, notably krill (*Euphausia superba*), in Antarctica.[103] Krill is the principal food supply of several species of baleen whale, and any diminution in its abundance could impede the recovery of Antarctic whale populations. Recognising the close link between whales and krill, the Convention requires its Commission to seek to develop a co-operating working relationship with the IWC.[104] Nothing in the Convention is intended to derogate

[100] See Chapter 12 below for a detailed analysis of CITES.
[101] Recommendation Conf. 2.7 of the second meeting of the Conference of the Parties to CITES, held in San José, Costa Rica in 1979. Recommendation Conf. 2.7 also recommended that Parties which do not currently adhere to the Whaling Convention be encouraged to do so.
[102] Council Regulation No. 348/81, Article 1; *O.J. Eur Comm.* No. L 39 (12 February 1981), p. 1, corrected by No. L 132 (19 May 1981), p. 30.
[103] 19 *I.L.M.* 841; *T.I.A.S.* no. 10240; *U.K.T.S.* no. 48 (1982), Cmd. 8714. See Chapter 9 below for a detailed discussion of the Convention.
[104] The Convention on the Conservation of Antarctic Marine Living Resources, Article 24(3).

from the rights and obligations of Parties under the Whaling Convention.[105]

8. *Conclusion*

On one hand, it could be stated with some justification that the Parties to the Whaling Convention have failed to achieve its objectives. The IWC has neither overseen an orderly development of the whaling industry nor effectively conserved whale stocks. On the other hand, the IWC has stimulated a substantial amount of research into whales and whaling, the system of enforcement established by the IWC has ensured that, on the whole, its regulations have been complied with relatively well, and the annual meetings of the Commission have ensured that problems such as "pirate" whaling have been rapidly brought to the attention of Party governments. Most importantly of all, the IWC has proved itself able, albeit belatedly, to decide to bring at least a temporary halt to commercial whaling in order to give depleted stocks the opportunity to recover.

Whether the IWC remains a powerful force depends primarily on whether the whaling States agree to abide by this decision and continue to participate in the Commission. If they eventually withdraw their objections and accept the decision, the expense of maintaining a non-operational whaling fleet may cause whaling States to disband their fleets and to end commercial whaling for the foreseeable future. If they do not, the whaling States may establish a commission of their own, leaving the IWC as a defunct body composed only of non-whaling members.

---

[105] *Ibid.*, Article 6.

CHAPTER 3

SEALS AND POLAR BEARS

"The old grey music doctors of the ocean, their holy happy eyes shining
devotion, applaud and blow in foam and soft commotion."
(L.A.G. Strong, *The Seals*)

1. *Seals*

Sealing is one of the oldest forms of commercial exploitation of
wildlife. Starting in the late eighteenth century,[1] commercial sealing
expanded steadily during the course of the nineteenth century,
reaching a peak about 1890. By the early 1900s, so many seal
populations had been depleted — some were on the verge of
extinction — that the need for controls on their exploitation had
become imperative. Since many seals either occurred outside areas
of national jurisdiction or migrated from one State's jurisdiction to
another, international cooperation was vital if controls were to be
successful. A number of sealing treaties have been concluded since
the turn of the century, and this chapter examines four which are
now in force. They are the Interim Convention on the Conservation
of North Pacific Fur Seals, the Convention for the Conservation of
Antarctic Seals, the Agreement on Measures to Regulate Sealing
and to Protect Seal Stocks in the Northeastern Part of the Atlantic
Ocean and the Agreement on Sealing and the Conservation of Seal
Stocks in the Northwest Atlantic.

These four treaties are concerned exclusively with seals, but it
should be emphasised that they are not the only treaties governing
the conservation and exploitation of seals. There are several more
which are considered elsewhere in this book because they cover
other species as well as seals. The Convention on International
Trade in Endangered Species of Wild Fauna and Flora ("CITES"),
for example, prohibits international commercial trade in monk seals
(*Monachus* spp.) and limits international trade in southern elephant
seals (*Mirounga leonina*) and southern fur seals (*Arctocephalus* spp.) to a
level which will not be detrimental to their survival.[2] In addition, the

---

[1] The first commercial sealing operation began in 1786 when Gerassim Pribilof, a
Russian navigator, discovered the breeding grounds of the northern fur seal (*Callorhinus
ursinus*) on St. George and St. Paul Islands, which are part of the group known today as the
Pribilof Islands. When the U.S.A. bought Alaska in 1867, the Pribilof Islands were included as
part of the package and they are now U.S. property.

[2] Monk seals are listed in Appendix I of CITES, while southern elephant seals and
southern fur seals are in Appendix II. See Chapter 12 below for further discussion of the
trading restrictions imposed by CITES on species listed in Appendix I and II of the
Convention.

Convention Concerning the Protection of the World Cultural and Natural Heritage, the Convention on the Conservation of European Wildlife and Natural Habitats and the Convention on the Conservation of Migratory Species of Wild Animals each protect various seal breeding grounds.[3]

a)   *Northern fur seals (Callorhinus ursinus)*

i)   *Background*

The first formal sealing treaty was concluded in 1891. It was a bilateral agreement between the U.K. (on behalf of Canada) and the U.S.A. Its objective was to limit the exploitation of northern fur seals (also known as North Pacific fur seals) whose populations had been seriously depleted by over-harvesting in the nineteenth century. It lasted less than a year and was followed by various other bilateral agreements until in 1911 Japan, the U.K. (on behalf of Canada), the U.S.A. and the U.S.S.R. concluded the multilateral Treaty for the Preservation and Protection of Fur Seals ("the 1911 Treaty").[4]

The most important provision of the 1911 Treaty was its strict curtailment of pelagic sealing,[5] a widespread and particularly wasteful method of sealing which involved killing seals on their migratory routes at sea rather than when they were out of the water on their breeding grounds. Many animals were wounded or killed without being retrieved, and most seals taken at sea were females, thus further reducing the population's breeding potential.[6]

The 1911 Treaty did not limit the number of seals which could be killed on their breeding grounds, but it required the countries on whose islands the killing took place to supervise the harvest. The most important northern fur seal breeding grounds are the Pribilof Islands (owned by the U.S.A.) and Commander, Robben and Kurile Islands (owned by the U.S.S.R.). A treaty restricting pelagic sealing was obviously beneficial to the two Parties with access to the breeding grounds, so the 1911 Treaty established a system of compensation whereby they were required to share a portion of their harvest with the two other Parties in return for the latters' agreement to stop pelagic sealing.

[3] For detailed discussion of these three conventions, see Chapters 11, 8 and 13 respectively.

[4] 37 *Stat.* 1542; *Treaty Series*, no. 564.

[5] I.e. killing seals at sea. Pelagic sealing was prohibited except by "Indians, Ainos, Aleuts, or other aborigines ... in canoes ... propelled entirely by oars, paddles or sails ... in the way hitherto practiced and without the use of firearms."

[6] See *Final Environmental Impact Statement on the Interim Convention on the Conservation of North Pacific Fur Seals* (U.S. Department of Commerce, Sept. 1980), p. 1.

The 1911 Treaty terminated in 1941, but it was replaced in February 1957 by the Interim Convention on the Conservation of North Pacific Fur Seals (the "Interim Convention"). The Interim Convention has the same Parties as the 1911 Treaty (with the exception that Canada is a Party in her own right and the U.K. is not a Party), has retained the basic principles of the 1911 Treaty and, as amended, is still in force today.[7] The Interim Convention established the North Pacific Fur Seal Commission to oversee implementation of the Convention. Each Party is a member of the Commission,[8] which meets annually.[9]

Initially the northern fur seal conventions proved extremely successful, overseeing a steady recovery in seal populations from their depleted state at the turn of the century. But in the last twenty years populations have undergone a marked decline, and the Parties to the Interim Convention have been unable, so far, to stem the downward trend. The total pre-exploitation population is estimated to have been 3-4 million seals, the majority of which bred in the Pribilof Islands.[10] By 1911 seal numbers had been reduced to about 300,000.[11] From 1911 until the 1950s, helped by a complete ban on commercial sealing from 1912-1917, the Pribilof population steadily recovered to a point where it reached its estimated pre-exploitation level of 2-2.5 million.[12] It has now dwindled to about 1.2 million.[13] The initial decline is thought to have resulted from a six year period of killing females between 1956 and 1962. Since the 1960s, the entanglement of seals in fishing nets and other debris is thought to have been the major problem, although there may be other factors involved which have not yet been identified.[14] The Soviet fur seal

---

[7] 314 *U.N.T.S.* 105. Signed on 9 February 1957, the Interim Convention came into force on 14 October 1957. After six years it was renewed for a further six years by the Protocol Amending the Interim Convention (8 October 1963, *T.I.A.S.* no. 5558) and again by the Agreement Extending the Interim Convention (3 September 1969, *T.I.A.S.* no. 6774). It was then extended for four years by the Protocol Amending the Interim Convention (7 May 1976, *T.I.A.S.* no. 8368) and for four more years by the Protocol Amending the Interim Convention (14 October 1980, *T.I.A.S.* no. 10020). A Protocol to extend the Interim Convention for a further four years is currently being negotiated.

[8] Interim Convention, Article V(1).

[9] *Ibid.*, Article V(6). Additional meetings may be held if requested by two members of the Commission.

[10] See *Draft Environmental Impact Statement on the Interim Convention on Conservation of North Pacific Fur Seals,* (U.S. Departments of State and Commerce, Oct. 1983), (hereinafter referred to as *Draft E.I.S.*), pp. 23-4. The Pribilof population is thought to have numbered 2-2.5 million, and the Commander population is estimated at 1-1.7 million.

[11] *Draft E.I.S.,* note 10 above, pp. 23-4.

[12] *Ibid.,* p. 23.

[13] See *Annual Report of the Marine Mammal Commission, Calendar Year 1983, a Report to Congress,* p. 23 (published by the Marine Mammal Commission, 1625 I St. NW, Washington DC, 1984).

[14] See *Draft E.I.S.,* note 10 above, pp. 21-4, 26, 106 and 108.

population increased from 1911 until the late 1960s when it experienced a similar period of decline, although Soviet scientists believe the population has now stabilised.[15] Entanglement is thought to have been the main problem for the Soviet population as well.

The killing of northern fur seals for commercial purposes has been reduced in recent years. The fact that it takes place at all has been criticised in some quarters because of declining seal populations, although North Pacific Fur Seal Commission scientists are adamant in their view that the harvest of bachelor seals, which form the majority of seals killed, has no impact on population trends.

ii)   *Objective of the Interim Convention*

The objective of the Interim Convention is to maximise harvest levels of northern fur seals. The preamble states that the Parties desire

> ...to take effective measures towards achieving the maximum sustainable productivity of the fur seal resources of the North Pacific Ocean so that the fur seal populations can be brought to and maintained at the levels which will provide the greatest harvest year after year, with due regard to their relation to the productivity of other living marine resources of the areas.

iii)   *Research*

Article II(1) of the Interim Convention states that in order to realise the objectives of the Convention the Parties agree to coordinate and cooperate in their research programmes to determine

> a) what measures may be necessary to make possible the maximum sustainable productivity of the fur seal resources so that the fur seal populations can be brought to and maintained at the levels which will provide the greatest harvest year after year; and
> b) what the relationship is between fur seals and other living marine resources and whether fur seals have detrimental effects on other marine living resources substantially exploited by any of the Parties and, if so, to what extent.

The North Pacific Fur Seal Commission is responsible for deciding on research programmes to achieve these objectives and for

---

[15] *Ibid.*, pp. 25 and 108. See also K. Yoshida and N. Baba, *Trend Analysis of Fur Seal Pup Population of Robben Island* (1982), submitted to the 25th Annual Meeting of the North Pacific Fur Seal Commission.

collecting and analysing the results.[16] Feeding habits, migratory patterns, population trends, reproductive cycles and the entanglement of seals in fishermen's nets are just some of the areas into which research has been carried out. Article IV of the Interim Convention states that each Party shall bear the expense of its own research and that sealskins taken during research activities belong to the Party conducting the research.

iv) *Pelagic sealing*

Except in two limited circumstances, the Interim Convention prohibits all pelagic sealing in the Pacific Ocean north of 30° north including the Bering, Okhotsk and Japan seas.[17]

The first exception is when it is carried out for research purposes, although Article II(3)(b) states that no more than 2,500 seals in the Eastern Pacific and 2,200 seals in the Western Pacific may be taken pelagically for research purposes in any one year without the express authorisation of the North Pacific Fur Seal Commission. In practice much fewer seals are taken pelagically for research purposes than the maximum allowed by the Interim Convention. Neither Canada, the U.S.A. nor the U.S.S.R. have taken significant numbers in recent years. Japan took about 1,000 animals in the early 1980s but agreed at the 1984 meeting of the North Pacific Fur Seal Commission to limit its future take to 200 males.[18]

The second exception is for

Indians, Ainos, Aleuts or Eskimos dwelling on the coast of the waters mentioned in Article III who carry on pelagic sealing in canoes not transported by or used in connection with other vessels, and propelled entirely by oars, paddles, or sails, and manned by not more than five persons each, in the way hitherto practiced and without the use of firearms; provided that such hunters are not in the employment of other persons or under contract to deliver the skins to any person.[19]

Prior to the renewal of the Interim Convention in 1980,[20] it was suggested in the U.S.A. that it might be better to replace the Interim Convention with a bilateral treaty between the U.S.A. and Canada on the grounds that the U.S. Marine Mammal Protection Act had been extended to apply to a zone up to 200 miles from the U.S.

[16] Interim Convention, Article V(2).

[17] *Ibid.*, Article III.

[18] *Summary Record, North Pacific Fur Seal Commission, Fourth Plenary Session, 11 April 1984,* Doc. SR/27/4.

[19] Interim Convention, Article VII.

[20] See note 7 above.

coastline and that the threat of pelagic sealing by other countries had consequently been greatly reduced.[21] Evidence that as many as 85% of northern fur seals travel beyond 200 miles from U.S. coastlines during all or part of their life cycle ultimately caused the U.S.A. to seek a renewal of the Interim Convention in 1980, although there is some doubt as to whether pelagic sealing would in fact recur at a significant level in any event because of the costs involved.

v)   *Share of harvest*

The Interim Convention has a similar system to the one established by the 1911 Treaty whereby the two Parties with jurisdiction over the northern fur seal breeding grounds (U.S.A. and U.S.S.R.) are obliged to share a portion of their commercial seal harvest with Canada and Japan in return for the latters' restraint on pelagic sealing. Article IX(1) of the Interim Convention requires the U.S.A. and U.S.S.R. to give Canada and Japan 15% each of the gross number of skins that they take commercially each year.[22] The 1911 Treaty required the U.S.A. and U.S.S.R. to pay Canada and Japan U.S.$10,000 each for every year that they did not hold a seal harvest, but the Interim Convention imposes no such penalty.

Comments made by the U.S. Commissioner at the 1984 meeting of the North Pacific Fur Seal Commission imply a belief on the part of the U.S.A. that once the Commission has recommended a quota, and the U.S.A. has accepted it, the U.S.A. is obliged to give Canada and Japan 15% of that quota even if the U.S.A. decides to forego its share of the harvest. He told the Commission that

from a marketability standpoint, the U.S. has noted difficulties in recent years in skin sales and might forego its share of the harvest and harvest only that portion which would be due to other Party governments.[23]

The Japanese Commissioner replied that Japan was only entitled to a percentage of skins actually taken, an interpretation which is more consistent with the wording of the Convention. Article IX(1) states:

The respective Parties agree that, *of the total number of sealskins taken* commercially each season on land, there shall at the end of the season

---

[21] See M. Bean, *The Evolution of National Wildlife Law* (Praeger, 1983), p. 260.

[22] Articles IX(2) and (3) establish a system whereby the amounts of sealskins delivered to Canada and Japan may change in certain circumstances in order to divide the cost of pelagic research more equitably.

[23] *Summary Record, North Pacific Fur Seal Commission, Fifth Plenary Session, 11 April 1984*, Doc. SR/27/5, para 4.

be delivered a percentage of the gross in number and value thereof as follows... (emphasis added)

The words "of the total number of sealskins taken" make it quite clear that the sharing system only applies to skins which are actually taken and not to a theoretical quota which may not, in practice, be reached.

vi)   *Size of harvest*

Article V(2)(d) of the Interim Convention makes the North Pacific Fur Seal Commission responsible for recommending, among other things,

> ...measures regarding the size and the sex and age composition of the seasonal commercial kill from a herd and regarding a reduction or suspension of the harvest of seals on any island or group of islands in case the total number of seals on that island or group of islands falls below the level of maximum sustainable productivity; provided, however, that due consideration be given to the subsistence needs of Indians, Ainos, Aleuts or Eskimos who live on the islands where fur seals breed, when it is not possible to provide sufficient seal meat for such persons from the seasonal commercial harvest or research activities.

Article V(2)(d)'s call for a reduction or suspension of the harvest when seal populations fall below the level of maximum sustainable productivity is particularly interesting because there is now clear scientific evidence that many of the populations still being harvested are below maximum sustainable productivity.[24] The dilemma is what to do about it. One obvious option is to end the harvest, yet of the 30,000 seals still killed each year the vast majority are bachelor males, and Commission scientists believe there is no evidence that this harvest is contributing to the population decline.[25] On the other hand, the rate of decline on St. Paul Island, where there is a substantial harvest, is higher than on St. George Island where only a relatively small subsistence kill is permitted,[26] and it is claimed by some that the population is expanding on the San Miguel Islands where no killing of bachelor males is allowed at all.[27] Whatever the answer, there is no doubt that the Interim

[24] See *Draft E.I.S.*, note 10 above, pp. 25 and 113.

[25] *Ibid.*, pp. 26 and 114. See also *Summary Record, North Pacific Fur Seal Commission, Fifth Plenary Session, 11 April 1984*, Doc. SR/27/5, para 3.

[26] See *Draft E.I.S.*, note 10 above, p. 109.

[27] See *Petition to the U.S. National Marine Fisheries Service to list the northern fur seal as a threatened species under the U.S. Endangered Species Act* (5 January 1984), presented by the Humane Society of the United States, 2100 L St. NW, Washington DC, pp. 11-12.

Convention imposes a responsibility on the Commission to take the necessary remedial measures if, as has happened, seal populations do fall below levels necessary for maximum sustainable productivity.

vii) *Other functions of the North Pacific Fur Seal Commission*

In addition to its formal responsibilities, the Commission performs an invaluable informal function in the sense that its annual meetings keep the Parties constantly aware of their obligations under the Interim Convention and provide an excellent opportunity for the Parties to take appropriate action when problems arise. For example, the U.S.A. was under internal political pressure in the early 1970s to look for more humane methods of killing and tagging seals. The other Parties were able to respond to this concern, and an appropriate amendment was incorporated into the 1976 Protocol to the Interim Convention.[28] The Commission has also provided a useful forum for Parties to discuss the problem of entanglement in fishing debris. The problem is far from solved, but Commission meetings do at least give the Parties the opportunity to share information on research carried out and to exchange ideas on possible solutions.

viii) *Enforcement*

The Interim Convention contains a number of provisions which are designed to assist enforcement of the Convention. Each Party is required to prohibit any person or vessel from using any part of its territory for any purpose designed to violate the Convention's restrictions on pelagic sealing,[29] and each Party must prohibit the import of, and internal trade in, skins of seals taken other than in accordance with the Convention.[30] All skins must be officially marked and duly certified by the authorities of the Party concerned before they can be legally traded.[31] Duly authorised officials of any Party may search and seize any vessel which they have reasonable cause to believe is offending against the Convention's restrictions on pelagic sealing, provided it is not within the territorial waters of another State.[32] However, the vessel must then be handed over for

[28] See note 7 above. Article X of the 1976 Protocol replaced Article IX(3) of the Convention with the following: "The respective Parties will seek to ensure the utilization of those methods for the capture and killing and marking of fur seals on land or at sea which will spare the fur seals pain and suffering to the greatest extent practicable."
[29] Interim Convention, Article VIII(1).
[30] *Ibid.*, Article VIII(2).
[31] *Ibid.*
[32] *Ibid.*, Article VI(1) and (2).

trial to the State to which it belongs.[33] Each Party is required to enact and enforce "such legislation as may be necessary to guarantee the observance of this Convention and to make effective its provisions with appropriate penalties for violation thereof",[34] and if any Party considers that another Party is not complying with its obligations, it has the right to notify all other Parties to that effect and the Parties must then meet within three months to discuss remedial measures.[35]

The fact that the Parties must report to the Commission the numbers of northern fur seals that they have killed each year[36] and the fact that the proceedings of Commission meetings are published are also important enforcement tools because they ensure that any violations will be rapidly brought to the public attention. Parties are likely to prefer to comply with the terms of the Convention than to face the wrath of public opinion if they do not — especially since the killing of seals is an issue which arouses such strong public sentiment.

ix) *Conclusion*

For the first sixty years of their existence, the various northern fur seal treaties can rightly claim to have been extremely successful. They oversaw a steady growth in seal populations, while at the same time supervising substantial seal harvests. The Interim Convention has not worked so well. It has neither achieved its objective of "the greatest harvest year after year" nor maintained the high seal populations of the early 1950s. The annual harvest is half what it was twenty years ago and so is the size of the population, at least in the Pribilofs. On the other hand, the situation might have been much worse without the Interim Convention. Very few female seals have been killed in recent years, the Convention has restricted pelagic sealing to a minimal amount for research purposes and useful research work has been carried out.

The real test of the Interim Convention may still lie ahead. Will the Commission have the ability and willpower to identify the causes of the population decline and to take the necessary measures to counteract them? Will it end the annual commercial harvests on the basis that the benefit of any doubt as to the impact of any harvest should go to the seals rather than to the harvest until the populations recover? If northern fur seal breeding grounds are

[33] *Ibid.*, Article VI(2) and (3).
[34] *Ibid.*, Article X.
[35] *Ibid.*, Article XII.
[36] *Ibid.*, Article II(4).

targeted for oil and gas development, will the Commission be able to do anything about it? These questions pose very real dilemmas, and the outlook for the northern fur seal may be rather gloomy unless they can be answered affirmatively.

b) *Antarctic seals*

i) *Background*

Of the six species of seals found in Antarctica, four — Ross seal (*Ommatophoca rossi*), crabeater seal (*Lobodon carcinophaque*), leopard seal (*Hydrurga leptonyx*) and Weddell seal (*Leptonychotos weddelli*) — have never been subjected to significant exploitation by man.[37] Southern elephant seals (*Mirounga leonina*) and southern fur seals (*Arctocephalus* spp.) were heavily exploited in the nineteenth and early twentieth centuries and the populations of both were seriously depleted, but the exploitation ceased several decades ago and populations have now recovered almost to their estimated pre-exploitation level.[38]

In 1959 twelve nations which had traditionally been interested in Antarctica signed the Antarctic Treaty.[39] Article IX(1)(f) of the Treaty authorises its Parties to make recommendations for the "preservation and conservation of living resources in Antarctica", and the Parties have made a number of recommendations to restrict the exploitation of seals and other fauna.[40] However, when an exploratory Norwegian commercial sealing operation began in 1964, the Parties to the Antarctic Treaty became sufficiently nervous of the possibility of a new era of uncontrolled sealing as to begin negotiations for a binding legal instrument to regulate sealing in Antarctica, rather than relying on non-binding recommendations. The result of their negotiations was the Convention for the Conservation of Antarctic Seals (the "Antarctic Seals Convention"),[41] which was concluded in February 1972 and came into force on 11 March 1978.[42] In addition to its strict regulation of

[37] Indeed the populations of some of these species may now be higher than they have ever been because of the increased availability of food resulting from the depletion of Antarctic stocks of the large baleen whales.

[38] See Mitchell and Sandbrook, *The Management of the Southern Ocean* (International Institute for Environment and Development, 1980), pp. 34-40.

[39] 12 *U.S.T.* 794; *T.I.A.S.* no. 4780.

[40] For a more detailed analysis of the Antarctic Treaty and the conservation measures adopted pursuant thereto, see Chapter 9 below.

[41] 11 *I.L.M.* 251; *T.I.A.S.* no. 8826; *U.K.T.S.* no. 45 (1978) Cmd 7209; 29 *U.S.T.* 441.

[42] As required by Article 13(1), the Antarctic Seals Convention entered into force on the thirtieth day following the date of deposit of the seventh instrument of ratification or acceptance. The Convention has now been ratified by Argentina, Belgium, Chile, France, Japan, Norway, Poland, South Africa, U.K., U.S.A. and U.S.S.R. Australia and New Zealand have signed but have not yet ratified.

sealing, the Antarctic Seals Convention is noteworthy as the first international conservation agreement to have been concluded prior to any significant commercial exploitation of the resource it is intended to protect. This is important because conservation is much easier to achieve *ab initio* than after vested interests have become established and over-exploitation has become the norm.[43]

ii) *Provisions of the Antarctic Seals Convention*

In contrast to the Interim Convention which aims to secure the greatest harvest year after year, the Antarctic Seals Convention emphasises protection. "Rational use of Antarctic seals" is one of the objectives of the Convention but it is on a par with "protection", "scientific study" and the maintenance of "a satisfactory balance with the ecological system".[44]

The Annex to the Antarctic Seals Convention, which is an integral part of the Convention, forbids the killing or capture of Ross seals, southern elephant seals and southern fur seals.[45] However, Parties are allowed to permit "limited quantities" of any species to be killed or captured in order "to provide indispensable food for men or dogs or to provide for scientific research or to provide specimens for museums and educational or cultural institutions."[46] The Annex allows crabeater seals, leopard seals and Weddell seals to be taken in any given year up to a maximum of 175,000, 12,000 and 5,000 animals respectively.[47] However, it prohibits pelagic sealing except in limited numbers for research purposes.[48] The Annex also establishes closed seasons,[49] sealing zones[50] and sealing reserves.[51] It invites the Scientific Committee on Antarctic Research of the International Council of Scientific Unions (SCAR) to make recommendations on humane methods of killing and capturing,[52] and it requires the Parties to report, by 31 October each year, all seals that they have killed or captured in the area covered by the Antarctic Seals Convention during the preceding period of 1 July-30

---

[43] The Convention on the Conservation of Antarctic Marine Living Resources, which came into force in 1982, is probably the only other "pre-exploitation convention" to have been concluded. See Chapter 9 for further discussion of this Convention.

[44] Preamble to the Antarctic Seals Convention.

[45] Annex to the Antarctic Seals Convention, section 2(a).

[46] Antarctic Seals Convention, Article 4(1).

[47] Annex to the Antarctic Seals Convention, section 1. These numbers are subject to review in the light of scientific assessments.

[48] *Ibid.*, section 7(b).

[49] *Ibid.*, section 3.

[50] *Ibid.*, section 4.

[51] *Ibid.*, section 5.

[52] *Ibid.*, section 7(a).

June.[53] Each Party must also notify other Parties and SCAR by 31 October each year of any steps they have taken to implement the Convention during the preceding period of 1 July-30 June.[54] Even if it has nothing to report, each Party must indicate this formally before 31 October every year.[55]

Any Party may propose an amendment to the Annex. It will be adopted if approved by two thirds of the Parties but will not bind any Party who notifies the Depository (the U.K. government) of its objection.[56] The Antarctic Seals Convention specifically authorises the Parties to adopt any domestic measures other than those already in the Annex which they deem to be appropriate for the "conservation, scientific study and rational and humane use of seal resources."[57]

The Antarctic Seals Convention did not establish a Commission, but it authorises any Party to propose a meeting of Parties to establish a Commission after commercial sealing has begun.[58] The strict reporting requirements of the Convention should ensure that any commercial sealing operation is rapidly brought to the attention of the Parties if one does begin.

iii) *Relationship with other treaties*

The Antarctic Seals Convention is closely tied to the system established by the Antarctic Treaty. All Parties to the Antarctic Seals Convention are also Parties to the Antarctic Treaty,[59] and no State can accede to the Antarctic Seals Convention without the consent of all existing Parties.[60] Furthermore, Article 1(1) requires the Parties to affirm the provisions of Article IV of the Antarctic Treaty, thus obliging them to accept the Antarctic Treaty's foreclosure of claims to territorial sovereignty in Antarctica.[61]

The Antarctic Seals Convention has not been superceded by the recently concluded Convention on the Conservation of Antarctic Marine Living Resources,[62] although the latter does have some jurisdiction over Antarctic seals. The Antarctic Seals Convention

[53] *Ibid.*, section 6(a).
[54] Antarctic Seals Convention, Article 5(2).
[55] *Ibid.*, Article 5(3).
[56] *Ibid.*, Article 9.
[57] *Ibid.*, Article 3(1).
[58] *Ibid.*, Article 6(1).
[59] See p. 156 below.
[60] Antarctic Seals Convention, Article 12.
[61] See pp. 159-160 below.
[62] Indeed, the Antarctic Marine Living Resources Convention specifically provides that nothing therein shall derogate from the rights and obligations of Parties under the Antarctic Seals Convention. See pp. 162-163 below.

applies to "the seas south of 60 degrees South Latitude",[63] while the Antarctic Marine Living Resources Convention includes the area between that latitude and the Antarctic Convergence.[64] Therefore, any exploitation of seals north of 60 degrees South latitude and south of the Antarctic Convergence will now be covered by the Antarctic Marine Living Resources Convention.

iv) *Conclusion*

Sealing in Antarctica has not taken place to any significant degree since the Antarctic Seals Convention was concluded, and it may never develop into a serious commercial venture. However, if it does, the system established by the Convention should ensure that over-harvesting does not occur.

c) *Bilateral sealing agreements*

Two bilateral agreements relating to the conservation and exploitation of seals are in force and operational. They are the Agreement on Measures to Regulate Sealing and to Protect Seal Stocks in the Northeastern Part of the Atlantic Ocean, which was concluded by Norway and the U.S.S.R. in 1957 (the "1957 Agreement"),[65] and the Agreement between Canada and Norway on Sealing and the Conservation of Seal Stocks in the Northwest Atlantic which was concluded in 1971 (the "1971 Agreement").[66]

i) *The 1957 Agreement*

The preamble to the 1957 Agreement states that the objective of the Agreement is to

[63] Antarctic Seals Convention, Article 1(1). It should be noted that the Antarctic Seals Convention does not cover seals which are hauled out on land, but they are covered by the Agreed Measures for the Conservation of Antarctic Fauna and Flora. See Chapter 9 at pp. 174-175.

[64] See Chapter 9 for a detailed analysis of the Convention on the Conservation of Antarctic Marine Living Resources.

[65] 309 *U.N.T.S.* 269.

[66] U.N. LEG/SER.B/16, p. 655. An Agreement between Finland and the U.S.S.R. Concerning Fishing and Sealing is also in force. First concluded in 1922, it was subsequently amended in 1959 and 1969. It is of no real conservation value because it merely grants Finnish nationals the right to hunt seals in certain areas of the Gulf of Finland which are within the jurisdiction of the U.S.S.R. The Convention between Denmark and Norway Concerning East Greenland, which was signed on 9 July 1924, and entered into force the next day, (27 *L.N.T.S.* 203) is also still in force but has apparently had little practical impact with respect to seals. Article 3 of the Convention provides that "hunting, sealing and fishing may not be carried on recklessly, in such a way as might result in the extermination of seals or other useful animals, such as musk oxen or eider ducks" and also that "the Contracting Parties agree that they will, when the occasion arises, enter into negotiations for the introduction of uniform regulations in regard to such matters". However, Denmark and Norway have apparently never entered into such negotiations.

...establish international cooperation for the purpose of achieving the optimum productivity of seal stocks in the waters of the north eastern part of the Atlantic Ocean, so that the size of these stocks may be increased and maintained at a level ensuring the maximum sustained catch and...to broaden and to coordinate scientific research for the purpose of studying the condition of the seal stocks in that area.

The 1957 Agreement applies to harp seal (*Pagophilus groenlandica*), hooded seal (*Cystophora cristata*) and walrus (*Odobaenus rosmarus*).[67] The Annex, which is an integral part of the Agreement, restricts the hunting of harp and hooded seal to certain specific areas and seasons and prohibits the taking of walrus in all areas throughout the year.[68] Licenses for taking walrus may be issued, however, for purposes of scientific research or to meet the needs of local indigenous inhabitants and expeditions provided that the raw materials are used for food, animal feed and other local domestic purposes only.[69] Article 3 of the Agreement establishes a Commission which meets annually and consists of not more than three representatives from each country. The primary functions of the Commission are to recommend measures for the regulation of hunting operations, such as quotas on the annual harvest of harp and hooded seals,[70] to submit proposals relating to scientific research,[71] and, if necessary, to submit proposals for measures to ensure that the provisions of the Agreement are properly enforced.[72] These recommendations and proposals are generally based on the advice of a Scientific Committee which meets in advance of the annual meetings of the Commission.

The exact geographic scope of the 1957 Agreement is somewhat confusing. As drafted, it regulates sealing in large areas of the Greenland Sea, Barents Sea, Denmark Straits and Jan Mayen region, which in 1957 were outside the jurisdiction of both Norway and the U.S.S.R. However, in line with the emerging Law of the Sea, Norway and the U.S.S.R. now exercise coastal State jurisdiction over marine living resources in zones up to 200 miles from their respective coastlines. The 1957 Agreement has not yet been

---

[67] Under Article 1(3) of the 1957 Agreement, the Commission has the authority to propose that the application of the Agreement be extended to cover bearded seals (*Erignathus barbatus*), ringed seals (*Pusa hispida*) and polar bears (*Ursus maritimus*). The Commission has not yet exercised this authority.

[68] 1957 Agreement, Annex, sections 1-4.

[69] The 1957 Agreement, Article 9(1). Article 9(2) requires the Parties to inform the Commission of the issuance of all such licenses. See also section 4 of the Annex.

[70] The 1957 Agreement, Article 4(a). In 1983, for example, the annual quota was set at 40,000 harp seals and 20,000 hooded seals.

[71] *Ibid.*, Article 4(b).

[72] *Ibid.*, Article 4(c).

amended to revise the areas within its scope but much of the pack ice used by seals in the Denmark Straits and East Barents Sea is now within coastal State jurisdiction.

ii) *The 1971 Agreement*

The 1971 Agreement also recognises the need for international cooperation with respect to sealing and scientific research into seal stocks in the Northwest Atlantic. However, its preamble puts greater emphasis on conservation than the preamble to the 1957 Convention, declaring that it is the desire of Canada and Norway to develop and maintain "the most effective conservation measures in order to secure the best possible protection of the seal stocks in this area and a rational utilisation of these resources", to ensure that "humane catching methods are used in sealing" and to extend and coordinate their scientific research concerning seal stocks in the Northwest Atlantic.

Like the 1957 Agreement, the 1971 Agreement applies to harp seal, hooded seal and walrus but it also applies to bearded seal (*Erignathus barbatus*).[73] In practice, however, the quotas established pursuant to the 1971 Agreement are made up entirely of harp and hooded seal, and neither Norway nor Canada allow bearded seal or walrus to be hunted commercially.[74] The 1971 Agreement set up a Commission which meets annually, consists of three representatives of each country and theoretically has almost indentical functions to those of the Commission established by the 1957 Agreement. However, the practical importance of the Commission under the 1971 Agreement was severely curtailed when, in 1977, Canada and Greenland extended their coastal State jurisdiction over marine living resources to zones up to 200 miles from their coastlines. Populations of harp and hooded seal, which had traditionally been hunted by Norwegian sealers in areas of the Northwest Atlantic which had been on the high seas, were suddenly no longer on the high seas but were under Canada's total control. This effectively removed the need for the 1971 Agreement since the Norwegians no longer had the option of pulling out of the Agreement and indulging in uncontrolled sealing in the Northwest Atlantic even if they wished to do so.

[73] As orginally drafted, the 1971 Agreement applied only to harp seal. However, pursuant to Article II of the Agreement which vests authority in the Commission to extend the application of the Agreement to hooded seal, bearded seal and walrus, the Agreement was so extended in 1976.

[74] Article IX of the 1971 Agreement allows local people to take both bearded seal and walrus and to sell their parts and products.

Because of Norway's traditional sealing in the area and the mutual desire for amicable relations between the two countries, the 1971 Agreement has remained in force, but the role of the Commission, in which Norway and Canada have equal votes, has been greatly reduced. For example, in contrast to its counterpart under the 1957 Agreement, the Commission does not recommend quotas for the annual harvest of harp and hooded seals in the Northwest Atlantic. Total Allowable Catch limits ("TACs") for these populations are recommended by the Scientific Council of the Northwest Atlantic Fisheries Organisation whose membership includes several countries in addition to Norway and Canada and whose scope covers various species of fish as well as harp and hooded seal. The ultimate decision on TACs for harp and hooded seal is made after informal mutual consultation between Canada and the European Economic Community. The EEC represents the interests of Greenland in her new 200 mile coastal zone. Once the TACs have been agreed, Canada and the EEC then negotiate an agreement as to how the TACs will be divided between Canada and Greenland. The primary function of the Commission under the 1971 Agreement is now to negotiate the percentage of the Canadian share of the TACs which Norwegian sealers will be allowed to take inside the Canadian 200 mile coastal zone and also to discuss the regulations which Canada will apply to the sealing operations. In 1982, for example, Canada was allocated 186,000 harp seals and 15,000 hooded seals out of which it was agreed that Norwegian sealers would be allowed to take 24,000 harp seals and 6,000 hooded seals. However, the recent dramatic decrease in numbers of harp and hooded seals harvested, caused primarily by the European Economic Community ban on imports of harp and hooded seal skins which came into effect on 1 October 1983,[75] has reduced the importance of the Commission still further.

iii) *Conclusion*

The importance of the 1957 and 1971 Agreements has been diminished both by the general extension of coastal State jurisdiction over marine living resources in the 1970s and by the recent decrease in numbers of seals harvested. However, the fact that both Agreements are still in force reflects the recognition by the countries concerned of the value of continuing international cooperation in whatever the future holds with respect to the protection and exploitation of seal stocks in the North Atlantic.

[75] Council Directive 83/129/EEC; *O.J. Eur. Comm.* No. L 91 (9 April 1983), p. 30.

2. Polar Bears (Ursus maritimus)

a) Background

In 1965, representatives of the five circumpolar States in whose territory polar bears occur '(Canada, Denmark (including Greenland), Norway, the U.S.A. and the U.S.S.R.) met in Fairbanks, Alaska to discuss the growing concern over the future of the species. The U.S.S.R., which had banned all hunting of polar bears since 1955, stated at the meeting that

> the world's total polar bear population has decreased sharply over the past 50-60 years. This in our view has been a result of economic penetration of the North, an increase in harvesting and the warming up of the Arctic ... it is important to note that the reduction of numbers has been observed equally in all Arctic regions, without exception.

As a result of that and later meetings, the International Union for Conservation of Nature and Natural Resources ("IUCN") prepared a draft treaty for the protection of polar bears. Called the Agreement on the Conservation of Polar Bears (the "Polar Bear Agreement"), it was eventually signed by the five circumpolar States in Oslo on 15 November 1973.[76] The Polar Bear Agreement entered into force on 26 May 1976, ninety days after three of the signatories had deposited instruments of ratification,[77] but it was not until 25 January 1978 that all five States had ratified. The Agreement has three main objectives: to persuade the Parties to coordinate with respect to their research programmes, to restrict the killing and capturing of polar bears and to protect the ecosystems of which polar bears are a part. The latter objective is particularly significant because of the increasing exploration of the Arctic for oil and other minerals, which will inevitably bring the disturbance of men and machines and the danger of pollution to important polar bear habitats.[78]

There has been one formal meeting of the Parties since the Polar Bear Agreement entered into force. Held in Oslo in January 1981, it was called a "Consultative Meeting" and made several recommendations to improve implementation of the Agreement.

[76] 13 I.L.M. 13, T.I.A.S. no. 8409; 27 U.S.T. 3918.

[77] As required by Article X(4) of the Polar Bear Agreement.

[78] See Consultative Meeting of the Contracting Parties to the Agreement on the Conservation of Polar Bears (1981), Report of the Meeting: Summary and Conclusions; Oslo, 20-22 January 1981 (hereinafter referred to as Report of the Consultative Meeting). See also The IUCN Mammal Red Data Book Part I (IUCN, 1196 Gland, Switzerland, 1982), pp. 343-5; and T. Larsen, Polar Bears of the World (Hamlyn, 1978), pp. 86-7.

b)   *Research and consultation*

Article VII of the Polar Bear Agreement requires the Parties to coordinate with each other on their research programmes and on their management of polar bear populations and to exchange information on "research results and data on bears taken." Article IX obliges the Parties to "continue to consult with one another with the object of giving further protection to polar bears."

Since the Agreement was concluded, a substantial amount of research has been carried out into population dynamics, denning areas, bear-human interactions and the effects of increased industrial activities in the Arctic on bears and their habitats.[79] Much of this has involved international cooperation, and the IUCN Polar Bear Specialist Group, which contains scientists from each of the five Parties to the Agreement, meets formally every two years to discuss polar bear research and management on an international basis. However, important gaps still remain. The worldwide population of polar bears, for example, remains largely unknown. Recent estimates have varied from 10,000[80] to "about 20,000 or more".[81] Recognising the need for further research, the Consultative Meeting recommended that "high priority" should be given to the development of assessment methods for estimating polar bear populations. The Meeting also recommended that "national efforts should be directed towards identification of important denning and feeding areas" and that "investigations for the development of appropriate measures which would minimise bear-human interactions in the future should be intensified".[82] More work also needs to be done on the effects of industrial activities, particularly exploitation of minerals and fossil fuels, in offshore areas. Heavy metals and toxic chemicals have been found in tissue samples from polar bears checked for these contaminants, but their effect on the survival of polar bears is unknown.[83]

c)   *Regulation of "taking"*

Article I(1) of the Polar Bear Agreement prohibits the "taking" of polar bears, which is defined to include hunting, killing and

---

[79] *Report of the Consultative Meeting*, note 78 above, p. 5.

[80] S.M. Uspenskii, *The Polar Bear* (Nanka, Moscow, 1977) (English translation by Canadian Wildlife Service, 1978).

[81] *The IUCN Mammal Red Data Book Part I* (IUCN, 1982), p. 343.

[82] *Report of the Consultative Meeting*, note 78 above, Summary and Conclusions.

[83] *The IUCN Mammal Red Data Book Part I* (IUCN, 1982), pp. 344-5. The section of the IUCN Mammal Red Data Book dealing with polar bears was compiled primarily by Dr. Ian Stirling, Chairman of the IUCN Polar Bear Specialist Group.

capturing,[84] "except as provided by Article III." Article III(1) authorises any Party to allow the taking of bears in circumstances where the taking is carried out

(a) for <u>bona fide</u> scientific purposes; or

(b) by that Party for conservation purposes; or

(c) to prevent serious disturbance of the management of other living resources, subject to forfeiture to that Party of the skins and other items of value resulting from such taking; or

(d) by local people using traditional methods in the exercise of their traditional rights and in accordance with the laws of that Party; or

(e) wherever polar bears have or might have been subject to taking by traditional means by its nationals.[85]

The Polar Bear Agreement allows the skins and other products of polar bears taken pursuant to paragraphs (a), (d) and (e) of Article III(1) to be sold for profit, but not skins taken under paragraphs (b) and (c).[86] Special exemptions for taking by native peoples is a common feature of wildlife treaties, but the Agreement is unusual in that commercial use of specimens taken under such exemptions is normally totally prohibited.[87] However, notwithstanding that the Agreement allows commercial trade in polar bear products in certain circumstances, trade within each of the five Parties is in fact strictly regulated by national legislation, and international trade is controlled by the Convention on International Trade in Endangered Species of Wild Fauna and Flora ("CITES"). All five Parties to the Agreement are Parties to CITES. The polar bear is listed in Appendix II of CITES which means that exports of bears

---

[84] Polar Bear Agreement, Article I(2).

[85] Paragraph (e) of Article III(1) is rather ambiguous. M. Bean suggests in *The Evolution of National Wildlife Law* (Praeger, 1983), at p. 268, that it could be interpreted either to allow taking by anyone using any means, provided it is done only in the area where it has or might have been done in the past by traditional means, or to allow taking by a country's own nationals, but only by traditional means and only where taking has or may have previously been done. Bean indicates that the U.S. appears to have adopted the latter view. However, Canada seems to favour the former interpretation since it allows limited sport hunting of polar bears by non-residents, provided it is done as part of the Inuit quota and is guided by Inuit hunters. See "Resume of the Trade in Polar Bear Hides in Canada, 1975-76", *Canadian Wildlife Service, Progress Notes*, No. 82 (Canadian Wildlife Service, December 1977), p. 3; see also Canada's *National Report to the Consultative Meeting of the Contracting Parties to the Agreement on the Conservation of Polar Bears (1981)*, p. 38.

[86] Polar Bear Agreement, Article III(2). Article V of the Agreement prohibits all trade in bears, or their parts or products, which have been taken in violation of the Agreement.

[87] See the migratory bird treaties considered in Chapter 4 below, all of which make exceptions for taking by native peoples and all of which prohibit birds taken thereunder from being used for commercial purposes. Whales taken pursuant to the International Convention for the Regulation of Whaling's provisions for aboriginal whaling may be used for local consumption only. See Chapter 2 above, p. 26.

or their parts and products must be limited to a level which is not detrimental to the survival of the species.[88]

Although Article III(1) of the Agreement lists five circumstances in which polar bears may be taken, it is careful to restrict the numbers of bears that may be killed even when these circumstances apply. It stipulates that any taking must always be subject to the provisions of Articles II and IV of the Agreement. Article II is particularly important because it states that each Party "...shall manage polar bear populations in accordance with sound conservation practices based on the best available scientific data." The Agreement does not define "sound conservation practices", but it is reasonable to suppose that the quantity of polar bears killed should therefore never be allowed to exceed a number which the population cannot sustain.[89] Article IV states that "the use of aircraft and large motorized vessels for the purpose of taking polar bears shall be prohibited except where the application of such prohibition would be inconsistent with domestic laws." Article IV is less important because the last thirteen words of the Article, which effectively exempt any Party from the ban on aircraft or large motor vessels if such a ban contravenes domestic law, empty it of any real meaning.

In practice, most Parties to the Polar Bear Agreement allow very few polar bears to be killed, even by native peoples or pursuant to the other exceptions authorised by Article III(1). The U.S.S.R. and Norway have prohibited the taking of polar bears by anyone since 1955 and 1973 respectively.[90] The U.S.A. and Greenland permit some native subsistence hunting, but the total number of bears killed annually in both these countries is not much more than 200.[91] By far the largest subsistence hunt occurs in Canada which accounts for over 75% of all polar bears killed each year. Canada's annual quotas for Inuit and Indians have averaged between 650

---

[88] See Chapter 12 below for further discussion of CITES. The trade in polar bears hides in Canada from 1972-78 was summarised annually by P.A. Smith in *Canadian Wildlife Service Progress Notes* for those years. Larsen reports that up to $10,000 was paid for a good pelt in 1973-4 but that in 1974-5 less than $600 was the average price paid at auctions in Canada and Denmark (see Larsen, note 78 above, p. 84.).

[89] The essence of conservation, as defined by the *World Conservation Strategy* (published in 1980 by IUCN, World Wildlife Fund and the United Nations Environment Programme), is that any exploitation of a wildlife resource should be sustainable.

[90] Article VI(2) of the Agreement specifically authorises Parties to take domestic measures which are stricter than the provisions of the Agreement. Norway in fact allows polar bears to be killed in self-defence or emergency, but Norway's *Report to the Consultative Meeting* states that no more than 20 bears were killed between May 1976 and December 1980. Recent press reports have indicated that the U.S.S.R. plans to recommence polar bear hunting, but it is not known whether there is any substance to the reports.

[91] See *Report of the Consultative Meeting*, note 78 above.

and 700 in recent years, and in 1981-82 the total number of bears killed was reported to be 726.[92] These figures do not include any animals which may have been killed illegally. The current level of polar bear hunting in Canada may well be sustainable and compatible with "sound conservation practices" — indeed the Chairman of the Polar Bear Specialist Group, a research scientist with the Canadian Wildlife Service, stated in a letter to the author dated 6 April 1983 that "overall the polar bear population in Canada is healthy although there are concerns in a couple of local areas. Hopefully, the results of new research will resolve these difficulties." However, if current levels of polar bear killing prove to be incompatible with sound conservation practices,[93] the Agreement imposes a clear obligation on Canada to take appropriate remedial measures.

d) *Protection of ecosytems*

In addition to insisting that polar bear populations shall be managed in accordance with sound conservation practices, Article II of the Polar Bear Agreement stipulates that

Each Contracting Party shall take appropriate action to protect the ecosystems of which polar bears are a part, with special attention to habitat components such as denning and feeding sites and migration patterns.

This sentence is strongly drafted, imposing a mandatory duty on the Parties to protect the ecosystems of polar bears and to give special attention to particularly important habitat components. The means by which each Party carries out its duty is discretionary — by "appropriate action" — but the underlying obligation is firm, and the Agreement makes no provision for any exceptions to be made to it. This duty is particularly significant because of the increasing

[92] *The IUCN Mammal Red Data Book Part I* (IUCN, 1982), p. 345.

[93] The Polar Bear Specialist Group reported to the Consultative Meeting that "Canadian harvest levels in some areas may exceed 5%" and that "recent analyses using a mathematical model indicate that sustained yield may be less than 2% of the total population" of polar bears. However, Dr. Stirling points out that all these values are hypothetical and are produced by models which are still in the preliminary stages of development. He states that "the sustainable yield of any of these models depends on the assumptions that are made so that it is misleading to focus on 2%, 5% or any other value at present. For example, the sustained yield may differ greatly depending on whether or not adult females are taken. The proportion of adult females, or any other age and sex class of bear, varies between areas and is influenced by local traditions, annual changes in ice conditions, and the kinds of polar bear habitat accessible to the Inuit when they hunt. Ultimately, these variables must be modelled for each subpopulation since it appears that the harvest patterns vary between areas. The research on modelling is continuing but it is premature to draw firm conclusions."

exploration of the Arctic for oil, gas and other minerals which will inevitably disturb at least some polar bear habitats and is likely to cause at least some pollution of their environment. Worried about the effects of mineral exploration and exploitation, the Consultative Meeting emphasised the need to protect important denning and feeding areas and acknowledged "the desirability of providing adequate protected zones around identified denning areas, where disturbances due to human activities otherwise may occur".[94]

Each Party to the Agreement has taken at least some measures to protect important polar bear habitats. To give just a few examples, Denmark has proclaimed the largest national park in the world in east Greenland (700,000 square kilometers) and a game reserve in Melville Bay in northwest Greenland to protect polar bears. The 15,000 square kilometre Polar Bear Provincial Park in the Hudson Bay/Cape Henrietta Maria area of Ontario was established primarily for the protection of denning sites, and the U.S.S.R. has protected several important denning areas in the Wrangel Island Republic Reserve.[95] However, the establishment of protected areas may not always be enough. Polar bears are wideranging animals[96] which will not reside permanently in sanctuaries, and even sanctuaries will not always be safe from the effects of pollutants emanating from a source that is some distance away. In order to be sure of complying with Article II, Parties will have to do what they can to restrict pollution throughout the Arctic.

e)   *Administration*

There is no administrative body such as a Secretariat or a Commission to promote enforcement of the Agreement. Neither are the Parties required to meet regularly to review its implementation, although they are obliged to consult with each other with a view to convening a meeting if one Party makes an appropriate request to the Depositary Government.[97] In these respects, the Agreement lacks the mechanisms which have proved critical to the enforcement of similar conventions concerned with wildlife conservation. However, the fact that the Parties decided to hold the Consultative Meeting within five years of the entry into force of the Agreement, notwithstanding that they were not under a legal obligation to do so, is encouraging evidence that the Parties

---

[94] *Report of the Consultative Meeting*, note 78 above, Summary and Conclusions.
[95] See Larsen, note 78 above, pp. 85-6.
[96] *The IUCN Mammal Red Data Book Part I* (IUCN, 1982), p. 83.
[97] Polar Bear Agreement, Article X(6). The Norwegian government is the Depositary government.

still have the political will to take the provisions of the Agreement seriously.

f) *Conclusion*

The Agreement has proved very successful as a legal conservation instrument in many respects. It covers most of the existing and potential threats to the survival of polar bears, and compliance with its terms is generally mandatory as opposed to being couched in the non-binding terminology used by so many other wildlife treaties. Furthermore, the Agreement has undoubtedly contributed to the establishment of protected areas for bears, to restrictions on hunting and to the substantial amount of scientific research that has been carried out in recent years. Its only real defect is the lack of a permanent administrative structure to oversee enforcement of its terms. The fact that Parties are not required to hold regular meetings to recommend ways of making the Agreement more effective has not yet been a serious hindrance, but it may make it easier for Parties to ignore the provisions of the Agreement if they prove to be a serious stumbling block to future industrial development in the Arctic.

CHAPTER 4

BIRDS

"But for the treaty and the statute there soon might be no birds for any powers to deal with."
(Justice Holmes, United States Supreme Court, 1920)[1]

1. *Background*

Man's recognition of the need to protect birds goes back many centuries, although man's reasons for protecting them have changed over the years. Birds were originally valued as a source of food, as controllers of insect pests and as sport hunting targets. In 1907, O. Herman claimed that the preservation of birds for gentlemen's sport had been a tradition in Germany since the thirteenth century and that the Lords of Europe's great grain region in Hungary had long understood the value of birds "against the perpetual insect foe".[2] More recently, increasing importance has been attached to their ecological and aesthetic qualities.

Since so many species of birds are migratory and cross international borders during the course of their migration, it is not surprising that numerous international agreements have been concluded to promote their conservation. Several of these treaties cover more than just birds, and they are considered later in this book.[3] This chapter examines ten legal instruments — three multilateral European treaties, a European Economic Community Directive and six non-European bilateral treaties — which are all concerned exclusively with birds. The main objective of the earliest treaties was to prohibit the killing, capturing or trading of insectivores and birds of obvious agricultural value. Numerous other birds, particularly birds of prey, were considered "noxious" and unworthy of protection. More recent treaties recognise the value of all species (ironically, birds of prey are now among the most strictly protected birds) and cover a much greater variety of threats, concentrating particularly on habitat protection.

---

[1] Justice Holmes in the United States Supreme Court case of *Missouri v. Holland*, 252 U.S. 416, 435 (1920). He was referring to the Convention for the Protection of Migratory Birds of 1916 between the U.S.A. and Great Britain, on behalf of Canada, and to the Migratory Bird Treaty Act which implements the Convention in the U.S.A.

[2] O. Herman, *The International Convention for the Protection of Birds and Hungary* (1907), p. 32.

[3] Every treaty examined in Parts III and IV of this book covers birds as well as other species.

This chapter looks first at the three European treaties, then at the European Community Directive and finally at the six non-European treaties.

2. The Convention for the Protection of Birds Useful to Agriculture

The first international initiative to conserve birds was made at the 26th General Assembly of German agriculturists and foresters in Vienna in 1868. The Assembly passed a resolution urging the Government of Austria-Hungary to procure agreements with other countries for the protection of animals useful to agriculture and forestry. The resolution was sent to the Foreign Minister who agreed to follow it up on condition that the agreements were limited to birds useful to agriculture. It took many years of further negotiations before a treaty was concluded, but in 1902 twelve European countries finally signed the Convention for the Protection of Birds Useful to Agriculture (the "1902 Convention").[4] It entered into force on 6 December 1905.

a) Objectives

As its title implies, the 1902 Convention was strictly utilitarian in approach. It protected some 150 species which were listed in a special Annex to the Convention as "useful to agriculture". They were predominantly passerines, owls and birds of obvious agricultural value. Eagles, hawks, most falcons, pelicans, herons and pigeons were deemed "nuisible" and unworthy of protection.

b) Conservation measures

Conservation measures for those species fortunate enough to be thought useful were aimed principally at regulating their killing, capturing and selling.

Article II of the 1902 Convention prohibited the taking, capturing, import, transit, transport and sale of nests, eggs and young of species in the Annex, although the owner of a house or building was allowed to destroy nests constructed inside or against his house or building. Article III prohibited the use of all methods designed to capture or destroy birds "en masse". This was aimed at stopping some of the extraordinary trapping and netting devices, such as the riccolo, which were apparently capable of killing birds in enormous numbers.[5] Article V outlawed the killing or capturing

---

[4] 102 B.F.S.P. 969. Austria-Hungary, Belgium, France, Germany, Greece, Lichtenstein, Luxembourg, Monaco, Portugal, Spain, Sweden and Switzerland signed the 1902 Convention.

[5] See S. Hayden, *The International Protection of Wildlife* (Columbia University Press, 1942), pp. 90-1.

or sale of all specimens of species in the Annex between 1 March and 15 September,[6] and Article X required each Party to conform its national legislation to the terms of the Convention within three years of signature.

c) *Practical impact*

Even "useful" birds have in fact received little practical benefit from the 1902 Convention. Any initiative to protect European migratory birds requires the cooperation of all the major stepping stones along the flyways in order to be successful, and neither Italy, the Netherlands, Norway, the U.K. nor the U.S.S.R. signed the Convention. Italy's absence was especially significant because Italy acts as a funnel along the migratory route of many European species, and the hunting of migratory birds has long been practiced there.[7] In addition, the 1902 Convention contained an "escape clause" which allowed Parties to avoid being bound by any of the conservation provisions of the Convention if they so desired.[8] The escape clause may have been necessary in order to secure the signature of twelve governments, but the French delegation claimed at an international conference in 1932 that the escape clause had been sufficient to make the Convention little more than a dead letter in France.[9]

Indeed, the 1902 Convention appears to have had little influence anywhere. In the decades following 1902, the U.K., which did not sign, and Germany, which did, were both notable for relatively strong national conservation legislation, while France, Spain and Portugal, all of which were Parties to the Convention, had virtually none.[10]

3. *The International Convention for the Protection of Birds*

Dissatisfaction with the shortcomings of the 1902 Convention and concern with the increasing threats to birds in Europe led to a series of conferences which culminated on 18 October 1950 in the signing of the International Convention for the Protection of Birds (the "1950 Convention").[11] The 1950 Convention represents considerable

---

[6] Northern European countries were permitted to modify this period, presumably because migratory patterns might otherwise allow them almost no open season at all.

[7] See Hayden, note 5 above, pp. 90-1.

[8] Article IV of the 1902 Convention allows Parties to mitigate the severity of the provisions of the Convention as they judge necessary.

[9] See Hayden, note 5 above, pp. 100-101.

[10] *Ibid.*, pp. 97-8.

[11] 638 *U.N.T.S.* 186. The Convention came into force on 17 January 1963. Belgium, Iceland, Italy, Luxembourg, Netherlands, Spain, Sweden, Switzerland, Turkey and Yugoslavia are full Parties to the Convention. Austria, Bulgaria, France, Greece, Monaco and Portugal have signed but have not yet ratified.

progress from the 1902 Convention in terms of the values given to birds and the obligations imposed on Parties to protect them, but its practical impact has also been very limited.

a) *Objectives*

Gone is the idea that certain birds are "nuisible", and highlighted are the concepts that endangered and migratory species merit special attention and that "*all* birds should in principle be protected" (emphasis added).[12]

b) *Conservation measures*

Article 2 of the 1950 Convention requires its Parties to protect all birds at least during the breeding season, migratory birds during the period of return to their nesting areas, especially March — July,[13] and species threatened with extinction throughout the year. The Convention allows Parties to make exceptions to Article 2 in limited circumstances,[14] but Article 6 stipulates that use of the exceptions clause must not lead to the "total destruction of resident or migratory species referred to in this Article, in any given country."[15]

In contrast to the 1902 Convention, the 1950 Convention is not limited to regulating the killing, capturing and trading of birds. It encourages Parties to promote conservation education[16] and to establish protected areas as well.[17] It also requires Parties to

> adopt appropriate measures to prevent the destruction of birds by waste oil or other sources of pollution of waters, by lighthouses, by electric cables, by insecticides, by poisons, or any other cause.[18]

c) *Practical impact*

As with the 1902 Convention, the lack of widespread accession to the 1950 Convention destroyed its prospects of becoming a dynamic legal conservation instrument. In addition, the terms of the Convention are too vague. For example, the Convention requires year-round protection for species which are "threatened with extinction", but there is no list of threatened species attached to the

[12] Preamble to the 1950 Convention.

[13] The intention was to protect migratory birds from spring shooting, a well established practice in parts of Southern Europe.

[14] Exceptions may be made for species causing agricultural damage and for the interests of science, education, game bird rearing and falconry.

[15] The Parties were concerned that without this safeguard measures to keep down birds that were agricultural pests might lead to their total eradication.

[16] 1950 Convention, Article 10.

[17] *Ibid.*, Article 11.

[18] *Ibid.*, Article 10.

Convention, and the Convention does not specifically require Parties to apply its terms to their own national lists. As a result, the Convention may have stimulated the adoption of conservation measures for threatened species in some Party countries, but there are no species about which one can state with certainty that the Convention helped to secure their survival. Finally, and perhaps most importantly, the Convention neither demands regular meetings of the Parties, nor requires Parties to submit reports on what they have done to implement the Convention, nor employs any of the other techniques used by more modern conservation treaties to keep themselves at the forefront of their Parties' attention. Accordingly, even if the 1950 Convention had some influence shortly after it came into force, it has become a "sleeping treaty" which no longer has a significant, if any, practical impact on the policies of its Party governments.

4. *The Benelux Convention on the Hunting and Protection of Birds*

The Benelux Convention on the Hunting and Protection of Birds (the "Benelux Convention")[19] was signed on 10 June 1970 and came into force on 1 July 1972. It harmonizes the rules of the three Benelux countries[20] with respect to the hunting of game birds,[21] and it regulates the exploitation of such other wild birds as are determined by the Committee of Ministers of the Benelux Economic Union.[22] On 30th August 1972, the Committee of Ministers gave limited protection from capture to sixteen species,[23] allowed unlimited exploitation of three species[24] and gave total protection from killing, selling and transport to all other non-game species.[25] The Benelux Convention is exclusively concerned with killing, capturing, trading and other forms of exploitation. It makes no provision for the protection of habitat, for the prevention of pollution, for the control of pesticides or for counteracting any of the other threats to wild birds.[26]

[19] 847 *U.N.T.S.* 255.

[20] Belgium, Netherlands and Luxembourg.

[21] Benelux Convention, Article 1.

[22] *Ibid.*, Articles 7-9.

[23] Decision de l'Union economique Benelux relative à la protection des oiseaux (Decision M. (72)), 30 aout 1972, Article 1(a).

[24] *Ibid.*, Article 1(b).

[25] *Ibid.*, Articles 2 and 3.

[26] The Benelux Convention has been modified by a Protocol (3 May 1977), which sets out rules of hunting in further detail and deals with various procedural matters. The text of the Protocol is reprinted in *International Environmental Law Multilateral Treaties* (Eric Schmidt Verlag, Berlin), 970:44. At the time of writing, only Netherlands has ratified the Protocol.

5. *Directive of the Council of the European Economic Community on the Conservation of Wild Birds*

On 2 April 1979 the Council of the European Economic Community (EEC) adopted a Directive on the conservation of wild birds (hereinafter called the "Birds Directive").[27] An EEC Directive is binding in the sense that each Member State of the EEC[28] is required to comply with its terms, but Member States are allowed to choose the means by which they implement their obligations.[29] They are normally allowed a time limit within which to take appropriate implementing measures. Article 18 of the Birds Directive required Member States to bring into force the laws, regulations and administrative provisions necessary to comply with its terms by 2 April 1981.

The Birds Directive by no means guarantees the future protection of European birds. The combined territories of Member States of the EEC cover only a portion of the migratory range of many species, and already there are signs that the Birds Directive will not always be properly enforced. Nevertheless, the Birds Directive is a very important step forward from the three earlier treaties. It imposes strict legal obligations on Member States to maintain populations of naturally occuring wild birds at levels corresponding to ecological requirements, to preserve a sufficient diversity and area of habitats for their conservation, to regulate trade in birds (including their parts and products), to limit hunting to species able to sustain exploitation and to prohibit certain methods of capture and killing. Member States are allowed to make exceptions to some of these provisions but only in carefully limited circumstances. Just as importantly, there is an administrative machinery responsible for keeping enforcement of the Birds Directive under close supervision. Although enforcement problems have arisen, the Directive's system of administration should ensure that the level of enforcement is considerably better than that of the older treaties.

---

[27] Council Directive 79/409/EEC; *O.J. Eur. Comm.* No. L 103 (25 April 1979), p. 1.

[28] The Member States of the European Economic Community are Belgium, Denmark, Federal Republic of Germany, France, Greece, Ireland, Italy, Luxembourg, Netherlands and the U.K.

[29] A careful distinction needs to be drawn between an EEC Directive and an EEC Regulation. The latter is directly binding on all Member States of the EEC and does not require implementing legislation in order to enter into force in the Member States.

The Birds Directive applies to all species of naturally occuring wild birds in the European territories of EEC Member States except Greenland.[30]

a) *Population levels*

Article 2 of the Birds Directive requires Member States to take appropriate measures to maintain populations of all species of wild birds that occur naturally in their European territories

> ...at a level which corresponds in particular to ecological, scientific and cultural requirements, while taking account of economic and recreational requirements, or to adapt the population of these species to that level.

Article 2, which corresponds closely to Article 2 of the Convention on the Conservation of European Wildlife and Natural Habitats,[31] is significant for two reasons. Firstly, it sets a standard corresponding to ecological requirements at which population levels of birds must be maintained or to which they must be adapted if they are depleted. Secondly, Article 2 obviously intends Member States to cater for economic and recreational needs in fulfilling their obligations under the Article whenever possible. However, a careful reading of Article 2 makes it absolutely clear that the primary duty of Member States is to maintain bird populations at levels corresponding to ecological, scientific and cultural requirements and that economic and other considerations are secondary. If it had been intended to give the latter equal weight to the former, it would have been easy for Article 2 to oblige Member States to maintain bird populations at levels corresponding to "ecological, scientific, cultural, economic, recreational etc." requirements. But this is not how the Article is drafted. The words "while taking account of", which start the second clause, are qualifying words which require Member States to consider the needs expressed in the second clause (economic and recreational) but do not put these needs on a par with the duty (ecological, scientific and cultural) expressed in the first clause. Therefore, in the event of an irreconcilable conflict between economic and ecological needs, Member States have a legal obligation to give priority to the latter.

[30] Birds Directive, Articles I(1) and I(3). The preamble to the Directive states that Greenland was excluded because conditions of life for birds there "are fundamentally different from those in the other regions of the European territory of the Member States on account of the general circumstances and in particular the climate, the low density of population and the exceptional size and geographical situation of the island."

[31] See Chapter 8 below, pp. 131-133.

The Birds Directive does not define a population level which corresponds to ecological, scientific and cultural requirements, but it can be safely assumed to be well above a level where a species is in danger of extinction.[32] At a minimum, therefore, Member States have a legal duty to ensure that no species of bird becomes extinct through means within their control, to help threatened species of birds to recover to a point where their numbers are once again large enough to perform their ecological functions and to ensure that presently healthy populations are not reduced below that point. Given the hundreds of activities in modern Europe, particularly economic pressures, which are capable of seriously depleting bird populations, the obligations imposed on Member States by Article 2 are extremely important and may not always be easy to implement.

b) *Conservation of habitat*

(i) *In general*

Article 3(1) of the Birds Directive requires Member States to take measures to preserve, maintain or re-establish a sufficient diversity and area of habitats for all species of wild birds naturally occuring in their European territories. Article 3(2) states that these measures shall include

(a) creation of protected areas;
(b) upkeep and management in accordance with the ecological needs of habitats inside and outside the protected zones;
(c) re-establishment of destroyed biotopes;
(d) creation of biotopes.

(ii) *Species in Annex I of the Directive.*

Article 4(1) stipulates that species listed in Annex I of the Birds Directive shall be the subject of "special conservation measures concerning their habitat" in order to ensure their survival and reproduction in their area of distribution. Article 4(1) goes on to require Member States to classify the most suitable territories in number and size as "special conservation areas" for these species, although it does not impose any time limit within which such classification should be completed.

The Birds Directive does not lay down any criteria for the inclusion of a species in Annex I, and the species so far listed suggest that the Member States did not intend to limit Annex I to species that are threatened, or even potentially threatened, with extinction.

[32] See p. 132 below.

The 74 species in Annex I range from threatened species such as peregrine falcon (*Falco peregrinus*) to relatively abundant species such as common tern (*Sterna hirundo*).

(iii)   *Migratory species*

Article 4(2) requires Member States to take similar measures for

> regularly occuring migratory species not listed in Annex I, bearing in mind...their breeding, moulting and wintering areas and staging posts along their migration routes. To this end, Member States shall pay particular attention to the protection of wetlands and particularly to wetlands of international importance.

The latter sentence is clearly intended to promote the Convention on Wetlands of International Importance Especially as Waterfowl Habitat, which is discussed in detail in Chapter 10.

(iv)   *Reporting requirements*

Article 4(3) obliges Member States to send the EEC Commission all information necessary for it to perform a coordinating role in ensuring that special protection areas established for Annex I species and for regularly occuring migratory species form a coherent whole which meets the conservation needs of those species.

(v)   *Avoidance of pollution or habitat deterioration*

Article 4(4) stipulates that Member States shall take appropriate steps to "avoid pollution or deterioration of habitats or any disturbances affecting the birds, in so far as these would be significant having regard to the objectives of this Article" in areas established as special protection areas for Annex I species or regularly occuring migratory species. Article 4(4) goes on to state that outside these protection areas Members States "shall also strive to avoid pollution or deterioration of habitats".

c)   *Regulation of exploitation*

As a general rule, the Birds Directive requires Member States to prohibit the deliberate killing or capture of all species of wild birds naturally occuring in their European territories, the damaging of nests or eggs, the taking or keeping of eggs, the keeping of birds and the deliberate disturbance of birds, particularly during the breeding season.[33]

---

[33] Birds Directive, Article 5(a)-(e).

There are a few exceptions to this rule. Species listed in Annex II of the Birds Directive may be hunted if the legislation of the State concerned allows them to be hunted.[34] Species in Annex II/1 may be hunted throughout the area to which the Directive applies,[35] but those in Annex II/2 may only be hunted in those States that are specifically indicated.[36] However, the Birds Directive insists that hunting must not be allowed to jeopardise conservation efforts anywhere in the distribution area of a species,[37] that it must comply with the principles of "wise use and ecologically balanced control of the species of birds concerned" and that it must also comply with the requirements of Article 2 with respect to population levels of birds.[38] The Directive also requires Member States to prohibit hunting during the rearing season or during the various stages of reproduction and, in the case of migratory species, during their return to their rearing grounds — i.e. spring shooting is prohibited.[39] Member States are required to send the Commission all relevant information on their hunting regulations.

The Birds Directive prohibits hunting from the modes of transport and under the conditions specified in Annex IV(b) of the Directive.[40] It also outlaws methods of hunting, capture or killing listed in Annex IV(a) and all other methods "used for the large-scale or non-selective capture or killing of birds or capable of causing the local disappearance of a species".[41]

In principle, the Directive bans the sale, transport for sale, keeping for sale and offering for sale of live or dead birds and of any readily recognisable parts or derivatives thereof.[42] However, it permits such activities in respect of species listed in Annex III/1 provided that the birds have been legally killed or captured or otherwise legally acquired.[43] It also authorises Member States to permit such activities in respect of species listed in Annex III/2 provided that the same conditions as to legal acquisition have been met. In the latter instance, however, Member States must first consult with the Commission in order to check whether marketing could result in population levels, geographic distribution or reproductive rates of

---

[34] *Ibid.*, Article 7(1).

[35] *Ibid.*, Article 7(2). Annex II(1) consists of 24 species most of which are game birds.

[36] *Ibid.*, Article 7(3). Annex II/2 consists of 48 species.

[37] *Ibid.*, Article 7(1).

[38] *Ibid.*, Article 7(4).

[39] *Ibid.*

[40] Birds Directive, Article 8(2).

[41] *Ibid.*, Article 8(1).

[42] *Ibid.*, Article 6(1).

[43] *Ibid.*, Article 6(2). Annex III/1 consists of ring-necked pheasant, wood pigeon, red grouse, mallard and three species of partridge.

the species concerned becoming endangered in the European Community as a whole.[44]

Article 9 of the Birds Directive allows Member States to make exceptions from any of its provisions regulating exploitation of birds in certain circumstances. These include situations where the interests of public health, the prevention of serious damage to crops or the promotion of scientific research are at stake. However, the Birds Directive allows Member States to invoke Article 9 only "where there is no other satisfactory solution", and Member States are obliged to send an annual report to the Commission giving details of any exceptions they have made under Article 9. The Commission is responsible for ensuring that usage of Article 9 is not incompatible with the Directive. It should also be noted that the Birds Directive does not allow Member States to make exceptions from its provisions dealing with the protection of habitat (Articles 3 and 4) or the maintenance of bird populations at levels corresponding to ecological, scientific and cultural requirements (Article 2).

d) *Research and the introduction of exotic species*

Article 10 requires Member States to encourage research into matters relating to the protection and management of wild birds, especially those matters that are listed in Annex V of the Birds Directive.

Article 11 obliges Member States to ensure that the introduction of any species of bird, which does not occur naturally in the wild in the European territory of any Member State, does not prejudice the local flora and fauna. Article 11 requires them to consult the Commission on proposed introductions.

e) *Reporting requirements*

In addition to the reporting requirements which have already been mentioned, the Birds Directive obliges Member States to provide the Commission with copies of the texts of the main provisions of their national laws governing bird conservation[45] and a report every three years on measures they have taken to implement the Birds Directive.[46] The first reports are due on 2 April 1985. The Commission must itself prepare a composite report every three years based on information received by the Member States and must

---

[44] *Ibid.*, Article 6(3). Annex III/2 consists of greylag goose, ptarmigan, coot and six species of ducks.

[45] *Ibid.*, Article 19.

[46] *Ibid.*, Article 12(1).

circulate it to all Member States.[47] These reporting requirements will ensure that the Birds Directive remains at the forefront of Member States' attention, and the contents of the reports will help the Commission to check how forcefully the Directive is being applied.

f) *Enforcement*

In addition to informal enforcement aids such as reporting requirements (Member States may prefer to implement the Directive rather than face the public embarrassment of having to report that they have done nothing to enforce it), there are more formal enforcement weapons available to the Commission. Article 169 of the Treaty of Rome authorises the Commission to bring an action in the European Court of Justice against any Member State which fails to comply with the terms of a Directive. Interested individuals or organisations cannot initiate proceedings in the European Court of Justice in such circumstances.[48] A heavy responsibility, therefore, rests on the shoulders of the Commission to monitor compliance with the Birds Directive and to take appropriate action against any Member State which is in breach of its terms. At the time of writing there is some doubt as to how forcefully the Commission will implement its enforcement responsibilities. The French government, for example, authorised a hunting season for turtle doves (*Streptopelia turtur*) from 1-15 May in 1982 and again in 1983. Since turtle doves are either starting to breed or are on their way north to their breeding grounds in May, the French government was in clear violation of Article 7(4) of the Directive.[49] Although plans for a similar season in May 1984 were announced several months beforehand, the Commission did nothing beyond writing a letter of protest and failed to prevent the season from going ahead. If the Birds Directive is not to suffer from the same lack of practical impact as the three earlier European bird treaties, it is essential that the Commission plays a more positive enforcement role — even if

[47] *Ibid.*, Article 12(2).

[48] They may, however, be able to seek some remedy under Article 177 of the Treaty of Rome. Under Article 177, a national court or tribunal may (and, if it is a court of last instance, must) refer questions of interpretation of acts of the institutions of the European Community (e.g. a Council Directive) to the European Court of Justice. The latter will then deliver a preliminary ruling on those questions which should be adopted by the national court or tribunal in its judgment in the case before it. If interested individuals or organisations can initiate an action in the national courts of a Member State which is in breach of the terms of the Directive, they may be able to obtain an appropriate ruling from the European Court of Justice by means of this route.

[49] See p. 71 above.

this means bringing actions against recalcitrant governments in the European Court of Justice.

Surprisingly, there is no requirement that Member States should meet regularly in order to review implementation of the Birds Directive and to recommend ways of making it more effective — a technique that has been used by a number of wildlife treaties to promote their enforcement. Such meetings, in which non-governmental conservation organisations are often allowed to participate, may also render reporting requirements more effective because governments know that their reports will be subjected to scrutiny in an international forum and that there will be organisations present which are ready to publicise examples of poor enforcement. Member States do meet on the Committee for the Adaptation to Technical and Scientific Progress, established by Article 16 of the Birds Directive, but the jurisdiction of this Committee is limited to considering proposals to amend the Annexes.

6.   *Non-European bilateral conventions for the conservation of birds*

Six non-European bilateral conventions for the conservation of birds have now been signed. The oldest is the Convention for the Protection of Migratory Birds which was concluded by Canada and the U.S.A. in August 1916 (the "1916 Convention").[50] It was followed in February 1936 by a similar agreement between Mexico and the U.S.A. called the Convention for the Protection of Migratory Birds and Game Mammals (the "1936 Convention").[51] The remaining four conventions were all concluded in the 1970s. They are the Convention for the Protection of Migratory Birds and Birds in Danger of Extinction and their Environment which was concluded by Japan and the U.S.A. in March 1972 (the "1972 Convention"),[52] the Convention for the Protection of Migratory Birds and Birds under Threat of Extinction and on the Means of Protecting Them which was concluded by the U.S.S.R. and Japan in October 1973 (the "1973 Convention"),[53] the Agreement for the Protection of Migratory Birds and Birds in Danger of Extinction and their

---

[50] 39 *Stat.* 1702; *Treaty Series* no. 628. Technically, the 1916 Convention was between the U.S.A. and Great Britain. Great Britain signed and ratified the Convention on behalf of Canada because Canada was still a British dominion at that time.

[51] 178 *L.T.S.* 309, *Treaty Series* no. 912. An Agreement Supplementing the Convention of February 7 1936 for the Protection of Migratory Birds and Game Mammals (837 *U.N.T.S.* 125) was effected by an exchange of notes between Mexico and the U.S.A. on 10 March 1972 and came into force the same day. The objective of the 1972 Agreement was to make substantial additions to the list of species protected by the 1936 Convention.

[52] 25 *U.S.T.* 3329; *T.I.A.S.* no. 7990; entered into force on 19 September 1974.

[53] The 1973 Convention is not yet in force.

Environment which was concluded by Japan and Australia in February 1974 (the "1974 Convention"),[54] and the Convention Concerning the Conservation of Migratory Birds and their Environment which was concluded by the U.S.S.R. and the U.S.A. in November 1976 (the "1976 Convention").[55]

The U.S.A. and Japan have the biggest interests in these six conventions, being Parties to four and three respectively. The U.S.S.R. is a Party to two, while Canada, Mexico and Australia are Parties to one each. Rather than examine the six conventions one by one, this section looks at the most important elements of each and makes comparisons between them.

The terms of a seventh bilateral migratory bird treaty — between the U.S.S.R. and India — have been finalised, and at the time of writing it is expected to be concluded shortly.[56] This represents a very useful expansion of the area covered by existing treaties and will hopefully stimulate the conclusion of yet more agreements.

a)   *Values placed on birds*

In contrast to the first European bird treaty, which only valued birds of direct agricultural use, the 1916 Convention states that birds are "...of great value as a source of food or in destroying insects which are injurious to forests and forage plants on the public domain, as well as to agricultural crops in both the United States and Canada."[57] The North American emphasis on birds as a source of food, as well as an asset to agriculture, derives from the enormous quantities of migratory waterfowl which breed in Canada, winter in the U.S.A. and have been traditionally prized by hunters. Food and sport are also emphasised by the 1936 Convention which states that "...it is necessary to employ adequate measures which will permit a national utilization of migratory birds for the purpose of sport as well as for food, commerce and industry."[58]

By the 1970s the values attributed to birds had expanded considerably. The 1972 Convention refers to the "aesthetic" and "scientific" qualities of birds as well as to their recreational and economic importance.[59] The 1973 Convention says that "...birds constitute an important element of the natural environment, [and]

---

[54] *A.T.S.* 1981, no. 6; entered into force on 30 April 1981.
[55] 29 *U.S.T.* 4647; *T.I.A.S.* no. 9073; entered into force on 13 October 1978.
[56] See S. Singh, *Conservation of India's Wildlife Heritage* (Department of the Environment, Government of India, New Delhi, 1984), p. 6.
[57] Preamble to the 1916 Convention.
[58] Preamble to the 1936 Convention.
[59] Preamble to the 1972 Convention.

that they play a significant role in enriching it...",[60] and the 1974 Convention makes an almost identical statement.[61] The 1976 Convention grants birds an even broader set of values including, for the first time, educational values. Its preamble states that "...migratory birds are a natural source of great scientific, economic, aesthetic, cultural, educational, recreational and ecological value."

The evolution of values placed on birds is important both because it demonstrates a growing awareness of ecological factors and because it may have practical consequences. The 1972 Convention, for example, states that the hunting of migratory birds shall be regulated "to maintain their populations in optimum numbers."[62] "Optimum numbers" are not further defined by the Convention, nor does the history of the Convention's negotiations explain what was intended. In 1975, a U.S. non-governmental conservation organisation brought a legal action against the U.S. government on the grounds that the latter had decided to allow certain species of migratory birds to be hunted in numbers which, in the opinion of the organisation, would cause populations of those species to fall below the "optimum numbers" provided for by the Convention.[63] The court dodged the issue, deciding the case on other matters, but it has been suggested that in construing what is meant by optimum numbers, consideration should be given to the reasons for which the birds are being protected. Thus "optimum numbers" would have a certain meaning in the context of a convention designed only for recreational hunting purposes and a different meaning where the convention considered the primary value of birds to be ecological or aesthetic in nature.[64]

b)   *Species covered*

All six conventions list the species that they cover and all, except the 1916 Convention, contain a procedure for amending their lists.

The 1916 Convention covers groups of birds rather than individual species. Some of the groups that it lists, such as "phalaropes" and "robins", are relatively clear but others, such as "all other perching birds which feed entirely or chiefly on insects", make it difficult to decipher exactly which species are covered. The 1916 Convention, whose stated objective is to protect migratory

---

[60] Preamble to the 1973 Convention.

[61] The preamble to the 1974 Convention states that "...birds constitute an important element of the natural environment and play an essential role in enriching the natural environment."

[62] The 1972 Convention, Article III(2).

[63] *Fund for Animals, Inc. v. Frizzell*, 402 F. Supp. 35 (D.D.C. 1975).

[64] See M. Bean, *The Evolution of National Wildlife Law* (Praeger, 1983), pp. 86-7.

birds,[65] is also rather confusing in that it does not specify whether it applies to all species in the listed groups or only to those that migrate between the U.S.A. and Canada. By way of comparison with the first European bird treaty, it is interesting to note that the 1916 Convention does not list any falcons, hawks or eagles notwithstanding that many of them cross the Canada-U.S. border during the course of their migration. Clearly, the Europeans were not the only people to view birds of prey as "noxious" in the early twentieth century.

The 1936 Convention lists the birds that it covers in families such as *Familia Mimidae* and *Familia Rallidae*. It stipulates that all species in these families shall be deemed migratory for the purposes of the Convention irrespective of whether they in fact migrate between Mexico and the U.S.A.[66] The 1936 Convention originally listed 33 families of birds, but a further 32 families were added under a supplementary agreement concluded on 10 March 1972.[67]

The four conventions concluded in the 1970s each have an Annex in which the species that they cover are individually listed. The general intention of all four conventions is to protect species which migrate between the countries concerned, but each of them also allows species that are common to the countries concerned to be listed in certain circumstances notwithstanding that they do not migrate from one to the other. The 1972 Convention allows species or subspecies "common to both countries" (i.e. Japan and the U.S.A.) to be listed in the Annex to that Convention.[68] The 1973 and 1974 Conventions allow species that are common to Japan and the U.S.S.R. and to Japan and Australia respectively to be listed in the absence of biological evidence that they do not migrate. The 1976 Convention allows species or subspecies common to the U.S.A. and the U.S.S.R. to be listed provided that they share common flyways or breeding or feeding grounds so that there is some potential for exchange of individual specimens among the populations of both countries.[69] All four conventions authorise the establishment of special lists for endangered species of birds whether or not they are migratory and require that they be given special protection.

c) *Regulation of exploitation*

All six conventions restrict the circumstances in which migratory birds may be traded or taken.

[65] Preamble to the 1916 Convention.
[66] 1936 Convention, Article IV.
[67] See note 51 above.
[68] See Articles II(1) and II(2)(a) of the 1972 Convention.
[69] 1976 Convention, Article I(1)(b).

(i)   *Trade*

The 1916 Convention prohibits interstate or international trade in migratory birds covered by the Convention or in their eggs during the close season.[70] With limited exceptions, the five subsequent conventions all prohibit trade in specimens of species that they cover at all times of the year. They also prohibit trade in the parts and products of specimens of these species and in their eggs.[71] International trade in many of the birds concerned is also regulated by the Convention on International Trade in Endangered Species of Wild Fauna and Flora.[72]

(ii)   *Taking*

The 1916 Convention requires Canada and the U.S.A. to prohibit the "taking" of nests or eggs of birds covered by the Convention at all times[73] and to prohibit hunting during close seasons.[74] The close season is year-round for migrating insectivorous and other non-game birds covered by the Convention, and the maximum allowable hunting season for migrating game birds is three and a half months.[75] The 1936 Convention requires Mexico and the U.S.A. to prohibit the "taking" of nests or eggs of listed species during close seasons and to prohibit the "taking" of the birds themselves during close seasons and in refuges.[76] The 1936 Convention sets the maximum permissible hunting season at four months,[77] forbids hunting of wild ducks between 10 March and 1 September[78] and outlaws hunting from aircraft.[79]

The four 1970s conventions all prohibit the "taking" of listed birds or their eggs, with limited exceptions for the hunting of a few species in certain circumstances. In contrast to the two older conventions which both specify the dates of close seasons, the four 1970s conventions leave these dates to the discretion of the countries concerned but lay down the principles according to which they should be set. For example, the 1972 Convention requires Japan and the U.S.A. to time their hunting seasons so as to avoid "principal nesting seasons" and to maintain "populations in optimum

---

[70] 1916 Convention, Article VI.

[71] Article II(1) of the 1976 Convention also requires the U.S.A. and the U.S.S.R. to prohibit trade in the nests of species listed in the Appendix to the Convention.

[72] See Chapter 12 below.

[73] 1916 Convention, Article V.

[74] *Ibid.*, Article II.

[75] *Ibid.*, Article II(1)-(2).

[76] 1936 Convention, Article II(a).

[77] *Ibid.*, Article II(c).

[78] *Ibid.*, Article II.

[79] *Ibid.*, Article II(f).

numbers".[80] The 1973 and 1974 Conventions require the U.S.S.R., Japan and Australia to set hunting seasons with due consideration for protecting the normal annual reproduction of migratory birds. The 1976 Convention obliges the U.S.S.R. and the U.S.A. to set hunting seasons "so as to provide for the preservation and maintenance of stocks of migratory birds."[81]

Although all six conventions regulate the "taking" of birds or their nests or eggs, not one of them defines the word "take". This is surprising because the extent of the obligations imposed on the countries concerned varies tremendously according to how the word "take" is interpreted. If "taking" is deemed only to cover activities such as shooting or trapping, the conservation obligations imposed by the conventions are relatively limited. However, if "taking" is deemed to include any kind of killing, the obligations imposed by the conventions take on a totally new perspective. There are many ways to kill birds other than by shooting or trapping — introducing toxic chemicals such as DDT into their environment or causing oil spills which foul their feathers are just two examples — and a broad interpretation of "take" could mean that any activity which led to the death of a specimen of a listed species is prohibited.

There is some evidence to suggest that the word "take" should be interpreted in the broadest sense. The U.S. Migratory Bird Treaty Act, which implements the 1916, 1936, 1972 and 1976 Conventions in the U.S.A., prohibits hunting *and* killing of migratory birds,[82] and other international conventions have defined "taking" to include killing as well as hunting and trapping.[83] Furthermore, two recent cases in the U.S.A. involving the Migratory Bird Treaty Act suggest that the word "killing" does cover the kinds of activities involving environmental pollutants mentioned above and even that people who kill birds unintentionally by these means have violated the law. The first case, *United States v. FMC*,[84] concerned the operator of a pesticide manufacturing plant which pumped water into a holding pond. Without the knowledge of the operator the water became contaminated, and migratory birds using the pond died. The operator was found guilty because he was responsible for the death of the birds and the court held that his lack of intent to cause their death was irrelevant. When instructing the jury the judge stated that

[80] 1972 Convention, Article III(2).
[81] 1976 Convention, Article II(2).
[82] Section 3 of the Migratory Bird Treaty Act, 16 U.S.C. §§703-711 (1976 & Supp. V 1981).
[83] See Article 1(2) of the Agreement on the Conservation of Polar Bears (see pp. 56-57 above) which defines "taking" to include hunting, killing and capturing.
[84] 572 F. 2d. 902 (1978).

...good will and good intention and measures taken to prevent the killing of the birds are not a defense. Therefore, if you find that the birds were killed by the products emitted from the FMC plant, then you must return a verdict of guilty.

The second case, *United States v. Corbin Farm Service*,[85] involved manufacturers of a pesticide which, when sprayed on a field, caused the death of approximately 1,100 American widgeon (*Mareca americana*). Again, in spite of the manufacturer's lack of intent to kill the birds, their death was considered enough for the manufacturer to be guilty of an offence under the Migratory Bird Treaty Act.[86]

Both of these cases laboured with the question of how to avoid carrying the potential logical conclusions of their holdings to the point of absurdity. Both courts suggested that bird deaths caused by collisions with motor vehicles etc. should not form the basis for prosecution under the Act.[87] The court circumvented the "extension to the absurd" argument in *United States v. FMC* on the grounds that dealing with pesticides was an ultrahazardous activity to which the concept of strict liability was applicable.[88]

If the interpretations of the Migratory Bird Treaty Act made by the U.S. courts are applied to the similar prohibitions made by the six conventions, the Parties to those conventions will be legally obliged to prohibit all activities under their respective jurisdictions which cause the death of birds covered by the conventions or destruction of their eggs.[89] Furthermore, at least in regard to ultrahazardous activities such as the use of pesticides, those countries may be obliged to prohibit such death or destruction even in cases where the person responsible did not intend his actions to result in such death or destruction.[90]

(iii) *Exceptions*

All six conventions allow exceptions to be made to their provisions in limited circumstances. In addition to exceptions for hunting which have already been mentioned, each convention allows the taking of birds for scientific or similar purposes. These include

[85] 444 F. Supp. 510 (1978).

[86] For further discussion of the cases and points of law involved, see Margolin, "Liability Under the Migratory Bird Treaty Act", 7 *Ecology Law Quarterly* 989 (1979).

[87] See M. Bean, note 64 above, pp. 83-4.

[88] 572 F. 2d. at 907.

[89] Note that the 1916 Convention regulates the "taking" of nests or eggs of species covered by the Convention but not of the birds themselves. Only "hunting" of birds is regulated. The other five conventions regulate the "taking" of birds as well as their nests or eggs.

[90] See "The Migratory Bird Treaty: Another Feather in the Environmentalist's Cap", 19 *South Dakota Law Rev.* 307, 321-31 (1974); see also Bean, note 64 above, p. 84.

educational and other purposes designed to promote the propagation of a species. Each convention also allows exceptions to be made in order to protect property. The 1916 Convention allows birds to be killed in "extraordinary conditions" when they are "seriously injurious to the agricultural or other interests in any particular community."[91] The 1936 Convention allows migratory insectivorous birds to be killed "when they become injurious to agriculture and constitute plagues."[92] It also authorises the live capture and use of insectivorous birds "in conformity with the laws of each contracting country."[93] The purpose of this exception was to cater for the well established Mexican practice of trading in caged live birds.[94] The four conventions concluded in the 1970s allow exceptions to be made for the protection of "persons and property".

The most important exceptions, however, are those which allow the taking of migratory birds for subsistence purposes. They are important because spring hunting is a well established tradition in parts of Alaska, Canada and the U.S.S.R., and large numbers of birds are shot every year as they return to their nesting sites. It is thought that spring hunting of some species of waterfowl in parts of Alaska may account for as much as 15% of their spring populations,[95] and approximately one million birds are taken in Canada each year for subsistence purposes.[96]

The 1936 and 1973 Conventions make no exceptions at all for subsistence hunting. The other four conventions all authorise subsistence hunting in some form, but there are significant differences in the exact provisions of each one. Articles II(1) and II(3) of the 1916 Convention allow Eskimos and Indians to take scoters, auks, auklets, guillemots, murres, puffins and their eggs at any time provided that the taking is for food and that the birds and eggs are neither sold nor offered for sale.[97] The problem with this exception is that Eskimos and Indians do not hunt these species in significant numbers, but they do hunt other species, notably ducks and geese, which are not included in Articles II(1) or II(3). Accordingly, much of the spring hunting in both Alaska and Canada has been illegal since 1916, although neither the U.S. nor Canadian governments have ever seriously attempted to enforce the law. In order to make

[91] 1916 Convention, Article VII.
[92] 1936 Convention, Article II(e).
[93] 1936 Convention, Article II(e).
[94] See Hayden, note 5 above, p. 87.
[95] See Copp and Smith, *A Preliminary Analysis of the Spring Take of Migratory Waterfowl by Yupik Eskimos on the Yukon-Kuskokwim Delta, Alaska* (U.S. Fish and Wildlife Service, 1981).
[96] See *Final Environmental Assessment, Subsistence Hunting of Migratory Birds in Alaska and Canada* (U.S. Fish and Wildlife Service, 1980), p. iv.
[97] 1916 Convention, Articles II(1) and (3).

this spring hunting legal, Canada and the U.S.A. signed a Protocol in Ottawa on 30 January 1979 amending the 1916 Convention and authorising both countries to allow any species of migratory bird and its eggs to be taken "by the indigenous inhabitants of the State of Alaska and the Indians and Inuit of Canada for their own nutritional and other essential needs."[98] However, Article II of the Protocol specifies that it will not enter into force until both countries have exchanged instruments of ratification, and at the time of writing this has still not been done.

The 1972 Convention authorises Japan and the U.S.A. to allow Eskimos, Indians and "indigenous peoples of the Trust Territory of the Pacific Islands" to take any species of migratory bird provided that the taking is for their own food and clothing.[99] The 1974 Convention is less specific as to the type of people which Australia and Japan can allow to take birds or eggs that are otherwise protected by the Convention, but it insists that such taking must be compatible with the maintenance of optimum numbers of the population concerned and must not prejudice the preservation of the species. Article II(1)(d) of the 1974 Convention permits

...the hunting and gathering of specified birds or their eggs by the inhabitants of certain regions who have traditionally carried on such activities for their own food, clothing or cultural purposes provided that the population of each species is maintained in optimum numbers and that adequate preservation of the species is not prejudiced.

Recognising the problems caused by the 1916 Convention over spring shooting in Alaska and Canada, the 1976 Convention authorises the U.S.A. and the U.S.S.R. to allow any species to be taken for subsistence purposes.[100] The Convention also extends the type of people who can utilise this provision from Eskimos and Indians to "indigenous inhabitants" of specified regions, thus including people of other racial origins who have moved to those regions. Article II(1)(c) of the 1976 Convention authorises

...the taking of migratory birds and the collection of their eggs by the indigenous inhabitants of the Chukchi and Koryaksk national regions, the Commander Islands and the state of Alaska for their own nutritional and other essential needs.

[98] See Article I of the Protocol Amending the Convention of August 16, 1916 for the Protection of Migratory Birds in Canada and the United States of America (text available from U.S. Fish and Wildlife Service, Washington D.C.).

[99] 1972 Convention, Article III(1)(e).

[100] For further information on the motives behind the provisions of the 1976 Convention from a U.S. viewpoint, see the *Negotiation Report from the American Delegation* (16 March 1977), available from the U.S. Fish and Wildlife Service or the U.S. Department of State.

d) *Protected areas*

In the early twentieth century, excessive shooting and egg-collecting was a greater threat to birds than loss of habitat, and it is not surprising that both the 1916 and 1936 Conventions were more concerned with regulating the "taking" of birds than with the establishment of protected areas. Nevertheless both do make some provision for habitat conservation. The 1916 Convention recommends the establishment of refuges for wood ducks and eider ducks as part of the "special protection" that it awards to those species,[101] and the 1936 Convention calls for the establishment of refuges in which the taking of migratory birds is prohibited.[102]

Drainage of wetlands and degradation of other important habitats have proceeded at such a rate in recent years that habitat loss is now the greatest threat to most migratory birds. Recognising the pressing need for habitat conservation, each of the four 1970s conventions urges its Parties to establish protected areas for migratory birds, and each Party has created a number of sanctuaries for this purpose. In 1980, for example, 21,740,500 hectares were added to the U.S.A.'s National Wildlife Refuge system in Alaska alone.[103] Most of the important migratory bird habitats in Alaska are now covered by refuges or other protected areas — a very important achievement considering that some 200-300 million migratory birds nest or pass through Alaska each year.[104] Between 1976 and 1979 the U.S.S.R. established nature reserves totalling 800,000 hectares on Wrangel Island (snow goose nesting area), 211,000 hectares in the southern Chitin Oblast and 1.3 million hectares in the northern Krasnoyarsk area in the vicinity of Lake Taimyr (a massive nesting area for swans, snow geese and other waterfowl).[105]

The 1976 Convention is the only one of the six conventions to require its Parties to list especially important habitats in an Appendix to the Convention. Article IV(2)(c) requires the U.S.A. and the U.S.S.R. to "identify areas of breeding, wintering, feeding and moulting which are of special importance to the conservation of migratory birds within the areas under their jurisdiction" within one

---

[101] 1916 Convention, Article IV.

[102] 1936 Convention, Article II(8).

[103] Pursuant to the Alaska National Interest Lands Conservation Act of 1980, Public Law No. 96-487; 94 Stat. 2371 (partially codified in scattered sections of 16 and 43 U.S.C.).

[104] See *United States Statement on Implementation of the U.S.-U.S.S.R. Convention Concerning the Conservation of Migratory Birds and Their Environment for the Year 1980*, p. 6 (available from the U.S. Fish and Wildlife Service, Washington, D.C.).

[105] See *Implementation by the Soviet Side of the Terms of the U.S.-U.S.S.R. Convention Concerning the Conservation of Migratory Birds and their Environment*, a statement which was presented to the Eighth Annual Meeting of the U.S.-U.S.S.R. Joint Committee for Cooperation in the Field of Environmental Protection in 1979.

year of the entry into force of the Convention and to include them "in list number I on the Appendix to this Convention entitled 'Migratory Bird Habitat'." Article IV(2)(c) also obliges the U.S.A. and U.S.S.R. "to the maximum extent possible...to protect the ecosystems in those special areas...against pollution, detrimental alteration and other environmental degradation."

Notwithstanding the one year deadline, the U.S.A. had still not submitted a list of areas of special importance at the time of writing, although the existing system of U.S. National Wildlife Refuges and National Parks goes a long way towards fulfilling U.S. obligations under the Convention.[106] The U.S.S.R., on the other hand, submitted a list of Soviet areas of special significance for migratory birds to the eighth meeting of the Joint Committee of the U.S.-U.S.S.R. Environmental Agreement in 1979.[107] Article IV(3) of the 1976 Convention authorises the U.S.A. and U.S.S.R. to designate areas of special importance to the conservation of migratory birds outside their areas of national jurisdiction and stipulates that areas so designated shall be included on "list number II on the 'Migratory Bird Habitat' Appendix to this Convention." Article IV(3) also states that each country "shall, to the maximum extent possible, undertake measures necessary to ensure that any citizen or person subject to its jurisdiction will act in accordance with the principles of this Convention in relation to such areas."

e)   *Protection of the environment*

In the early twentieth century, oil spills, pesticides and other forms of environmental pollution were a minimal threat to birds, and the 1916 and 1936 Conventions make no mention of them. However, the 1972 Convention requires Japan and the U.S.A. "to endeavour to take appropriate measures to preserve and enhance the environment" of birds covered by the Convention and, in particular, requires both countries to endeavour to prevent "damage resulting from pollution of the seas."[108] The other conventions concluded in the 1970s contain similar provisions, although the 1976 Convention uses stronger terminology stating that the U.S.A. and the U.S.S.R. "*shall* undertake...to the extent possible...measures necessary to protect and enhance the environment of migratory birds and to prevent and abate the pollution or detrimental alteration of that

---

[106] See *United States Statement on Implementation of the U.S.-U.S.S.R. Convention,* note 104 above, p. 4.

[107] See *Implementation by the Soviet Side of the Terms of the U.S.-U.S.S.R. Convention,* note 105 above. The U.S.S.R. also submitted a list of migratory birds, endangered species and endangered sub-species requiring special protective measures.

[108] 1972 Convention, Article VI.

environment" (emphasis added).[109] Again, every Party to the four
1970s Conventions has taken at least some steps to protect the
environment of migratory birds. Particularly damaging pesticides
such as DDT have been widely banned, and measures have been
taken to control and mitigate the effects of oil pollution. In Alaska,
for example, a prior environmental review is required for all
developmental activity in the North Slope area along the Arctic
coast, including an evaluation by the U.S. Fish and Wildlife Service
on the projected effects of a given action on migratory birds.
Approximately 300 proposed development projects in Alaska,
ranging from small individual home development projects to major
oil and gas ventures, were examined by the Fish and Wildlife Service
in 1980.[110]

f) The introduction of exotic species

The introduction of exotic species can play havoc with the
ecological balance established by native fauna and flora. The
damage can be particularly serious when predators such as rats or
cats are introduced on to islands that are important nesting colonies
for seabirds.[111] Recognising this, the four 1970s Conventions all
require their respective Parties to control the introduction of species
which might disturb the ecological balance of natural environments
and also require them to control the import of live animals and
plants which might be detrimental to the preservation of migratory
or endangered birds. Again, all the Parties have enacted measures to
control the introduction of exotic species. To give just two examples,
Japan has taken steps towards eradicating introduced species from
coastal islands with important seabird nesting colonies, and the
U.S.A. has prohibited further introduction of grass carp
(*Ctenopharyngodon idella*) because it may have an adverse impact on
the food resources of migratory birds.[112]

g) Research and cooperation

The 1916 and 1936 Conventions make no mention of research or
cooperation with respect to the conservation of migratory birds,
although Canada, the U.S.A. and Mexico do in fact conduct joint
research programmes and cooperate extensively in their

[109] 1976 Convention, Article IV(1).
[110] See *United States Statement on Implementation of the U.S.-U.S.S.R. Convention*, note 104
above, p. 2.
[111] In Japan, for example, predation by rats and cats has threatened the breeding success of
the endangered short-tailed albatross (*Diomeda albatrus*) on Torishima Island.
[112] See *United States Statement on Implementation of the U.S.-U.S.S.R. Convention*, note 104
above, p. 4.

conservation efforts. For example, these three countries recently helped develop a management plan for the Pacific coast brant goose (*Branta bernicla nigricans*), and they all participate in the North American Bird Banding Programme which has been active since the 1920s.[113] Canada and the U.S.A. frequently cooperate with respect to management plans for migratory birds — the lengthy management plan prepared by the Canadian Wildlife Service and the U.S. Fish and Wildlife Service on the once-threatened greater snow goose (*Anser caerulesceus atlanticus*) in July 1981 is just one of many examples of such cooperation.[114] Mexico and the U.S.A. currently have some fifteen on-going joint projects involving migratory birds, ranging from waterfowl surveys, to identifying suitable habitats for wildlife management areas, to research into the effects of pesticides, to protection of endangered species such as the masked bobwhite (*Colinus virginianus ridgwayi*).[115]

The four 1970s Conventions all specifically require their respective Parties to cooperate in their research programmes. As a result, information obtained from bird banding programmes has been exchanged between the countries concerned and a number of specific joint research projects have been established. Since 1978, for example, Japan has arranged for officials from the U.S. Fish and Wildlife Service to accompany Japanese fishing boats in order to assess the extent of the accidental drowning of seabirds in the gill-nets of Japanese fishing fleets operating in the North Pacific and Bering Sea.[116]

h) *Enforcement mechanisms*

It is evident from the examples cited above that considerable efforts have been made to enforce the six bilateral conventions examined in this chapter. However, far from being assisted by some of the measures employed by other wildlife treaties to promote their enforcement, the progress made has been achieved without any enforcement aids. Not one of the six conventions requires its Parties to meet regularly or to submit regular reports on steps they have taken to implement the convention. The four 1970s conventions all

[113] See Appendix II of the *Memorandum of the Seventh Meeting of the U.S.A.-Mexico Joint Committee on Wildlife Conservation*, held in Culiacan in October 1981, available from the U.S. Fish and Wildlife Service.

[114] Copies of the management plan, which was prepared with the help of the Technical Section of the Atlantic Flyway Council, are available from the U.S. Fish and Wildlife Service.

[115] See Appendix II of the *Memorandum of the Seventh Meeting of the U.S.A.-Mexico Joint Committee on Wildlife Conservation*, note 113 above.

[116] See *Report on the Joint U.S.-Japan Cooperative Program on Development and Utilization of Natural Resources*, Panel on Conservation, Recreation and Parks (17 December 1980), available from the U.S. Fish and Wildlife Service.

require that "consultations" on implementation should be held if any Party requests them, but such a request has never been made and formal meetings have never taken place although informal talks occur relatively frequently. It may be that the enforcement mechanisms adopted by other conventions are not necessary in the context of these bilateral conventions, particularly as several of the countries concerned share close political and geographical ties. If relations between East and West deteriorate further, however, one wonders whether some of the conventions will continue to be effective without a formal forum in which their Parties must meet on a regular basis.

i) *Conclusion*

Although birds are receiving a considerable degree of legal and actual protection in Australia, Canada, Japan, Mexico, the U.S.A. and the U.S.S.R., the range of hundreds of species of migratory birds extends far beyond the jurisdictional limits of these countries. It almost goes without saying that the loss of habitat in South and Central America or in South East Asia, or the ingestion of pesticides in those regions, may be sufficient to devastate populations of migratory birds which breed in North America or North Asia however much protection they receive during the breeding period. It is crucial, therefore, that the six countries which have taken the initiative in concluding these bilateral conventions do their utmost to conclude similar agreements with other range states of the birds concerned.

CHAPTER 5

VICUNA

"Are we to allow the vicuna, one of the most beautiful animals in the world, to suffer the same fate as the chinchilla?"
(Sr. Felipe Benavides, 1975)

1. *Background*

Few species are as well covered by international law as the vicuna (*Vicugna vicugna*), a South American cameloid closely related to the llama and reputed to have the finest and most expensive wool in the world. Three international conventions have been concluded in the last fifteen years specifically to promote its conservation. They are the Convention for the Conservation of Vicuna (concluded in La Paz in October 1969 and hereinafter called the "La Paz Agreement")[1] to which Argentina, Bolivia, Chile, Peru and Ecuador are Parties, the Convention for the Conservation and Management of Vicuna (signed in Lima on 16 October 1979 and hereinafter called the "Lima Convention")[2] to which Bolivia, Chile, Ecuador and Peru are Parties, and the bilateral Agreement Between the Bolivian and Argentinian Governments for the Protection and Conservation of Vicuna (signed in Buenos Aires on 16 February 1981 and hereinafter called the "Buenos Aires Agreement").[3] In addition, vicuna are listed in Appendix I of the Convention on International Trade in Endangered Species of Wild Fauna and Flora ("CITES").[4]

The extraordinary attention lavished on vicuna by lawmakers reflects the heated debate which has raged in recent years as to whether or not controlled exploitation of the species should be allowed. Vicuna populations, which are found in the wild in Argentina, Bolivia, Chile and Peru[5] with by far the largest

---

[1] Diaro Oficial (Chile) No. 28504 (1973). Also reprinted in *International Environmental Law Multilateral Treaties* (Eric Schmidt Verlag, Berlin), 969:61.

[2] Reprinted in *International Environmental Law Multilateral Treaties* (Eric Schmidt Verlag, Berlin), 979:94.

[3] Not yet in force.

[4] See Chapter 12 below for a detailed analysis of CITES. Non-Peruvian populations of vicuna are listed in Appendix I of the Convention on the Conservation of Migratory Species of Wild Animals (see Chapter 13 for a description of this Convention). However, none of the countries with wild populations of vicuna are as yet Parties to this Convention.

[5] Vicuna may also have existed in Ecuador at one time. They are extinct there now, although plans to reintroduce them have been put forward. See A. Brack Egg, *Estudio de Viabilidad Tecnica para la Reintroduccion de la Vicuna en el Ecuador* (1980), a study prepared for the Food and Agriculture Organization of the United Nations.

concentration of the species occuring in Peru's Pampa Galeras National Vicuna Reserve, were reduced by persecution to a low of some 6,000 specimens in 1965 from a pre-Colombian population which may have been more than one million.[6] The La Paz Agreement was concluded when concern for the survival of the species was at its height, and it strictly prohibits the killing of vicuna for their meat, skins or wool. When the La Paz Agreement was signed it was hoped that if vicuna were given an opportunity to recover it might then be possible to live capture and shear them for their wool. In order to promote this objective Peru signed a technical cooperation agreement with the Federal Republic of Germany in 1972 for the "rational utilisation of the vicuna in Peru".

By the mid-1970s vicuna populations had increased substantially from the nadir of the 1960s, although the exact nature of the increase was the subject of considerable dispute. Amid much controversy, Peru began a limited culling programme in the Pampa Galeras in 1977 which continued until 1981.[7] Since any exploitation involving the killing of vicuna violated the protectionist provisions of the La Paz Agreement, Peru initiated negotiations for a new international arrangement. The resulting discussions led to the conclusion of the Lima Convention in 1979 which superceded the La Paz Agreement and allows culling in limited circumstances. Argentina was the only Party to the La Paz Agreement not to sign the Lima Convention. Argentina did not sign because it wanted to maintain strict protection for vicuna, and in 1981 Bolivia committed itself to a similar policy by signing the Buenos Aires Agreement

[6] *The IUCN Mammal Red Data Book Part I* (IUCN, 1196 Gland, Switzerland, 1982), p. 453.
[7] The numbers of vicuna killed under the programme were:
1977 — 210
1978 — 400
1979 — 1,558
1980 — 3,012
1981 — 1,467
In 1977 there were reports that drought, combined with the increased population, had decreased available forage in the central part of the Pampa Galeras National Vicuna Reserve and that vicuna were dying of starvation. The Peruvian authorities justified the initiation of their culling programmes on the basis that not only had numbers increased sufficiently to allow the population to sustain a harvest but also that a cull was essential if the rangeland was to be preserved. Others challenged the true extent of the increase in population and disputed the need for a cull. For further details, see *The IUCN Mammal Red Data Book Part I* (IUCN, 1982), pp. 454-5; Ashevou and Jackman, "One Angry Man and his 40,000 Vicunas", *The Sunday Times* (London) (24 February 1980), p. 50; N. Sitwell, "Go Shoot A Vicuna", *New Scientist* no. 1240 (1981), pp. 413-5; R. Telander, "Riding Herd on Peru's Vicunas", *International Wildlife* no. 11 (1981), pp. 36-43. See also S.K. Eltringham, *An Aerial Count of Vicuna in the Pampa Galeras National Reserve and Surrounding Regions, Ayacuho, Peru, Final Report to the International Fund for Animal Welfare* (April 1980); see also Norton-Griffiths and Torres Santibaez, *Evaluation of Ground and Aerial Census Work on Vicuna in Pampa Galeras, Peru* (results of a WWF/IUCN evaluation mission, 17 September — 7 October 1980).

with Argentina. The latter is rigorously protectionist in its terms and expressly stipulates that Bolivia will not exercise any rights that it may have incurred to exploit vicuna under the Lima Convention.[8] The Buenos Aires Agreement has not been ratified by Argentina and is therefore not yet in force[9], but Bolivia has already incorporated the terms of this Agreement into Bolivian law, thereby granting vicuna as strict legal protection in Bolivia as if the Agreement were in force.

2.   *Provisions of the Conventions*

a)   *Conservation of habitat*

The La Paz Agreement, the Lima Convention and the Buenos Aires Agreement each require their respective Parties to establish national parks, reserves and other protected areas for vicuna. Once they have been set up, each Agreement stipulates that these areas should remain protected. In addition, the Buenos Aires Agreement requires Argentina and Bolivia to evaluate the possibility of establishing a bilateral vicuna reserve within one year, and the Lima Convention requires its Parties to extend areas of repopulation managed as wildland areas. The Lima Convention added this provision because of projects undertaken in the 1970s to relocate vicuna in areas where the species was underpopulated or had disappeared.[10]

There are now five protected areas for vicuna in Argentina, two in Bolivia, one in Chile and three in Peru. Some were created prior to the La Paz Agreement — the Pampa Galeras National Vicuna Reserve was set up in 1967 for example — but most have been set up since 1969.[11] Although it is impossible to be certain whether these protected areas were set up in response to the three vicuna conventions rather than other factors, the habitat provisions of the conventions almost certainly contributed to their establishment.

b)   *Regulation of exploitation*

The La Paz Agreement prohibited international trade in vicuna wool, hides, skins and manufactured items thereof for ten years[12] and banned hunting and internal trade in vicuna wool, fur, skins

---

[8] Buenos Aires Agreement, Article 7.

[9] When it comes into force, the Buenos Aires Agreement will remain in force for twenty years.

[10] See Article 5 of the La Paz Agreement, Article 5 of the Lima Convention and Article 2 of the Buenos Aires Agreement. A bilateral Argentinian — Bolivian reserve has not yet been created.

[11] See *The IUCN Mammal Red Data Book Part I* (IUCN, 1982), p. 456.

[12] La Paz Agreement, Article 2.

and manufactured items thereof indefinitely.[13] It also prohibited the export of live animals except for limited numbers of specimens which were "not suitable for reproduction".[14]

The Lima Convention adopted a new approach. Article 1 states:

> The Signatory Governments agree that the conservation of the vicuna provides an economic production alternative for the benefit of the Andean population and commit themselves to its gradual use under strict governmental control, applying such technical methods for the management of wildlife as the competent official authorities may determine.

Although the Lima Convention has been hailed as an important step towards utilisation of vicuna, the circumstances in which they can legally be exploited are in fact still very limited. Article 3 authorises Parties to trade in vicuna under strict government control if populations of the species reach a level "which in terms of management would allow the production of meat, viscera and bones, as well as the processing of skins and wool into cloth." "Management" is defined as

> the application of methods to increase the vicuna population until the grazing capacity of a specific region, zone or area has been reached, and thereafter to maintain a balance between those two factors, employing technically accepted methods such as the translocation and/or culling of vicunas.[15]

Culling vicuna is therefore legally impermissible until the grazing capacity of a particular area has been reached, and trade is allowed only in the parts and products of specimens culled under such circumstances. Furthermore, the lucrative international market for vicuna products is still closed because the species is listed in Appendix I of CITES. Argentina, Bolivia, Chile and Peru are all Parties to CITES, and international commercial trade in specimens of Appendix I species or their parts and derivatives is prohibited except in a few very limited circumstances.[16] As a result, Peru, the only country to have allowed culling in recent years, has had to stockpile the wool, skins and other products which have been collected.

---

[13] *Ibid.*, Article 1.

[14] *Ibid.*, Article 3.

[15] Lima Convention, Article 9.

[16] See Chapter 12 below at pp. 247-249. However, reports of illegal international trade in vicuna cloth still persist. See *Will the Vicuna Survive?* (International Fund for Animal Welfare, 1983).

c)   *Research, technical assistance and education*

The La Paz Agreement, the Lima Convention and the Buenos Aires Agreement each require their respective Parties to carry out research on vicuna, and a number of ecological and conservation-oriented studies, primarily concerned with the establishment of protected areas, have been undertaken.[17] In addition, the Lima Convention requires "an active interchange of information through the Multinational Center for Documentation with headquarters in the Republic of Bolivia" and requires its Parties to provide each other with technical assistance for the conservation and management of vicuna, including the training of personnel.[18] The Buenos Aires Agreement requires Argentina and Bolivia to cooperate in their vicuna research programmes, and Article 3 of the Agreement states that the Argentinian government will finance studies in relation to the establishment of a bilateral vicuna reserve.[19]

With respect to education, Article 7 of the La Paz Agreement required the Parties to

> endeavour to conduct an active propaganda campaign on vicuna conservation, including the organisation of training courses for protection staff and the incorporation in school text books at all levels of reading matter designed to inculcate the idea of conservation in the minds of the pupils.

Several public education programmes on the conservation of vicuna were initiated in the 1970s, particularly in Chile and Argentina.[20] Although it is difficult to judge the degree to which the La Paz Agreement, rather than other factors, was responsible for these programmes, it was probably a useful stimulant. The Lima Convention makes no mention of conservation education, but the Buenos Aires Agreement requires Argentina and Bolivia to cooperate in this field.[21]

---

[17] See *The Vicuna in Argentina*, presented to the Reunion de Los Paroses Signatarios del convenio para la conservacion de la Vicuna, La Paz-Lima, 9-19 October 1979; see also W.L. Franklin, *Socioecology of the Vicuna* (Utah State University, Logan, Utah); and C. Koford, "The Vicuna and the Puna", 27 *Ecol. Mon.* 153-219 (1977).

[18] Lima Convention, Articles 6 and 7.

[19] Buenos Aires Agreement, Article 3. These studies have not yet been carried out nor has the bilateral reserve been set up. Technically, however, this does not mean that Argentina has violated Article 3 since it has not yet ratified the Agreement.

[20] See "South America: Vicuna projects", *World Wildlife Yearbook*, 1974-5, pp. 247-9, 252, 261; 1975-6 at pp. 187, 195-6; 1976-7 at pp. 203, 208, 217-9, 222. In Chile, various television programmes — such as "La tierra en que vivimos" — have covered the subject.

[21] Buenos Aires Agreement, Article 4.

d) *Commission*

The La Paz Agreement did not establish an administrative mechanism to oversee implementation of the Agreement, but, perhaps in recognition of the value of such mechanisms in the context of other conventions concerned with the conservation of wildlife, the Lima Convention states:

> In order to evaluate the implementation of the Convention, to keep the Parties informed and to recommend solutions for problems resulting from its application, the Signatory Governments agree to create the Technical-Administrative Commission of this Convention, composed of representatives of each of the countries. The Commission shall meet annually and its statutes shall be approved at its first meeting.[22]

The Technical-Administrative Commission met for the first time from 1-6 May 1981 in Arica, Chile and La Paz, Bolivia. It published a report of the proceedings which included information on population statistics, habitat protection and research programmes. The publication of similar reports each year should ensure that changes in the status of vicuna populations or their habitats are rapidly brought to the attention of Party governments, and that appropriate remedial action can be taken before any problems arising become irreversible. The Buenos Aires Agreement also established a Commission which will meet annually and is responsible for reviewing implementation of the Agreement and for making such recommendations as are necessary to improve its effectiveness.[23]

3. *Conclusion*

It is often difficult to establish a direct link between the provisions of an international convention and actual protection of the species concerned. Measures taken to conserve a species are as likely to stem from the requirements of domestic legislation or from private enterprise as from international obligations. However, there is no doubt that vicuna populations have increased dramatically since the La Paz Agreement came into force, nor is there any question that the prospects for the survival of the species are better than they were in 1969. The three vicuna conventions and CITES can reasonably claim considerable credit for this. Without them it is unlikely that an international commission would meet regularly to monitor vicuna conservation, that international trade in vicuna products would be

[22] Lima Convention, Article 8.
[23] Buenos Aires Agreement, Article 6.

prohibited and that the killing of vicuna for meat and wool would have been as limited as it has been in the last fifteen years. It would certainly be hard to give the vicuna more comprehensive international legal protection than it receives at present, and if the species does not prosper it would raise serious questions as to the worth of negotiating any international wildlife treaties at all.

PART III

Part III examines four treaties which are concerned with the conservation of wildlife in four distinct geographical areas. The oldest is the Convention on Nature Protection and Wildlife Preservation in the Western Hemisphere (the "Western Hemisphere Convention"). It was concluded in 1940 and is open to countries in North, Central and South America. Next came the African Convention on the Conservation of Nature and Natural Resources (the "African Convention"), which was adopted in Algiers in 1968 and is open to Member States of the Organization of African Unity. The other two treaties are much newer. The Convention on the Conservation of European Wildlife and Natural Habitats (generally known as the "Berne Convention" because it was concluded in Berne in Switzerland) was opened for signature in 1979 but only came into force in June 1982. It is open to Member States of the Council of Europe, although there are certain circumstances in which other countries may become Parties. The Convention on the Conservation of Antarctic Marine Living Resources ("CCAMLR") was signed in 1980 and came into force in April 1982. CCAMLR emanated from the Antarctic Treaty and has so far been signed only by Parties to the Antarctic Treaty, but other countries are allowed to join if they satisfy certain conditions.

The Western Hemisphere Convention, the African Convention and the Berne Convention have much in common. The most important link between them is the special emphasis that they each give to habitat protection. All three conventions require their Parties to establish protected areas for wildlife and to utilise all wildlife habitats wisely, including those outside specially designated protected areas. In addition, they all regulate trade in wildlife, prohibit the killing or capture of certain species and demand their

Parties to cooperate with each other in promoting the objectives of the conventions.

CCAMLR has a different emphasis. Its foremost aim is to limit fishing in Antarctic waters to a level which will not harm the Antarctic marine ecosystem. This "ecosystem approach" to fishing — which requires that catch quotas are set at a level which will neither damage populations of the species being caught nor populations of other dependent species — is particularly interesting because it represents a radical change from the traditional approach of fisheries treaties which is to consider only the stocks being fished when setting quotas. The Parties to the Convention were especially anxious to prevent krill (*Euphausia superba*), the principal diet of baleen whales, from being fished in quantities which would impede the recovery of depleted whale populations.

The Berne Convention and CCAMLR have been in operation for such a short time that it is difficult to judge how effective they will be, although some trends are already apparent. The Western Hemisphere and African Conventions have both resulted in the adoption of a number of conservation measures, but both have suffered from the lack of an administrative body to supervise and promote their enforcement with the result that their practical value has not been as great as it might have been. Recent initiatives have been made to amend these two conventions, particularly with a view to providing them with a system of administration and so improve their level of implementation, but nothing concrete has so far come of these moves.

Efforts have also been made in recent years to conclude a convention for the conservation of wildlife in south-east Asia and thereby close an important part of the geographical gap left by the four existing regional treaties. A draft agreement has been prepared and is being considered by the Member States of the Association of South-East Asian Nations, but nothing has been signed at the time of writing.

CHAPTER 6

THE CONVENTION ON NATURE PROTECTION AND WILDLIFE PRESERVATION IN THE WESTERN HEMISPHERE
(THE "WESTERN HEMISPHERE CONVENTION")

"Fully implemented, the Convention would provide an extraordinary commitment to preserve and protect the hemisphere's natural diversity." (R. Michael Wright, 1980)[1]

1. *Background*

In December 1938 the Eighth International Conference of American States met in Lima and recommended to the Pan American Union that it should establish a committee of experts to study problems relating to nature and wildlife in the American republics and should prepare a draft convention for their protection.[2] The recommendation was adopted, and the committee of experts drew up the Convention on Nature Protection and Wildlife Preservation in the Western Hemisphere (the "Western Hemisphere Convention").[3] The Western Hemisphere Convention was opened for signature to Member States of the Pan American Union (now called the Organization of American States, hereinafter referred to as the "OAS") on 12 October 1940 and entered into force on 30 April 1942.[4] At the time of writing, it has been signed by twenty one Member States of OAS and ratified by eighteen of them.[5]

The Western Hemisphere Convention was a visionary instrument, well ahead of its time in terms of the concepts it espouses. The protection of species from man-induced extinction,

---

[1] This comment was made in a paper included in the *Final Report of the Technical Meeting on Legal Aspects Related to the Western Hemisphere Convention* (held in Washington D.C. from 28 April-2 May 1980).

[2] Resolution XXXVIII: Protection of Nature and Wildlife, Eighth International Conference of American States.

[3] 161 *U.N.T.S.* 193, *U.S.T.S.* 981, 56 *Stat.* 1374.

[4] As required by Article XI(3) of the Western Hemisphere Convention, this was three months after the fifth instrument of ratification had been deposited with the Pan American Union.

[5] Argentina, Brazil, Chile, Costa Rica, Dominican Republic, Ecuador, El Salvador, Guatemala, Haiti, Mexico, Nicaragua, Panama, Paraguay, Peru, Trinidad and Tobago, Uruguay, U.S.A., and Venezuela are Parties to the Convention. Bolivia, Colombia and Cuba have signed the Convention but have not yet deposited instruments of ratification with OAS.

the establishment of protected areas, the regulation of international trade in wildlife, special measures for migratory birds and the need for international cooperation are all elements of wildlife conservation which are covered by the Convention — many of them for the first time by an international treaty — and which have reappeared time and again in other conventions concluded since 1940. The greatest weakness of the Convention, which plagues it still, was its failure to set up an administrative structure to review and promote enforcement of its terms. In consequence, although the Convention has stimulated the establishment of some protected areas, the enactment of some national conservation legislation and the development of some international cooperative programmes, it has become a "sleeping Convention" which, with a few notable exceptions, is now of limited practical value in most Party countries.

2. *Objectives*

The Parties had two main objectives in signing the Western Hemisphere Convention. The first was to protect all native animals and plants from extinction through means within man's control. Not only was the Western Hemisphere Convention the first international agreement to have such an objective, but it expresses it more clearly and in a more all-embracing fashion than do any other wildlife treaties concluded since. The preamble to the Convention states that it is the desire of the Parties to

> ...protect and preserve in their natural habitat representatives of all species and genera of native flora and fauna, including migratory birds, in sufficient numbers and over areas extensive enough to assure them from becoming extinct through any agency within man's control.

This objective is especially significant in light of the fact that a) the combined territories of the Parties to the Convention probably contain over 25% of all species on earth and b) between 1 — 2% of tropical forest (the richest of all habitat types in terms of species diversity) in South and Central America may be disappearing each year.[6] Such a rate of deforestation clearly threatens the survival of, if it has not already extinguished, thousands of native species. The Parties have therefore committed themselves to the ambitious goal of conserving the natural diversity of the largest and one of the most threatened "reservoirs" of species in the world.

[6] See *Tropical Moist Forests* (Earthscan, London, 1982), pp. 5-7. See also *Technical Meeting on Conservation of Migratory Animals of the Western Hemisphere and their Ecosystems* (held in June 1979 in Panama), OAS Doc. SG/Ser.P/111.3, p. 14, para. D(1).

A second objective of the Convention, also stated in the preamble, is to

> ...protect and preserve scenery of extraordinary beauty, unusual and striking geologic formations, regions and natural objects of aesthetic, historic or scientific value, and areas characterized by primitive conditions in those cases covered by this Convention.

3. *Conservation of habitat*

The Western Hemisphere Convention was one of the first international agreements to emphasise the need to conserve habitats as a means of protecting species, and its primary focus is on the establishment of "national parks, national reserves, nature monuments and strict wilderness reserves".

a) *Definitions*

Article I of the Western Hemisphere Convention defines "national parks" as

> areas established for the protection and preservation of superlative scenery, flora and fauna of national significance which the general public may enjoy and from which it may benefit when placed under public control;[7]

and "national reserves" as

> regions established for conservation and utilization of natural resources under government control, on which protection of animal and plant life will be afforded in so far as this may be consistent with the primary purpose of such reserves;[8]

and "nature monuments" as

> regions, objects or living species of flora or fauna of aesthetic, historic or scientific interests to which strict protection is given. The purpose of nature monuments is the protection of a specific object, or a species of flora or fauna, by setting aside an area, an object or a single species, as an inviolate nature monument, except for duly authorised scientific investigations or government inspection;[9]

---

[7] Western Hemisphere Convention, Article I(1).
[8] *Ibid.*, Article I(2).
[9] *Ibid.*, Article I(3).

and a "strict wilderness reserve" as

> a region under public control characterized by primitive conditions of flora, fauna, transportation and habitation wherein there is no provision for the passage of motorised transportation and all commercial developments are excluded.[10]

b) *Establishment of protected areas*

Article II of the Convention requires its Parties to

> ...explore at once the possibility of establishing in their territories national parks, national reserves, nature monuments and strict wilderness reserves as defined in the preceding article. In all cases where such establishment is feasible, the creation thereof shall be begun as soon as possible.[11]

Where such establishment is impractical, it shall be done "as soon as ... circumstances will permit."[12] Parties are required to notify the OAS of any national parks, national reserves, nature monuments and strict wilderness reserves which they have established, and of the legislation and methods of administrative control adopted in connection therewith.[13]

Each of the four categories of protected area described by the Western Hemisphere Convention has been established by one or more Parties.[14] National parks are the most widespread. The majority of Parties have at least one and some have considerably more — Costa Rica, for example, has twelve national parks covering over 400,000 hectares (a considerable achievement in view of the size of the country) and Brazil has twenty three covering over eight million hectares.[15] "National reserves" are less common, and where the term "national reserve" has been used it has not always had the same meaning. In Peru, for example, national reserves denote an area set aside for the protection and propagation of species such as vicuna (*Vicugna vicugna*) where the intention is to promote controlled exploitation of the animal, whilst in Argentina they denote buffer zones between national parks and surrounding farmland. However, the practice of setting aside areas for the

---

[10] *Ibid.*, Article I(4).

[11] *Ibid.*, Article II(1).

[12] *Ibid.*, Article II(2).

[13] *Ibid.*, Article II(3).

[14] For details of the current state and classification of the world's protected areas, see the *United Nations List of National Parks and Protected Areas* (prepared by the IUCN Commission on National Parks and Protected Areas and published by IUCN, 1196 Gland, Switzerland).

[15] *Ibid.*

purpose of rational use of their natural resources, which is the basic concept behind the Convention's definition of national reserves, is widespread even if the terminology varies. The "national forests" of Brazil, Peru and the U.S.A., the "fiscal forests" of Uruguay and the "forest reserves" of Venezuela all have this kind of management objective.[16]

Argentina, Chile, Paraguay and Venezuela all use the term "nature monument" or "natural monument" to describe an object or area which is strictly protected in much the same sense as is intended by the Western Hemisphere Convention. They are generally smaller than national parks, although the U.S. government's designation of 22.7 million hectares in Alaska as a "national monument" in 1978 is a major exception to this rule. Chile has also used the term to protect individual species — all specimens of Chilean false larch (*Fitzroya cupressoides*) and araucaria (*Araucaria araucana*) have been declared "natural monuments" under Chilean law.[17]

The term "strict wilderness reserve" is not used by any Party *per se*, although the scientific zones of national parks that are closed to the public and many of the scientific and biological reserves of Brazil, Chile and Ecuador are all designed to protect remote and primitive land, which is the basic objective of a strict wilderness reserve.[18] The U.S.A. comes closest to using the terminology of the Western Hemisphere Convention. The Wilderness Act of 1964 establishes a National Wilderness Preservation System in the U.S.A. and defines wilderness as "an area where the earth and its community of life are untrammelled by man, where man is himself a visitor who does not remain". To qualify as wilderness, an area must, among other things, be under the control of the U.S. government and be at least five thousand acres in size. Wilderness areas may be established within national parks or national forests or as separate units.[19]

In conclusion, a point of caution should be noted. There are many factors which may have influenced the decisions of Party governments to set up national parks, national reserves, nature monuments or strict wilderness reserves, and a desire to implement

[16] See G. Wetterberg and M.T. Jorge Padua, "Vocabulary of the Western Hemisphere Convention", *Final Report of Technical Meeting on Legal Aspects Related to the Convention on Nature Protection and Wildlife Preservation in the Western Hemisphere* (March 1980), OAS Doc. OEA/Ser.J/XI, CICYT/Doc. 199, p. 44 (hereinafter referred to as *Final Report of Technical Meeting on Legal Aspects*).

[17] *Ibid.*, pp. 44-5.

[18] *Ibid.*, p. 45.

[19] See The Wilderness Act of 1964, 16 U.S.C. §§1131-1136 (1976 & Supp. V 1981).

the Western Hemisphere Convention may or may not have been of practical significance. It is impossible to be certain how important the Convention has been to the establishment of protected areas in Party countries because Parties have never submitted reports to the OAS on measures they have taken to implement the Convention, and only a few of the domestic legislative or administrative instruments used by Parties to create protected areas refer back to the Convention as a source of legal authority or command. Nevertheless, correspondence with bureaucrats in national parks departments in Party countries indicates that the Convention has been of considerable value both in the conceptual development of habitat protection since 1940 and as a leverage to support their efforts to get protected areas established.[20]

c) *Management*

The Western Hemisphere Convention makes specific requirements regarding the management of national parks and strict wilderness reserves (but not of national reserves or nature monuments):

(i) *National Parks*

Article III stipulates that boundaries of national parks "shall not be altered, or any portion thereof be capable of alienation except by the competent legislative authority" and their resources "shall not be subject to exploitation for commercial profit." It also prohibits the "hunting, killing and capturing of members of the fauna and destruction or collection of representatives of the flora in national parks except by or under the direction or control of the park authorities or for duly authorised scientific investigations." The latter is particularly interesting because grazing by domestic animals and felling of trees for domestic use both pose problems in a number of national parks. Unless these activities are directed or controlled by the park authorities, they appear to be prohibited by Article III since they cause the destruction of flora. Another problem in some parks is siltation, erosion or pollution originating from a source outside the park boundaries. It could be argued that Article III also prohibits activities outside parks which cause siltation, erosion or pollution inside parks on the grounds that they result in destruction of the parks' flora.

---

[20] This is purely the personal opinion of the author based on correspondence with government officials in North, Central and South America during the course of research for this Chapter.

The Western Hemisphere Convention does not, however, intend national parks to be wilderness areas devoid of human presence. Recognising that they should be used for educational and recreational purposes provided that this does not conflict with conservation needs, Article III requires each Party "to provide facilities for public recreation and education in national parks consistent with the purposes of this Convention."

(ii)   Strict wilderness reserves

Article IV of the Western Hemisphere Convention stipulates that strict wilderness reserves shall be maintained "inviolate, as far as practicable, except for duly authorized scientific investigations or government inspection, or such uses as are consistent with the purposes for which the area was established." In contrast to its designs for national parks, the Convention clearly intends that strict wilderness reserves shall remain primitive areas to which man can gain access only with some difficulty.

4.   Conservation of species

The Western Hemisphere Convention selects three categories of species for special attention: species found outside national parks, national reserves, nature monuments or strict wilderness reserves; migratory birds; and species listed in a special Annex to the Convention.

a)   Species found outside national parks, national reserves, nature monuments or strict wilderness reserves

Article V(1) states:

> The Contracting Governments agree to adopt, or to propose such adoption to their respective appropriate law-making bodies, suitable laws and regulations for the protection and preservation of flora and fauna within their national boundaries, but not included in the national parks, national reserves, nature monuments, or strict wilderness reserves referred to in Article II hereof. Such regulations shall contain proper provisions for the taking of specimens of flora and fauna for scientific study and investigation by properly accredited individuals and agencies.

From the point of view of the legal obligations it imposes on Party governments, Article V(1) is weakly drafted. It does not require Party governments to adopt laws and regulations to protect wildlife outside parks and reserves, only that they "propose such adoption."

Neither does it set any standards which should apply in relation to exploitation of wildlife, modification of natural habitats, use of toxic chemicals and the many other threats to wildlife populations. It requires only that the laws and regulations should be "suitable" and that provisions for the taking of specimens for scientific research by accredited individuals and agencies should be "proper". Accordingly, every Party which has any sort of legislation to protect wildlife outside parks and reserves can justifiably claim to have fulfilled its obligations under Article V(1), however weak that legislation may be. However, as with much of the Convention, the value of Article V(1) lies not so much in its specific legal requirements as in its general recognition of the need to protect wildlife outside parks and reserves and in the authority it provides for Parties to do something about it. The U.S.A.'s Endangered Species Act, for example, protects endangered species from harmful activities even if they are carried out in an area which is not a national park or a specially protected zone, and the preamble to the Act specifically refers to the Western Hemisphere Convention as a source of legal authority for its enactment.[21]

b) *Migratory birds*

Article VII states:

> The Contracting Governments shall adopt appropriate measures for the protection of migratory birds of economic or aesthetic value or to prevent the threatened extinction of any given species. Adequate measures shall be adopted which will permit, in so far as the respective governments may see fit, a rational utilization of migratory birds for the purpose of sports as well as for food, commerce and industry, and for scientific study and investigation.

Although Article VII allows Parties to choose the methods ("appropriate measures") by which they implement their obligations, it nevertheless imposes on them a legal duty to protect economically or aesthetically valuable migratory birds and to prevent the extinction "of any given species".[22] However, the exact scope of Article VII is unclear because "economic and aesthetic" are undefined, and there is no list of economically and aesthetically valuable migratory birds attached to the Convention. Neither is "any given species" defined and could refer to migratory birds in

---

[21] See Endangered Species Act of 1973, as amended, 16 U.S.C. §§1531-1543 (1976 & Supp. V 1981).
[22] See Chapter 11 below at pp. 223-225.

general or only to those which are economically or aesthetically valuable.[23]

Enforcement of Article VII has been patchy. Some Parties, notably the U.S.A., have enacted strong domestic measures to protect migratory birds,[24] and some cooperative programmes have been established. To give two examples, information obtained from bird ringing programmes is regularly exchanged between countries in the Western Hemisphere, and the U.S.A. assisted in the development of a management plan for Palo Verde National Refuge in Costa Rica when the Refuge was created in 1979. It is estimated that approximately 240 species of birds use Palo Verde, at least 83 of which are migrants from North America.[25] On a less optimistic note, notwithstanding evidence that tropical deforestation and other habitat changes in Central and South America are having serious adverse effects on migratory birds[26] and that more than 170 species of North American breeding birds winter in Central and South America, only two international agreements have been concluded for the protection of migratory birds in the Western Hemisphere — one between Canada and the U.S.A. and the other between Mexico and the U.S.A. — and both were signed before the Convention came into force.[27]

c) *Species included in the Annex*

Article VIII states that

the protection of the species mentioned in the Annex to the present Convention, is declared to be of special urgency and importance. Species included therein shall be protected as completely as possible, and their hunting, killing, capturing or taking, shall be allowed only with the permission of the appropriate government authorities in the country. Such permission shall be granted only under special circumstances, in order to further scientific purposes, or when essential for the administration of the area in which the animal or plant is found.

---

[23] It is noteworthy that Article VII is limited to migratory birds. Migratory fish, sea turtles and marine mammals might also benefit from inclusion within its scope.

[24] See Migratory Bird Treaty Act, 16 U.S.C. §§703-711 (1976 & Supp. V 1981).

[25] See C. Freese, "U.S. Fish and Wildlife Service Participation in the Convention on Nature Protection and Wildlife Preservation in the Western Hemisphere", *Report of Fourth International Waterfowl Symposium* (January 1981), pp. 37-42 (available from Ducks Unlimited, P.O. Box 66300, Chicago, Illinois).

[26] *Ibid.* See also M. Wright, "The Convention and an Analysis of Problems not Covered by the Previous Meetings", *Final Report of Technical Meeting on Legal Aspects*, note 16 above, p. 33.

[27] See Chapter 4 above for a more detailed description of these two bilateral agreements.

The Annex is particularly confusing. It is not a single comprehensive list of species agreed by the Parties (the normal system adopted by wildlife treaties) but is a compilation of national lists submitted separately by individual Parties. Some of the lists are long, others are short, some species appear on more than one list and about half the Parties have not submitted a list at all. Neither the Convention nor the Annex establish criteria for the inclusion of a species in the Annex, although most Parties have limited their selections to species occuring within their territories which they deem to be threatened or potentially threatened with extinction. There are no procedures for amending the Annex although, since Parties may submit their own lists, there is no apparent reason why they should not amend them unilaterally. The U.S. government has adopted this attitude, stating:

> It is understood by this Government that such lists are to be considered as flexible rather than permanent in character and may from time to time be altered by the respective Governments by the addition or removal of such species from their several lists as changes and conditions may seem to them to warrant.[28]

Finally, it is not clear whether Parties must apply the provisions of Article VIII to all species in the Annex or only to those included in their own national lists.

In practice, the Annex has had very limited conservation value. Parties have naturally tended to include species in the Annex which are already protected under their national legislation, with the result that the Annex has tended to reflect the status quo rather than stimulate additional protection. Most national lists were submitted to OAS many years ago (no revisions have been submitted since 1967)[29] and probably do not reflect present conservation needs. In addition, there is no provision for the circulation of lists to Parties with the result that even if a Party wishes to help protect species listed by other Parties it may not know what those species are.

5. *International trade*

The provisions of Article IX, which regulate international trade in wildlife, have been largely superseded by the more recent Convention on International Trade in Endangered Species of Wild

---

[28] See *Treaties and other International Agreements on Fisheries, Oceanographic Resources and Wildlife Involving the United States* (U.S. Government Printing Office, 1977) p. 150, note 1.

[29] Comment made to the author by V. Yackovlev, Director, Department of Scientific and Technical Affairs, OAS.

Fauna and Flora ("CITES"),[30] but since several Parties to the Western Hemisphere Convention have not yet acceded to CITES, Article IX merits brief consideration.

Article IX requires each Party to regulate the export or transit of "protected species" or parts thereof by issuing export or transit certificates as appropriate. The Convention is more restrictive than CITES with respect to transit since CITES exempts specimens in transit from permit requirements.[31] Article IX also obliges each Party to prohibit the import of species or parts thereof which are "protected by the country of origin" unless they are accompanied by a lawful export certificate. "Protected species" are not defined but apparently refer to species listed in the Annex, again raising the problem as to how an importing country can discover which species are protected in the country of origin.

Even if this information can be obtained, Article IX causes other difficulties. In contrast to CITES it does not require, and there has apparently not been developed, a standard form for an export certificate in order to help enforcement officers in an importing country recognise a bogus certificate immediately. Neither does it require Parties to designate specific government agencies with responsibility for the issue of export permits. Without such designation it will be difficult for Parties to assist each other in the interception of illegal trade because an enforcement officer in an importing country needs to know the identity of the agency responsible for issuing permits in the exporting country in order to be able to check the legality of documents accompanying a shipment.[32]

Finally, the scope of Article IX is limited to species that are listed as protected in the Annex to the Convention. Since El Salvador is the only non-Party to CITES to have submitted a list for inclusion in the Annex, Article IX will have absolutely no practical value until other non-Parties to the CITES also submit lists. As the rate of accession to CITES has been considerably quicker than the rate of submission of lists of species to OAS for inclusion in the Annex, it seems unlikely that the future effect of Article IX will be more significant than it is at present.

---

[30] See Chapter 12 below.

[31] See pp. 256-257 below.

[32] For further discussion of some of these problems, see M. Bean, "The Western Hemisphere Convention and its Relation to Other International Conservation Agreements", *Final Report of Technical Meeting on Legal Aspects*, note 16 above, p. 36.

6. *Cooperation*

Article VI requires Parties "to cooperate among themselves in promoting the objectives of the present Convention" and, in particular, to assist each other with scientific research and field study, to "enter in to agreement with one another...in order to increase the effectiveness of this collaboration" and to "make available to all the American Republics equally through publication or otherwise the scientific knowledge resulting from such cooperative effort."

Article VI is one of the most important articles of the Western Hemisphere Convention. So many of the species found in the Western Hemisphere are either migratory or are found in more than one country that mutual cooperation between Parties is essential if efforts to protect them are to succeed. In addition, the financial resources and technical expertise in wildlife management are so heavily weighted in favour of a few countries in the region that assistance to the poorer countries is vital if the latter are to be able to carry out sound scientific conservation policies. In 1976, after many years of relative inactivity in the field of cooperation, the General Assembly of OAS unanimously agreed

> ...to urge the implementation of the Convention by the member states through mutual cooperation in activities such as scientific research and technical cooperation and assistance relating to wild flora and fauna, the creation, planning and training in the management of parks and reserves, the adoption of measures to conserve wild flora and fauna, and to protect species which are in danger of extinction.[33]

Whether as a result of the OAS resolution or not, there has unquestionably been an expansion in cooperative activities under the aegis of the Western Hemisphere Convention since the mid 1970s. For example, pursuant to an Executive Order issued by the President in relation to the Convention in 1976,[34] the U.S.A. has substantially increased its cooperative activities in the area of technical assistance and training through its National Park Service and Fish and Wildlife Service. A U.S. government lawyer has assisted El Salvador in drafting its first national wildlife law, and U.S. biologists have visited Ecuador to help initiate a population survey of the American crocodile (*Crocodylus acutus*) and Chile to

[33] See C. Freese and G. Wetterberg, "Cooperative Action under the Aegis of the Western Hemisphere Convention", *Final Report of Technical Meeting on Legal Aspects*, note 16 above, p. 69.

[34] Executive Order 11911 of 1976. For further details of the Order and subsequent action taken by the U.S. government, see Freese and Wetterberg, note 33 above, pp. 68-9.

assist in a study of the pudu (*Pudu pudu*).[35] At the request of the Paraguayan government, U.S. scientists helped conduct a survey of fauna and flora in Paraguay in 1980 and assisted in the establishment of the first Paraguayan natural history museum. In 1981, trainees from Guatemala, Costa Rica, Panama, the Dominican Republic, Ecuador and Brazil visited ten national wildlife refuges in the U.S.A. as part of a one month course in wildlife management.[36] The U.S.A. sponsored a Ranger Skills Training Course for fifteen Panamanian Park Rangers in 1982 and organised the first international workshop on environmental interpretation which was attended by representatives of thirteen Parties to the Convention. Using the Convention to authorise its actions, the U.S. National Park Service has provided instructors for two "Central American Mobile Seminars on Wildland Planning and Management", an urban park planner for a month in Caracas, guidance on management and interpretation of limestone cave formations to the Parks Directorate of the Dominican Republic, and a landscape architect to assist with development plans in Trinidad and Tobago's Caroni Swamp National Park.[37]

Cooperative programmes involving countries other than the U.S.A. have also been activated. Costa Rica and Panama have initiated the establishment of contiguous national parks on either side of their borders. The adjacent national parks of Pico da Neblina in Brazil and Serrania de la Neblina in Venezuela mutually enhance each other's objective of protecting the important ecosystems of that region. The Centro Agronomico Tropical de Investigacion y Ensenanza in Costa Rica and the Instituto Nacional de Pesquisas da Amazonia in Brazil are academic and research institutions which play an important role in international training in various aspects of wildland management.[38] Research in Peru on captive-bred Andean condors (*Vultur gryphus*) is supplying knowledge which has helped the successful captive breeding of the highly endangered California condor (*Gymnogyps californianus*).[39] The "First Regional Central American Meeting on Wildlife" was held in Nicaragua in 1978 in order to exchange information on the best methods of protecting and using wildlife in the Central American region.[40]

[35] See Freese and Wetterberg, note 33 above, p. 73.
[36] See C. Freese, "The Western Hemisphere Convention: International Framework for Wildlife Conservation", *Endangered Species Technical Bulletin*, Vol. VII, No.1 (January 1982, Department of the Interior, Washington D.C.), pp. 4-5.
[37] See Freese and Wetterberg, note 33 above, p. 74.
[38] *Ibid.*
[39] See Freese, note 36 above, p. 7.
[40] See Freese and Wetterberg, note 33 above, p. 76.

In response to the resolution on cooperation passed at its General Assembly in 1976, OAS has also been active. It sponsored five technical meetings on implementation of the Convention in cooperation with the national park and wildlife agencies of several Parties between 1977 and 1979. These meetings covered marine mammals, terrestrial ecosystems, migratory animals, education and training in relation to the administration of protected areas, and legal aspects of the Convention.[41] However, much as they may have achieved by way of an exchange of information and an analysis of what needs to be done to implement the Convention, many of the recommendations made by these meetings have not been acted upon. The meeting on legal aspects, for example, recommended that OAS should perform the functions of a Secretariat and, in particular, should collect and disseminate relevant information, update the lists of protected species and submit an annual report on enforcement of the Convention. It also suggested that representatives of Party governments should meet every two years to review enforcement of the Convention and to make appropriate recommendations on how to improve it.[42] However, not one of these recommendations has yet been implemented.

The examples of cooperative efforts mentioned above indicate that a useful initiative towards implementation of Article VI has been made in recent years, but there is still much to do.

7. Administration

One of the themes appearing consistently throughout this book is that conventions with an administrative mechanism to promote their enforcement are generally far more effective than those without one. Unfortunately, the Western Hemisphere Convention falls into the latter category. It neither requires its Parties to meet regularly in order to review implementation of the Convention (with the result that they have never formally met for this purpose since the Convention was signed), nor requires them to submit regular reports on the domestic measures that they have taken to enforce its provisions. In comparison with the wide-ranging

[41] Detailed reports on the results of these meetings are available from OAS. Their full titles are: *Meeting of Experts on Conservation of Marine Mammals and their Ecosystems* (held Sept. 1977 in Argentina), OAS Doc. OEA/Ser.J/XI, CICYT/Doc. 183; *Final Report, Meeting of Experts on Conservation of the Major Terrestrial Ecosystems of the Western Hemisphere*, April 10-14, 1978, San Jose, Costa Rica (OAS, 1978); *Technical Meeting on Conservation of Migratory Animals of the Western Hemisphere and their Ecosystems* (held June 1979 in Panama), OAS Doc. SG/Ser.P/III.3; *Technical Meeting on Education and Training for the Administration of National Parks, Wildlife Reserves and other Protected Areas* (held Sept. 1978 in Venezuela), OAS Doc. SG/Ser.P/III.1; and *Final Report of Technical Meeting on Legal Aspects*, note 16 above.

[42] See *Final Report of Technical Meeting on Legal Aspects*, note 16 above, pp. 6-8.

responsibilities of the permanent Secretariats or Commissions established by other treaties, the role of OAS within the Convention is very limited. It acts as a depositary for the original text of the Convention, for instruments of ratification and for denunciations, and it is responsible for receiving notification of protected areas which have been established and of species which have been listed in the Annex. Its only other function is to notify the Parties of any relevant information communicated to it by national museums or other interested organisations.[43]

The recommendations made by the technical meeting on legal aspects of the Convention, mentioned above, were designed to remedy some of the major deficiencies in its administration, and implementation of those recommendations is clearly essential if the Convention is to become a legal instrument of which Party governments are forced to take more active notice.

8. *Conclusion*

The Western Hemisphere Convention is more than forty years old, but most of the concepts which it espouses are sufficiently relevant for it still to be a legal instrument of considerable potential value to wildlife in the Americas. Its provisions, particularly its emphasis on the protection of habitat and the need for international cooperation, would benefit an enormous number of species and ecosystems if they were fully implemented by all the Parties. Some of its potential has already been fulfilled in the sense that protected areas have been established, several Parties have given special attention to migratory birds and some cooperative programmes have been successfully carried out, although the degree to which the Convention stimulated, or provided the legal authority for, these activities is difficult to judge. However, in many areas the Convention has become a "sleeping treaty" of little or no practical value and, unless and until changes are made in its administrative structure so as to force the Convention to the forefront of the attention of Party governments, it is likely to remain that way. This is a tragic waste, and it can only be hoped that every effort will be made to establish a system of administration capable of resurrecting the Convention from its present state of semi-retirement and pressing it into to full active service.

---

[43] Western Hemisphere Convention, Article X(2).

CHAPTER 7

THE AFRICAN CONVENTION ON THE CONSERVATION OF NATURE AND NATURAL RESOURCES
(THE "AFRICAN CONVENTION")

"We are the fire which burns the country. The calf of the elephant is exposed on the plain."
(Bantu saying)

1. *Background*

The first international agreement to conserve African wildlife was signed in London on 19 May 1900. It was called the Convention for the Preservation of Wild Animals, Birds and Fish in Africa.[1] It was signed by the colonial powers then governing much of Africa — France, Germany, Great Britain, Italy, Portugal and Spain — and its objective was "to prevent the uncontrolled massacre and to ensure the conservation of diverse wild animal species in their African possessions which are useful to man or inoffensive."[2] As long ago as 1900 the teeming herds of African wild animals were starting to diminish, and the primary goal of the Convention was to preserve a good supply of game for trophy hunters, ivory traders and skin dealers.

The 1900 Convention prohibited the killing of all specimens of species listed in Table 1 of the Convention and "all other animals which each local government judges necessary to protect, either because of their usefulness or because of their rarity and danger of disappearance."[3] Table 1 was divided into Series A ("useful animals") and Series B ("animals that are rare and in danger of disappearance"). Series A contained the secretary bird and all vultures, owls and oxpeckers. Series B consisted of "giraffe, gorillas, chimpanzee, mountain zebra, wild asses, white tailed gnu and pygmy hippopotamus." The Convention also prohibited the killing of non-adults[4] and females "when accompanied by their young"[5] of "elephant, rhinoceros, hippopotamus, zebra other than mountain zebra, buffalo, antelope and gazelles, ibex and mouse deer."

---

[1] 94 *B.F.S.P.* 715.
[2] Preamble to the 1900 Convention.
[3] 1900 Convention, Article II(1).
[4] *Ibid.*, Article II(2).
[5] *Ibid.*, Article II(3).

Certain methods of killing, including the use of explosives for fishing, were also outlawed.[6] The 1900 Convention was the first treaty to encourage the establishment of nature reserves, and it prohibited the hunting, killing or capture of any bird or animal "except those specifically excepted by the local authorities" in nature reserves.[7] However, the 1900 Convention considered numerous species unworthy of protection, and it urged signatory governments to destroy the eggs of crocodiles, poisonous snakes and pythons[8] and to "reduce" certain other species including lion (*Panthera leo*), leopard (*Panthera pardus*), spotted hyaena (*Crocuta crocuta*), wild dog (*Lycaon pictus*) and birds of prey except owls and vultures.[9]

The 1900 Convention was superseded in 1933 by the Convention Relative to the Preservation of Fauna and Flora in their Natural State,[10] which was also signed in London and became known as the "London Convention". Like its predecessor, the London Convention was a treaty between African colonial governments, and Belgium, Egypt, France, Great Britain, Italy, Portugal, South Africa and Sudan became Parties to it.[11] The London Convention expanded on the requirements of the 1900 Convention, but its principal objective — to preserve supplies of species which were economically valuable or popular with trophy hunters — was much the same except that it ended the concept of nuisance species.

The main emphasis of the London Convention was on the creation of protected areas. It required its Parties to explore the possibility of establishing "national parks" and "strict natural reserves" forthwith.[12] In cases where such establishment was possible, the Convention stipulated that work should begin within two years of the Convention coming into force.[13] Where it was "impracticable at present, suitable areas should be selected as early as possible...and transformed into national parks or strict nature reserves as soon as...circumstances will permit."[14] The Convention

[6] *Ibid.*, Article II(9). Article II(8) states that the use of nets and traps for animal capture shall be "restricted".

[7] *Ibid.*, Article II(5).

[8] *Ibid.*, Article II(15).

[9] *Ibid.*, Article II(13). The full list of species to be "reduced" is contained in Table V of the Convention.

[10] 172 *L.N.T.S.* 241; *U.K.T.S.* no. 27 (1930), Cmd. 5280. The London Convention was signed on 8 November 1933 and came into force on 14 January 1936.

[11] India acceded to the London Convention on 9 May 1939, and Tanzania (then Tanganyika) acceded on 3 December 1963. Spain signed on 8 November 1933 but never ratified.

[12] London Convention, Article 3(1).

[13] *Ibid.*

[14] *Ibid.*, Article 3(2).

prohibited the hunting, killing or capture of fauna and the collection or destruction of flora in parks and reserves,[15] and it required Parties to establish "intermediate zones" around the borders of parks and reserves in which the killing or capture of animals was to be controlled by the park or reserve authorities and in which no person "shall have any claim in respect of depredations caused by animals."[16] The intention of this latter provision was to create buffer zones around the parks where farmers farmed at their own risk and where any animal migrating out of the park would not immediately be shot. It is noteworthy that these provisions are very similar to the habitat provisions of the Western Hemisphere Convention which was signed seven years later.[17] The Western Hemisphere Convention was probably heavily influenced by its African counterpart.

Like its predecessor, the London Convention highlighted certain species for special protection. They were listed in an Annex to the Convention and consisted of one plant and forty animals (mostly ungulates) plus all lemurs and pangolins. The Convention prohibited the hunting, killing and capture of these species except with a special license.[18] It also regulated internal and international trade in their trophies,[19] which were defined to include parts and products.[20] The Convention banned certain methods of hunting, killing and capture including the use of poison, nets and dazzling lights.[21]

As more and more African States gained independence, the need for a new treaty, more relevant to modern Africa, became increasingly evident. In 1968 the London Convention was superseded by the African Convention on the Conservation of Nature and Natural Resources (the "African Convention").[22] This new Convention was signed on 15 September 1968 in Algiers on the recommendation of the Organization of African Unity (hereinafter called the OAU) and entered into force on 7 May 1969.[23] At the time

---

[15] *Ibid.*, Article 2(1) and (2).

[16] *Ibid.*, Article 4(2).

[17] See Chapter 6 above, pp. 100-103.

[18] London Convention, Article 8(1).

[19] *Ibid.*, Article 9(2).

[20] *Ibid.*, Article 9(8). However, a trophy which "by process of *bona fide* manufacture...has lost its original identity" is not covered by the Convention.

[21] *Ibid.*, Article 10.

[22] 1001 *U.N.T.S.* 3.

[23] Article XXI of the African Convention states that the London Convention shall cease to have effect in countries in which the African Convention has come into force.

of writing, 28 States are Parties to the African Convention. A further 14 have signed but have not yet ratified.[24]

The African Convention is primarily concerned with wildlife, but it also embraces the conservation of other natural resources such as soil and water, making it the most comprehensive multilateral treaty for the conservation of nature yet negotiated. Like the London Convention, the African Convention emphasises the need for protected areas and special conservation measures for species listed in an Annex to the Convention, but it also covers topics such as conservation education, research and the need to integrate conservation into development plans. Unfortunately, it made the same mistake as both the London and Western Hemisphere Conventions and did not establish an administrative structure to oversee its enforcement. As a result, little has been done to encourage Parties to implement its provisions. The African Convention should not be lightly dismissed because it has stimulated useful conservation measures in some countries and remains the framework on which a substantial body of national legislation is based, but its practical value for African wildlife might have been considerably greater if it had established a central body with responsibility for overseeing and promoting its enforcement.

2. Objectives

Article II, which is entitled "Fundamental Principle", sets out the basic objective of the African Convention. It states that Parties

...shall undertake to adopt the measures necessary to ensure conservation, utilization and development of soil, water, flora and faunal resources in accordance with scientific principles and with due regard to the best interests of the people.

Article VIII(1) sets out another objective which is more specifically relevant to wildlife. It is

...to accord a special protection to those animal and plant species that are threatened with extinction, or which may become so, and to the habitat necessary to their survival.

[24] Cameroon, Central African Republic, Comoros Islands, Djibouti, Egypt, Ghana, Ivory Coast, Kenya, Liberia, Madagascar, Malawi, Mali, Morocco, Mozambique, Niger, Nigeria, Rwanda, Senegal, Sudan, Swaziland, Tanzania, Togo, Tunisia, Seychelles, Uganda, Upper Volta, Zaire and Zambia are full Parties to the African Convention. Algeria, Botswana, Benin, Burundi, Chad, Congo, Ethiopia, Gabon, Gambia, Guinea, Lesotho, Libya, Mauritania, Mauritius, Sierra Leone and Somalia have signed but have not yet ratified.

These are exemplary conservation goals since they envisage conservation *and* development of African natural resources (the integration of conservation and development is a key theme of the World Conservation Strategy)[25] and special protection for threatened species. The emphasis on preserving habitat is particularly significant because degradation and loss of habitat is the main threat to the vast majority of African species.

3. *Conservation areas*

The African Convention emphasises the need to establish "conservation areas".

a) *Definition*

Article III(4) defines a "conservation area" as "any protected natural resource area, whether it be a strict natural reserve, a national park or a special reserve."

Article III(4)(a) defines a "strict nature reserve" as an area

> under State control...throughout which any form of hunting or fishing, any undertaking connected with forestry, agriculture or mining, any grazing, any excavation or prospecting, drilling, levelling of the ground or construction, any work tending to alter the configuration of the soil or the character of the vegetation, any water pollution and, generally, any act likely to harm or disturb the fauna or flora, including introduction of zoological or botanical species, whether indigenous or imported, wild or domesticated, are strictly forbidden.

Strict nature reserves are the most strictly protected type of conservation area and are similar in concept to the "strict wilderness reserves" established by the Western Hemisphere Convention.[26]

Article III(4)(b) defines a "national park" as an area

> under State control...exclusively set aside for the propagation, protection, conservation and management of vegetation and wild animals as well as for the protection of sites, landscapes or geological formations of particular scientific or aesthetic value, for the benefit and enjoyment of the general public, and...in which the killing, hunting and capture of animals and the destruction or collection of plants are prohibited except for scientific and management purposes and on the

[25] The *World Conservation Strategy* (IUCN, 1980) was launched in 1980 as a blueprint of modern conservation philosophy. It was prepared by the International Union for Conservation of Nature and Natural Resources with advice, cooperation and financial assistance from the United Nations Environment Programme and the World Wildlife Fund. It explains at length the interdependence of conservation and development.

[26] See Chapter 6 above, pp. 100-103.

condition that such measures are taken under the direction or control of the competent authority.

Article III(4)(b) goes on to state that acts prohibited in strict nature reserves are equally prohibited in national parks, except that a) sport fishing in national parks is permissable provided that it is authorised and controlled by the competent authority and b) national park authorities are permitted to do what is appropriate for the purpose of managing the parks, including allowing the public to visit them. National parks in the context of the African Convention are also comparable to national parks in the context of the Western Hemisphere Convention since they are areas set aside for the protection of wildlife but in which public recreation is encouraged to the extent that it is compatible with conservation requirements.[27]

Article III(4)(c) defines a "special reserve" as an area

> set aside for the conservation, management and propagation of wild animal life and the protection and management of its habitat...where settlement and other human activities shall be controlled or prohibited...to protect characteristic wildlife and especially bird communities, or to protect particularly threatened animal or plant species and especially those listed in the Annex to this Convention, together with the biotopes essential for their survival.

In contrast to strict nature reserves and national parks, a special reserve need not be under State control, and Article III(4)(c)(i)(b) permits the hunting, killing or capturing of wildlife in special reserves if it is done "by or under the direction or control of the reserve authorities".

b) *Establishment*

The Convention stipulates that Parties should establish conservation areas in order to

> i) ...undertake the conservation of plant species or communities, which are threatened and/or of special scientific or aesthetic value;[28]
> ii) ...protect those ecosystems which are most representative of and particularly those which are in any respect peculiar to their territories;[29]
> iii) ...ensure the conservation of all species and more particularly of those listed or which may be listed in the Annex to this Convention.[30]

[27] See pp. 102-103 above.
[28] African Convention, Article VI(2).
[29] *Ibid.*, Article X(1)(i).
[30] *Ibid.*, Article X(1)(ii).

The latter obligation is particularly interesting because, literally interpreted, it requires each Party to ensure that every species within its jurisdiction has enough habitat set aside as a conservation area in order to ensure its survival. Since habitat loss is the major threat to most species in the Annex to the Convention as well as to many other non-listed African species, the Convention has imposed a very important responsibility on Party governments.

Article X(2) of the Convention requires the Parties to establish, where necessary, buffer zones around the borders of conservation areas "within which the competent authorities shall control activities detrimental to the protected natural resources".

4.   *Habitats outside conservation areas*

The African Convention is not only concerned with the establishment of parks and reserves but also with the wise use of natural habitats outside specially designated protected areas.

Article VI of the Convention, entitled "Flora", requires each Party to adopt

> ...scientifically based conservation, utilization and management plans of forests and rangeland, taking into account the social and economic needs of the States concerned, the importance of the vegetation cover for the maintenance of the water balance of an area, the productivity of soils and the habitat requirements of the fauna.[31]

Article VI also requires each Party to

> ...pay particular attention to controlling bush fires, forest exploitation, land clearing for cultivation, and overgrazing by domestic and wild animals...[to] set aside areas for forest reserves and carry out afforestation programmes where necessary...[to] limit forest grazing to seasons and intensities that will not prevent forest regeneration; and ...establish botanical gardens to perpetuate plant species of particular interest.[32]

Article VII, entitled "Faunal Resources", emphasises the conservation of aquatic habitats. It requires Parties to

> manage aquatic environments, whether in fresh, brackish or coastal water with a view to minimise deleterious effects of any water and land use practice which might adversely affect aquatic habitats.[33]

---

[31] African Convention, Article VI(1)(a).
[32] *Ibid.*, Article VI(1)(b)-(e).
[33] African Convention, Article VII(1)(b).

5.   *Protected Species*

a)   *Species in the Annex to the Convention*

Article VIII(1) of the African Convention stipulates that Parties shall take special measures to protect species listed in the Annex to the Convention. The Annex is sub-divided into Class A and B.

(i)   *Criteria for including species in the Annex*

The African Convention does not directly establish criteria for the inclusion of a species in the Annex nor for the inclusion of a species in Class A as opposed to Class B or vice versa. However, Article VIII(1) infers that the Annex should include species which are or may become threatened with extinction. It states:

> The Contracting States recognise that it is important and urgent to accord a special protection to those animal and plant species that are threatened with extinction, or which may become so, and to the habitat necessary to their survival...These species which are, or may be listed, according to the degree of protection that shall be given to them are placed in Class A or B of the Annex to this Convention.

Furthermore, the fact that the African Convention requires stricter protection for Class A species than Class B species implies that Class A is intended to include species in greater danger than Class B.

Class A includes all Malagasy lemuroids, all African palm squirrels and forty three other species of mammals. It also contains all pelicans, storks, hammerkops, ibises, spoonbills, herons, egrets, bitterns, flamingoes, vultures, cranes and ground hornbills as well as lammergeyer (*Gypaetus barbatus*), crowned hawk-eagle (*Stephanoaetus coronatus*), Teita falcon (*Falco fasciinucha*), white-headed guineafowl (*Agelastes meleagrides*), Congo peacock (*Afropavo congensis*), white-necked rockfowl (*Picarthartes oreas*), grey-necked rockfowl (*Picarthartes gymnocephalus*) and Warsangli linnet (*Warsanglia johannis*). Although mammals and birds comprise the bulk of species in Class A, ten species of reptiles, six species of blind fish, two species of toads and three species of plants are also listed. Class B is heavily biased towards mammals. Over seventy species are individually listed, and Class B also includes all oribis, Malagasy tenrecs, shrews of the family Potamogalidae, prosimians of the family Lorisidae, Malagasy mongooses of the subfamily Galidiinae, otters of the subfamily Lutrinae and all monkeys except common baboons. The only birds in Class B are ostrich (*Struthio camelus*), bustards and birds of prey and owls not in Class A, and the only other species listed are "all crocodiles".

The Annex has not been amended since the Convention came into force and clearly needs restructuring. The black rhinoceros (*Diceros bicornis*), for example, is in Class B although its numbers have drastically declined in the last fifteen years to a point where it may be in serious danger of extinction in some parts of its range.[34] Yet Class B also includes relatively common mammals such as impala (*Aepyceros melampus*) and buffalo (*Syncerus caffer*). It is also noteworthy that plants, fish and amphibians are poorly represented in the Annex and that no invertebrates are listed at all.

(ii)   *Protective measures for species in the Annex*

Article VIII(1)(i) stipulates that

> species in Class A shall be totally protected throughout the entire territory of the Contracting States; the hunting, killing, capture or collection of specimens shall be permitted only on the authorization in each case of the highest competent authority and only if required in the national interest or for scientific purposes.

Article VIII(1)(ii) states that species in Class B shall also "be totally protected", but it goes on to say that hunting, killing, capturing or collecting of Class B species is permissible "under special authorization granted by the competent authority." Furthermore, in contrast to Article VIII(1)(i), Article VIII(1)(ii) does not insist that such authorisation shall only be granted when in the national interest or for scientific purposes.

Finally, Article VIII(1) states that where a species is or may become threatened with extinction and is found only in the territory of one Party to the Convention, that Party "has a particular responsibility for its protection."

b)   *Species not in the Annex to the Convention*

Article VII(1) of the Convention allows Parties to exploit populations of species that are not listed in the Annex and are situated outside conservation areas, provided that the populations are managed "for an optimum sustainable yield, compatible with and complimentary to other land uses."[35]

Article VII(2) of the Convention requires each Party to adopt "adequate legislation on hunting, capture and fishing under which (a) the issue of permits is properly regulated; (b) unauthorised

---

[34] This information is stored in IUCN's Mammal Red Data Base at 219c Huntingdon Rd, Cambridge, England.

[35] African Convention, Article VII(1)(a).

methods are prohibited." Article VII(2) also lists certain prohibited methods of hunting, capture and fishing. These include the use of drugs, mechanically propelled vehicles (in the case of hunting and capture only), fire, explosives and poisoned bait as well as "any method liable to cause a mass destruction of wild animals."[36] Hunting or capture at night is also forbidden.[37] However, Article VII(2) permits the capture of animals with the aid of drugs or mechanically propelled vehicles, or hunting or capture by night "if carried out by, or under the control of, the competent authority."[38] In order to ensure the fullest use of game meat, Article VII(2) prohibits "the abandonment by hunters of carcasses of animals, which represent a food resource."[39]

6. *Trade*

Article IX of the African Convention regulates trade in wildlife. Like the comparable clause of the Western Hemisphere Convention (also Article IX), it has been largely superseded by the Convention on International Trade in Endangered Species of Wild Fauna and Flora ("CITES"). However, since there are some differences and since not all Parties to the African Convention are Parties to CITES, Article IX merits brief consideration.

Article IX(2)(b) prohibits the export of a "specimen" (the term "specimen" is not defined, and it is therefore unclear whether trade in parts or derivatives such as ivory is covered by Article IX) or a "trophy" (also undefined) of species listed in the Annex without a permit. Permits must indicate the destination of specimens or trophies, must be on a standard form, must be examined prior to export and "shall not be given unless the specimens or trophies have been obtained legally." Article IX(2)(c) makes the import and transit of such specimens and trophies subject to the same conditions but adds the clause "with due provision for the confiscation of specimens and trophies exported illegally, without prejudice to the application of other penalties." Like Article IX of the Western Hemisphere Convention, Article IX(2)(c) of the African Convention is stricter than CITES in the sense that it regulates transit. CITES exempts transit from permit requirements.[40]

Article IX(1) requires the Parties "to regulate trade in and transport of specimens and trophies" of species not listed in the Annex. It also requires Parties to "control the application of these

[36] *Ibid.*, Article VII(2)(c).
[37] *Ibid.*, Article VII(2)(c)(iv)(4).
[38] *Ibid.*, Article VII(2)(e).
[39] *Ibid.*, Article VII(2)(d)(iii).
[40] See Chapter 12 below at pp. 256-257.

regulations in such a way as to prevent trade in specimens and trophies which have been illegally captured or killed or obtained." The Convention gives no further details as to how trade should be regulated.

7. *Research, education and development plans*

a) *Research*

Article XII of the African Convention stipulates that Parties "shall encourage and promote research in conservation, utilization and management of natural resources" and "shall pay particular attention to ecological and sociological factors."

b) *Education*

Article XIII obliges Parties to "ensure that their peoples appreciate their close dependence on natural resources and that they understand the need, and rules for, the rational utilization of those resources."[41] It also requires Parties to include conservation principles "in education programmes at all levels",[42] to establish "information campaigns capable of acquainting the public with, and winning it over to, the idea of conservation",[43] and to "make maximum use of the educational value of conservation areas."[44]

c) *Development plans*

Article XIV states that Parties "shall ensure that conservation and management of natural resources are treated as an integral part of national and/or regional development plans",[45] and that "in the formulation of all development plans, full consideration shall be given to ecological, as well as to economic and social factors."[46] Where any development plan is "likely to affect the natural resources of another State, the latter shall be consulted."[47]

8. *Exceptions*

In contrast to the Western Hemisphere Convention which does not allow its Parties to make exceptions from its provisions in any circumstances, Article XVII(1) of the African Convention states that its provisions

[41] African Convention, Article XIII(1)(a).
[42] *Ibid.*, Article XIII(1)(b)(i).
[43] *Ibid.*, Article XIII(1)(b)(ii).
[44] *Ibid.*, Article XIII(2).
[45] African Convention, Article XIV(1).
[46] *Ibid.*, Article XIV(2).
[47] *Ibid.*, Article XIV(3).

...shall not affect the responsibilities of Contracting States concerning (i) the paramount interest of the State, (ii) "*force majeure*", (iii) defence of human life.

Article XVII(2) allows Parties to enact measures contrary to the provisions of the Convention in time of famine, for the protection of public health and in defence of property provided that their application is precisely defined in respect of aim, time and place.

Article XVII(1) neither defines "the paramount interest of the State" nor limits the circumstances in which it may be applied. There is therefore nothing in the Convention to prevent a Party from building a hydro-electric plant in a national park or from clear-cutting a section of tropical forest if it decides that such a course of action is in the paramount interest of the State. It is interesting to note that Article XVII is not qualified in the same way as the "exception clause" of the Convention on the Conservation of European Wildlife and Natural Habitats which insists that the use of exceptions must not in any circumstances be detrimental to the survival of a species or a population thereof.[48] In addition there is no provision in the African Convention corresponding to the article in the European Convention which requires Parties to report every two years on any exceptions they have made.[49] This is an important omission because the knowledge that a government will have to justify in public any exceptions that it makes may serve to deter it from making them.

9. *Administration*

Like the Western Hemisphere Convention, the African Convention has no permanent Secretariat responsible for overseeing its implementation. The OAU acts as a recipient of information and is responsible for calling meetings of the Parties on request[50] but has no permanent oversight role. There is no requirement for regular meetings of the Parties, and no formal meeting has been held since the Convention came into force. Nor are Party governments required to submit regular reports on their implementation of the Convention. They have to supply the OAU with reports "on the results achieved",[51] but the Convention makes no provision as to

[48] See Chapter 8 below at p. 139.
[49] *Ibid.*
[50] Article XVI(3) of the African Convention provides that the OAU shall organise meetings of the Parties, but only on request from at least 3 Parties and with the approval of two thirds of all Parties.
[51] African Convention, Article XVI(2)(b).

how often this should be done and there is no record of any having been formally submitted.

The importance of a good system of administration to the enforcement of wildlife treaties is emphasised many times in this book. The positive impact that effective administrative structures have had on the Convention on International Trade in Endangered Species of Wild Fauna and Flora and the Convention for the Protection of the World Cultural and Natural Heritage, to name just two, are discussed in detail in other chapters.[52] The reversion of the Western Hemisphere Convention to a "sleeping treaty" is very largely due to the lack of a system of administration to oversee its implementation,[53] and there is clearly a danger of the same happening to the African Convention. As the section below on "Implementation" demonstrates, the African Convention may have stimulated useful conservation measures in some African States. But it has undoubtedly been forgotten in many others, where the conservation policies and actions of governments are derived more from internal considerations than from a desire to implement the provisions of the Convention. Unless and until a system of administration is created to constantly remind Parties of the existence of the Convention and of the need to comply with its terms, the Convention is likely to become more and more of a "sleeping treaty" with relatively little practical influence on government policies and activities in Africa.

10. *Implementation*

There was no lack of African interest or action in wildlife conservation before the African Convention came into force. Most Parties had already enacted conservation legislation, set aside protected areas and regulated the taking and trading of certain species prior to 1969. The key question is whether or not they have updated their conservation measures in tune with the provisions of the Convention.

a) *Legislation*

Considerable progress has been made since the Convention came into force. For example, Ghanaian wildlife legislation (the Wild Animal Preservation Act, 1961)[54] was already in accordance with the general spirit of the Convention by 1969, and there was no need to repeal it. However, Legislative Instruments adopted in Ghana

---

[52] See Chapters 11 and 12 below.
[53] See Chapter 6 above.
[54] Wild Animal Preservation Act, Act 43 of 1961.

pursuant to the Wild Animal Preservation Act since 1969 have reflected the terms of the Convention more closely. For instance, the Act provided only for the "establishment of reserves within which it shall be unlawful to hunt, capture or kill any bird or other wild animal except those which shall be specially exempt from protection." Ghana's Wildlife Reserves Regulations of 1971[55] gave effect to the African Convention by reclassifying "reserves" into national parks, strict nature and wildlife sanctuaries and game production reserves. The African Convention does not employ the term "game production reserve", but the intent — that of allowing different forms of land use in the reserves provided that they are compatible with conservation needs — is similar to the intent behind the concept of the Convention's "special reserves". The Regulations also prohibit any person from entering a reserve "except with the consent of the Chief Game and Wildlife Officer and subject to such conditions as he may determine". This corresponds closely with the requirement of Articles III(4)(a), (b) and (c) of the Convention that entry to and activities in conservation areas shall be prohibited except under the direction and control of the appropriate authorities.

There has been conservation legislation in Tanzania for decades, but the principal Tanzanian wildlife law, the Wildlife Conservation Act,[56] was enacted in 1974 and coincides with the African Convention's entry into force in Tanzania in the same year. The Act authorises the declaration of game reserves, game controlled areas and partial game reserves to give protection to certain specified animals or class of animals. The division of protected areas into these different categories is similar, although the names used are different, to the three types of conservation area described by the Convention. The Act also restricts the hunting and capture of animals listed in a schedule to the Act, although the species in the schedule differ considerably from those listed in Annex A and B of the Convention, requires the registration of trophies and prohibits their export without a permit.

The principal wildlife law of Sierra Leone, the Wildlife Conservation Act of 1972,[57] probably reflects the provisions of the African Convention as closely as the laws of any African State although, ironically, Sierra Leone has not ratified its signature of the Convention in 1968 and is therefore not yet a Party to it. Indeed this Act is the only law which states specifically that it is intended to give

[55] Legislative Instrument 710.
[56] Act 12 of 1974.
[57] Act 27 of 1972.

effect to the Convention.[58] The Act authorises the declaration of various categories of protected area, prohibits the hunting or capture of animals listed in a schedule to the Act (with exceptions for defence of human life or property), requires the registration of trophies and prohibits the possession of any protected animal without a license.

b) *In practice*

It is very difficult to ascertain the extent to which the provisions of the African Convention are enforced in practice. Since Parties are not required to submit reports to the OAU on their implementation of the Convention, and have never formally met to review implementation, very little published material is available.

Some progress has undoubtedly been made. Many Parties have established new protected areas since 1969 and have tightened up on hunting and trading regulations. However, it is impossible to state categorically that the Convention, rather than other factors, has been directly responsible for the progress made. Few of the new laws and regulations refer back to the Convention as a source of legal authority or command, and there are no records of Party governments publicly stating that the Convention was responsible for conservation measures which they have adopted. However, correspondence with officials in Party countries has indicated that the Convention has been a useful stimulant behind the progress made over the last fifteen years. In a letter to the author dated 21 March 1983, the Chief Administrator of Ghana's Forestry Commission stated "it is also relevant to note the tremendous increase in conservation areas in Africa since 1968. I would attribute this to the Convention as one of the major factors."

On the other hand, serious problems still remain. The clearing of tropical forests in central and western Africa[59] seems inconsistent with the Convention's demand for "scientifically based conservation...plans of forests and rangeland, taking into account...the importance of the vegetation cover for the maintenance of the water balance of an area, the productivity of soils

[58] The full title of the Act is An Act to Make Further and Better Provisions for the Control of Fauna and Flora of Sierra Leone and to Give Effect to the International Convention relating to the Protection of Fauna and Flora in a Natural State (1933) as amended by the International Convention for the Protection of Fauna and Flora of Africa of 1968.

[59] Ivory Coast, for example, is reported to have lost between a third and a half of its virgin forests already and still to be losing over 5,000 square kilometers a year. It has been said that this rate of exploitation could cause Ivory Coast to lose almost all its primary forest by 1985. See *International Biosciences Network, African Biosciences Network, Proceedings of the Symposium on the State of Biology in Africa* (a joint International Council of Scientific Unions and United Nations Educational, Scientific and Cultural Organization publication, 1981), pp. 23-7, especially p. 25. See also N. Myers, *The Sinking Ark* (Pergamon Press, 1979), p. 137.

and the habitat requirements of the fauna."[60] Poaching and illegal trading of rhino horn, ivory and other wildlife products has reached alarming proportions in many areas. The massive project to build the Jonglei Canal, which involves draining part of the Sudd swamp in the southern Sudan, may damage a large aquatic habitat.[61]

A meeting of Party governments to review implementation of the Convention and to take appropriate steps to improve it is an essential first step. Meetings alone cannot solve enforcement problems — that is always a task for each individual Party — but they have proved to be an extremely important stimulant in the context of other wildlife treaties. As the Norwegian delegate told the first meeting of the Parties to the Convention on the Conservation of European Wildlife and Natural Habitats, "the future importance of this Convention will greatly depend on the way the Standing Committee [the technical term for a meeting of the Parties] is able to utilise this article [for the protection of European habitats] to encourage national efforts in achieving concrete results in the countries involved."[62] The same principle applies equally well to the African Convention.

11. *Conclusion*

The provisions of the African Convention cover most of the threats to African wildlife and most of the actions that need to be taken by African governments to counteract those threats. To this extent, the Convention is a legal instrument of considerable potential value to wildlife. Furthermore, it may have already been of some practical value in the sense that a number of Party governments have taken some of the steps required by the Convention — although it is not clear to what extent the Convention has been directly responsible for the measures taken.

On the other hand, there is no question that enforcement of the Convention is a very serious problem in many African States. The obstacles to implementation are many, ranging from rapidly increasing population to changing agricultural practices. Lack of money and technical expertise are also crucial factors. The need for a permanent Secretariat and regular meetings of the Parties has been mentioned, but the permanent Secretariat established under the Convention on International Trade in Endangered Species of Wild Fauna and Flora, for example, has an annual budget of over

---

[60] African Convention, Article VI(1)(a). See p. 118 above.

[61] See N. Myers, *The Sinking Ark* (Pergamon Press, 1979), p. 41.

[62] See Appendix X of the *Report of the First Meeting of the Standing Committee of the Convention on the Conservation of European Wildlife and Natural Habitats*, Council of Europe Doc. T-PVS(82) Misc.1 (1982), available from the Council of Europe, Strasbourg, France.

U.S.$500,000 which is financed predominantly by the industrialised nations. The OAU simply does not have the financial resources to help the African Convention in the same way. More importantly, most African governments have insufficient funds and technical expertise to prevent overgrazing and deforestation, to promote conservation and education and to enforce the many other obligations required of them by the Convention. In consequence, natural habitats in most of Africa are likely to continue to decline in both size and quality unless African governments drastically rearrange their priorities for the limited financial resources available to them or receive considerable foreign assistance.

CHAPTER 8

THE CONVENTION ON THE CONSERVATION OF EUROPEAN WILDLIFE AND NATURAL HABITATS
(THE "BERNE CONVENTION")

"And God said unto the serpent: 'because thou has done this, thou art cursed above all cattle, and I will put enmity between thee and the woman and between thy seed and her seed, subject only to the provisions of the Convention on the Conservation of European Wildlife and Natural Habitats of 1979.'"
(*The Times*, London, 5 June 1982)

1. *Background*

In March 1976 the Second European Ministerial Conference on the Environment advised the Committee of Ministers of the Council of Europe[1] to set up a committee of experts to draft the text of a treaty for the conservation of wildlife "which would obviate the difficulties encountered in the implementation of existing conventions."[2] A committee was duly convened, a draft of the Convention on the Conservation of European Wildlife and Natural Habitats was drawn up,[3] the text was finally agreed by the Committee of Ministers in June 1979 and the Convention was opened for signature on 19 September 1979 in Berne — hence the name "Berne Convention". It came into force on 1 June 1982.[4] At the time of writing, thirteen European States and the European Economic Community are Parties to the Convention. A further seven States have signed but not yet ratified.[5]

The aims of the Berne Convention are to "conserve wild flora and fauna and their natural habitats", to promote cooperation between countries in their conservation efforts and to give "particular

[1] The Council of Europe was established in 1949 and currently has a membership of 21 European countries. The Committee of Ministers of Foreign Affairs acts as its executive body.

[2] Resolution No. 2, Second European Ministerial Conference on the Environment, Conclusions (Brussels, 23-24 March, 1976) See pp. 62-66 above for details of the deficiencies of earlier European bird treaties.

[3] *Europ. T.S.* no. 104; *U.K.T.S.* no. 56 (1982), Cmd. 8738.

[4] As required by Article 19(2), the Berne Convention came into force three months following the date the fifth signatory State had deposited an instrument of ratification.

[5] Austria, Denmark, Greece, Ireland, Italy, Liechtenstein, Luxembourg, The Netherlands, Portugal, Sweden, Switzerland, Turkey and the U.K. are full Parties to the Convention. Belgium, Cyprus, Finland, France, Federal Republic of Germany, Norway and Spain have signed but not ratified.

emphasis to endangered and vulnerable species, including endangered and vulnerable migratory species."[6] In order to achieve its objectives, the Convention provides for the conservation of wildlife and wildlife habitats in general and for the special protection of species listed in Appendix I (strictly protected plants), Appendix II (strictly protected animals) and Appendix III (protected animals) of the Convention.

The Berne Convention is an extremely important conservation treaty. It imposes a clear and unequivocal legal obligation on Parties to protect all important breeding and resting sites of the hundreds of species of animals in Appendix II. It imposes an equally clear obligation on Parties to prohibit the picking, collecting, cutting or uprooting of the 119 species of plants in Appendix I, and it requires Parties to take such measures as are necessary to maintain populations of all species of animals and plants at levels corresponding to ecological, scientific and cultural requirements — even if this means over-riding economic interests. The Convention permits Parties to exempt themselves from these obligations in certain limited circumstances, but in no event are Parties allowed to exercise their right of exemption if the result will be detrimental to the survival of a species or population thereof.

There are two aspects of the Berne Convention which are particularly noteworthy. The first is that almost every one of its provisions is mandatory as opposed to being couched in the hortatory language used by so many wildlife treaties. Rather than simply encouraging Parties to do this and that, the Berne Convention almost always requires Parties to do this and that. The second important aspect of the Berne Convention is the system of administration it has created to promote and oversee its implementation. It cannot be over-emphasised how vital it is to the enforcement of a wildlife treaty that there are mechanisms — such as a Secretariat, regular meetings of Parties, attendance by non-governmental observers at these meetings, reporting requirements, etc. — to keep Parties on their toes and to make them feel that they will be publicly castigated if they do not comply with the terms of the treaty. It is in this respect, in particular, that the Berne Convention has made major advances from the Western Hemisphere and African Conventions. It established a Standing Committee which meets annually to review implementation of the Convention and to recommend ways of making it work more effectively. Each Party is represented on the Standing Committee, and approved non-governmental conservation organisations may attend meetings as

[6] Berne Convention, Article 1.

observers. The Council of Europe provides Secretariat services for the Convention.

This chapter looks initially at the general conservation provisions of the Berne Convention. It then discusses the species listed in the three Appendices and the special provisions made by the Convention for protecting them. It goes on to consider various supplementary clauses of the Convention which cover, among other things, migratory species and the introduction of exotic species, and then looks at the very important question of the area to which the Convention applies. Finally it examines the administrative structure set up to promote enforcement of the Convention.

2. General conservation provisions

Although the Berne Convention is primarily concerned with the protection of species in the three Appendices, Articles 2 and 3 of the Convention impose certain obligations on the Parties with respect to the protection of all wildlife, including species not in the Appendices.

a) Article 2: Population levels

Article 2 states:

> The Contracting Parties shall take requisite measures to maintain the population of wild flora and fauna at, or adapt it to, a level which corresponds in particular to ecological, scientific and cultural requirements, while taking account of economic and recreational requirements and the needs of sub-species, varieties or forms at risk locally.

Article 2, which was taken from and is almost identical to Article 2 of the 1979 EEC Directive on the conservation of wild birds,[7] is significant for two reasons. Firstly, it sets a standard corresponding to ecological requirements at which population levels of wildlife must be maintained, or to which depleted or excessive populations must be raised or lowered. Secondly, although it intends Parties to cater for economic and recreational needs in fulfilling their obligations under the Article whenever possible, a careful reading of Article 2 makes it clear that the primary duty of the Parties is to maintain wildlife populations at levels corresponding to ecological, scientific and cultural requirements and that economic and recreational considerations are secondary. In the event of an

---

[7] Council Directive 79/409/EEC; *O.J. Eur. Comm.* No. L 103 (25 April 1979), p. 1. See Chapter 4 above at p. 68.

irreconcilable conflict between economic and ecological requirements, therefore, Parties have a legal obligation to give priority to
the latter.

Both the Explanatory Report concerning the Convention on the
Conservation of European Wildlife and Natural Habitats
(hereinafter called the "Explanatory Report"[8]) and a plain reading of
the English in Article 2 support this view. Paragraph 21 of the
Explanatory Report states that Article 2 contains "a main obligation
that follows from the aims stated in Article 1, paragraph 1." Article 1,
paragraph 1 states that "the aims of this Convention are to conserve
wild flora and fauna and their natural habitats, especially those
species and habitats whose conservation requires the cooperation of
several States, and to promote such cooperation." Thus Article 2
follows from a clearly expressed objective to conserve wildlife and
should be interpreted with that aim in mind. Under a plain reading
of the English, the Parties' duty to take the necessary measures to
maintain wildlife populations at, or adapt them to, levels
corresponding to ecological, scientific and cultural requirements
could not be more clearly stated than in the first clause of Article 2.
The words "while taking account of", which start the second clause,
are qualifying words which require the Parties to consider the needs
expressed in the second clause but do not put these needs on a par
with the duty expressed in the first clause. If it had been intended to
give equal weight to the needs expressed in the second clause, the
Article would require that population levels correspond to
"ecological, scientific, cultural, economic, recreational etc."
requirements, and the fact that the Article does not do this
emphasises the primary importance of the first clause.

The Convention does not define a population level which
corresponds to "ecological, scientific and cultural requirements",
but it can be safely assumed to be well above a level where a species
is in danger of extinction.[9] At a minimum, therefore, Parties have a
legal duty to ensure that species do not become extinct through
agencies within their control, to help endangered species recover to a
point where their numbers are once again large enough to perform

---

[8] *The Explanatory Report Concerning the Convention on the Conservation of European Wildlife and
Natural Habitats* (Council of Europe, 1979) is based on the discussion of the committee of
experts responsible for drafting the Berne Convention and was submitted to the Committee of
Ministers of the Council of Europe who authorised its publication. It is not an official
legislative history nor conclusive on matters of interpretation of the Berne Convention but it is
a useful guide to its terms. It is hereinafter referred to as the *Explanatory Report.*

[9] See Berne Convention, Article 7(2) which requires that exploitation of Appendix III
species be regulated "to keep populations out of danger". See also Article IV(3) of the
Convention on International Trade in Endangered Species of Wild Fauna and Flora,
discussed in Chapter 12 below at p. 250.

their ecological function, and to ensure that presently healthy populations are not reduced below that point. Given the hundreds of activities in the modern world which are capable of seriously reducing wildlife populations, the obligations imposed on the Parties by Article 2 are extremely important and will not be easy to implement.

b) *Article 3: National policies, development and education*

Article 3(1) obliges Parties "to promote national policies for the conservation of wild flora, wild fauna and natural habitats". It states that these policies should give particular attention to "endangered and vulnerable species, especially endemic ones, and endangered habitats". Article 3(1) is particularly significant for Parties with a federal system of government such as the Federal Republic of Germany and Austria, and for Parties with a system of regional autonomy such as Belgium, Spain and Italy, because it requires *national* governments to take whatever action they deem to be appropriate. By requiring the formation of *national* (as opposed to regional) policies, Article 3(1) effectively prohibits Party governments from delegating their responsibility to a local level.

Article 3(2) requires Parties to have regard to wildlife conservation in their planning and development policies and in their measures against pollution.

Article 3(3) requires Parties to promote education and disseminate general information on the need to conserve species and their habitats.

The Berne Convention gives no further details as to how these provisions should be implemented. This has the advantage of giving Parties maximum flexibility and the disadvantage of allowing reluctant Parties to do very little. For example, a Party which promotes an educational campaign in schools and in the media on the importance of conserving wildlife will clearly be implementing Article 3(3) more fully than a Party which places a single notice outside a nature reserve indicating the need to maintain the area's natural values. Yet both could justifiably claim to be complying with the Convention's requirements. In practice, Article 3 is likely to be a valuable tool for non-governmental conservation organisations and the Standing Committee to use to persuade governments to promote conservation education, national conservation policies etc. However, it also allows Parties where pressure groups are not so active to limit their contribution to a few token gestures if they so desire.

3. *Species included in the Appendices of the Convention*

This section looks at the species listed in the three Appendices and at the criteria for including species in the Appendices.

a) *Appendix I*

Appendix I is reserved exclusively for plants and contains 119 species. The concern of the Berne Convention with flora as well as fauna is a major step forward because plants have historically suffered as the poor relation of animals in terms of conservation priorities. Indeed the Berne Convention is the first international agreement to provide any kind of protection for European plants other than by the regulation of international trade.[10] Appendix I is currently heavily biased towards Southern European species, primarily because most threatened endemic European plants occur in Southern Europe, although some additions may be necessary to include threatened plants in other areas. Appendix I, as it stands, is based on a list of species drawn up by the Threatened Plants Committee of the International Union for Conservation of Nature and Natural Resources — demonstrating the important role played by non-governmental organisations in the drafting of the Convention.[11]

b) *Appendix II*

Appendix II is reserved for animals and contains several hundred species of mammals, birds, reptiles and amphibians. Again, there are gaps in Appendix II, particularly in relation to invertebrates and threatened freshwater fish. The Standing Committee did not amended the Appendices at any of its first three meetings, but it recognised that gaps existed and agreed to consider additions at future meetings.[12] In establishing Appendix II, account was taken of the lists of threatened fauna drawn up by the European Committee for the Conservation of Nature and Natural Resources (known as "CDSN"), and the Standing Committee has recommended that in considering further additions to Appendix II special attention should be given to the CDSN study on freshwater fish in Europe.[13]

[10] International trade in many plants is regulated by the Convention on International Trade in Endangered Species of Wild Fauna and Flora, discussed in Chapter 12 below.

[11] See *Explanatory Report*, note 8 above, para. 74.

[12] See *Report of the First Meeting of the Standing Committee of the Convention on the Conservation of European Wildlife and Natural Habitats* (4 October 1982), Council of Europe Doc. T-PVS (82) 3, para. 10.7 (available from the Council of Europe, Strasbourg, France and hereinafter referred to as *Report of the First Meeting of the Standing Committee*). See also *Report of the Second Meeting of the Standing Committee of the Convention on the Conservation of European Wildlife and Natural Habitats* (29 November 1983), Council of Europe Doc. T-PVS (83) 23, para. 8.

[13] *Ibid.*

In contrast to Appendix I, which includes plants that are mostly endemic to Europe, Appendix II contains numerous species which are migratory and spend only a portion of their life cycle in Europe — including the humpback whale (*Megaptera novaengliae*), Kemp's ridley turtle (*Lepidochelys kempii*) and dozens of species of birds. Appendix II also includes the leopard (*Panthera pardus*), a non-migratory species whose range is primarily non-European, and the tiger (*Panthera tigris*) which does not occur in Europe at all.[14]

c) *Appendix III*

Appendix III is something of a "catch-all" list for animals not in Appendix II. It includes all reptiles and amphibians not in Appendix II, all birds not in Appendix II except for eleven very common species and a number of relatively common European mammals.

d) *Listing criteria*

The Explanatory Report indicates that the Appendices are not intended to be comprehensive as they presently stand and that the Parties decided initially to list only those species which were "generally acceptable" on the basis that additions could be made more easily after the Berne Convention had come into force.[15] The Berne Convention does not establish criteria for the inclusion of species in, or their deletion from, the Appendices, and such criteria have not yet been established by the Standing Committee. Particularly conspicuous by its absence is the lack of any requirement that species should be threatened with extinction or even potentially threatened with extinction in order to merit inclusion in the Appendices. Furthermore, the kinds of species currently in the Appendices suggest that it was positively not the intention of the Parties to limit their selections to threatened or potentially threatened species — the hedge sparrow (*Prunella modularis*), for example, is listed in Appendix II although it is widespread and common throughout much of Europe.

In contrast to some wildlife treaties, the Berne Convention does not specifically provide for sub-species or geographically separate populations of species to be separately listed in the Appendices.

[14] The tiger was probably listed in the belief that a few Caspian tigers (*Panthera tigris virgata*) survive in Turkey, although information stored in IUCN's Mammal Red Data Base (located at 219c Huntingdon Rd., Cambridge, England) suggests that this sub-species is extinct in Turkey (if in fact it ever occurred there) and may now be extinct everywhere in the wild. See also G. Mountfort, *Saving the Tiger* (Calmann and Cooper, 1981), p. 16.

[15] *Explanatory Report*, note 8 above, paras. 68-70.

However, it does not prohibit such listings, and paragraph 78 of the Explanatory Report points out that one sub-species, *Rupicapra rupicapra ornata*, has already been included in Appendix II. This is an encouraging sign because listing sub-species or separate populations can be extremely useful, particularly in the case of plants where certain populations of a species are threatened with extinction — such as the U.K. population of lady slipper orchid (*Cypripedum calceolus*) — although the species is relatively secure in Europe as a whole.

4.   *Conservation of habitat*

The Berne Convention places its heaviest emphasis on the protection of habitats, especially habitats of species in the Appendices and endangered habitats. Some of its habitat conservation provisions are rather general, while others, particularly Article 6(b) which prohibits deliberate damage to breeding or resting sites of Appendix II species, are very specific. This section looks first at the general habitat provisions of the Berne Convention and then at Article 6(b).

a)   *In general*

Article 4(1) requires each Party to "take appropriate and necessary legislative and administrative measures to ensure the conservation of the habitats of the wild flora and fauna species, especially those specified in the Appendices I and II and the conservation of endangered natural habitats."

Recognising that Article 4(1) is rather general in its terms and aware that a "systematic establishment of nature reserves" in each Party would help fulfil the aims of Article 4(1), Norway urged the first meeting of the Standing Committee to consider the development of guidelines on how each Party should apply Article 4(1). The Standing Committee requested Norway to transmit details of its proposals to other Parties and to the European Committee on the Conservation of Nature and Natural Resources for comment and to produce a document for examination at the second meeting of the Standing Committee held in November 1983.[16] The latter announced its "full support" for the Norwegian proposals as a guideline for action but deferred the adoption of any specific recommendations on the implementation of Article 4(1) until the third meeting.

---

[16] *Report of the First Meeting of the Standing Committee*, note 12 above, para. 8.1.5.2.

b)   *Planning and development policies*

Article 4(2) states that the Parties "in their planning and development policies shall have regard to the conservation requirements of the areas protected under the preceding paragraph [Article 4(1)] so as to avoid or minimise as far as possible any deterioration of such areas." Neither the Explanatory Report nor the Standing Committee have clarified the meaning of Article 4(2), but the maintenance of buffer zones around protected areas seems to be what is intended — i.e. Parties should not locate an airport or industrial complex in an area where it will damage the value of a nearby national park.

c)   *Migratory species in Appendices II and III*

Article 4(3) stipulates that the Parties "undertake to give special attention to the protection of areas that are of importance for the migratory species specified in Appendices II and III and which are appropriately situated in relation to migration routes as wintering, staging, feeding, breeding or moulting areas."

Article 4(3) is particularly interesting because many of the migratory species in Appendices II and III winter in Africa and Asia. Areas important to these species therefore include many areas outside the jurisdiction of Parties to the Convention. Since there is nothing in Article 4(3) to suggest that the scope of the Parties' obligations to protect areas important to migratory species in Appendices II and III is restricted to areas within their own national borders — indeed such a restriction would make very little sense because migratory species clearly need to be protected at all stages of their migratory route — Parties are apparently required by Article 4(3) to do what they can to protect areas important to these species whether they are located inside or outside their territories.

There is clearly much that Parties can do for migratory species in their own territories by, amongst other things, controlling the use of pesticides and increasing protection for wetlands and other important habitats. There is also much that Parties can do outside their territories. In particular, they can give much needed assistance to the protection of important wintering habitats by providing financial and technical assistance to the countries concerned. Recognising the need for close cooperation with non-European States, particularly African States, it was suggested at the first meeting of the Standing Committee that Parties "should consider closer cooperation with less developed countries in the field of nature conservation in relation to their development aid programmes and the urgent need for assistance in improving natural resources management in the developing countries."[17]

d) *Coordination in frontier areas*

Article 4(4) requires the Parties to coordinate their efforts to protect habitats situated in frontier areas. The first meeting of the Standing Committee had three examples of such coordination brought to its attention. The first involved the Netherlands, Denmark and the Federal Republic of Germany and concerned joint efforts to conserve the natural values of the Wadden Sea. The second involved Italy and Yugoslavia and concerned joint efforts to protect brown bears (*Ursus arctos*) in frontier areas, and the third involved the Agreement on the Conservation of Polar Bears which was signed by the five circumpolar States in 1973.[18]

e) *Article 6(b)*

(i) *Requirements*

Article 6(b) is probably the most important habitat protection clause in the Berne Convention. Unlike the general provisions of Article 4, Article 6(b) is specific, clear and very strict. It prohibits "the deliberate damage to or destruction of breeding or resting sites [of Appendix II species]."

Article 6(b) has far reaching implications. Appendix II lists hundreds of species, their breeding and resting sites occur in countless different locations throughout Europe, and Article 6(b) imposes an unequivocal obligation on each Party to protect them from deliberate damage or destruction.[19] There are dozens of cases of agricultural or industrial development which must now be controlled in order to protect breeding or resting sites of Appendix II species. For example, the U.K. must now prohibit deliberate damage to breeding and resting sites of the corncrake (*Crex crex*), a requirement which could severely inhibit the proposed agricultural development of certain habitats in the Western Isles off the Scottish coast.[20] The consequences of Article 6(b) become even more overwhelming in the case of very widespread Appendix II species such as the hedge sparrow, which uses most hedgerows in Europe as

[17] *Ibid.*, para. 8.1.4.
[18] *Ibid.*, para. 5.f. See Chapter 3 above for a detailed discussion of the Agreement on the Conservation of Polar Bears,.
[19] See *Explanatory Report*, note 8 above, para. 29.
[20] For an analysis of the proposed development and its likely environmental impact, see *An Integrated Development Programme for the Western Isles of Scotland (Outer Hebrides), a Five Year Programme 1982-7* (30 March 1982, available from the Scottish Office, New St. Andrews House, Edinburgh).

either a breeding or resting site. Must every hedgerow now be protected?

The answer is no. There are two balancing factors designed to prevent Article 6(b) from having absurd consequences. Firstly, paragraph 29 of the Explanatory Report states that Article 6(b) should apply only to *important* breeding and resting sites. Secondly, Article 9(1) of the Convention allows each Party to make exceptions to Article 6(b) in a few limited circumstances. These include for the protection of crops, for the "judicious exploitation of certain wild animals and plants in small numbers" and to satisfy the "overriding public interest" — but only if "there is no other satisfactory solution". However, Article 9(1) prohibits Parties from making an exception if it will be "detrimental to the survival of the population concerned", and each Party must report to the Standing Committee any exceptions that it makes together with details of the circumstances.[21]

In conclusion, therefore, each Party must either protect important breeding and resting sites of every Appendix II species or publicly justify why it is entitled to make an exception under Article 9.

(ii)   *Implementation*

In order to implement Article 6(b), each Party will have to identify important breeding and resting sites of Appendix II species situated within its territory and then take appropriate measures to ensure that they are adequately protected. Since each Party has hundreds of such sites within its territory, and since many of them are outside existing protected areas, implementing Article 6(b) will not be an easy task.

To illustrate the problems and the progress made to date, it is interesting to consider what has happened in the U.K. The Nature Conservancy Council, the official government body responsible for nature conservation in the U.K., has initiated an inventory of important U.K. breeding and resting sites of Appendix II species, although the process is likely to take several years. The U.K. has also gone some way towards protecting some of these sites, but the protection is less than absolute in most cases. Protection is provided by the Wildlife and Countryside Act of 1981 which was intended, among other things, to implement the U.K.'s responsibilities under the Berne Convention. There are three main categories of protected areas for wildlife in the U.K. — national nature reserves, marine nature reserves and sites of special scientific interest. National and marine nature reserves are strictly protected by the Wildlife and

[21] Berne Convention, Article 9(2).

Countryside Act,[22] and the U.K. can justifiably claim to have satisfied its obligations under Article 6(b) with respect to breeding and resting sites of Appendix II species situated in these reserves. However, sites of special scientific interest (generally known as, and hereinafter called, "SSSIs"), which are far more numerous than national or marine nature reserves, receive only limited statutory protection. The Wildlife and Countryside Act requires the Nature Conservancy Council to notify every owner and occupier of every SSSI of operations likely to damage the features which justified the site's designation as an SSSI,[23] and it prohibits owners and occupiers from carrying out such operations without notifying the Nature Conservancy Council in writing at least three months beforehand[24] in order to give the Council time to persuade the owner or occupier to modify his plans or to enter into a management agreement with him. If voluntary negotiations break down, the Secretary of State has the power to issue a conservation order prohibiting damaging activities on the land in question for a period of up to twelve months to allow further time to reach an agreement.[25] As a last resort, the Nature Conservancy Council has the power to purchase the land (or an interest therein) compulsorily.[26]

The problem in relation to Article 6(b) of the Convention is that the Nature Conservancy Council is under-financed and may not always have the funds to pay compensation under a management agreement or to make a compulsory purchase. In addition, the Nature Conservancy Council has notified less than 25% of owners or occupiers of SSSIs of operations likely to damage those sites in the three years following the entry into force of the Act. Only owners or occupiers who have been so notified are prohibited by the Act from carrying out damaging operations. Therefore, important breeding and resting sites of Appendix II species which are situated in SSSIs do not always enjoy strict legal protection in the U.K., and already there is evidence that SSSIs are being damaged in spite of the Act. A report published in July 1984 documents examples of damage to 133 SSSIs since the Act became law, including several important areas for species listed in Appendix II of the Berne Convention. These include the Berwyn Mountains in Wales where merlin (*Falco*

---

[22] Wildlife and Countryside Act, 1981, sections 35-7.

[23] *Ibid.*, section 28(1).

[24] *Ibid.*, section 28(5)-(6).

[25] *Ibid.*, section 29(1)-(6). Since the Act came into force in October 1982 the Secretary of State has used this power to halt potentially damaging operations on four sites of special scientific interest — Baddesley Common in Hampshire, Tedham Moors in Somerset, Annesley Woodhouse Quarry in Nottinghamshire and Sandford Heath in Dorset.

[26] Wildlife and Countryside Act, 1981, section 29(7).

columbarius) breed, Trigon in Dorset, an important smooth snake (*Coronella austriaca*) breeding site, and the River Wye in Wales where otters (*Lutra lutra*) still survive.[27]

If an area is not in a category which is specially covered by the Wildlife and Countryside Act, such as an SSSI, but is an important breeding or resting site of an Appendix II species, there is nothing in the Act to prevent the owner or occupier from damaging the site, provided the damage is caused "incidentally" to an otherwise lawful operation such as ploughing for agricultural reasons or clearing for building purposes.

In conclusion, the U.K. is going in the right direction in the sense that an inventory of important breeding and resting sites of Appendix II species is being prepared, sites in national and marine nature reserves are strictly protected and sites which have been designated as SSSIs have some, if not an absolute, degree of protection. However, the U.K. will not be able to claim to have fully implemented its obligations under Article 6(b) of the Berne Convention until all important breeding and resting sites of Appendix II species in the U.K. have, at a minimum, been designated as SSSIs. And even that may not be enough unless the Wildlife and Countryside Act is strengthened to give SSSIs stricter legal protection or unless the spending power of the Nature Conservancy Council is greatly increased.

5. *Regulation of exploitation*

The Berne Convention strictly limits the killing, capture and other forms of exploitation of species listed in the three Appendices. It imposes a general duty on Parties to take "appropriate and necessary legislative and administrative measures" to ensure the "special protection" of species in Appendices I and II and the "protection" of species in Appendix III.[28] It also imposes a number of more specific obligations on Parties which are examined below.

Parties are allowed to make exceptions to these obligations in the same limited circumstances and subject to the same conditions which apply to exceptions to Article 6(b) and have already been mentioned.[29]

a)   *Appendix I*

Article 5 of the Berne Convention stipulates that "deliberate picking, collecting, cutting or uprooting of such [Appendix I] plants

---

[27] Sites of Special Scientific Interest: 1984, The Failure of the Wildlife and Countryside Act (Friends of the Earth, 1984), available from Friends of the Earth, 377 City Road, London EC1.

[28] Berne Convention, Articles 5, 6 and 7(1).

[29] *Ibid.*, Article 9(1). See p. 139 above.

shall be prohibited." Article 5 also states that "each Contracting Party shall as appropriate prohibit the possession or sale of these species [of Appendix I flora]." According to the Explanatory Report, "sale" is intended to include "exchange" and "barter" and the regulation of "sale" is to be limited to internal trade on the basis that international trade restrictions should be left to the Convention on International Trade in Endangered Species of Wild Fauna and Flora ("CITES").[30] This leaves a small loophole because four of the signatories to the Berne Convention are not yet Parties to CITES.[31]

An interesting question posed by Article 5 is whether its ban on "uprooting" means that activities such as bulldozing an Appendix I plant site for a road or ploughing it up for agricultural purposes are prohibited. The question is important because the biggest danger to Southern European plants, which comprise the bulk of species in Appendix I, comes not so much from collectors or the plant trade as from road building and hotel construction which have accompanied the growth of tourism in the Mediterranean region.[32] It may be that the habitat provisions of Articles 4(1) and (2) of the Berne Convention[33] are sufficient to oblige Parties to prohibit any activity that will damage the site of an Appendix I plant. But it is certainly arguable that Article 5, although it is aimed primarily at collectors, also outlaws bulldozing or ploughing such sites on the basis that roots will be upended or torn from the soil, and therefore plants will be "uprooted", as a result.[34]

b) *Appendix II*

Article 6 of the Berne Convention prohibits four activities in order to give Appendix II species special protection from exploitation. They are

...all forms of deliberate capture and keeping and deliberate killing; (Article 6(a))

...the deliberate disturbance of wild fauna particularly during the period of breeding, rearing and hibernation, insofar as disturbance would be

[30] See *Explanatory Report*, note 8 above, para. 25. For a detailed discussion of CITES, see Chapter 12 below.
[31] Greece, Ireland, Spain and Turkey are not Parties to CITES at the time of writing.
[32] Comment made to the author by G. Lucas, Secretary, Threatened Plants Committee of the International Union for Conservation of Nature and Natural Resources.
[33] See pp. 136-137 above.
[34] It might also be argued, because "killing" or "damaging" is not prohibited, that there is nothing to prevent a person from poisoning plants and then developing the area on the basis that there are no longer any plants to uproot. However, such a strict interpretation seems inconsistent with Article 5's general requirement that the Parties ensure the "special protection" of Appendix I plants.

significant in relation to the objectives of this Convention; (Article 6(c))

...the deliberate destruction or taking of eggs from the wild or keeping these eggs even if empty; (Article 6(d))

...the possession of and internal trade in these animals, alive or dead, including stuffed animals and any readily recognisable part or derivative thereof, where this would contribute to the effectiveness of the provisions of this Article (Article 6(e)).

Article 6 raises several problems of interpretation. Article 6(a) prohibits the "keeping" of Appendix II species in all circumstances yet Article 6(e) envisages some situations where "possession" and "internal trade", which both involve "keeping", would be allowed. The two sub-articles seem to be contradictory. It might be argued that Article 6(a) does not prohibit "keeping" but only "capture and keeping", and that if the initial act of capture and keeping was accidental or was done in a non-Party country, "possession" and "internal trade" should be allowed unless their prohibition "would contribute to the effectiveness of" Article 6. However, it seems more likely that the word "deliberate" was put before the word "capture" and the word "killing" but not the word "keeping" in Article 6(a) because capture and killing could both be accidental whereas keeping can only be deliberate.

Article 6(e) raises the question of whether internal trade should be regulated only in the State of origin. For example, if specimens of an Appendix II species are legally imported into the U.K. from Turkey under CITES, is the U.K. obliged by Article 6(e) to ban trade in the species within the U.K. if this would contribute to the effectiveness of Article 6? On one hand, one could argue that the U.K. should ban internal trade under Article 6(e) if this will make protection of the species more effective. On the other hand, however, one might claim that Article 6(e) applies only to internal trade in the State of origin on the basis that CITES covers international trade and that it would be inconsistent for an importing State to ban internal trade under Article 6(e) in specimens which have been legitimately imported under CITES. The Explanatory Report does not address this problem, and it has not yet been considered by the Standing Committee.

c) *Appendix III*

The Berne Convention does not prohibit the killing, capture or trade of species in Appendix III, but Article 7(2) stipulates that any exploitation must be regulated "in order to keep the populations out of danger, taking into account the requirements of Article 2." Article 7(3) requires Parties to take various measures to implement Article 7(2) including closed seasons, temporary or local prohibition of exploitation where necessary to restore satisfactory population levels and "the regulation as appropriate of sale, keeping for sale, transport for sale or offering for sale of live and dead wild animals." Paragraph 36 of the Explanatory Report states that Parties must also, in accordance with Article 2 of the Convention, have regard for sub-species and varieties which are at risk locally when implementing Article 7(2).

Article 8 bans the use of large-scale and non-selective killing methods either to kill animals in Appendix III or to kill animals in Appendix II in cases where the exception procedure under Article 9 has been invoked. Article 8 requires the Parties to "prohibit the use of all indiscriminate means of capture and killing and the use of all means capable of causing local disappearance of, or serious disturbance to, populations of a species [in Appendix II or III] and, in particular, the means specified in Appendix IV." Prohibited methods listed in Appendix IV include snares, gassing, poisoned baits and several other means of capture and killing.

Protection for species in Appendix III is much less strict than for species in Appendix II, but Parties must still be careful to ensure that they have an adequate regulatory mechanism at their disposal to control exploitation of Appendix III species if necessary. The U.K.'s Wildlife and Countryside Act, for example, does not presently regulate the killing or collecting of grass snakes (*Natrix helvetica*), adders (*Vipera berus*), slow worms (*Anguis fragilis*), common frogs (*Rana temporaria*), common toads (*Bufo bufo*), palmate newts (*Triturus helveticus*) or smooth newts (*Triturus vulgaris*), all of which are in Appendix III. However, the Act does contain a mechanism whereby their killing or collection can be subjected to controls in the future by order of the Secretary of State.[35]

6. *Supplementary provisions*

a) *Special attention for migratory species*

It has already been mentioned that the Berne Convention requires its Parties to give special attention to protecting areas important for migratory species.[36] In addition, Article 10(3) of the Convention requires Parties "to co-ordinate their efforts for the

[35] Wildlife and Countryside Act, 1981, section 22(3)-(4).
[36] See pp. 137-138 above.

protection of the migratory species specified in Appendices II and III whose range extends into their territories", and Article 10(2) obliges them to ensure that closed seasons and other measures regulating the exploitation of Appendix III species "are adequate and appropriately disposed to meet the requirements of the migratory species specified in Appendix III." The Explanatory Report does not explain this requirement any further, but it appears to be intended to ensure that shooting and trapping seasons are set at times which will not be unduly damaging to populations of migratory birds.

b) *Co-operation, research and introduction of species*

Article 11(1) requires Parties to "co-operate wherever appropriate and in particular where this would enhance the effectiveness of measures taken under the articles of this Convention" and to "encourage and co-ordinate research related to the purposes of this Convention." Article 11(2) obliges the Parties "to strictly control the introduction of non-native species" and "to encourage the re-introduction of native species of wild flora and fauna when this would contribute to the conservation of an endangered species." The Berne Convention is the first wildlife treaty to urge its Parties to consider re-introduction of native species as a method of promoting their conservation.

7. *The area to which the Convention applies*

There are three important questions concerning the geographic scope of the Convention which need to be addressed:

1) Are the obligations of the Parties to conserve Appendix II species limited to activities taking place within their own areas of national jurisdiction or do they extend to the activities of their citizens within the jurisdiction of other States or on the high seas?

2) Appendix II lists "all species" of a number of families, including *Ursidae* and *Falconiformes*. Does Appendix II therefore include the South American spectacled bear (*Tremarctos ornatus*) and the Mauritius kestrel (*Falco punctatus*), or does it refer only to bears and falcons that occur in Europe?

3) Several Articles of the Convention require the Parties to take measures to conserve "wild flora and fauna". Are the Parties therefore required to do what they can to help wildlife in an Indonesian tropical forest or an African savannah, or are their obligations limited to European species?

The answer to these questions is of more than academic importance. Article 6(a), for instance, requires each Party to prohibit "all forms of deliberate capture and keeping and deliberate killing" of Appendix II species, and Article 6(d) requires Parties to prohibit the taking of eggs of Appendix II species from the wild. If the Parties' obligations extend to acts committed by their citizens within the jurisdiction of foreign States, the implications will be far-reaching. To take just two of many possible examples concerning Appendix II species found outside Europe, Parties will be required to prohibit their nationals from shooting a leopard in Africa or from taking the eggs of green turtles (*Chelonia mydas*) from any of the hundreds of green turtle nesting beaches around the world — unless, of course, they make an exception under Article 9 and report it, together with reasons, to the Standing Committee. The application of Article 6(b) to the non-European breeding or resting sites of Appendix II species would be even more significant because numerous European companies and governments are involved in development projects affecting non-European wintering areas of Appendix II birds.

Few States currently have legislation prohibiting their citizens from taking actions damaging to wildlife outside the jurisdiction of the State concerned. It is also rare for a State to require prior environmental assessments of development projects financed by its foreign aid programmes. However such requirements are not unprecedented. New Zealand, for example, has enacted a law prohibiting New Zealand citizens from killing whales wherever they may be — even if within the coastal waters of another State where the killing is legal under local law.[37] The U.S.A. requires an environmental impact assessment prior to funding a development project through its foreign aid programme,[38] and the World Bank, to which most Party governments contribute funds, requires an environmental review of most of its projects prior to their implementation.[39] Some European governments have also taken

[37] See New Zealand's Marine Mammal Protection Act (1978), No. 80, section 1. Australia's Whale Protection Act of 1980 (sections 3(1), 6(2) and 9(1)) contains similar provisions. Canadian law prohibits Canadian citizens or residents, with limited exceptions, from engaging in pelagic sealing in any waters covered by the Interim Convention on Conservation of North Pacific Fur Seals (The Pacific Fur Seals Convention Act (1957), c.31 S.1. as amended, section 5).

[38] See *Aiding the Environment, A Study of the Environmental Policies, Procedures and Performances of the U.S. Agency for International Development* (Natural Resources Defense Council, Washington, D.C., February 1980); see also 22 C.F.R. Part 216.

[39] See *Declaration of Environment Policies and Procedures Relating to Economic Development*, a document which has been signed by nine development agencies including the World Bank.

steps towards limiting harmful environmental consequences of their bilateral aid contributions.[40]

a) *Question 1 — the scope of the Parties' obligations to conserve Appendix II species*

Whether the negotiators of the Berne Convention intended that acts prohibited by the Convention in relation to Appendix II species should include acts committed by a Party's citizens outside that Party's area of national jurisdiction is not clear from the meeting reports of the Interim Committee or from the Explanatory Report. Nevertheless, there is a convincing case to support the argument that the Convention does require each Party to apply Article 6 (the most important Article for the protection of Appendix II species) to acts committed by its citizens within the jurisdiction of other States or on the high seas.

The generally accepted rule of international law with respect to the interpretation of a treaty is that it should be interpreted according to the "ordinary meaning to be given to the terms of the treaty in their context and in the light of its object and purpose".[41] With minor exceptions which have already been discussed, the ordinary meaning of Article 6 is clear and makes no limitations whatsoever with respect to the geographical area in which its provisions should be applied. The object and purpose of the Convention is stated by Article 1(1) to be "to conserve wild flora and fauna and their natural habitats" and to give "particular emphasis ... to endangered and vulnerable species, including endangered and vulnerable migratory species," many of which are included in Appendix II. It goes without saying that migratory species must be protected both in their European and non-European habitats if conservation measures are to be successful. Consequently, the object and purpose of the Convention will only be fulfilled to a very limited degree if each Party restricts its application of Article 6 to acts committed within its borders. Furthermore, paragraph 17 of the Explanatory Report makes it clear that the negotiators were well aware of the need not to restrict the application of the Convention to Europe. It states that it was deliberately decided not to qualify the Convention's objective of the conservation of "wild flora and fauna and their natural habitats" with the words "in Europe" or "European" for two reasons:

[40] See B. Johnson and R. Blake, *The Environment and Bilateral Development Aid; The Environmental Policies, Programs and Performances of the Development Assistance Agencies of Canada, the Federal Republic of Germany, the Netherlands, Sweden, the United Kingdom and the United States* (International Institute for Environment and Development, London, 1980).

[41] Vienna Convention on the Law of Treaties, Article 31(1); see pp. 7-8 above.

i) not to restrict the geographical coverage of the convention to the European continent, with a view to the fact that many species of flora and fauna of Europe are found outside Europe;

ii) to include visiting migratory animals that are not confined to Europe.

There are, therefore, strong legal grounds for suggesting that the Parties' obligations to protect Appendix II species do not stop at their national borders. Although few Parties currently apply Article 6 to acts committed by their nationals within the jurisdiction of other States or on the high seas, at least two governments have shown signs of realising that they ought to do so. The observer from the Federal Republic of Germany stated at the first meeting of the Standing Committee that the provisions of the Convention apply to acts "performed on the high seas on vessels navigating under the flag of the Contracting Parties or in no-man's land". He said that the Federal Republic of Germany would not ratify the Convention until its domestic legislation covered this point.[42] In a letter dated 21 September 1983, the U.K.'s Nature Conservancy Council wrote to the Department of the Environment, the government department responsible for implementing the Convention in the U.K., stating:

We have studied this Article [6] and our interpretation is that it applies to the overseas activities of Governments which are Contracting Parties. This would therefore require any exceptions to Article 6 arising from development projects funded by the U.K. to be reported under Article 9.2.[43]

b)   *Questions 2 and 3 — "all species" of Appendix II families and "wild flora and fauna"*

Questions 2 and 3 can be considered together because they raise similar issues. It is certainly arguable that "all species" of *Falconiformes* and *Ursidae* is clear and unambiguous and must therefore include species such as the Mauritius kestrel and South American spectacled bear which have no connection with Europe. It is also arguable that "wild flora and fauna" clearly include wildlife in an Indonesian forest or an African savannah. However, the full title

[42] See *Report of the First Meeting of the Standing Committee*, note 12 above, para. 8.1.5.3. Section 3(1) of the Bill Relating to the Convention on the Conservation of European Wildlife and Natural Habitats, passed by the German Bundestag in 1983, states that: "It shall be prohibited, in areas which do not form part of the territory of any sovereign State, to take from the wild any of the species of flora listed in Appendix I or the species of fauna listed in Appendix II. This prohibition applies in particular with respect to activities carried out from a ship or aircraft entitled to fly the federal flag or carry the nationality mark of the Federal Republic of Germany."

[43] This letter was written by Dr. Peter Gay, Head Scientific Services Division, to Keith Dow, Wildlife Division of the Department of the Environment.

of the Convention — the Convention on the Conservation of *European Wildlife and Natural Habitats* (emphasis added) — together with the reference in paragraph 17(1) of the Explanatory Report to the fact that many species "of Europe" are found outside Europe suggests an intention to limit the application of the Convention to species which have some European connection.

8. *Administration*

It was suggested in Chapters 6 and 7 that the relative ineffectiveness of the African and Western Hemisphere Conventions was caused at least in part by deficiencies in the administrative structures of the treaties themselves, particularly their failure to require regular meetings of, and regular reports from, the Parties and their failure to establish a permanent Secretariat to oversee enforcement. Prospects for the Berne Convention appear much brighter if only because it has succeeded, for the most part, in the administrative areas where the other two Conventions failed.

a) *Standing Committee*

The Standing Committee, established by Article 13(1), is responsible for monitoring implementation of the Berne Convention and, in particular, may:

(i) keep under review the provisions of this Convention, including its Appendices, and examine any modifications necessary;

(ii) make recommendations to the Contracting Parties concerning measures to be taken for the purposes of this Convention;

(iii) recommend the appropriate measures to keep the public informed about the activities undertaken within the framework of this Convention;

(iv) make recommendations to the Committee of Ministers concerning non-member States of the Council of Europe to be invited to accede to this Convention;

(v) make any proposal for improving the effectiveness of this Convention, including proposals for the conclusion, with the States which are not Contracting Parties to the Convention, of agreements that would enhance the effective conservation of species or groups of species.[44]

In order to discharge its functions the Standing Committee is authorised to arrange for meetings of groups of experts.[45]

The broad powers given to the Standing Committee inevitably mean that much will depend on it as to how effectively the

---

[44] Berne Convention, Article 14(1).
[45] *Ibid.*, Article 14(2).

Convention is implemented. A hint of its potential strength was provided by the Interim Committee which was established in 1979 and met four times between then and 1982 to prepare the way for the day the Convention came into force and to encourage voluntary implementation of its terms in the meantime.[46] Although merely a provisional body, the Interim Committee helped persuade the Austrian government to take action to protect *Artemisia laciniata* (an endangered plant). After the Interim Committee had expressed concern that the plant's last remaining natural Western European habitat near Lake Neusiedl in Austria was under threat, the Austrian delegation reported that "the competent authorities [in Austria] have undertaken to ensure its strict protection in an integrated nature reserve."[47] The first meeting of the Standing Committee continued the trend established by the Interim Committee in the sense that the Standing Committee proved itself willing to aim two specific recommendations at the Italian government in circumstances where a breach of the terms of the Convention seemed likely. The first recommended that the Italian government ensure the protection of Gran Sasso and its wildlife and the second reminded the Italian government of its obligations under the Convention in relation to a proposal to re-open hunting in the Valle Furlana.[48] If the Standing Committee continues to make similar recommendations in similar circumstances at future meetings, it could prove to be a very potent weapon in ensuring that the Convention is enforced by all Party governments.

The Standing Committee, on which each Party has the right to be represented, must meet at least every two years and whenever a majority of the Parties so request.[49] Only Parties may vote, but the Convention allows a number of countries and organisations to be represented at meetings by observers. These include any member State of the Council of Europe which is not a Party to the Convention and States which have signed but not yet ratified the Convention. Non-member States of the Council of Europe which are not Parties to the Convention may be invited to be represented

---

[46] Resolution No. 3 on the Implementation of the Recommendations of the Previous Conferences and Future Action to be taken in the Environmental Field, 3rd European Ministerial Conference on the Environment, 19-21 September 1979. See Conference report drawn up by the Secretariat of the Council of Europe, Strasbourg, 1980.

[47] *Report of the Fourth Meeting of the Interim Committee of the Convention on the Conservation of European Wildlife and Natural Habitats*, Council of Europe Doc. T-VS(81)9 (21 January 1982), paras. 35-38 (hereinafter referred to as *Report of the Fourth Meeting of the Interim Committee*).

[48] See *Report of the First Meeting of the Standing Committee*, note 12 above, Appendix VII and VIII.

[49] Berne Convention, Article 13(4).

by an observer by unanimous decision of the Standing Committee.[50] National and international governmental and non-governmental agencies or bodies who are "technically qualified in the protection, conservation, or management of wild fauna and flora and their habitats" have the right to be admitted to meetings upon their own request unless at least one third of the Parties have registered an objection at least a month before the meeting. Applications to attend meetings must be filed at least three months beforehand.[51] The ability of non-governmental organisations interested in the conservation of wildlife to attend meetings of the Parties has been particularly important from a conservation viewpoint in the context of other treaties because of their scientific expertise, their ability to motivate public interest, their willingness to lobby governments to adopt conservationist positions and their capacity to publicise incidents where governments adopt positions antipathetic to conservation or fail to enforce the terms of a treaty. Non-governmental conservation organisations participated in the drafting of the Berne Convention, attended the first three meetings of the Standing Committee and there is every reason to believe that their influence will be just as real in the context of this Convention as it has been in other fora.

b)   *Reporting requirements*

The Convention's reporting requirements are not as strict as they might be to the extent that the Parties do not have to submit reports to each meeting of the Standing Committee on measures they have taken to enforce the Convention, although the Standing Committee has the authority to recommend that this be done. However, the Parties must report to the Standing Committee every two years on any exceptions they have made to the provisions of the Convention, and after each meeting the Standing Committee must itself transmit a report "on its work and the functioning of the Convention" to the Committee of Ministers of the Council of Europe.[52] The report of the final meeting of the Interim Committee contained a survey of measures taken by signatory states to prepare implementation of the Convention, based on information received from those States,[53] and the Standing Committee may invite Parties to continue to submit reports on their national implementing measures in order to make its own report more comprehensive.

[50]   *Ibid.*, Article 13(3).
[51]   *Ibid.*
[52]   Berne Convention, Article 15.
[53]   *Report of the Fourth Meeting of the Interim Committee*, note 47 above, pp. 30-36.

c)   *Secretary General of the Council of Europe*

The Berne Convention does not specifically establish a Secretariat, but the Depositary for the Convention (the Secretary General of the Council of Europe) has been authorised by the Committee of Ministers to perform all the normal functions of a Secretariat. Expenses incurred by the Secretary General in performing these functions will be met out of the general funds of the Council of Europe.

The Secretariat has already demonstrated its effectiveness by convening four meetings of the Interim Committee before the Convention came into force and by following up on the recommendations of those meetings. For example, upon the recommendation of the Interim Committee, the Secretary General wrote to the French, Spanish and Italian authorities to draw their attention to the imminent danger of extinction of the brown bear in the Pyrenees and the Alps.[54] The Secretary General also wrote to the appropriate national authorities urging that they take the necessary measures to prevent the disappearance of certain populations of black grouse (*Lyrurus tetrix*) caused by changes in its low-lying peatland habitat in Belgium, Denmark and the Netherlands and by increasing disturbance from tourism and forestry in the Alpine States.[55] Again, there is no reason to believe that the Secretariat will not continue its active role in following up on the recommendations of the Standing Committee.

9.   *The Committee of Ministers*

The Committee of Ministers of the Council of Europe, which played an important role in the conclusion of the Berne Convention, retains an unusual authority in two respects. Normally the Parties have sole power to make decisions on the implementation of wildlife treaties, but final decisions concerning certain amendments to the Convention and the choice of States to be invited to accede to the Convention are in the hands of the Committee of Ministers and not the Parties.

Most of the procedures for amending the Convention are not unusual. Any Party may propose an amendment to the Appendices provided it is communicated to the Secretary General in time for him to circulate it to other Parties at least two months before the meeting of the Standing Committee at which it will be considered.[56] If adopted by a two-thirds majority of the Parties, it will enter into

[54] *Report of the Fourth Meeting of the Interim Committee*, note 47 above, para. 23.
[55] *Ibid.*
[56] Berne Convention, Article 17(1).

force three months later for all Parties unless at least a third of the Parties notify objections.[57] Similarly, any Party may propose an amendment to any of the Convention's substantive provisions,[58] and provided the same procedural conditions are satisfied and a three quarter majority of votes cast approve it, the amendment will enter into force thirty days after all Parties have informed the Secretary General that they have accepted it.[59] However, the Committee of Ministers may also propose an amendment to the Appendices or to one of the substantive provisions of the Convention, although the proposal must go through the normal procedures in order to come into force.[60] In addition, any proposal to amend the operational provisions of the Convention must be approved by the Committee of Ministers before it can come into force.[61] According to the Explanatory Report, this is because of the "political and financial implications" for the Council of Europe of amendments to the operational provisions.[62]

The procedures by which a State becomes a Party to the Berne Convention are also normal to the extent that it is open for signature by member States of the Council of Europe and by non-member States which participated in its elaboration.[63] The Convention is subject to ratification, acceptance or approval, and signatory States must deposit instruments of ratification, acceptance or approval with the Secretary General in order to become full Parties.[64] However, non-member States of the Council of Europe may only accede to the Convention upon the invitation of the Committee of Ministers, rather than upon the invitation of the Parties.[65] Although there are valid reasons for the retention of these powers by the Committee of Ministers,[66] some East European and African States, whose

[57] *Ibid.*, Article 17(2)-(3).
[58] *I.e.* to Articles 1 — 12; Berne Convention, Article 16(2)(a).
[59] Berne Convention, Article 16(3).
[60] *Ibid.*, Articles 16(1) and 17(1).
[61] *I.e.* to Articles 13-24; Berne Convention, Article 16(2)(b).
[62] *Explanatory Report*, note 8 above, para. 57.
[63] Berne Convention, Article 19(1). Finland is the only non-member State who participated in the negotiation of the Convention — and has now signed it. Yugoslavia was invited to sign but has not yet done so.
[64] Berne Convention, Article 19(1).
[65] *Ibid.*, Article 20(1).
[66] The Statute of the Council of Europe states that the main objective of the organisation is to achieve greater unity between its members. To this end the Committee of Ministers, its executive body, may, among other things, conclude international conventions. Such conventions — more than 100 have been concluded so far — are normally signed only by member States, but in some cases non-member States are invited to accede after the convention has entered into force (so-called "open conventions"). Because of its responsibilities within the structure of the Council of Europe, the Committee of Ministers always plays a dominant role in the implementation of these conventions.

accession to the Convention is essential from the point of view of conservation because of the importance of their territories to migratory species, may be reluctant to accede to a treaty which is not totally controlled by the Parties themselves.

10. *Final Clauses*

There are a number of standard clauses in the Convention which have not been considered but merit brief mention. The Parties may adopt stricter measures for the conservation of wildlife and natural habitats than those provided under the Convention,[67] any disputes should be settled by negotiation or arbitration,[68] and Parties may make reservations at the time of their signature, ratification, acceptance, approval or accession regarding species listed on the Appendices or methods of exploitation listed in Appendix IV.[69] Parties may also make reservations on amendments to the Appendices that have been adopted by the Standing Committee [70] but may not make reservations of a general nature.[71] Finally, Parties may, at the time of their signature, ratification, acceptance, approval or accession, specify territories, for whose international relations they are responsible other than their own main territories, to which the Convention shall apply.[72] They can extend the application of the Convention to any other such territories at a later date.[73]

11. *Conclusion*

The Berne Convention is undeniably of great potential value. Hundreds of species are included within its scope, it emphasises the protection of habitat which is the vital factor in the conservation of most animals and plants, and it imposes strict conservation obligations on the governments of contracting Parties. Because the Convention has only recently come into force, the extent to which wildlife will in fact benefit from it is still uncertain. Much will depend on the Standing Committee. So far the signs have been reasonably promising. In the two and a half years that the Berne Convention has been in force the Standing Committee has met three times, suggesting there is little danger of the Berne Convention suffering from the "sleeping sickness" that has afflicted the Western Hemisphere and African Conventions. In addition, the Standing

[67] Berne Convention, Article 12.
[68] *Ibid.*, Article 18.
[69] *Ibid.*, Article 22(1).
[70] *Ibid.*, Article 17(3).
[71] *Ibid.*, Article 22(1).
[72] *Ibid.*, Article 21(1).
[73] *Ibid.*, Article 21(2).

Committee has already displayed a considerable enthusiasm for ensuring the Convention is properly enforced — its public reminder to the Italian government of its obligations under the Convention in circumstances where that government appeared likely to breach them was a most unusual step in the context of international wildlife law and is particularly noteworthy. Whether the Standing Committee maintains its early trends and continues to promote enforcement in all Party countries remains to be seen, but it is vital for the future success of the Berne Convention that it does.

CHAPTER 9

THE CONVENTION ON THE CONSERVATION OF ANTARCTIC MARINE LIVING RESOURCES ("CCAMLR")

"Great God! This is an awful place."
(Captain Robert Scott, South Pole, 17 January 1912)

1. *Introduction*

The origins of the Convention on the Conservation of Antarctic Marine Living Resources ("CCAMLR")[1] can be traced back to the Antarctic Treaty,[2] which was signed in 1959, came into force in June 1961 and established the legal framework for dealing with a wide variety of issues involving Antarctica. The Antarctic Treaty applies to the entire area south of 60° South latitude except for the high seas[3] and is a kind of self-denying ordinance under which the twelve "Consultative Parties" agreed to use Antarctica for peaceful purposes only, to prohibit the disposal of nuclear waste there, to freeze the legal status quo with respect to territorial claims and to promote free scientific research in the continent. The twelve Consultative Parties are Argentina, Australia, Belgium, Chile, France, Japan, New Zealand, Norway, South Africa, U.K., U.S.A., and U.S.S.R. They have since been joined by Brazil, Poland, the Federal Republic of Germany and India.

The Antarctic Treaty does not address the exploitation, ownership or management of living or non-living resources, although it does authorise the Consultative Parties to recommend measures with respect to the "preservation and conservation of living resources in Antarctica".[4] Pursuant to this authority, the Consultative Parties adopted several conservation measures in the early 1960s,[5] and when Japan and the U.S.S.R. began fishing for

---

[1] 19 *I.L.M.* 841; *T.I.A.S.* no. 10240; *U.K. T.S.* no. 48 (1982), Cmd. 8714.

[2] 402 *U.N.T.S.* 71; *T.I.A.S.* no. 4780; *U.K. T.S.* no. 97 (1961), Cmd. 1535; 12 *U.S.T.* 794.

[3] Antarctic Treaty, Article VI.

[4] *Ibid.*, Article IX(I)(f).

[5] The most notable of these are the Agreed Measures for the Conservation of Antarctic Fauna and Flora, which were adopted by the Third Consultative Meeting of the Consultative Parties to the Antarctic Treaty in 1964 (hereinafter referred to as the Agreed Measures). The Agreed Measures are reprinted in *Treaties and Other International Agreements on Fisheries, Oceanographic Resources, and Wildlife Involving the United States* (U.S. Govt. Printing Office, 1977), pp. 28-34. They are discussed in more detail later in this chapter at pp. 174-176.

krill (*Euphausia superba*) in the late 1960s and early 1970s the Consultative Parties decided to take it upon themselves to develop a legal regime to control the emerging fishery.

Negotiations for such a regime began in the early 1970s and ended with the conclusion of CCAMLR in Canberra in May 1980.[6] CCAMLR was signed by the twelve original Consultative Parties to the Antarctic Treaty and by the German Democratic Republic, the Federal Republic of Germany and Poland. It came into force on 7 April 1982 being thirty days after the date of deposit of the eighth instrument of ratification.[7] At the time of writing there are eighteen Parties to the Convention.[8] They consist of the fifteen signatories plus Spain, Sweden and the European Economic Community which have all acceded since May 1980.

The objective of CCAMLR is "the conservation of Antarctic marine living resources",[9] and Article II(2) states that "for the purposes of this Convention, the term 'conservation' includes rational use". The Convention established a Commission which meets annually and is responsible for adopting the necessary measures to implement this objective. It also established a Scientific Committee as a consultative body responsible for providing the Commission with scientific advice.

CCAMLR is particularly noteworthy in two respects. Firstly, a major Antarctic fishery had not emerged by the time the Convention was signed in 1980, making it one of the few international treaties concerned with wildlife conservation to be concluded prior to heavy commercial pressure on the species it was designed to protect.[10] This is important because experience with whaling and fishing industries throughout the world has proved how difficult it is to conserve a living resource (i.e. ensure that exploitation is sustainable) once the industry has become over-capitalised and over-exploitation has become the norm. The Convention provided a unique chance to manage Antarctic marine living resources wisely from the very beginning. Secondly, CCAMLR obliges its Parties to adopt an

[6] The issue of exploitation of Antarctic marine living resources was raised informally by the Antarctic Treaty Consultative Parties at their Seventh Consultative Meeting in 1972. However, it was not until the Ninth Consultative Meeting called for a "definitive regime" for the conservation of the marine living resources of the Antarctic ecosystem as a whole (Recommendation IX (2)) that negotiations began in earnest.

[7] As required by Article XXVIII of CCAMLR.

[8] They are: Argentina, Australia, Belgium, Chile, European Economic Community, France, Federal Republic of Germany, German Democratic Republic, Japan, New Zealand, Norway, Poland, South Africa, Spain, Sweden, U.K., U.S.A., and U.S.S.R. Brazil has told the Secretariat to CCAMLR that it intends to accede to the Convention in the near future.

[9] CCAMLR, Article II(1).

[10] Another such treaty is the Convention for the Conservation of Antarctic Seals. See Chapter 3, pp. 48-51 above.

"ecosystem approach" to the exploitation of Antarctic marine living resources. This means, for example, that when the Commission sets catch limits on krill fishing, it must not only consider the impact on krill populations but also the impact on populations of other animals, such as whales and penguins, which depend upon krill for food. The traditional approach of fisheries treaties is to consider only the stock being fished when setting harvest levels. If strictly applied, an ecosystem approach is likely to mean much lower harvest levels than would result from the traditional approach since substantial krill harvesting may affect the recovery of the already depleted populations of large baleen whales in Antarctica.

At the time of writing CCAMLR has been in force for less than three years, and the Commission has met just three times. It is too early to judge whether its objective will be achieved, although the early signs are not particularly promising. The Commission has not yet agreed even interim catch limits, which means that any State, whether or not a Party to CCAMLR, is still free, in practice, to take as much fish as its trawlers can catch throughout almost the entire Convention area — notwithstanding the conservation objective of the Convention and notwithstanding the legal duty imposed on Parties to adopt an ecosystem approach to the harvesting of living resources within the area. This chapter examines the provisions of CCAMLR in detail and looks at some of the obstacles facing implementation of its objective.

2.   Background biological and territorial concerns

a)   Biological

The negotiators of CCAMLR were primarily concerned about krill, a protein-rich shrimp-like crustacean which is the central link in the Antarctic marine food chain. It feeds on tiny phytoplankton and is itself the principal food supply of numerous species of birds, seals, squid, fish and whales.[11] Experimental krill fishing began in the 1960s, and annual catches grew to some 200,000 tonnes in the mid 1970s amid estimates that, if technical and marketing problems could be solved,[12] krill might sustain an annual yield of up to 150 million tonnes (which would have tripled the world fish catch). Such estimates have since been lowered, and krill fishing has not

[11] See B. Mitchell and J. Tinker, *Antarctica and its Resources*, (Earthscan, London, 1980), p. 38. See also SCAR/SCOR Group of Specialists on Living Resources of the Southern Ocean, *Biological Investigations of Marine Antarctic Systems and Stocks* (BIOMASS, 1977); and McWhinnie, "The High Importance of the Lowly Krill", 89 *Nat. Hist.* 66 (1980).

[12] The most serious technical problems have arisen from processing and from difficulties in detecting krill. Persuading people to eat krill in large quantities will also mean inducing a change in dietary habits. See Mitchell and Tinker, note 11 above, pp. 42-7.

expanded as rapidly as was anticipated, although annual catches have reached nearly one million tonnes. Nevertheless, aware that human over-exploitation was responsible for the near extinction of southern fur seals (*Arctocephalus* spp.) in the nineteenth century and for the drastic depletion of Antarctic stocks of blue (*Balaenoptera musculus*), fin (*Balaenoptera physalus*), right (*Baleana glacialis*) and humpback whales (*Megaptera novaeangliae*) in this century, the Consultative Parties to the Antarctic Treaty were anxious to prevent over-harvesting of krill. Their main concern was not so much for krill itself as for the effects that overharvesting krill might have on other species, particularly whales, which depend upon krill for food.[13] Reflecting this concern for the Antarctic marine ecosystem as a whole, the preamble to CCAMLR acknowledges "the increased interest in the possibilities offered by the utilisation of these [marine living] resources as a source of protein" and "the importance of...protecting the integrity of the ecosystem of the seas surrounding Antarctica."

b)   *Territorial*

By the time the Antarctic Treaty was concluded in 1959, seven of the signatories to the Treaty (Argentina, Australia, Chile, France, New Zealand, Norway and the U.K.) had made formal territorial claims in Antarctica. The other five signatories had all been active in the area but had either refrained from making claims themselves or had rejected all existing claims. Article IV of the Antarctic Treaty stipulates that no new territorial claims shall be asserted while the Treaty is in force, that nothing done during this period shall constitute a basis for asserting, supporting or denying such claims and that previously asserted claims shall not be affected. This solution presented few problems until the discovery of the potential for exploitation of krill and, possibly, oil and gas in Antarctic waters. The issue was complicated further in the late 1970s by the general acceptance as customary international law, in line with the emerging Law of the Sea Convention, of the rights of coastal States to exercise jurisdiction over 200 mile exclusive economic zones. The possibility of being able to exploit resources within 200 miles of "their" coastlines was of enormous importance to claimant States in Antarctica, particularly in view of the fact that these resources may include valuable minerals and huge fish stocks. None of the claimant

---

[13] See D. Edwards and J. Heap, "Convention on the Conservation of Antarctic Marine Living Resources: A Commentary", *Polar Record*, Vol. 20, no. 127 (1980), p. 354. Edwards and Heap were both members of the U.K. delegation at meetings where the text of the Convention was negotiated.

States have yet displayed a serious inclination to depart from the system established by the Antarctic Treaty, but they were anxious to ensure that CCAMLR did not prejudice their territorial claims or their rights to exercise coastal State jurisdiction. Non-claimants were equally anxious to ensure that it did not give claimant States a preferred status regarding the exploitation of marine zones off the Antarctic mainland and did nothing else which could be interpreted as acknowledging the validity of territorial claims.

CCAMLR attempted to solve the claims question by adopting the so-called "bi-focal approach". This approach was made possible by the existence of a number of islands north of 60° South and south of the Antarctic Convergence over which all Parties agree that national sovereignty is exercisable.[14] These islands are outside the scope of the Antarctic Treaty because they are north of 60° South but are within the scope of CCAMLR since they are south of the Antarctic Convergence.[15] Article IV(2)(b) of CCAMLR, which implements the bi-focal approach, is deliberately ambiguous. It states that nothing in the Convention, nor acts or activities taking place while the Convention is in force, shall be interpreted "as prejudicing any right or claim or basis of claim to exercise coastal State jurisdiction under international law within the area to which this Convention applies." Claimant States can interpret Article IV(2)(b) as referring both to undisputed islands north of 60° South and to disputed or unrecognised territorial claims south of 60° South. Non-claimant States, on the other hand, can argue that Article IV(2)(b) applies only to waters and islands north of 60° South where the existence of national sovereignty, and therefore coastal State jurisdiction, is recognised. Furthermore, Articles IV(2)(a), IV(2)(c) and IV(2)(d) of CCAMLR contain very similar provisions to those in Article IV of the Antarctic Treaty with the result that nothing done pursuant to CCAMLR will prejudice claims to territory or coastal State jurisdiction south of 60° South. Equally, these Articles ensure that the legal basis of the position from which non-claimants may protest is safeguarded should a claimant State attempt to exercise coastal State jurisdiction pursuant to its territorial claims south of 60° South.

3. *Scope*

a) *Area covered by CCAMLR*

Article I(1) states that CCAMLR will apply

---

[14] Sovereignty over some of these islands is disputed by two States — for example, South Georgia is disputed by Argentina and the U.K. — but the fact that sovereignty is exercisable by one of the two is not disputed.

[15] See p. 161 below.

...to the Antarctic marine living resources of the area south of 60° South latitude and to the Antarctic marine living resources of the area between that latitude and the Antarctic Convergence which form part of the Antarctic marine ecosytem.

The Antarctic Convergence was chosen as the outer limit because it is a natural biological frontier where warmer waters flowing south meet the colder Antarctic waters, separating distinct marine communities on either side. The Convergence moves slightly from year to year but, for the purposes of the Convention, is deemed to be a line joining certain parallels of latitude and meridians of longitude.[16] The application of CCAMLR as far as the Antarctic Convergence represents a considerable extension northwards from the boundary of the Antarctic Treaty area at 60° South and is particularly important because many of the known concentrations of krill are situated between the Convergence and 60° South.[17]

In practice, however, CCAMLR may not apply to all waters south of the Antarctic Convergence. The owners of the numerous islands between the Convergence and 60° South over which the existence of national sovereignty is undisputed have the right to exclude measures adopted by the Commission if they so desire. The statement incorporated into the Final Act of the Convention in order to confirm French jurisdiction over fishing in waters adjacent to the French islands of Kerguelen and Crozet makes it clear that any State with sovereignty over islands south of the Antarctic Convergence retains the authority to exclude measures adopted by the Commission from application to waters adjacent to those islands.[18] If all States with sovereignty over islands south of the Antarctic Convergence decide to apply their own fishing regimes to waters within 200 miles of their coastlines, a large area of krill-rich ocean will be excluded from the control of the Commission.[19]

From a conservation viewpoint, such exercise of coastal State jurisdiction may prove to be beneficial — the statement incorporated into the Final Act implies that France envisages circumstances where it may wish to take national measures that are stricter than

[16] CCAMLR, Article I(4). The parallels of latitude and meridians of longitude chosen by CCAMLR in fact only approximate the Convergence, and the lines originally proposed were adjusted to some extent in the Argentine area in order to avoid disputes with Argentina.

[17] See Mitchell and Tinker, note 11 above, p. 67.

[18] Statement Regarding the Application of the Convention on the Conservation of Antarctic Marine Living Resources to the Waters Adjacent to Kerguelen and Crozet over which France has Jurisdiction and to the Waters Adjacent to Other Islands Within the Convention Area over which the Existence of State Sovereignty is Recognised by all Contracting Parties (hereinafter referred to as Statement Regarding Application of the Convention); attachment to the Final Act of CCAMLR, final paragraph.

[19] See Mitchell and Tinker, note 11 above, p. 67.

those adopted by the Commission.[20] Indeed, until the Commission establishes catch limits, the imposition of national limits in as many areas as possible would be infinitely preferable to the current situation where fishing is being allowed to proceed without any controls whatsoever throughout most of the region. On the other hand, once the Commission has agreed on catch limits, coastal State jurisdiction may be exercised at a future date to allow higher catch levels than those set by the Commission.[21]

b) *Species covered by CCAMLR*

CCAMLR applies to "Antarctic marine living resources". These are defined by Article I(2) as "populations of fin fish, molluscs, crustaceans and all other species of living organisms, including birds, found south of the Antarctic Convergence". In spite of this broad definition, CCAMLR will not govern the protection and exploitation of as many Antarctic species as Article I(2) implies. Article VI expressly provides that nothing in the Convention shall derogate from the rights and obligations of the Parties under the International Convention for the Regulation of Whaling, which regulates whaling throughout Antarctica, or under the Convention for the Conservation of Antarctic Seals (the "Antarctic Seals Convention"), which regulates sealing south of 60° South at sea but not on land.[22] The scope of CCAMLR is further limited by the fact that all its Parties are bound by the Agreed Measures for the Conservation of Antarctic Fauna and Flora (the "Agreed Measures"), which were promulgated pursuant to the Antarctic Treaty in 1964. The Agreed Measures, which are considered in more detail later in this chapter,[23] prohibit the killing, capturing or molesting of any native mammal or bird south of 60° South on land, including all ice shelves, except in strictly limited circumstances.

---

[20] Statement Regarding the Application of the Convention, note 18 above, para. 3(a).

[21] The Parties to CCAMLR were also concerned that conservation measures established by the Commission should be in harmony with conservation measures adopted in waters outside, but adjacent to, the area to which the Convention applies. Article XI requires the Commission to cooperate with "Parties which may exercise jurisdiction in marine areas adjacent to the area to which this Convention applies in respect of the conservation of any stock or stocks of associated species which occur both within those areas and the area to which this Convention applies, with a view to harmonising the conservation measures adopted in respect of such stocks".

[22] For further discussion of the International Convention for the Regulation of Whaling and the Antarctic Seals Convention, see Chapters 2 and 3 above.

[23] See pp. 174-176 below. The Agreed Measures are reprinted in *Treaties and Other International Agreements on Fisheries, Oceanographic Resources, and Wildlife Involving the United States* (U.S. Govt. Printing Office, 1977), pp. 28-34.

Any future Parties which are not also Parties to the Antarctic Treaty must agree to observe the Agreed Measures.[24]

In practice, therefore, the most significant impact of CCAMLR is likely to be in relation to the harvest of fish, molluscs and crustaceans, and the conservation of whales, seals and penguins will generally be covered by other legal instruments. However, even this may not always be true. For example, if sealing operations began between 60° South and the Antarctic Convergence, or in any area south of the Antarctic Convergence by nationals of non-Parties to the Antarctic Seals Convention, they would be outside the scope of the Antarctic Seals Convention but within the scope of CCAMLR. CCAMLR would also cover any pelagic killing of penguins since the Agreed Measures do not apply to the high seas. Furthermore, the Agreed Measures did not establish a Commission to oversee their implementation, and if land-based operations to kill penguins did start, the Commission established by CCAMLR would be responsible for taking appropriate action.

4.   *Conservation standard*

The objective of most international fisheries agreements is to achieve the maximum sustainable yield of the stock being fished. CCAMLR not only stipulates that harvesting shall be regulated so as to prevent populations of target species from decreasing below their level of maximum sustainable yield but also that equal consideration shall be given to the likely effects of proposed harvest levels on non-target species and on the marine ecosystem as a whole. Article II(3), which gives effect to the "ecosystem approach", is worth quoting in full. It states as follows:

> Any harvesting and associated activities in the area to which this Convention applies shall be conducted in accordance with the provisions of this Convention and with the following principles of conservation:
> (a) prevention of decrease in the size of any harvested population to levels below those which ensure its stable recruitment. For this purpose its size should not be allowed to fall below a level close to that which ensures the greatest net annual increment;
> (b) maintenance of the ecological relationships between harvested, dependent and related populations of Antarctic marine living resources and the restoration of depleted populations to the levels defined in sub-paragraph (a) above; and
> (c) prevention of changes or minimisation of the risk of changes in the marine ecosystem which are not potentially reversible over two or three

---

[24] CCAMLR, Article V(2).

decades, taking into account the state of available knowledge of the direct and indirect impact of harvesting, the effect of the introduction of alien species, the effects of associated activities on the marine ecosystem and of the effects of environmental changes, with the aim of making possible the sustained conservation of Antarctic marine living resources.

The level below which Article II(3)(a) requires that a harvested population shall not be allowed to fall is essentially its level of maximum sustainable yield. Articles II(3)(b) and II(3)(c) give effect to the "ecosystem approach", and Article II(3)(b) is particularly significant because of the depleted populations of large baleen whales south of the Antarctic Convergence. Clearly, krill may not be harvested at a level which would impede the recovery of these depleted populations.

At the final Conference held in Canberra immediately prior to the adoption of CCAMLR in May 1980, there was some concern that Article II(3) might not be read as a whole and that the Commission might interpret Article II(3)(a) as a mandate to proceed along the traditional paths of maximum sustainable yield notwithstanding Articles II(3)(b) and II(3)(c). To ensure that the interdependence of species was treated as a factor of equal importance to maximum sustainable yield, the U.K. delegation proposed an addition to Article II(3)(a) to the effect that where a species is subject to significant natural predation it may not be reduced by harvesting "to a level below which the stable recruitment of species dependent on it cannot be ensured". The U.K. delegation withdrew its amendment on the understanding, agreed by the Conference and recorded in the Conference documents, that Article II should be read as a whole and that their proposed amendment was therefore unnecessary.[25]

5. *The Commission*

CCAMLR established a Commission with wide-ranging powers to give effect to the objective and principles of the Convention. The Commission must meet at least once a year[26] and has a Secretariat,[27] a Scientific Committee and permanent headquarters in Hobart[28] in order to assist it in its tasks. The Commission is authorised to establish any subsidiary bodies that are necessary for the performance of its functions.[29] None have yet been set up, but they

---

[25] See Edwards and Heap, note 13 above, pp. 355-6.

[26] CCAMLR, Article XIII(2). Extraordinary Meetings of the Commission will be held at the written request of one third of its members.

[27] CCAMLR, Article XVII.

[28] *Ibid.*, Article XIII(1).

[29] *Ibid.*, Article XIII(6).

might include bodies such as a Technical Expert Committee or an Infractions Committee both of which have been formed by Commissions of other wildlife treaties.[30] The Commission is responsible for adopting a budget for itself and for the Scientific Committee at each annual meeting.[31] The financial arrangements are rather unusual in that each member of the Commission must contribute equally to the budget until 1987, but contributions thereafter will be determined according to the amounts harvested by each member and according to "an equal sharing among all members of the Commission". The Commission is responsible for deciding by consensus the proportion in which these two criteria will apply.[32]

a) *Functions*

Article IX(1) of CCAMLR states that "the function of the Commission shall be to give effect to the objective and principles set out in Article II of this Convention". It is worth emphasising that Article II imposes a legal obligation on Parties to conserve Antarctic marine living resources and to adopt an ecosystem approach to any exploitation.[33] Therefore, if the Commission fails to take the necessary action to conserve Antarctic marine living resources or to adopt an ecosystem approach in so doing, it will be failing in its legal duty. If, for example, scientific evidence suggests that harvesting even relatively small levels of krill in certain critical areas could impede the recovery of populations of baleen whales, the Commission will be legally obliged to prohibit harvesting in those areas.

Article IX(1) specifies eight activities which the Commission shall undertake in particular. These include research, compilation and analysis of data, implementation of a system of observation and inspection, and the formulation of conservation measures on the basis of the best scientific evidence available. Article IX(1) also authorises the Commission to "carry out such other activities as are necessary to fulfil the objective of this Convention".[34] Article IX(2) stipulates that the conservation measures to be taken by the Commission shall include, but are not limited to, designation of catch limits for harvested species, designation of protected species, designation of open and closed seasons, designation of protected

---

[30] The International Whaling Commission, for example, has established both a Technical Committee and an Infractions Committee. See Chapter 2 above at pp. 28 and 32.

[31] CCAMLR, Article XIX(1).

[32] *Ibid.*, Article XIX(3).

[33] See p. 163 above.

[34] CCAMLR, Article IX(1)(h).

areas and "regulation of the effort employed and methods of harvesting, including fishing gear, with a view, *inter alia*, to avoiding undue concentration of harvesting in any region or sub-region". This latter provision may be particularly useful in preventing over-exploitation of the swarms of krill which tend to form in the Antarctic summer. The Commission is obliged to publish and maintain a record of all conservation measures in force[35] and to notify all members of the Commission of these measures.[36] Conservation measures become binding upon all members of the Commission 180 days after such notification,[37] although CCAMLR, like many treaties concerned with the conservation of wildlife, contains a procedure whereby individual members of the Commission may avoid being bound by specific measures which they feel unable to accept.[38]

b)　*Scientific Committee*

The Scientific Committee is an advisory body to the Commission.[39] The latter is authorised to direct the Scientific Committee to conduct such activities as it considers appropriate, but the Committee has certain mandatory functions under the Convention. These include obligations to assess the status and trends of populations of Antarctic marine living resources, to analyse data concerning the direct and indirect effects of harvesting on these populations and to make recommendations to the Commission with respect to conservation measures and research that are necessary to implement the objective of the Convention.[40] The Committee is composed of representatives of members of the Commission who may seek the advice of other scientists and experts as may be required on an *ad hoc* basis.[41] In particular, Article XXIII(3) of CCAMLR requires the Committee to seek to develop cooperative working relationships with a number of organisations including the Scientific Committee on Oceanic Research and the International Whaling Commission.

---

[35]　*Ibid.*, Article IX(3).
[36]　*Ibid.*, Article IX(6)(a).
[37]　*Ibid.*, Article IX(6)(b).
[38]　*Ibid.*, Article IX(6)(c). In order to avoid being bound by a specific conservation measure, a member of the Commission must inform the Commission within 90 days of being notified of the measure under Article IX(6)(a) that it is unable to accept it. If this procedure is invoked, any other member has the right to have the Commission meet to review the measure and within 30 days of such meeting any other member also has the right to notify the Commission that it is no longer able to accept the measure (Article IX(6)(d)).
[39]　CCAMLR, Article XIV(1).
[40]　*Ibid.*, Article XV(2).
[41]　*Ibid.*, Article XIV(3).

The work of the Scientific Committee is crucial, primarily because the Convention establishes an "ecosystem approach" to conservation and relatively little is known about the Antarctic marine ecosystem. Even such basic information as the life span and breeding cycle of krill is incomplete.[42] The key to the effectiveness of the Scientific Committee lies in its relationship with the Commission and, as is often the case in the context of such treaties, the negotiators of CCAMLR spent a lot of time in coming to an agreement on the precise nature of that relationship.[43] If the Committee is nothing but a pawn of the Commission, which is essentially a political body, there is a danger that "politically inconvenient" data might be excluded from the consideration of the Committee or that the Committee might make recommendations that are politically acceptable to the Commission but may not be scientifically advisable. The result could be increased exploitation in the short term accompanied by over-capitalisation of the fishing industry, which could make rational use difficult to implement in the long term. On the other hand, the negotiators were concerned that the Scientific Committee should not be given such a degree of independence that the Commission would have an excuse to ignore its advice. As finally drafted, CCAMLR vests control of the Committee's budget in the Commission, requires the Committee to conduct such activities as the Commission may direct and, in the final instance, allows the Commission to take such action as it deems appropriate notwithstanding any scientific advice it has received. However, Article IX(4) requires the Commission to take "full account" of the recommendations and advice of the Scientific Committee, and the reports of the Committee must be published.[44] In this way, the negotiators hoped to avoid a credibility gap from opening up between Committee and Commission.[45]

c) *Decision-making*

The decision-making bodies established by most treaties concerned with the conservation of wildlife employ a two thirds or three quarters majority voting procedure. In contrast, decisions of the Commission on all matters of substance require a consensus, and if a question arises as to whether a matter is one of substance it

[42] See J. Barnes, *The Emerging Convention on the Conservation of Antarctic Marine Living Resources: An Attempt to Meet the New Realities of Resource Exploitation in the Southern Ocean* (Center for Law and Social Policy, Washington D.C., 1982), p. 266.
[43] See Edwards and Heap, note 13 above, p. 357.
[44] CCAMLR, Article IX(1)(d).
[45] See Edwards and Heap, note 13 above, p. 357.

will be treated as a matter of substance.[46] The consensus voting system was adopted as a compromise which it was thought would not fatally prejudice the interests of either the conservation-oriented members of the Commission or those most interested in fishing. The latter were apparently concerned that with a three quarters majority voting system they might be consistently outvoted.[47]

It may be that the tradition of cooperation among the Parties to the Antarctic Treaty is sufficient to ensure that the Commission does in fact take such measures as are necessary to implement the conservation objectives of CCAMLR. However, this will not be easy under a consensus voting system where just one member of the Commission can prevent any conservation measure from being adopted. The system makes the initial decisions of the Commission especially significant because just as it may be difficult to agree on harvest levels, protected zones, fishing seasons etc. it will be equally difficult to undo a decision after it has been made. If, for example, a krill fishing industry develops and quotas are set at a level which are subsequently found to be too high from an ecological viewpoint, it may be very difficult to achieve an appropriate reduction if just one member of the Commission has a vested economic interest in maintaining high quotas. The consensus system does not render fulfilment of the objectives of the Convention impossible by any means, but it may make the achievement of an already difficult goal still harder.

Two members of the U.K. delegation to the final conference held to conclude CCAMLR in May 1980 have published an article suggesting that neither a three quarters majority voting system nor a consensus voting system is demonstrably superior to the other.[48] They argue that the Convention allows each Party to avoid being bound by a measure to which it is opposed by filing an objection or reservation[49] and that neither voting system can therefore bind a Party which does not wish to be bound by a specific conservation measure. It is certainly true that no decision-making procedure can of itself force a State to accept a conservation measure which it deems to be contrary to its vital interests, but it is also true that States which oppose proposals made in the context of other wildlife treaties, but

[46] CCAMLR, Article XII(1). Any other decisions will be taken by simple majority (Article XII(2)). If a regional economic integration organisation, such as the European Economic Community, participates in the taking of a decision, the number of Parties participating shall not exceed the number of member States of the regional economic integration organisation which are members of the Commission (Article XII(3)). A regional economic integration shall have only one vote (Article XII(4)).

[47] See Edwards and Heap, note 13 above, pp. 357-8.

[48] See Edwards and Heap, note 13 above.

[49] See note 38 above and accompanying text.

are outvoted, do not always lodge objections or reservations. Decisions of meetings of the Conference of the Parties pursuant to the Convention on International Trade in Endangered Species of Wild Fauna and Flora, for example, require a two thirds majority to be adopted and are frequently not unanimously approved, yet relatively few reservations have been taken. Furthermore, a State may be more reluctant to lodge a formal objection or reservation, with all the international publicity that will accompany its action, than quietly to prevent the decision being made in the first place by refusing to agree to it. This is particularly likely in the context of CCAMLR where, except for the International Union for Conservation of Nature and Natural Resources, non-governmental conservation organisations have not been admitted to Commission meetings as observers, with the result that there is every chance that a State's refusal to make up a consensus will receive the minimum adverse publicity.

d) *Meetings of the Commission*

At the time of writing the Commission has met three times — in May 1982, September 1983 and September 1984 — but has made only limited progress towards making CCAMLR operational. The first meeting was monopolised by procedural matters, and its only concrete achievements were to adopt rules of procedure for the Commission and to agree on a budget of U.S.$380,000 for the second half of 1982 and U.S.$780,000 for 1983.[50] The second meeting quickly agreed on rules of procedure for the Scientific Committee but, although there was some discussion of possible over-exploitation of some species of fin fish in some areas, did not adopt any conservation measures.

Responding to evidence of depleted fin fish stocks around South Georgia, particularly of *Notothenia rossii*, the Commission finally adopted some limited conservation measures at its third meeting. It prohibited all fishing, other than for scientific research purposes, within twelve nautical miles of South Georgia.[51] With a view to protecting juveniles throughout Antarctic waters, the Commission also prohibited the use of pelagic and bottom trawls with mesh sizes less than 120 mm for any fishing directed at *Notothenia rossii* or

[50] The budget is just over half the amount proposed by Australia at the Preparatory Meeting held in October 1981. Some non-governmental organisations have expressed concern that the present funding level may be insufficient for adequate data analysis. See *ECO*, Vol. XIX, No. 4 (14 June 1982), available from Friends of the Earth, 377 City Rd., London.

[51] Report of the Third Meeting of the Commission, CCAMLR-III/16, 19 September 1984, para. 48. Official Reports of all Commission meetings may be obtained from the CCAMLR Secretariat, Hobart, Tasmania.

Dissostichus eleginoides and less than 80 mm for any fishing directed at *Notothenia gibberifrons*, *Notothenia kempi*, *Notothenia squamifrons* or *Champsocephalus gunnari*. These measures apply as of 1 September 1985 but do not apply to fishing for scientific research purposes.[52] However, they will have little practical significance, and their contribution to the development of the Convention should not be over-estimated. The U.S.S.R., the main fishing nation in the South Georgia area, opposed the adoption of more far-reaching conservation measures at the third Commission meeting and only agreed to the limited measures because it had already stopped fishing within 12 miles of South Georgia and already operated the mesh size restrictions.

There are still no catch limits, no open and closed seasons, no non-fishing zones except the one around South Georgia, no protected species and no restrictions on mesh sizes for fishing operations directed at species other than the ones mentioned above. It is to be expected that procedural issues should dominate initial meetings of the Commission, but it should also be emphasised that the Commission has a legal duty to ensure that Antarctic marine resources are not over-fished, and future meetings of the Commission will need to make considerably greater progress if member States are to be sure of complying with their obligations.

6. *Enforcement*

Article XXI(1) of CCAMLR requires each Party to "take appropriate measures within its competence to ensure compliance with the provisions of this Convention and with conservation measures adopted by the Commission to which the Party is bound". Article XXII(1) goes on to require each Party "to exert appropriate efforts...to the end that no one engages in any activity contrary to the objective of this Convention". More specifically, CCAMLR provides for the elaboration of a system of observation and inspection, requires the publication of misdeeds in certain circumstances and makes a number of reporting requirements, all of which are designed to increase the Convention's prospects of enforcement.

a) *Observation and inspection*

Article XXIV(2) requires the Commission to elaborate a system of observation and inspection in order to "ensure observance of the provisions of this Convention" and, in particular, to establish procedures for boarding and inspection, procedures for prosecution

---

[52] *Ibid.*, para. 49.

by the flag State concerned and procedures for reporting to the Commission any prosecutions or sanctions imposed by Parties. However, Article XXIV(2) also states that inspectors and observers shall remain subject to the jurisdiction of the Party of which they are nationals. This provision has been criticised by some commentators on the basis that inspectors and observers appointed by and responsible to the Commission may be more likely to do an effective enforcement job than those that are appointed by and are responsible to the State of which they are nationals.[53]

Pending elaboration of the system, Article XXIV(3) requires members of the Commission to seek to elaborate interim arrangements according to the principles established by Article XXIV(2). In spite of this, however, the Commission has still not elaborated even an interim system for either observers or inspectors.

b) *Article X*

Article X takes the unusual step of requiring the Commission to point a public finger at States, whether Parties or non-Parties to CCAMLR, whose activities adversely affect implementation of the objective of the Convention. In particular, Article X(1) requires the Commission to draw the attention of a non-Party "to any activity undertaken by its nationals or vessels which, in the opinion of the Commission, affects the implementation of the objective of this Convention". Article X(2) requires the Commission to draw the attention of

> ...all Contracting Parties to any activity which, in the opinion of the Commission, affects the implementation by a Contracting Party of the objective of this Convention or the compliance by that Contracting Parties with its obligations under this Convention.

Article X may prove to be an important deterrent to potential miscreants in that States may prefer to implement the objectives of the Convention, and, if they are Parties, to comply with their obligations under the Convention rather than face the adverse international publicity that would result from any action taken by the Commission pursuant to Article X. However, it should be noted that Article X cannot be invoked unless it is "the opinion of the Commission" that it should be invoked. Under the consensus voting system, a member of the Commission against which it was proposed to use Article X, could prevent it from being used simply by refusing to agree that it was the opinion of the Commission that it should be used.

[53] See Barnes, note 42 above, p. 267.

c) *Reporting requirements*

Reporting requirements made by other treaties concerned with the conservation of wildlife have proved to be a useful enforcement tool because they have resulted in the provision of information which has revealed whether or not Parties are complying with the terms of those treaties.[54] CCAMLR makes a number of reporting requirements which may also help ensure that the Convention is properly enforced. Members of the Commission are obliged to submit reports on their harvesting activities so as to enable reliable catch and effort statistics to be compiled,[55] and each year they must submit any other statistical or biological data as the Commission or Scientific Committee may require.[56] In addition, each Party must inform the Commission of the steps it has taken to ensure compliance with the provisions of the Convention and with the conservation measures adopted by the Commission, including information on the sanctions it has imposed for violations.[57] Observers and inspectors must report to the member of the Commission by which they have been designated which in turn must report to the Commission as a whole.[58] Article XXII(2) requires each Party to notify the Commission of any activity contrary to the objective of the Convention which comes to its attention, irrespective of whether the activity is being carried out by its own nationals or vessels or by those of another State.

The information supplied by these reports should greatly assist in the establishment of conservation measures and should ensure that incidents of non-compliance therewith, if they do occur, are rapidly brought to the attention of the Parties. Reporting requirements may also be useful as a preventative medicine since Parties may prefer to comply with their obligations under CCAMLR rather than face the public embarassment of having to report incidents of their own non-compliance.

7. *Accession to CCAMLR and membership of the Commission*

CCAMLR is subject to ratification, acceptance or approval by the fifteen States which signed the Convention[59] and is open to accession "by any State interested in research or harvesting activities in relation to the marine living resources to which this Convention

---

[54] See, for example, Chapter 12 below, pp. 268-269.
[55] CCAMLR, Article XX(2).
[56] *Ibid.*, Article XX(1).
[57] *Ibid.*, Article XXI(2).
[58] *Ibid.*, Article XXIV(2)(c).
[59] *Ibid.*, Article XXVII(1).

applies".[60] The Convention does not define what form the interest of a State should take before it is allowed to accede, and the Commission has not yet made any recommendations thereon. CCAMLR is also open for accession by "regional economic integration organisations constituted by sovereign States which include among their members one or more States Members of the Commission and to which the States members of the organisation have transferred, in whole or in part, competences with regard to the matters covered by this Convention".[61] In drafting this provision, the European Economic Community was uppermost in the minds of the negotiators,[62] and the EEC has now acceded.

Qualification for membership of the Commission is slightly different from qualification for accession to the Convention. Parties participating in the meeting at which the Convention was adopted — i.e. the fifteen signatories — are automatically entitled to be members of the Commission.[63] However, other States acceding to CCAMLR are only entitled to be members during such time as they are "engaged in research or harvesting activities in relation to the marine living resources to which this Convention applies".[64] A regional economic integration organisation is entitled to be a member if one or more of its member States is entitled to be a member.[65] The meaning of "engaged in harvesting activities" is fairly self evident, but the Convention does not define what a Party must do to be considered "engaged in research", and the Commission has not yet established any appropriate guidelines. Of the three Parties to CCAMLR which were not among the original signatories, only the EEC is a member of the Commission. Spain and Sweden are not yet members, although they were allowed to attend the 1984 meeting of the Commission as observers.

If a Party considers itself qualified for membership, it must notify the Depositary (the Australian government) of the basis of its claims and of its willingness to accept conservation measures already in force. The Depositary will transmit the notification and accompanying information to existing members, any one of which may request a special meeting of the Commission to consider the matter. If a meeting is not so requested, the Party concerned will be deemed to have satisfied the membership requirements.[66]

[60] *Ibid.*, Article XXIX(1).
[61] *Ibid.*, Article XXIX(2).
[62] See Barnes, note 42 above, pp. 256-259.
[63] CCAMLR, Article VII(2)(a).
[64] *Ibid.*, Article VII(2)(b).
[65] *Ibid.*, Article VII(2)(c).
[66] *Ibid.*, Article VII(2)(d).

These provisions of CCAMLR differ from most international fisheries agreements which do not normally restrict participation in their decision-making bodies.[67] They illustrate the deep concern of the Consultative Parties to the Antarctic Treaty that they should retain a powerful voice in the management of Antarctic fisheries. The Consultative Parties have also made very certain that the current situation in relation to the International Convention for the Regulation of Whaling, where the International Whaling Commission has recently been flooded by non-whaling States determined to alter the traditional course of whaling,[68] is not repeated in the context of Antarctica.

8.   Related treaties and measures

It has already been pointed out in this chapter how CCAMLR serves to bind its Parties to the system established by the Antarctic Treaty, and there are other provisions of the Convention not previously mentioned which cement the tie to that system. For example, Parties to CCAMLR are required not to engage in any activities south of 60° South contrary to the principles and purposes of the Antarctic Treaty, whether or not they are Parties to it.[69] They also undertake to be bound specifically by Articles I, IV, V, and VI of the Antarctic Treaty.[70] Article I requires that Antarctica be used for peaceful purposes only, Article IV freezes the legal status quo as it was in 1959 with respect to territorial claims, Article V prohibits the disposal of nuclear waste in Antarctica and Article VI describes the geographical area to which the Antarctic Treaty shall apply. CCAMLR also requires its Parties to acknowledge the "special obligations and responsibilities of the Antarctic Treaty Consultative Parties for the protection and preservation of the environment of the Antarctic Treaty area".[71]

The relationship of CCAMLR to the International Convention for the Regulation of Whaling and to the Convention for the Conservation of Antarctic Seals has already been discussed, and an earlier part of this chapter gave brief mention to the Agreed Measures for the Conservation of Antarctic Fauna and Flora.[72] The Agreed Measures, adopted by the Third Consultative Meeting of the

---

[67] In practice, however, coastal States within the geographical scope of an agreement and countries interested in fishing the stocks concerned tend to be the only ones which do participate.

[68] See Chapter 2 above at pp. 20-21.

[69] CCAMLR, Article III.

[70] *Ibid.*, Articles III and IV(1).

[71] *Ibid.*, Article V(1).

[72] See pp. 156 and 162 above.

Antarctic Treaty in 1964 and since approved by the governments of all the Consultative Parties, are particularly interesting. The preamble declares that the entire Antarctic Treaty area is to be considered a "Special Conservation Area", and Article V(1) requires participating governments to "prohibit within the Treaty Area the killing, wounding, capturing or molesting of any native mammal or native bird, or any attempt at any such act, except in accordance with a permit". Article V(2) stipulates that permits may only be issued to provide specimens for scientific study, for educational purposes or for cultural uses or to provide "indispensable food for men or dogs in the Treaty Area". Thus the circumstances in which penguins or other native birds may legally be killed on land south of 60° South are extremely limited. The enormous public fuss which followed reports in early 1984 that France had blasted an airstrip near its base at Dumont D'Urville and had killed and disturbed penguins in so doing was made, at least in part, because it was such a blatant violation of Article V of the Agreed Measures.[73]

Permits for "Specially Protected Species", listed in an Annex to the Agreed Measures, may only be granted "for a compelling scientific purpose" and may not "jeopardise the existing natural ecological system or the survival of that species".[74] In addition, "Specially Protected Areas" may be designated and are subject to similar stringent protection.[75] Criteria for reviewing specially protected areas and for establishing sites of special scientific interest were adopted at the seventh Consultative Meeting, and several such areas and sites have now been established.[76] Finally, "harmful interference" with the normal living conditions of any native mammal or bird must be "minimised". This is clearly less than absolute prohibition, but permissible harmful interference is defined to include only a few limited activities.[77]

The intention behind the Agreed Measures was to protect mammals and birds from undue slaughter and disturbance on land by personnel from the growing number of scientific bases established in Antarctica in the early 1960s. When the Agreed Measures were adopted in 1964, the question of exploration for or development of mineral resources in Antarctica had not become a

---

[73] See "France Dynamites Antarctic Penguins", *New Scientist* (26 January 1984), p. 4. The French Government subsequently set up an official inquiry into the construction of the airstrip.

[74] Agreed Measures, note 5 above, Article V(7).

[75] *Ibid.*, Article VIII.

[76] See *Handbook of Measures in Furtherance of the Principles and Objectives of the Antarctic Treaty* (U.S. Department of State, Washington D.C., 1979), pp. 2203-5 and 3101-17.

[77] Agreed Measures, note 5 above, Article VII.

serious issue, and the Consultative Parties did not consider the need to regulate such activities in order to protect Antarctic wildlife when negotiating the Measures. However, in view of the designation of the Antarctic Treaty Area as a "Special Conservation Area" and the prohibition of "molesting" native mammals or birds within the Area, the Consultative Parties will have to take account of the Agreed Measures if they develop a legal regime for the exploitation of minerals in Antarctica since drilling, oil spills etc. may well result in the "molesting" if not actually the "killing" of Antarctic wildlife.[78] It is also noteworthy that the legislation which implements the Agreed Measures in the U.S.A. makes it unlawful for a U.S. citizen to "harass, molest, harm...kill..." a native mammal or bird south of 60° South, irrespective of whether on land or at sea, or "to discharge, or otherwise dispose of, any pollutant within Antarctica", without a permit,[79] which may only be issued for the purpose of providing specimens for scientific study or for educational or cultural uses.[80] Given the hazardous physical conditions, which will make it very difficult to avoid oil spills and other forms of pollution, it is questionable whether substantial U.S. mineral exploitation in Antarctica will be possible under existing U.S. law.

9.   *Conclusion*

There is no question that CCAMLR imposes a strong and unequivocal obligation on its Parties to use Antarctic marine living resources wisely. This obligation, combined with the fact that krill fishing has not yet developed into a major commercial venture, raises some hope that Antarctic fish stocks will not be over-exploited in the same way as other fisheries have been and, indeed, that they will not even be exploited to an extent that will adversely affect other Antarctic species, notably the large baleen whales. However, the Convention will only succeed to the extent that its Commission wants it to succeed. The Commission also has a legal duty to ensure that Antarctic marine living resources are used wisely and to adopt an "ecosystem approach" in so doing, but the fact that there are still no catch limits, no open and closed seasons, only one relatively small

---

[78] Negotiations for the conclusion of an international agreement regarding the exploitation of mineral resources in Antarctica are already underway. Pursuant to Recommendation XI-1 of the Eleventh Antarctic Treaty Consultative Meeting held in 1981 which called for negotiation of a regime for Antarctic minerals "as a matter of urgency", representatives of the fourteen Consultative Parties to the Antarctic Treaty have held several consultative meetings. Negotiations are still at a relatively early stage, but the series of discussions held in 1983 and 1984 demonstrate the seriousness with which the Consultative Parties are treating the subject.

[79] Antarctic Conservation Act of 1978, 16 U.S.C. §§2401 *et. seq.*, sub-sections 4(a)(1)(A), 4(a)(1)(E) and (3)(13).

[80] *Ibid.*, sub-sections 5(e)(2)(A) and (B).

no-fishing zone and only limited restrictions on mesh sizes demonstrates that the Commission has made little progress so far towards complying with its obligations. There are many obstacles facing the Commission, the most serious of which may prove to be the capacity of any member to block any conservation measure to which that member is opposed. But if exploitation of the unique wildlife resources of one of the last unspoiled environments on earth is to be conducted without destroying its fragile ecological balance, it is imperative that the Commission succeeds in fulfilling its mandate.

PART IV

Part IV examines four treaties which form the centrepiece of international wildlife law and are the most important agreements considered in this book. They were all concluded in the 1970s and, in contrast to the treaties discussed in earlier chapters, they are neither restricted to a few individual species nor to certain geographical regions. They are the Convention on Wetlands of International Importance Especially as Waterfowl Habitat (generally known as "Ramsar", the name of the Iranian town where it was signed), the Convention Concerning the Protection of the World Cultural and Natural Heritage (the "World Heritage Convention"), the Convention on International Trade in Endangered Species of Wild Fauna and Flora ("CITES"), and the Convention on the Conservation of Migratory Species of Wild Animals (generally known as the "Bonn Convention" because it was signed in the West German capital city).

Each of the four has its limitations as a legal conservation instrument. Ramsar is limited to wetlands, the World Heritage Convention is concerned with a few select areas of "outstanding universal value", CITES is restricted to the regulation of international trade, and the Bonn Convention covers only migratory species. Together, however, the four treaties comprise a powerful body of international law affecting the conservation of an immense number and variety of wild animals and plants. Ramsar's broad definition of wetlands includes a wide diversity of important wildlife habitats. CITES is vitally important for parrots, crocodiles, cacti, sea turtles, cats, rhinos and dozens of other groups of species whose survival is threatened, or potentially threatened, by international trade. The World Heritage Convention provides an excellent mechanism for the protection and international recognition of particularly outstanding natural areas such as the Galapagos Islands and the Serengeti, and it establishes an unprecedented system whereby Parties can receive international financial and technical assistance to help them protect these unique places. The Bonn Convention establishes a system of international co-operation which is essential to the protection of hundreds of migratory species which cross international frontiers during their migration.

The four treaties had separate origins, but each is an indicator of the growing recognition amongst the international community in the 1970s that wild animals and plants are irreplaceable components of the earth's natural systems, that wildlife populations and habitats are declining because of man's activities, that countries should do their utmost to halt this trend and that international cooperation is essential to the achievement of this objective. The preambles to each of the four treaties reflect these sentiments very clearly. The preamble to CITES states that "wild fauna and flora in their many beautiful and varied forms are an irreplaceable part of the natural systems of the earth which must be protected for this and the generations to come" and that "international cooperation is essential for the protection of certain species of wild fauna and flora against over-exploitation through international trade". The preamble to the Bonn Convention contains similar acknowledgements, stating that "wild animals in their innumerable forms are an irreplaceable part of the earth's natural system which must be conserved for the good of mankind" and that "conservation and effective management of migratory species of wild animals require the concerted action of all States" through whose territory they pass. The preamble to Ramsar indicates that wetlands "constitute a resource of great economic, cultural, scientific and recreational value, the loss of which would be irreparable" and that the objective of the Convention is "to stem the progressive encroachment on and loss of wetlands now and in the future...by combining far-sighted national policies with co-ordinated international action". The preamble to the World Heritage Convention recognises that "the cultural heritage and the natural heritage are increasingly threatened with destruction", that "deterioration or disappearance of any item of the cultural or natural heritage constitutes a harmful impoverishment of the heritage of all nations of the world" and that "it is incumbent on the international community as a whole to participate in the protection of the cultural and natural heritage of outstanding universal value".

At least two of the four treaties are also indicators of a concept which became increasingly widely accepted during the 1970s. The concept is that wildlife is part of the common heritage of all people and that wildlife conservation is an international concern, rather than being solely of interest to the State in whose territory the wildlife occurs. This principle gained international recognition at the United Nations Conference on the Human Environment in Stockholm in 1972, but was perhaps best expressed by the representative of Lesotho, speaking on behalf of the African States at the final conference held to conclude the Bonn Convention in 1979, when he stated:

> The African States believe that wildlife as a whole and more especially migratory species of fauna, are the common heritage of humanity and that wherever they live they should throughout their lives be managed in the common interest and by the common consent of all peoples.

The gradual acceptance of the concept of a common wildlife heritage and of a common interest in its protection is particularly interesting because of the traditional sensitivity of States to international interference in their domestic affairs. The fact that a State is prepared to incur international obligations with respect to the conservation of wildlife found within its territory rather goes against the grain of normal international relations. However, it is an extremely important development from a conservation viewpoint because it gives the international community a right to put pressure on a State to protect its wildlife on the basis that the loss of that wildlife will be a loss to the world as a whole. Many species, such as migratory species, and many threats to species, such as international trade, are obvious candidates for international action, but the more widely accepted the concept of a common wildlife heritage becomes the more the scope of international law to cover all species and all threats to their survival will be opened up. There are still relatively few international treaties giving effect to the concept of a common wildlife heritage, but they do exist and the World Heritage Convention is a particularly good example of the growing willingness to convert the concept from an interesting idea to international law.

CHAPTER 10

THE CONVENTION ON WETLANDS OF INTERNATIONAL IMPORTANCE ESPECIALLY AS WATERFOWL HABITAT ("RAMSAR")

"The lasting benefits that society derives from wetlands often far exceed the immediate advantage their owners might get from draining or filling them."
(President Carter, 1977)

1. Background

Wetlands are amongst the most productive life-support systems on earth, and their conservation is important for biological, hydrological and economic reasons. They provide essential habitat for hundreds of species of waterfowl, fish, amphibians, reptiles, mammals and plants. They act as natural sponges which control floods and droughts. A sub-tropical saltmarsh may produce organic material at more than twice the rate of the most fertile hayfield, and two thirds of the commercially important fish and shellfish harvested along the U.S. Atlantic seaboard — and 98% of those harvested in the Gulf of Mexico — depend on estuaries and associated wetlands for food, spawning grounds and nurseries for their fry. In spite of their valuable functions, wetlands in many parts of the world have been destroyed at an alarming rate in recent decades by drainage, land reclamation and pollution.[1]

A series of international conferences and technical meetings were held in the 1960s, mainly under the auspices of the International Waterfowl Research Bureau ("IWRB"), in an effort to stem this tide of destruction. As a result of these discussions, the Convention on Wetlands of International Importance Especially as Waterfowl Habitat[2] was drawn up and was eventually signed on 2 February 1971 in the Iranian town of Ramsar (hence the name "Ramsar" by which the Convention is commonly known and hereinafter referred to). Ramsar came into force on 21 December 1975.[3]

[1] See *Proceedings, International Conference on Conservation of Wetlands and Waterfowl* (IWRB, 1972), pp. 65-264, available from the International Waterfowl Research Bureau, Slimbridge, Glos., England; see also *Liquid Assets* (IWRB, 1980); *World Conservation Strategy* (IUCN, 1980), available from IUCN, 1196 Gland, Switzerland; *The Ecology and Utilisation of African Inland Waters* (UNEP Reports and Proceedings Series 1, 1981); see also the preamble to Ramsar.

[2] 11 *I.L.M.* 963; *U.K.T.S.* no. 34 (1976), Cmd. 6465.

[3] Pursuant to Article 10(1) of the Convention, Ramsar came into force four months after the seventh State deposited its instrument of ratification.

At the time of writing there are 36 Parties to the Convention,[4] and 294 wetland sites covering almost 20 million hectares are in Ramsar's "List of Wetlands of International Importance" (the "List"). Since the Convention came into force there have been three formal meetings of the Parties. The first, an "ordinary" Conference of the Parties, was a technical meeting held at Cagliari in Italy in November 1980 (the "Cagliari Conference") at which a variety of recommendations were made in order to improve the effectiveness of the Convention. The next was an "extraordinary" Conference of the Parties with plenipotentiary delegates empowered to approve a Protocol to the Convention. It was held in Paris in December 1982 (the "Paris Conference"). The most recent meeting was a second "ordinary" Conference of the Parties which was held at Groningen in the Netherlands in May 1984 (the "Groningen Conference").

The preamble to Ramsar states that the objective of the Convention is "to stem the progressive encroachment on and loss of wetlands now and in the future." Article 2(1) defines wetlands as "areas of marsh, fen, peatland or water, whether natural or artificial, permanent or temporary, with water that is static or flowing, fresh, brackish or salt, including areas of marine water the depth of which at low tide does not exceed six metres", which may also include adjacent riparian and coastal zones.[5] This is a very broad definition, and Ramsar therefore aims to stem encroachment on habitats as diverse as mangrove swamps, peat bogs, water meadows, coastal beaches, coastal waters, tidal flats, mountain lakes and tropical river systems. To achieve its objective, Ramsar seeks to promote the wise use of all wetlands and special protection for wetlands in the List. It also encourages research into wetlands and their fauna and flora, seeks to promote the training of personnel competent in the fields of wetland research and management, and requires Parties to cooperate in implementing their obligations under the Convention.

Ramsar has been criticised in some quarters on the basis that it imposes few legally binding conservation obligations on its Parties, that there are too few non-European Parties and that its financial and administrative arrangements are woefully inadequate. There is no doubt that the Convention compares unfavourably with the financial and administrative arrangements of, and the conservation

---

[4] They are: Algeria, Australia, Austria, Bulgaria, Canada, Chile, Denmark, Federal Republic of Germany, Finland, German Democratic Republic, Greece, Hungary, Iceland, India, Iran, Italy, Japan, Jordan, Mauritania, Morocco, Netherlands, New Zealand, Norway, Pakistan, Poland, Portugal, Senegal, South Africa, Spain, Sweden, Switzerland, Tunisia, U.K., Uruguay, U.S.S.R. and Yugoslavia. Belgium and Ireland have signed but have not yet ratified.

[5] Ramsar, Article 2(1).

obligations imposed by, the other three conventions considered in Part IV of this book and that it needs more Parties, particularly from the tropical regions of the world. However, progress towards improving its system of administration and attracting more developing countries has been made in recent years and, as will become clear later in this chapter, Ramsar has had a very considerable positive impact on wetland conservation in many Party States.

2. The List of Wetlands of International Importance

a) Inclusion of sites in the List

In contrast to the World Heritage Convention, which has a screening procedure for the inclusion of sites in the World Heritage List, Ramsar allows its Parties to designate sites unilaterally in the List of Wetlands of International Importance. Ramsar obliges each Party to designate "suitable wetlands within its territory" for inclusion in the List,[6] including at least one at the time it signs, ratifies or accedes to the Convention.[7] The boundaries of each listed site must be "precisely described and also delimited on a map".[8] The Convention allows Parties to extend the boundaries of listed sites or add wetlands situated within their territory to the List at any time.[9] The List is maintained by the International Union for Conservation of Nature and Natural Resources ("IUCN") in its capacity as "Bureau" (a form of Secretariat) under the Convention.[10]

Recognising that the List should contain as many wetlands of international importance as possible in order to achieve the aims of the Convention, the Cagliari Conference called on Parties "to increase the number of wetlands in their territories to be included in the List, particularly as regards sites outside the western Palearctic and wetland types poorly represented in the western Palearctic."[11] This recommendation was prompted by the fact that

[6] Ibid.

[7] Ibid., Article 2(4).

[8] Ibid., Article 2(1).

[9] Ibid., Article 2(5).

[10] Copies of the List may be obtained from IUCN, 1196 Gland, Switzerland. For further discussion of the role played by IUCN under Ramsar, see pp. 203-204 below.

[11] Cagliari Conference, Recommendation 1.3. Conference recommendations are reprinted in Conference on the Conservation of Wetlands of International Importance Especially as Waterfowl Habitat (International Waterfowl Research Bureau, 1980), hereinafter referred to as Report on the Cagliari Conference. See also Proceedings of the Conference on the Conservation of Wetlands of International Importance Especially as Waterfowl Habitat (Cagliari, Italy, 24-29 November 1980) (M. Spagnesi, ed.), Supplement to Ricerche di Biologia della Selvaginna Vol. 8 (Istituto Nazionale di Biologia della Selvaginna, Ozzano Emilia, Italy, 1984). The "western Palearctic" is a geo/biological term covering Europe (east to the Urals), western Asia (including much of the Arabian peninsular and parts of Iran) and northern Africa.

over 80% of wetlands in the List in 1980 were in the western Palearctic, and even in that region the network was incomplete since tundra, peatlands, tidal estuaries and southern wintering areas for waterfowl were sparsely represented.

At the time of the Cagliari Conference there were 216 wetlands covering 6 million hectares in the List. At the time of writing, four years later, the List had increased to 294 wetlands totalling almost 20 million hectares. These figures illustrate both that most Parties have exceeded the legal minimum of listing one site and that considerable progress has been made since the Cagliari Conference. Italy now has 36 sites in the List; Australia, Canada, Denmark, Finland, the Federal Republic of Germany, Greece, Iran, Netherlands, Sweden, the U.K. and the U.S.S.R. all have at least 10; and 22 Parties have at least 2. Furthermore, the fact that Jordan has designated just one site — Azraq Oasis — is misleading because it is the only Jordanian wetland of international importance for waterfowl.[12] The addition of sites is an ongoing process and, either through their national reports or through the personal intervention of their delegates, 15 of the 36 Parties indicated to the Groningen Conference that they intended to add more sites in the near future. If promises made at Groningen are fulfilled, the List could swell to more than 500 sites and the area covered could be trebled.

The Italian, Canadian and Australian records are particularly impressive. Italy has regularly added sites to the List since her ratification in 1976, and the hectarage of listed Italian sites has quadrupled from 12,000 to almost 50,000. Canada designated just one site of 2,200 hectares on her accession in January 1981 but added a further 10 million hectares in 1982. Australia has added 22 sites to the List since the Cagliari Conference. The commitment made by the U.K. delegation to the Groningen Conference is also noteworthy. It stated that 132 sites had been identified as eligible for listing in the U.K., that 19 had already been listed and that "nearly all" would be listed by 1986.[13] These examples illustrate how States with small, densely populated land surfaces such as Italy and the U.K. as well as those with large, sparsely populated wetlands like Australia and Canada can put Ramsar to good use.

In terms of the recommendation made by the Cagliari Conference, the Canadian and Australian contributions are

---

[12] See *The Ramsar Convention, A Technical Review*, Cagliari Conference Doc. CONF/4, para. 36. Conference documents of the Cagliari, Paris and Groningen Conferences are available from either IWRB, Slimbridge, Glos., England or IUCN, 1196 Gland, Switzerland.

[13] Groningen Conference Plen. C2.3(Rev.1).

particularly encouraging since both are outside the western Palearctic. While the Palearctic still predominates, the proportion of sites there has decreased from 90% in 1980 to 77% in 1984. There has also been an improvement in areas which the Cagliari Conference identified as poorly represented in the western Palearctic. Peatlands are now better represented in the List following the U.K.'s recent listing of Claish Moss and Silver Flowe and Poland's listing of Karas Lake. The coverage of tidal estuaries was greatly improved when Mauritania listed the Banc d'Arguin, a major tidal zone, in 1982 and when the Netherlands listed the whole of the Dutch section of the Wadden Sea in 1984. The listing of the Banc d'Arguin, the Donana National Park in Spain and two of the important El Kala wetlands in Algeria since the Cagliari Conference has also greatly increased the coverage of southern wintering areas for waterfowl.[14]

b)   *Deletion of sites from the List*

In cases of "urgent national interests", Ramsar allows its Parties to delete or restrict the boundaries of sites which they have included in the List[15] but requires them "as far as possible [to] compensate for any loss of wetland resources" resulting from such deletion or reduction, either by creating "additional nature reserves" or by protecting "in the same area or elsewhere an adequate portion of the original habitat".[16] Parties are obliged to notify IUCN of any boundary changes "at the earliest possible time".[17] No site has yet been deleted from the List, although boundary reductions have been recorded by the Federal Republic of Germany, Iran, Italy and Norway. The Italian, Norwegian and German reductions were counterbalanced by corresponding extensions, but the Iranian report of reductions at Mian Kaleh and in the Shadegan marsh makes no mention of any extension.[18]

c)   *Criteria for the inclusion of a wetland in the List*

i)   *Biological criteria*

Article 2(2) of Ramsar states that

wetlands should be selected for the List on account of their international significance in terms of ecology, botany, zoology,

[14] See *Overview of National Reports submitted by Contracting Parties and Review of Developments since the First Conference of the Parties held in Cagliari, Italy in November 1980*, Groningen Conference Doc. C2.6, paras. 44-49.
[15] Ramsar, Article 2(5).
[16] *Ibid.*, Article 4(2).
[17] *Ibid.*, Article 2(5).
[18] See Groningen Conference Doc. C2.6, paras. 52-55.

limnology or hydrology. In the first instance, wetlands of international importance to waterfowl at any season should be included.

Recognising that more specific guidelines for the inclusion of wetlands in the List would be useful, the International Conference on Conservation of Wetlands and Waterfowl, held at Heiligenhafen in the Federal Republic of Germany a few months before Ramsar came into force and attended by representatives of most Parties to the Convention, agreed on the "Heiligenhafen criteria". These had no legal force but formed the basis for the selection of sites until 1980 when they were revised by the Cagliari Conference. The revised criteria, which have quasi-legal force,[19] are known as the "Cagliari criteria". They are sub-divided into three categories: quantitive criteria for identifying wetlands of international importance to waterfowl, general criteria for identifying wetlands of international importance to plants or animals and criteria for assessing the value of representative or unique wetlands.

In the first category, the Cagliari criteria state that a wetland should be considered of international importance for waterfowl if it:

a) regularly supports 10,000 ducks, geese and swans; or 10,000 coots; or 20,000 waders; or

b) regularly supports 1% of the individuals in a population of one species or sub-species of waterfowl; or

c) regularly supports 1% of the breeding pairs in a population of one species or sub-species of waterfowl.[20]

In the second category, the Cagliari criteria state that a wetland should be considered of international importance for plants or animals if it

a) supports an appreciable number of a rare, vulnerable or endangered species or subspecies of plant or animal; or

b) is of special value for maintaining the genetic and ecological diversity of a region because of the quality and peculiarities of its flora and fauna; or

c) is of special value as the habitat of plants or animals at a critical stage of their biological cycles; or

d) is of special value for its endemic plant or animal species or communities.[21]

[19] The Cagliari criteria are recommendations made by a formal meeting of the Parties to Ramsar and, although they do not have the same legal force as the provisions of the Convention itself, they constitute "soft law". The meaning of "soft law" is described in Chapter 1 above at pp. 10-11.

[20] See *Report on the Cagliari Conference*, note 11 above, Annex II, para. 1.

[21] *Ibid.*, Annex II, para. 2.

In the third category, the Cagliari criteria specify that a site which is a particularly good example of a specific type of wetland characteristic of its region should be considered of international importance.[22]

Under the Cagliari criteria, nesting beaches for endangered sea turtles, rivers containing rare endemic crustaceans, estuaries which are important breeding or feeding areas for commercial fisheries or other wetlands with similar qualities are just as worthy of inclusion in the List as habitats for waterfowl. Most of the sites now in the List were designated because of their importance to waterfowl, but this is at least partly because of the historical and continuing involvement of the IWRB in the negotiation and implementation of Ramsar. IWRB's extended network of observers and correspondents has amassed an immense amount of data on waterfowl from all over the world, while information on other wetland species is badly deficient, with the result that the limelight has tended to fall on areas known to be important to waterfowl. To be fair, Austria, Italy and the U.K. have selected sites for inclusion in the List because of their botanical and limnological quality, but these are exceptions rather than the rule. However, the Cagliari criteria make it abundantly clear that Ramsar is not just a waterfowl convention.

The Cagliari Conference recommended that appropriate international organisations should compile a "shadow" list of wetlands based on the Cagliari criteria in order to provide an objective assessment of which wetlands are of international importance.[23] IUCN has prepared a Directory of Western Palearctic Wetlands, IWRB has drawn up a Preliminary Inventory of Wetlands of International Importance for Waterfowl in West Europe and Northwest Africa, and both these organisations, together with the International Council for Bird Preservation, are at present cooperating in the compilation of wetland directories covering the Neotropical region, the Afrotropical region and the Asia/Indomalayan region.[24]

ii) *Conservation criteria*

The text of Ramsar does not specify whether Parties should only include sites in the List which are already protected by the State concerned, or whether they should also list biologically suitable sites which do not yet enjoy protection under domestic laws or regulations. In practice, different Parties have taken different

---

[22] *Ibid.*, Annex II, para. 3.
[23] Cagliari Conference, Recommendation 1.4.
[24] See Groningen Conference Doc. C2.6, paras. 118-121.

approaches on this point. Some (for example the U.K., Chile, Netherlands and Poland) have generally taken the view that they can only designate sites which already have extensive national legal protection on the basis that designation under Ramsar raises the national commitment to conserve a site to an international level and provides a valuable extra safeguard to its protected status.[25] There is no doubt that this "international" element of protection is much needed — the U.K. report to the Cagliari Conference indicated that 11 of the 13 sites originally listed by the U.K. were either threatened or potentially threatened, notwithstanding that they were all theoretically protected by national legislation.[26] Moreover, there is no doubt that designation under Ramsar can help such sites: in 1978 it was proposed to blow up a stricken oil tanker just off the coast adjacent to the listed site of Minsmere in Suffolk but, following representations to the U.K. government that the proposed act might damage a Ramsar site, the hulk was towed 20 miles out to sea and then blown up.[27]

Other Parties have adopted a different attitude. At the Cagliari Conference the Italian delegation strongly recommended listing unprotected wetlands which were biologically suitable on the grounds that the granting of "international" status under Ramsar can be an effective method of securing national protection for an unprotected site. He pointed to Lake Burano and Valle Cavanata as examples of listed wetlands which were privately owned and unprotected by Italian law but which were saved from proposed development by their designation under the Convention — not because listing the sites under Ramsar automatically protected them under Italian law, but because listing under Ramsar provided the necessary political stimulus to get the sites protected.[28] Canada has also adopted this approach and, in view of the size of the areas involved, her action takes on special significance. Almost one million hectares of the Canadian wetlands added to the List in 1982 do not yet have any special protection from developments under Canadian law.[29] Greece and Australia have also included unprotected wetlands in the List, and several Australian sites have subsequently received statutory protection at the national level.[30]

[25] See Cagliari Conference Doc. CONF/4, para. 24.
[26] See U.K. national report to the Cagliari Conference, p. 2.
[27] See Cagliari Conference Doc. CONF/4, para. 57.
[28] See *Report on the Cagliari Conference*, note 11 above, para. 25.
[29] See *Canadian Sites Designated as Wetlands of International Importance* (Canadian Wildlife Service, 24 May 1982).
[30] See Groningen Conference Doc. C2.6, paras. 67-68.

Although the Cagliari criteria do not specifically indicate which approach should be adopted, they imply that Parties should list biologically suitable wetlands irrespective of whether they already enjoy protection under domestic legislation. Section 4 of the Heiligenhafen criteria recommended that a wetland should only be designated under Ramsar if it was capable of being effectively conserved and was unlikely to be seriously damaged by land use or external pollution, and this was used by advocates of the "protected area only" approach to justify their position. The Cagliari criteria, however, which otherwise closely reflect the substance of the Heiligenhafen criteria, omit any provision similar to Section 4. This omission, especially when viewed in the context of Article 3(1) of the Convention which requires Parties to "promote the conservation of wetlands included in the List" and the proven success of several Parties in achieving such conservation by listing both protected and unprotected sites, suggests that Parties should now list biologically suitable wetlands even if they are not protected under domestic laws or regulations.

d) *Consequences of including a wetland in the List*

The legal obligations established by Ramsar with respect to sites included in the List are few. The Convention states that Parties shall formulate and implement their planning so as to "promote" the conservation of listed sites,[31] shall "promote" the establishment and adequate wardening of nature reserves thereon[32] and shall inform IUCN, in its capacity as Bureau, of any changes or likely changes in their ecological character.[33] If IUCN is so informed, the next Conference of the Parties has the competence to consider the information submitted.[34]

i) *Weaknesses*

From a strictly legal viewpoint, these provisions are weakly drafted. Requiring Parties to "promote" the conservation of listed sites by formulating and implementing their planning accordingly, to "promote" the establishment of nature reserves and to inform IUCN of any changes in the ecological character of listed sites does not legally oblige Parties to ensure that wetlands included in the List are actually protected nor does it oblige them to prohibit activities which will change, or are likely to change, their ecological

[31] Ramsar, Article 3(1).
[32] *Ibid.*, Article 4(1).
[33] *Ibid.*, Article 3(2).
[34] *Ibid.*, Article 6(2)(c).

character. Furthermore, by the time a Conference of the Parties meets to consider information submitted in relation to such changes or likely changes, it may well be too late to do anything about them.

ii)   *Promotion of conservation*

In spite of the weaknesses in the legal terminology used by Ramsar, there is no doubt that the Convention has had a positive impact on the conservation of numerous wetlands included in the List. The West German delegation to the Groningen Conference reported that Ramsar had had "a spectacular effect" at the listed site of the Rhine between Eltville and Bingen where a planned road bridge spanning the site had been re-routed, and the Italian delegation referred to the important impact of Ramsar on the recent decision to conserve habitat at the Stagno di Molentargius.[35] In 1979 a proposal to allow commercial development of Lake Haleji, a Wildlife Sanctuary in Pakistan listed under Ramsar in 1976, was withdrawn "owing to the international recognition of this lake as a wetland of international importance for waterfowl."[36] The Greek delegation told the Cagliari Conference that a project to reclaim the whole of Lake Mitrikou had been abandoned because it was listed under Ramsar and that a proposed leather factory at Visthonis Lake was switched to a site fifty kilometres away for the same reasons. The East German delegation told the Cagliari Conference that Ramsar had been responsible for securing an extension of the Darss wetland to include the site used by cranes and geese during their autumn migration from their Scandinavian nesting grounds.[37]

In 1976 Ramsar helped protect the Ouse Washes in the U.K. The Washes were threatened by the plans of the local Water Authority to dam the River Ouse, which would have caused incursion of tidal water from the sea and damaged the vegetation of the area and its suitability for waterfowl. When it was pointed out that the Ouse Washes were listed under Ramsar, the plans were changed to maintain a flow of fresh water to the area.[38] In September 1982 the U.K. government informed IUCN that a drainage pump affecting part of Hickling Broad and Horsey Mere, another listed site, would "be re-located to a site where ochre, salt and nitrogen-rich water would be released downstream rather than

[35] See Groningen Conference Plen. C2.4 (Rev.1).
[36] See Cagliari Conference Doc. CONF/4, para. 55. See also Groningen Conference Plen. C2.4 (Rev.1).
[37] See *Report on the Cagliari Conference*, note 11 above, para. 25.
[38] See Cagliari Conference Doc. CONF/4, para. 57.

upstream of the Ramsar site".[39] The U.K. also informed IUCN that where it had been unable to prevent drainage pumps from affecting other parts of the same site, "the possibility of taking legal proceedings ... will have to be considered".[40]

The latter two examples raise an important point since most wetlands are affected by factors operating over a much larger area than the site itself, and the U.K. is one of the few Parties to have enacted legislation to counteract threats to wetlands originating outside as well as inside the site. The U.K.'s Wildlife and Countryside Act requires Water Authorities to consult the Nature Conservancy Council, except in an emergency, before carrying out work or operations likely to destroy or damage wildlife in areas which they have been notified are of special wildlife interest, even if the work takes place outside the area.[41] The Act also requires Water Authorities to "further the conservation...of flora, fauna and geological and physiographical features of special interest" when they formulate or consider proposals relating to the discharge of their functions.[42] Other Parties would do well to consider taking similar legislative or administrative measures to protect their wetlands from harmful activities originating from a point outside the wetland boundaries.

iii)   *Establishment of nature reserves*

At the time of the Cagliari Conference more than 80% of wetlands in the List were wholly or partly within nature reserves or other protected areas, but Australia, Denmark, the Federal Republic of Germany, the U.K. and the U.S.S.R. have all established new nature reserves or extended existing reserves on listed sites since the date of their inclusion in the List.[43]

iv)   *Notification of changes or likely changes in the ecological character of listed sites*

Very little information has been formally submitted to IUCN on changes in the ecological character of listed wetlands. Only Denmark, Tunisia and the U.K. acknowledged detrimental changes

[39]   This quotation was taken from a letter sent by J.C. Goldsmith, Chief, Wildlife Division, Department of the Environment, to IUCN on 3 September 1982.

[40]   See note 39 above. Any legal proceedings would be brought pursuant to the Wildlife and Countryside Act, 1981, which implements the Convention in the U.K.

[41]   Wildlife and Countryside Act, 1981 section 48(3).

[42]   *Ibid.*, section 48(1).

[43]   See Cagliari Conference Doc. CONF/4, para. 49. See also Minutes of the 27th Executive Board Meeting of the International Waterfowl Research Bureau, 27 October 1981, Item 8(1) at p. 12.

or likely changes in their national reports to the Groningen Conference. However, information made available to IUCN and IWRB from other sources suggests that there have been changes for the worse to the ecological character of listed sites in several other Parties. IUCN and IWRB have received reports of potential changes to three of Austria's five recently designated wetlands,[44] of pollution in Pakistan's Lake Kheshki caused by a nearby paper mill[45] and of a reclamation project adversely affecting Quinto do Ludo in Portugal.[46] A "Review of Developments since the Cagliari Conference", prepared for the Groningen Conference, describes the situation in Greece as "extremely disturbing" with reports of major development projects in many wetlands including Mikra Prespa (which has National Park status) and Amvrakikos Gulf (described as "one of the most important Mediterranean wetlands with excellent potential as a national park").[47] This Review also reports that

> the famed Djoudj national park [in Senegal] will be severely affected by the construction of the Diama dam, due to be completed in about 1986. Unless major repairs and reconstruction work is carried out on the sluices and embankments — at a cost of several million dollars — the whole site will be submerged and the alternation of flooding and drying out, essential to its ecosystem, will be totally lost. The second Senegalese site, the N'daiel depression, has been deprived of water for several years because the principal water inlet was blocked during hydro-agricultural development work.[48]

On a more positive note, it should be pointed out that these examples comprise a small proportion of the 294 sites listed and that the ecological character of some Ramsar sites has actually improved since listing. The Coto Donana in Spain was badly affected in the 1960s and 1970s, prior to its designation under Ramsar, by agricultural projects which deprived the area of two thirds of its water supply. A Water Regeneration Plan was approved in 1983 which will restore much of the original water supply. According to the "Review of Developments since the Cagliari Conference", this project "must be regarded as one of the wetland events of the 1980s".[49] Comparable in importance is the plan to restore Lake Hornborga in Sweden by substantially increasing the water level.

---

[44] See Groningen Conference Doc. C2.6, para. 81.
[45] *Ibid.*, para 88.
[46] *Ibid.*, para 89.
[47] *Ibid.*, para 83.
[48] *Ibid.*, para 90.
[49] *Ibid.*, para 92.

Due to begin in 1985, the restoration work is scheduled for completion by 1987.[50]

v) *Geographical scope*

Ramsar's requirement that Parties shall "formulate and implement their planning so as to promote the conservation of the wetlands included in the List" raises an interesting question with respect to the geographical scope of the obligation thereby imposed. Are Parties required only to formulate and implement their planning so as to promote the conservation of wetlands situated within their own territories or are they required to do this for wetlands situated within the territories of other Parties as well? This question, which also arises in the context of the Convention on the Conservation of European Wildlife and Natural Habitats,[51] is of more than academic importance since many activities adversely affecting wetlands are carried out with the aid of finance or personnel originating outside the State in whose territory the wetland is situated. A Technical Review of Ramsar, specially prepared by IWRB for the Cagliari Conference, reported that two listed sites — Ichkeul in Tunisia and Djoudj in Senegal — were threatened by development financed by aid from foreign States. The Review states:

> At Ichkeul, dams are being built on feeder rivers outside the designated area with aid from other countries; unless some dammed water is released, the ecological character of the site will be gravely affected. At Djoudj, diking of the Senegal River with outside help has already destroyed natural wetlands complementary to Djoudj, and the proposed dam across the river downstream from Djoudj will have further far-reaching effects.[52]

In view of the fact that Parties are required to formulate and implement their planning so as to promote the conservation of wetlands in *the* List, as opposed to in *their* List or wetlands *designated by them* in the List, it is certainly arguable that the Parties' obligations do extend to all listed sites irrespective of where they are situated. Measures which Parties might take to promote the conservation of wetlands situated beyond their borders include the control of trans-frontier pollution and the attachment of environmental safeguards to development projects financed by their foreign aid contributions.

---

[50] *Ibid.*, para 93.
[51] See Chapter 8 at pp. 145-149 above.
[52] See Cagliari Conference Doc. CONF/4, para 81.

3.   *The conservation of wetlands in general, including non-listed sites*

a)   *Wise use of all wetlands*

Article 3(1) of Ramsar requires the Parties to "formulate and implement their planning so as to promote...as far as possible the wise use of wetlands in their territory" whether or not they are included in the List. The term "wise use" is not defined, but the preamble to Recommendation 1.5 of the Cagliari Conference states that "wise use of wetlands involves maintenance of their ecological character, as a basis not only for nature conservation, but for sustainable development". This recognition of the need to maintain the ecological character of a wetland as part and parcel of any development project represents a major advance from the widespread traditional practice of subsidised drainage.

Aware that "the establishment of comprehensive national policies would benefit the wise use of wetlands", the Cagliari Conference called on Parties "to prepare inventories of their wetlands and of their resources as soon as possible as an aid to the formulation and implementation of national wetland policies".[53] National reports submitted to the Cagliari and Groningen Conferences indicate that about half the Parties have made systematic inventories of important wetlands within their territories.[54] Fewer have drawn up a formal national policy on the wise use of wetlands, although some have taken steps in that direction.[55] Italy has adopted a particularly strong line. The Italian report to the Cagliari Conference states that no wetlands have been drained for agricultural purposes since Ramsar came into force in Italy, that the policy of drainage for such purposes ("*bonifica*") has been abandoned and that wetlands are now regarded as areas to be protected in relation to land use planning.[56]

Although the provisions of the Convention with respect to the wise use of wetlands are rather vague, they have helped to protect at least one site which was neither in the List nor protected by national law. In 1979 the Nature Conservancy Council, the U.K. government's official scientific advisory body, purchased 2,300 hectares of the Ribble Estuary to protect them from reclamation and diking for agricultural purposes because it acknowledged that the proposed development would have constituted a violation of the U.K.'s obligation to promote the "wise use" of all wetlands.[57]

[53]   Cagliari Conference, Recommendation 1.5.
[54]   See Groningen Conference Doc. C2.6, paras. 103-121 and *Summary of National Reports Submitted by Contracting Parties*, Cagliari Conference Doc. CONF/3, paras. 20-38; see also Cagliari Conference Doc. CONF/4, paras. 40-45.
[55]   See documents referred to in note 54 above.
[56]   See Italian national report to the Cagliari Conference, p. 2.
[57]   See Cagliari Conference Doc. CONF/3, para. 46.

b) *Establishment of nature reserves*

Article 4(1) requires Parties to establish nature reserves on non-listed as well as listed wetlands, and the reports submitted to the Cagliari Conference by Finland, Hungary, Iceland, Norway, Pakistan, Poland and the U.K. all give details of nature reserves established on non-listed sites. For example, eleven Hungarian wetlands comprising some 54,000 hectares which are not in the List have been made nature conservation areas. Four non-listed wetlands totalling 20,149 hectares have been set aside as nature reserves in Iceland, and in Pakistan 347,300 hectares of wetlands over and above those included in the List have been designated "Game Sanctuaries" under provincial wildlife legislation.[58] Since the Cagliari Conference, two unlisted wetlands under threat at the time of the Conference — Oostvaardersplassen in the Netherlands and Blar nam Faoileag in the U.K. — have been protected. In 1981 the Netherlands Government agreed to create a nature reserve of 5650 hectares in Oostvaardersplassen, an action which was hailed by Dutch conservationists as one of the most important decisions in the conservation field for many years.[59] Blar nam Faoileag is a blanket bog which was threatened by drainage in 1980, but the U.K.'s Nature Conservancy Council subsequently received funds enabling it to negotiate a renewable 99 year lease.[60]

4. *Research, training and cooperation*

Article 4(3) of Ramsar requires the Parties to "encourage research and the exchange of data and publications regarding wetlands and their flora and fauna", and Article 4(5) requires them to "promote the training of personnel competent in the fields of wetland research, management and wardening." Primarily because of pleas by Senegal and Tunisia that the developing world needs financial and technical assistance in those fields, the Cagliari Conference recommended that Parties and appropriate international aid organisations should help developing countries establish training programmes.[61]

Ramsar appears to have stimulated considerable progress with respect to both research and training. Most national reports submitted to the Cagliari and Groningen Conferences describe research programmes under way and refer to publications making research results available. In the Federal Republic of Germany and

[58] See Cagliari Conference Doc. CONF/4, paras. 39-50.
[59] See *IWRB Bulletin* No. 47 (IWRB, December 1981), p. 82.
[60] See Groningen Conference Doc. C2.6, para. 123.
[61] Cagliari Conference, Recommendation 1.2.

the German Democratic Republic, scientific conferences on wetland conservation have been held and information booklets on wetlands have been published.[62] Most Parties also reported that they are operating training programmes, and Jordan indicated an intention to send staff abroad for training.[63] Tunisia has agreed to host a field course on wetland conservation and waterfowl management for North and West Africa, and UNESCO is preparing a similar training seminar for neotropical wetlands management in Everglades National Park in the U.S.A.[64] National reports refer mainly to training opportunities for Parties' own citizens, in spite of the Cagliari Conference recommendation that richer Parties should help developing countries establish training programmes. However, the Hungarian report to the Groningen Conference indicated that Hungary would be happy to take part in training programmes for developing countries if requested. The U.K. report also stated that any request from a developing country involving conservation of wetlands and waterfowl, including requests for training, would be considered on its merits subject to availability of funds.[65]

With respect to cooperation, Article 5 requires Parties to

> ...consult with each other about implementing obligations from the Convention especially in the case of a wetland extending over the territories of more than one Contracting Party or where a water system is shared by Contracting Parties. They shall at the same time endeavour to coordinate and support present and future policies and regulations concerning the conservation of wetlands and their flora and fauna.

The best example of such cooperation is probably the joint efforts of Denmark, Netherlands and the Federal Republic of Germany to protect the Wadden Sea.

5.   *Conservation and development*

Disturbed by reports of development threats to many Ramsar sites and other internationally important wetlands,[66] and concerned that conservation is often inadequately considered in development planning, the Cagliari Conference recommended that "any projected large-scale wetland transformation" be delayed until "an assessment of all values involved has been made" and that "ecologists be involved in the planning process".[67]

[62] See Cagliari Conference Doc. CONF/3, para. 51.

[63] *Ibid.*, para 53.

[64] See Groningen Conference Doc. C2.6, para. 142.

[65] *Ibid.*, para. 141.

[66] See Cagliari Conference, Preamble to Recommendation 1.6.; see also *Report on the Cagliari Conference*, note 11 above, para. 29.

[67] Cagliari Conference, Recommendation 1.6.

Several Parties have already enacted national legislation requiring assessments of the likely environmental effects of major development projects prior to their construction, and others are planning similar legislation.[68] Furthermore, an environmental impact assessment has already been carried out in relation to the development of at least one Ramsar site — Ichkeul in Tunisia — where the government is building dams on tributary rivers which will affect the water supply and salinity in the lake and marshes.[69] Acceptance of the need for such assessments during the planning stages of a development project is an important precedent in the field of international wildlife law because it ensures that conservation values are identified at a time when something can still be done rather than after the project has started when major changes may be difficult to make.

6. *Priorities for action*

Recognising that guidelines on practical measures for implementing Ramsar would be useful to Parties, the Groningen Conference discussed a document entitled "Framework for Implementing the Convention".[70] This document outlined thirty steps for Parties to consider, varying from national measures such as the "development of a nationwide inventory of wetlands" to international measures such as the "development of international or regional databases to monitor the conservation situation of wetlands" and the "provision of special assistance to developing countries".

Taking note of the points raised in the Framework Document, the Groningen Conference decided that certain measures were of particular importance. The Conference therefore passed a resolution urging Parties to give priority attention to seven "Action Points". These Action Points, which are likely to determine the direction taken by Parties in their implementation of Ramsar over the next few years, are:

1) Elaboration of a system of wetland classification or typology;
2) Preparation of a standard data sheet on wetlands and of guidelines for its use in wetland inventories;

[68] See, for example, Canada's Government Organisation Act of 1979 and Japan's Basic Law for Environmental Pollution Control, No. 132 of 1967, as amended. Similar legislation is planned in the Federal Republic of Germany and the Netherlands, and a draft Directive to apply to all member States of the European Economic Community has been prepared.

[69] A major study, financed jointly by the French government, the EEC Commission and University College London, has been set up to assess the effect of the dam and to propose compensatory measures. See *Note on Wetland Conservation Measures Carried Out in the Framework of the Ramsar Convention since the Cagliari Conference*, Paris Conference Doc. E1. Inf.1, para. 15.

[70] Groningen Conference, CRP C2.3 (Annex).

3) Development of common criteria for evaluating the importance of wetlands at local, national or international level; and, in particular, expansion of the existing Cagliari Criteria to cover also ecological factors concerning life forms other than waterfowl;

4) Development of a common base for recording and evaluating long-term trends in the ecology of wetlands through monitoring of physical and biological parameters, taking into account the different levels of expertise and support in the various Contracting Parties;

5) Quantification of both direct (monetary) and indirect (non-monetary) values of wetlands and formulation of criteria to enable all values to be taken fully into account in the planning of conservation projects and projects which may lead to changes in the ecological character of wetlands;

6) Development of strategies and techniques for wetland management including measures to enable the retention of natural characteristics of wetland areas before, during and after execution of modification or transformation projects; and

7) Promotion of increased international cooperation among the Contracting Parties and interested States; in particular, development of a clearing-house function for special assistance for wetland conservation projects in developing countries.[71]

7. The need for more Parties

More than half the thirty six Parties to Ramsar are European, and there is now a relatively comprehensive network of listed wetlands along the Western Palearctic flyway. However, other areas of the world are not so well represented. Canada, Chile and Uruguay are the only American Parties, India and Pakistan are the only representatives from the Indomalayan region, and there are just six African Parties — Algeria, Mauritania, Morocco, Senegal, South Africa and Tunisia. Tropical wetlands, which are of immense importance to thousands of endemic and migratory species, are almost entirely unrepresented in the List. If any sort of network of important wetlands outside the Western Palearctic flyway is to be established under Ramsar, it is essential that Ramsar attracts more Parties. Recognising this, the Cagliari Conference urged existing Parties to "use their good offices with other States...with a view to obtaining their ratification of, or accession to, the Convention". The Conference recommended that special emphasis should be given to tropical regions and to the Americas.[72]

The Cagliari Conference recognised that there are three main problems in attracting more Parties to the Convention. One of these is Ramsar's stipulation that the English text of the Convention shall

[71] *Ibid.*, CRP C2.3.
[72] Cagliari Conference, Recommendation 1.1.

prevail in the case of any divergency between the English, French, German and Russian versions.[73] Several States had indicated that they could not accede to the Convention in these circumstances. The Cagliari Conference therefore recommended that the Parties should adopt a Protocol giving the languages parity.[74] The Paris Conference carried out this recommendation, adopting a Protocol which replaced the words "in any case of divergency the English text [shall prevail]" with "all texts equally authentic".[75] The revised text of the original French version of the Convention was reproduced in an Annex to the Protocol, and the Final Act of the Paris Conference required the Depositary (UNESCO) to prepare official versions of the Convention in Arabic, Chinese and Spanish and official versions of the Protocol in Arabic, Chinese, German, Russian and Spanish. With the exception of the German version of the Protocol, this has now been done.

The Protocol will come into force when two thirds of the Parties to Ramsar at the time of the Paris Conference have deposited instruments of ratification, acceptance or approval of the Protocol. Seventeen of the required 22 instruments of ratification, acceptance or approval have been deposited at the time of writing. The French observer told the Paris Conference that the adoption of the Protocol would enable France to accede to Ramsar and that the Camargue would be the first French wetland to be included in the List.[76] France acceded to the Protocol in August 1984 and will become a Party to the Convention when the Protocol comes into force.

The second problem is that Ramsar contains no amendment procedure. The Cagliari Conference recognised that a number of amendments to the Convention would be desirable,[77] so the Protocol adopted by the Paris Conference duly established an amendment procedure.[78] The Groningen Conference was unable to make any amendments because the Protocol was not yet in force, but it established a "Task Force" to consider and recommend future amendments.[79]

[73] Ramsar, Article 12.

[74] Cagliari Conference, Recommendation 1.7(1).

[75] Protocol to Amend the Convention on Wetlands of International Importance especially as Waterfowl Habitat, Article 2 (hereinafter referred to as Protocol to the Convention). The text of the Protocol is reprinted in *Convention on Wetlands of International Importance especially as Waterfowl Habitat, Extraordinary Conference of the Contracting Parties, Paris, France, 2-3 December 1982* (IUCN, 1982).

[76] See "Summary Report of the Plenary Sessions", *Convention on Wetlands of International Importance especially as Waterfowl Habitat, Extraordinary Conference of the Contracting Parties, Paris, France, 2-3 December 1982* (IUCN, 1982) p. 7.

[77] Cagliari Conference, Recommendation 1.7(2).

[78] Protocol to the Convention, note 75 above, Article 1.

[79] See pp. 204-206 below.

The third problem facing a wider participation in Ramsar, especially by the developing countries, concerns finance. Ramsar makes no provisions for financial contributions from its Parties either to help developing countries implement the objectives of the Convention or for any other purpose. As the delegate from Senegal told the Cagliari Conference, "there are too few developing countries in Ramsar because there is nothing in the Convention for them...the Sahel countries would like to sign a Convention which will bring aid. The world wants wetlands saved: poor countries cannot pay."[80] The handful of developing country Parties to Ramsar contrast markedly with the much larger number of developing country Parties to the World Heritage Convention which offers the prospect of financial and technical assistance to countries willing to protect their unique wildlife habitats but lacking the means to do so.[81] The experience of the World Heritage Convention suggests that many more developing countries would also accede to Ramsar if financial and technical assistance for wetland conservation were available.

Ramsar is not intended to be an "aid convention" in the same sense as the World Heritage Convention, but the Cagliari Conference acknowledged the need for poorer Parties to be given material help. The Cagliari Conference therefore recommended that Parties should give financial and technical assistance to developing countries for the purposes of wetland conservation, that aid programmes should help finance environmental impact assessments prior to the implementation of large-scale projects to develop wetlands and that developing countries should pay more attention to wetland conservation in any request for and programming of assistance.[82] The Conference also recommended that consideration should be given to amending the text of Ramsar so as to authorise meetings of the Parties to provide financial resources for any purpose that they deem to be appropriate.[83] The whole question of financial and technical assistance to developing countries was also discussed at the Groningen Conference, and the last of the "Action Points" adopted by the Conference urges "development of a clearing-house function for special assistance for wetland conservation projects in developing countries".[84] The Norwegian delegation told the Groningen Conference that environmental components were included within the aid

---

[80] This quotation was taken, with his permission, from the notes of Keith Dow, head of the U.K. delegation to the Cagliari Conference.

[81] See Chapter 11 below.

[82] Cagliari Conference, Recommendations 1.2. and 1.6.

[83] Cagliari Conference, Recommendation 1.8(3).

[84] See p. 200 above.

programmes of more and more industrialised nations, that Norway had £100,000 available for environmental support grants but that specific requests were needed and few had been received so far. The Dutch delegation reported the establishment of a small fund in the Netherlands for which applications were awaited and pointed out that UNEP had a new Clearing House Fund for environmental projects.[85]

These attempts to overcome the obstacles to a wider participation in Ramsar have proved moderately successful in that the number of Parties has increased, albeit slowly, since the Cagliari Conference, and Belgium, France and Costa Rica pledged to the Groningen Conference that they would soon become Parties. Six other States (Chad, Finland, Malawi, Mali, Nigeria and the U.S.A.) said they would give active consideration to becoming Parties in the near future.[86] However, the need for a major recruitment effort remains, especially in States with tropical wetlands, if Ramsar is to develop to anything like its full potenital.

8. *Administration*

The only significant administrative provisions of Ramsar are that Conferences of the Parties shall be convened "as the necessity arises"[87] and that IUCN shall be a temporary, unpaid "Bureau".[88] Ramsar imposes no obligation on Parties to submit periodic reports on their implementation of the Convention. Neither does it provide for the establishment of a scientific committee to coordinate research or to make appropriate recommendations on wetland conservation. Indeed the Federal Republic of Germany, although a Party to Ramsar, has not enacted any implementing legislation on the grounds that the Convention imposes no financial commitment for which consultation with the German legislature would be necessary and no administrative burden for which new laws would be required.

a) *Bureau*

The duties of the Bureau are comparable to those of the Secretariat under CITES, the World Heritage Convention and the Bonn Convention but are more limited. The only official requirements made of IUCN in its capacity as Bureau are to maintain the List, to assist in convening Conferences of the Parties,

---

[85] Groningen Conference Plen. C2.4 (Rev.1).
[86] *Ibid.*, Plen. C2.3 (Rev.1).
[87] Ramsar, Article 6(1).
[88] *Ibid.*, Article 8(1).

to receive official notifications of changes in the List or of changes in the ecological character of listed sites, to notify the Parties of such changes and to arrange for discussion of any changes at the next Conference of the Parties.[89]

The main practical difference, however, between the Bureau under Ramsar and the Secretariats provided for by the other three Conventions is that the former is temporary and unpaid while the latter are permanent and paid. The fact that Ramsar has been able to progress at all has been entirely due to the generosity of a few Party governments, who have hosted Conferences of the Parties and have made financial contributions to the Bureau on a voluntary basis, and to the time and money made available by IUCN, IWRB and other international organisations. IUCN and IWRB, in particular, have made tremendous efforts to help the Convention in spite of having to meet most of the costs involved themselves. However, given resources and a degree of permanency, there is no doubt that the Bureau would be able to play an even more effective role in improving the implementation of Ramsar, and in attracting more Parties to it, in the same way as the Secretariats to CITES and the World Heritage Convention have done.[90]

Recognising that the present situation is unsatisfactory, the Cagliari Conference recommended that as soon as the Protocol establishing an amendment procedure was in force a further Protocol should be adopted which, among other things, would establish a permanent Secretariat with wider duties including the authority to make recommendations to improve implementation of Ramsar.[91] The Cagliari Conference went on to recommend that this further Protocol should authorise meetings of the Parties to provide financial resources for the operation of the Secretariat[92] and that Parties should give "sympathetic consideration" to making voluntary contributions to IUCN to enable it to continue to perform its interim Bureau duties.[93] The Groningen Conference also urged Parties and international organisations concerned with wetland conservation "to give careful consideration to the possibilities of finding financial or other means to support the interim secretariat to the Convention."[94]

---

[89] *Ibid.*, Article 8(2).
[90] See Chapters 11 and 12 below.
[91] Cagliari Conference, Recommendation 1.8(6).
[92] *Ibid.*, 1.8(3).
[93] *Ibid.*, 1.10.
[94] Groningen Conference, CRP C2.4.

b)   *National reports*

Ramsar does not require its Parties to submit periodic reports on their implementation of the Convention, although most Parties responded to requests by the Bureau to submit such reports to the Cagliari and Groningen Conferences. Recognising the importance of these reports for purposes of monitoring implementation of the Convention and recognising the need for them to be submitted well in advance of Conferences of the Parties to enable the Bureau to prepare a review of them, the Groningen Conference recommended that all Parties should submit detailed national reports to the Bureau at least six months prior to each ordinary meeting of the Conference of the Parties. The Conference also recommended that a simplified questionnaire should be produced with a view to making reports easier to prepare while at the same time ensuring that they reveal the information desired.[95]

c)   *Meetings of the Parties*

Neither does Ramsar require its Parties to meet regularly to review implementation of the Convention, although the fact that one extraordinary and two ordinary Conferences have been held illustrates that Parties are well aware of the value of such meetings. Recognising the need to regularise these *ad hoc* Conferences, the Cagliari Conference recommended that the further Protocol, referred to in a) above, should also provide for "periodic ordinary meetings" of the Parties[96] and for the attendance of observers "especially from international non-governmental organisations" at such meetings.[97]

The importance of regular meetings of Parties to any wildlife treaty cannot be over-emphasised, especially when they are attended by non-governmental organisations as observers. Not only do they enable Parties to review implementation of the treaty and to take action to improve it but they serve to publicise and stimulate interest in its objectives. The Cagliari Conference, for example, led directly to several States becoming Parties to Ramsar. After an initial spate of ratifications and accessions between 1975 and 1977, little progress was made until shortly before the Cagliari Conference when Japan, the Netherlands, Morocco, Tunisia and Portugal acceded. Delegates representing Algeria, Canada, Chile and India told the Cagliari Conference that their governments intended to ratify or

[95] *Ibid.*, CRP C2.1.
[96] Cagliari Conference, Recommendation 1.8(1).
[97] *Ibid.*, 1.8(2).

accede in the near future,[98] and they all did so soon afterwards. Equally, there was a significant increase in the number and area of wetlands in the List shortly after the Cagliari Conference and, if promises are kept, there is likely to be a similar rise after Groningen.

d) Proposed amendments to Ramsar

Reference has already been made to the numerous recommendations made by the Cagliari Conference for amending the text of Ramsar as soon as the Protocol establishing an amendment procedure has come into force. The Netherlands government incorporated these recommendations into draft proposals for amending the Convention and presented them to the Groningen Conference. The proposals were discussed at length but were eventually referred for further consideration to a Task Force, consisting of representatives of six Parties, which will report back to the next ordinary Conference of the Parties.

9. Conclusion

Ramsar was the first conservation treaty to aim for a truly worldwide participation,[99] and it was the first to concern itself exclusively with habitat. Earlier treaties such as the African Convention and the Western Hemisphere Convention both contained provisions pertaining to habitat, but they concentrated on species protection as well. Furthermore Ramsar's attitude to habitat conservation is quite different to that of the earlier treaties. While the latter emphasised the establishment of strictly protected areas for wildlife, Ramsar leans towards a policy of "wise use" rather than "hands off". Although Ramsar acknowledges the need for nature reserves, it does not regulate hunting, trapping or fishing on wetlands in its List, and the only restriction on agricultural or other usage is that it should not harm the "ecological character" of a wetland. Ramsar is therefore very much in line with the concept of sustainable development which may be rather more acceptable than absolute protection in the modern world.

There is no doubt that Ramsar has deficiencies when compared with the other three conventions considered in Part IV of this book, particularly with regard to the small number of Parties from the tropical regions and the lack of a well financed administrative

---

[98] See Report on the Cagliari Conference, note 11 above, para. 21.

[99] The International Convention for the Regulation of Whaling was concluded 25 years before Ramsar, and any State may become a Party to it. However, until recently, only States interested in whaling participated in the Convention, and it was never aimed at such a broad range of States as Ramsar.

machinery to promote its implementation. However, it should be remembered that Ramsar was concluded before the other three conventions, which to a certain extent have been able to learn from Ramsar's mistakes. In addition, Ramsar has achieved some impressive practical results in spite of its deficiencies, and when the procedure for amending the Convention comes into force, as it soon will, the Parties will have every opportunity to make the necessary changes to improve its financial and administrative arrangements and to entice more States to accede to it. It is imperative that the Parties seize this chance if significant further progress is to be made.

CHAPTER 11

THE CONVENTION CONCERNING THE PROTECTION OF THE WORLD CULTURAL AND NATURAL HERITAGE
(THE "WORLD HERITAGE CONVENTION")

"Deterioration or disappearance of any item of the cultural or natural heritage constitutes a harmful impoverishment of the heritage of all nations of the world."
(Preamble to the World Heritage Convention)

1. *Background*

The Convention Concerning the Protection of the World Cultural and Natural Heritage (the "World Heritage Convention")[1] was adopted at the General Conference of the United Nations Educational, Scientific and Cultural Organization ("UNESCO") on 16 November 1972 and came into force on 17 December 1975.[2] Its origins can be traced to two separate but related factors. The first is that by 1972 the international community was becoming increasingly receptive to the concept of a "common heritage". In the context of the Convention this concept maintains that there are certain outstanding natural and man-made features such as the Serengeti or the Pyramids, the Galapagos Islands or the Taj Mahal, which are more than the heritage of just one State. They constitute part of the heritage of all people, and mankind as a whole has certain rights with respect to their conservation. The second factor is that by 1972 the international community had shown itself willing to take positive action to help protect these sites. When the Nubian monuments of the Upper Nile, including the 30 foot high statue of Ramses II at Abu Simbel, were threatened by flooding in 1960 as a result of the newly constructed Aswan High Dam, the response of the international community was prompt, and international campaigns were organised by UNESCO and others to save the famous monuments from destruction.[3] On the natural side, the International Union for Conservation of Nature and Natural Resources ("IUCN") was active in the 1950s and 1960s in securing

---

[1] 11 *I.L.M.* 1358; *T.I.A.S.* no. 8226; 27 *U.S.T.* 37.
[2] Pursuant to Article 33, the Convention entered into force three months after the twentieth country had deposited an instrument of ratification, acceptance or accession.
[3] See *Protection of Mankind's Cultural Heritage, Sites and Monuments* (UNESCO, 1970), pp. 39-60.

protection for important natural habitats, aided by the financial support of a variety of governments, companies and individuals. As the threats grew, however, it became increasingly evident that a permanent legal, administrative and financial framework for the identification and conservation of areas of outstanding cultural and natural importance would greatly assist the *ad hoc* efforts of UNESCO, IUCN and others.[4]

The World Heritage Convention provides such a framework. Its objective is the protection of natural and cultural areas of "outstanding universal value", and it established a World Heritage Committee, a World Heritage List, a List of World Heritage in Danger and a World Heritage Fund to help it achieve its goal. The World Heritage Committee is responsible for selecting cultural and natural sites of outstanding universal value and for including them in the World Heritage List or, if they are seriously threatened, in the List of World Heritage in Danger. The Committee is also responsible for using the money in the World Heritage Fund to help protect sites which have been or may be included in either of the World Heritage Lists. Each Party is required to contribute to the Fund according to the level of its contribution to the regular budget of UNESCO, which means that most of the money in the Fund is provided by a relatively few wealthy States and that the financial burden on developing countries is very small. The Convention imposes a legal duty on each Party to do its utmost to protect sites which have been included in the World Heritage Lists.

The value of the World Heritage Convention for wildlife will always be limited because the objective of the Convention is to protect only the world's most select cultural and natural areas. Natural habitats which contain some interesting animals and plants but are not of exceptional significance will not benefit, at least directly, from the Convention. However, within these limitations, the Convention has the potential to be of great importance to wildlife. The World Heritage Lists provide a mechanism for giving international recognition to some of the most outstanding natural habitats in the world, and the World Heritage Fund offers poorer Parties the prospect of receiving financial and technical assistance, worth far more than their own contributions to the Fund, to help them protect these areas. The World Heritage Convention is the only treaty to offer developing countries a material incentive to protect outstanding wildlife habitats.

---

[4] See R. L. Meyer, "Travaux Preparatoires for the UNESCO World Heritage Convention", 2 *Earth Law Journal* 45 (1976), which describes the background to the Convention and the history of its negotiation.

Although it has only been fully operational for a few years, there are already signs that the Convention will prove to be an extremely useful legal conservation instrument. Almost fifty areas of outstanding natural, as opposed to cultural, value have been included in the World Heritage List, and the Convention has already helped protect several of them. The role played by the Convention in halting construction of a dam on the Gordon-below-Franklin river, which would have flooded a large area of temperate rainforest in South West Tasmania, is probably the best known example.

This chapter looks first at the Parties to the World Heritage Convention and goes on to examine various factors relating to the two World Heritage Lists including the criteria and procedures for listing a site and the nature of the Parties' obligations to protect sites once they have been listed. It then considers the system of contribution to the World Heritage Fund and how the resources of the Fund may be used, and finally it examines the structure and operation of the World Heritage Committee. Because of the scope of this book, only those aspects of the Convention which are relevant to areas of natural, rather than cultural, importance are considered.

2. *Parties*

At the time of writing there are 83 Parties to the World Heritage Convention consisting of one Australasian, nineteen Asian, twenty six African, seventeen European and twenty American States.[5] There are three main reasons for the widespread appeal of the Convention: it provides a vehicle for all Parties to gain international recognition for areas of outstanding natural or cultural value situated within their territories; it provides the poorer Parties with the prospect of receiving financial and technical assistance for the protection of these sites; and the administrative structure established by the Convention provides an assurance to the wealthier Parties, whose contributions to the World Heritage Fund are likely to exceed the value of any financial or technical assistance which they may receive, that their money will be effectively spent on the conservation

---

[5] The Parties to the Convention are: Afghanistan, Algeria, Antigua and Barbuda, Argentina, Australia, Bangladesh, Benin, Bolivia, Brazil, Bulgaria, Burundi, Cameroon, Canada, Central African Republic, Chile, Colombia, Costa Rica, Cuba, Cyprus, Democratic Yemen, Denmark, Ecuador, Egypt, Ethiopia, France, Federal Republic of Germany, Ghana, Greece, Guatemala, Guinea, Guyana, Haiti, Holy See, Honduras, India, Iran, Iraq, Italy, Ivory Coast, Jamaica, Jordan, Lebanon, Libya, Luxembourg, Madagascar, Malawi, Mali, Malta, Mauritania, Mexico, Monaco, Morocco, Mozambique, Nepal, Nicaragua, Niger, Nigeria, Norway, Oman, Pakistan, Panama, Peru, Poland, Portugal, Qatar, Saudi Arabia, Senegal, Seychelles, Spain, Sri Lanka, Sudan, Switzerland, Syria, Tanzania, Tunisia, Turkey, U.K., U.S.A., Yemen, Yugoslavia, Zaire, Zambia and Zimbabwe.

of some of the most outstanding cultural and natural sites in the world.

A broad spectrum of Parties is vital to the success of the World Heritage Convention. Support from the industrialised world is essential to the existence of a well-endowed World Heritage Fund, but a large number of Parties from the developing world is equally important, particularly for wildlife, because so many of the world's outstanding natural areas are in the less developed regions. Countries with particularly important wildlife habitats which are not yet Parties include Botswana, Indonesia, Kenya, and Papua New Guinea. Other notable non-Parties from the point of view of the money they would contribute to the Fund or of the large areas within their control include China, Japan and the U.S.S.R.

3. *The World Heritage List*

The first and foremost responsibility of the World Heritage Committee is the compilation of the World Heritage List from sites nominated by the Party in whose territory they are situated. The latter twelve words are important because however much the Committee might think a site worthy of inclusion in the List, it only becomes eligible for selection after the Party in whose territory it is situated has made an appropriate proposal. Only sites situated in States which are Parties to the Convention can be included in the List. The Convention requires the Committee to "establish, keep up to date and publish" the List and to distribute an updated version at least every two years.[6] In practice, an updated version is published after each of the Committee's annual meetings.

One hundred and sixty five sites in 46 States are in the World Heritage List at the time of writing. Of these, 47 were listed wholly or primarily because of their outstanding natural, as opposed to cultural, value. They are: Los Glaciares National Park (Argentina); Kakadu National Park, the Great Barrier Reef, the Willandra Lakes Region, the Western Tasmania Wilderness National Parks and the Lord Howe Island Group (Australia); Srebarna Nature Reserve and Pirin National Park (Bulgaria); Nahanni National Park, Dinosaur Provincial Park, Wood Buffalo National Park and the Burgess Shale Site (Canada); Cape Girolata, Cape Porto and Scandola Nature Reserve (Corsica, France); Talamanca Range-La Amistad Reserves (Costa Rica); the Galapagos Islands and Sangay National Park (Ecuador); Simien National Park (Ethiopia); Tikal National Park (Guatemala); Mount Nimba Strict Nature Reserve (Guinea/Ivory

[6] World Heritage Convention, Article 11(2).

Coast); Rio Platano Biosphere Reserve (Honduras); Tai National Park and Comoe National Park (Ivory Coast); Sagarmatha National Park (Nepal); Darien National Park (Panama); Bialowieza National Park (Poland); Djoudj National Bird Sanctuary and Niokolo-Koba National Park (Senegal); Aldabra Atoll and Vallee de Mai Nature Reserve (Seychelles); Serengeti National Park, Ngorongoro Conservation Area and Selous Game Reserve (Tanzania); Ichkeul National Park (Tunisia); Mammoth Cave National Park, Olympic National Park, Grand Canyon National Park, Redwood National Park, Everglades National Park and Yellowstone National Park (U.S.A); Durmitor National Park and Plitvice Lakes (Yugoslavia); Virunga National Park, Garamba National Park and Kahuzi-Biega National Park (Zaire); and Kluane National Park/Wrangell and St. Elias National Monument, which was nominated jointly by Canada and the U.S.A.

In addition to these sites, Tassili N'Ajjer National Park (Algeria), Santuario Historico de Machu Picchu (Peru) and Lake Ohrid (Yugoslavia) are in the World Heritage List because of their cultural and natural values.

a) *Listing criteria*

(i) *Value of the site*

There are two hurdles to be overcome before a site can be considered worthy of inclusion in the World Heritage List. The first is that the Party in whose territory the site is situated must consider it to be part of the cultural or natural heritage. Articles 1 and 2 of the World Heritage Convention define what shall be considered as cultural or natural heritage for the purposes of the Convention, and Article 3 stipulates that "it is for each State Party to this Convention to identify and delineate the different properties situated on its territory mentioned in Articles 1 and 2". Article 1 is not relevant to this book because it deals only with cultural heritage, but Article 2 is important. It states that sites shall be considered part of the "natural heritage" if they are:

a) natural features consisting of physical and biological formations or groups of such formations, which are of outstanding universal value from the aesthetic or scientific point of view; or
b) geological and physiographical formations and precisely delineated areas which constitute the habitat of threatened species of animals and plants of outstanding universal value from the point of view of science or conservation; or

c) natural sites or precisely delineated natural areas of outstanding universal value from the point of view of science, conservation or natural beauty.

The essence of Article 2 is that only *physical areas* of *outstanding universal value* can qualify. One might argue, for example, that the blue whale (*Baleanoptera musculus*) should be considered part of the world's natural heritage because it is the largest creature ever to have inhabited our planet, but it does not qualify under Article 2 because it is a mobile animal and not immovable property. Similar conditions apply to the cultural heritage which cannot include paintings and other movable works of art.

However, just because a Party deems an area to be part of the natural heritage as defined by Article 2 does not necessarily mean that it will be selected for inclusion in the World Heritage List. The World Heritage Committee is responsible for compiling the List, and Article 11(5) of the Convention requires the Committee to establish criteria on the basis of which a property, deemed by the State in which it is situated to belong to the cultural or natural heritage as defined by Articles 1 and 2, may also be deemed worthy of inclusion in the List. The "Operational Guidelines", which the Committee first adopted in 1979 to guide it in all aspects of its work but which have since been revised,[8] state that sites qualifying under Article 2 will only qualify for the List if they:

(i) [are] outstanding examples representing the <u>major stages of the earth's evolutionary history</u>; or
(ii) [are] outstanding examples representing <u>significant ongoing geological processes, biological evolution and man's interaction with his natural environment</u>; as distinct from the periods of the earth's development, this focuses upon ongoing processes in the development of communities of plants and animals, landforms and marine areas and fresh water bodies; or
(iii) contain <u>superlative natural phenomena, formations or features</u>, for instance, outstanding examples of the most important ecosystems, areas of exceptional natural beauty or exceptional combinations of natural and cultural elements; or
(iv) contain <u>the most important and significant natural habitats where threatened species of animals or plants of outstanding universal value</u> from the point of view of science or conservation still survive.[9]

[7] See Article 1 of the World Heritage Convention and paras. 17-19 of the Operational Guidelines for the Implementation of the World Heritage Convention (Doc. No. WHC/2 Revised (January 1984)). These Guidelines, hereinafter referred to as the Operational Guidelines, may be obtained from UNESCO, 7 Place de Fontenoy, 75700 Paris, France.
[8] The most recent version is Doc. No. WHC/2 Revised (January 1984). See note 7 above.
[9] Operational Guidelines, note 7 above, para. 24. The sections underlined here are also underlined in the Operational Guidelines.

Criterion (iv) is especially interesting from a wildlife viewpoint because it means that an area is eligible for inclusion in the World Heritage List if it is an important habitat for a threatened species of outstanding universal value even if it has no other notable features. Criterion (iv) also presents an interesting problem. By referring to species "of outstanding universal value from the point of view of science or conservation", it implies that some species are of outstanding universal value whilst others are not. Yet who is to say that well known threatened species such as the mountain gorilla (*Gorilla gorilla beringei*) or giant panda (*Ailuropoda melanoleuca*) are more important for science and conservation than the tiny snail darter (*Percina tanasi*) in the Tennessee river or an undiscovered species of mouse? One might argue that a species such as the aye aye (*Daubentonia madagascariensis*) is particularly important since it is the only species in an endangered family of mammals (Daubentonidae), whereas the mountain gorilla is only a sub-species and mice and snail darters belong to prolific genera which speciate readily. Or one could claim that the mountain gorilla is especially valuable because tourists will pay to come and see it and their money pays for the protection of a habitat which is also important for other less glamorous species. The Operational Guidelines do not address the problem and, in practice, the Committee appears to have adopted the line that all species are of outstanding universal value. For example, Virunga National Park and Kahuzi-Biega National Park in Zaire were included in the World Heritage List at least in part because they contain important habitat for mountain gorillas.[10] However, Mount Nimba Strict Nature Reserve in Guinea was listed partly because of its importance to less well known endemic species such as the viviparous toad and dwarf African otter shrew.[11] Darien National Park in Panama, "the best available example of Central American rainforest ecosystems", was listed at least in part because "scientific opinion is that thousands of species remain to be discovered, and that many of these will prove to be endemic to Darien".[12] Most of these undiscovered endemics are certain to be "unglamorous" insects and plants.

(ii)   *Integrity*

The Operational Guidelines also insist that a site must fulfil certain "conditions of integrity" before it can qualify for inclusion in the World Heritage List.

[10] See *Nature and Resources*, Vol. XV, No. 4, October-December 1979, p. 22.
[11] See *IUCN Technical Review for 1981*, No. 155, para. 5 (available from IUCN, 1196 Gland, Switzerland).
[12] *Ibid.*, No. 159, paras. 8 and 5.

They vary according to which of the four criteria a particular site is deemed to meet, but the essence of the conditions is that a site must be large enough to include the key components of the process it represents and to be self-perpetuating.[13] For example, the Operational Guidelines state that an area of tropical rainforest nominated for inclusion under criterion (ii) "may be expected to include some variation in elevation above sea level, changes in topography and soil types, river banks or oxbow lakes, to demonstrate the diversity and complexity of the system."[14] An area proposed for inclusion under criterion (iv) "should be of sufficient size and contain necessary habitat requirements for the survival of the species."[15] Thus, in recommending Panama's Darien National Park for inclusion in the List on the basis that it satisfied criteria (ii) (iii) and (iv),[16] IUCN advised the Committee that the Park is "sufficiently large to ensure the continuation of evolutionary processes and the survival of the endangered species contained therein."[17] In the case of sites nominated for their importance to migratory species,

> ...seasonable sites necessary for their survival, wherever they are located, should be adequately protected. The Committee must receive assurances that the necessary measures be taken to ensure that the species are adequately protected throughout their full life cycle. Agreements made in this connection, either through adherence to international conventions or in the form of other multilateral or bilateral arrangements would provide this assurance.[18]

Finally, the Guidelines require that an adequate "buffer zone" around a property should be established and protected whenever necessary for the conservation of a nominated site.[19]

(iii) State of protection

Neither the Convention nor the Operational Guidelines insist that a site need be a protected area such as a national park or a nature reserve in order to qualify for inclusion in the World Heritage List, although the Guidelines stipulate that the nomination file of a

---

[13] Operational Guidelines, note 7 above, para. 25.

[14] Ibid., para. 25(ii).

[15] Ibid., para. 25(iv).

[16] See The World's Greatest Natural Areas, An Indicative Inventory of Natural Sites of World Heritage Quality (IUCN, 1982), p. 66; see also IUCN Technical Review for 1981, No. 156, paras. 5-8.

[17] IUCN Technical Review for 1981, No. 159, para. 6.

[18] Operational Guidelines, note 7 above, para. 25(v).

[19] Ibid., para. 14.

property which is under threat should include "an action plan outlining the corrective measures required" and that if the corrective measures are not taken within the proposed time by the Party concerned "the property will be considered by the Committee for delisting."[20]

As under Ramsar, some Parties have apparently decided only to nominate sites which are already protected at the time of their nomination. The seven U.S. sites in the List, for example, are all national parks which are strictly protected by the U.S. National Park Service Act. Furthermore, every one of the thirty four natural properties submitted to the World Heritage Committee by the U.S.A. in May 1982 as part of its inventory of properties which may qualify for future nominations to the List is either a national park, a national monument, a national seashore, a coast reserve or a national wildlife refuge, all of which are protected by U.S. law.[21] There are advantages to including an already protected area in the List. The Party concerned will be entitled to apply for assistance from the World Heritage Fund,[22] and the added status given by the Convention may help bolster protection for an area which is protected in name but is threatened in fact. Darien National Park in Panama is a case in point. Although national parks are protected by Panamanian Law, IUCN advised the Committee prior to the inclusion of Darien in the List that

> the area is under powerful pressures from north and south for a wide range of purposes, many of them inimical to the national park's interests (and the interests of Panama as a whole)...*Awarding World Heritage status to this unique and particularly important area will provide additional leverage for long-term protection of the area...* Panama is very concerned to establish political control over the area. The early awarding of support to the newly established naional park will help ensure its proper management and development, with particular reference to boundary demarcation and to integration of the area into overall regional development plans.[23] (Emphasis added).

Other Parties have nominated unprotected sites for inclusion in the List. Australia nominated almost the entire Great Barrier Reef in 1981, and the World Heritage Committee accepted the nomination notwithstanding that about half of the area was outside the scope of Australia's Great Barrier Reef Marine Park Act of 1975. It was

[20] *Ibid.*, para. 19.

[21] See "Indicative Inventory of Potential Future U.S. Nominations to the World Heritage List", U.S. Federal Register, Vol. 47, No. 88, pp. 19648-19655 (6 May 1982).

[22] See pp.229-235 below.

[23] See *IUCN Technical Review for 1981*, No. 159, para. 6.

shown in Chapter 10 how the designation of unprotected sites in Ramsar's List of Wetlands of International Importance has helped to secure their protection,[24] and the same may also be true with respect to the inclusion of sites in the World Heritage List. Noting that large areas of the Great Barrier Reef were not yet protected under national law, the Committee followed their acceptance of the nomination with a request to the Australian government

> ...to take steps to ensure that the whole area is proclaimed under relevant legislation as soon as possible and that the necessary environmental protection measures are taken.[25]

Undoubtedly stimulated by the new international status to be given to the Barrier Reef, the Prime Minister of Australia assured the 1981 meeting of the World Heritage Committee that the "Great Barrier Reef Marine Park will be progressively extended. The question is not whether but when."[26]

(iv)   *Other considerations*

The Operational Guidelines state that the criteria for the inclusion of a site in the List were designed to enable the World Heritage Committee to consider the site on its intrinsic merits only. The prospects of the nominating Party being eligible to receive assistance from the World Heritage Fund or any other such considerations are theoretically irrelevant. The objective of the Committee is to establish a List for educational and public information purposes which truly reflects the world's natural and cultural areas of outstanding universal value.[27] The Operational Guidelines also stipulate that efforts should be made "to avoid any disproportion between the cultural heritage and the natural heritage properties entered on the List."[28] So far there has been a bias towards the "cultural" aspects of the Convention, and efforts are required to redress this balance, while acknowledging that there may always be rather more cultural than natural properties of world heritage status.

---

[24] See p. 190 above.

[25] Report of the Rapporteur, World Heritage Committee, Fifth Session (1981), Conf. Doc. CC-81/CONF.003/6, para. 15.

[26] This statement was made in a Press Release issued by the Prime Minister of Australia on 26 October 1981 on his opening the Fifth Session of the World Heritage Committee in Australia. Other sites in the World Heritage List without a fully protected legal status under national legislation include the Willandra Lakes region in Australia and Ngorongoro in Tanzania.

[27] Operational Guidelines, note 7 above, para. 6(ii).

[28] *Ibid.*, para. 6(iii).

b) *Inventories*

Article 11(1) of the World Heritage Convention requires Parties "in so far as possible" to submit to the World Heritage Committee an inventory of sites situated on their respective territories which they deem suitable for inclusion in the World Heritage List. Inventories which are submitted will not be considered exhaustive[29] and submission of an inventory does not of itself constitute a formal nomination of the sites concerned. The inventory submitted by the U.S.A. in May 1982 goes to great lengths to explain that it is merely an

> indicative inventory of potential future U.S. nominations for the World Heritage List...The inventory will be used as the basis for selecting future United States nominations, and provides a comparative framework within which the outstanding universal value of a property may be effectively judged.[30]

Although a comprehensive list of "possible" sites based on inventories submitted by every Party would greatly assist the Committee in selecting those of outstanding universal value, relatively few Parties have complied with Article 11(1). At the time of writing only Brazil, Canada, the Federal Republic of Germany, France, India, Pakistan, Portugal and the U.S.A. have submitted inventories of possible natural sites, although IUCN has prepared a worldwide indicative inventory of natural sites of World Heritage quality.[31]

c) *Annual schedule for nominations*

The Operational Guidelines have established a very precise schedule for the processing of nominations for the World Heritage List. 1 January is the deadline for receipt by the Secretariat of nominations to be processed during that year. By 1 April the Secretariat registers and checks on the origin and contents of each nomination, transmits nominations of natural heritage sites to IUCN for evaluation, IUCN in turn transmits its evaluations back to the Secretariat which then transmits each nomination and evaluation to members of the "Bureau" of the World Heritage Committee. By July, the Bureau, which consists of representatives of

---

[29] World Heritage Convention, Article 11(1). Para. 7 of the Operational Guidelines suggests that inventories "should comprise those properties which the State intends to nominate during the following five to ten years."

[30] U.S. Federal Register Notice, Vol. 47, No. 88, p. 19648 (6 May 1982).

[31] *The World's Greatest Natural Areas, An Indicative Inventory of Natural Sites of World Heritage Quality* (IUCN, 1982).

seven members of the World Heritage Committee, transmits its recommendations to all Parties to the Convention and may ask Parties which submitted nominations to provide further information. The Secretariat collects any supplementary information on the nominations in August-September, and the World Heritage Committee meets in October-December to determine which sites should be listed.[32]

In view of the small size of the staff available to the Secretariat and to IUCN, the number of nominations which can be approved in any one year is clearly limited, and the Operational Guidelines make it clear that the listing process is intended to be a gradual one and that "no formal limit is imposed either on the total number of properties included in the List or on the number of properties any individual State can submit at successive stages for inclusion therein."[33]

d) *Territorial disputes*

The Convention's provision that it is for each Party to identify the heritage sites "situated on its territory"[34] and that the inclusion of a site in the World Heritage List requires "the consent of the State concerned"[35] has twice been the cause of heated debate among members of the World Heritage Committee.

When Jordan nominated "The Old City of Jerusalem and its Walls" for listing as a cultural heritage site without the consent of Israel, which is not a Party to the Convention, the Committee met in extraordinary session in September 1981 to consider the controversial issues involved. The U.S. delegation referred to Israel "as the State responsible for the administration and *de facto* control of the Old City of Jerusalem"[36] and opposed the Jordanian nomination on the basis that it contravened

> ...those articles [of the Convention] which provide that the nominating state submit only those sites which are "situated in its territory", which require that the consent of "the State concerned" be obtained, and which require that the nominating State provide an effective plan for the protection and management of the site. The Committee has taken an impermissible action...[37]

---

[32] Operational Guidelines, note 7 above, para. 43.

[33] *Ibid.*, para. 6(iv).

[34] World Heritage Convention, Article 3.

[35] *Ibid.*, Article 11(3).

[36] World Heritage Committee, First Extraordinary Session, UNESCO Doc. CC-81/CONF.008/2 Rev., Annex IV, para. 7.

[37] *Ibid.*, para. 9.

Other delegates argued that Israeli consent was not necessary on the basis that the occupied city of Jerusalem is Arab sovereign territory.[38] The Jordanian nomination was eventually approved.

There was also considerable argument following Argentina's nomination of Los Glaciares National Park. At the fifth ordinary session of the World Heritage Committee, held in October 1981, Chile stated that it would study the possibility of nominating "the sector of the Glaciers Region located within its national jurisdiction",[39] to which Argentina replied that "the whole area of the 'National Park Los Glaciares' is unquestionably situated in Argentinian territory".[40] Again, the Argentinian nomination was eventually approved.

Article 11(3) makes it clear that the listing of a site over which sovereignty or jurisdiction is claimed by more than one State "shall in no way prejudice the rights of the parties to the dispute." Nevertheless, some States may believe that political benefit can be derived from nominating a disputed site. Whatever the merits of the arguments in relation to the particular instances of Jerusalem and Los Glaciares, there is clearly a danger that such nominations might so aggravate political tensions that the effectiveness of the Convention as a legal instrument to promote the conservation of the world's cultural and natural heritage would be seriously reduced.

e)   Deletion of properties from the World Heritage List

The Operational Guidelines stipulate that the Committee shall delete properties from the List in the following circumstances:

> a) Where the property has deteriorated to the extent that it has lost those characteristics which determined its inclusion in the World Heritage List; and
> b) where the intrinsic qualities of a world heritage site were already threatened at the time of its nomination by action of man and where the necessary corrective measures as outlined by the State Party at the time have not been taken within the time proposed.[41]

When either of these circumstances arise, the Party on whose territory the property is situated should inform the Secretariat.[42] If the information comes from a source other than the Party concerned, the Secretariat will investigate the matter and report to

---

[38] *Ibid.*, para. 3.
[39] World Heritage Committee, Fifth Session, UNESCO Doc. CC-81/CONF.003/6, Annex III.
[40] *Ibid.*, Annex IV.
[41] Operational Guidelines, note 7 above, para. 26.
[42] *Ibid.*, para. 27.

the Chairman of the Committee who will decide whether the information is to be acted upon.[43] If the Chairman considers that further action is appropriate, the information, together with the comments of IUCN and the Party concerned, will be passed on to the Bureau for their recommendations and subsequently back to the Committee for a final decision.[44] The Operational Guidelines emphasise that "all possible measures should be taken to prevent the deletion of any property from the List" and that the Committee is "ready to offer technical cooperation as far as possible to States Parties in this connection".[45] No site has yet been deleted, or even proposed for deletion, from the List.

4. The List of World Heritage in Danger

Article 11(4) of the World Heritage Convention requires the Committee to establish, keep up to date and publish, "whenever circumstances shall require", a List of World Heritage in Danger. This List shall consist of sites in the World Heritage List which are "threatened by serious and specific dangers", which require major operations for their conservation and for which assistance has been requested under the Convention. It shall also contain an estimate of the cost of such operations. In cases of urgent need, the Committee is authorised to make a new entry in the List of World Heritage in Danger and to publicise such entry immediately.[46] Only two areas have been included in this List at the time of writing, and both are cultural sites. Kotor in Yugoslavia was listed in 1979 following an earthquake, and the Committee authorised U.S.$20,000 from the World Heritage Fund to assist with the restoration of its buildings.[47] The Old City of Jerusalem and its walls was listed in 1982. However, in 1983 the World Heritage Committee suggested that Senegal and Tanzania should respectively propose Djoudj National Bird Sanctuary and Ngorongoro Conservation Area for inclusion in the List of World Heritage in Danger because of threats facing both these sites, and Zaire has proposed the listing of Garamba National Park.[48]

Usage of the List of World Heritage in Danger may increase following the Committee's adoption in December 1982 of detailed

[43] Ibid., para. 28.
[44] Ibid., paras. 29-31.
[45] Ibid., para. 34.
[46] World Heritage Convention, Article 11(4).
[47] See World Heritage Committee, Fifth Session, UNESCO Doc. CC-81/CONF.003/INF.2, p. 5.
[48] See World Heritage Committee, Seventh Session, UNESCO Doc. SC/83/CONF.009/8, paras. 43-4.

guidelines for the inscription of properties in the List. These guidelines specify that a site is eligible if it is faced with a "specific and proven imminent danger" such as a development project (including major public works, mining, logging, firewood collection etc.) which threatens the integrity of the property or a serious decline in the population of an endangered species. A site is also eligible if it is faced with "major threats which could have deleterious effects on its inherent characteristics" such as modification of its legal protective status or planned development projects. Sites should only be listed if the threats are amenable to human correction — thus a site threatened by a natural disaster which man can do nothing to avoid is ineligible.[49]

5.   *The Nature of the Parties' Obligations to Protect World Heritage Sites*

a)   *Conservation of sites in the World Heritage List*

Articles 4 and 5 of the Convention set out the obligations on Parties to conserve sites in the World Heritage List which are situated in their territories.

Article 4 states:

> Each State Party to this Convention recognises that the duty of ensuring the identification, protection, conservation, presentation and transmission to future generations of the cultural and natural heritage referred to in Articles 1 and 2 and situated on its territory belongs primarily to that State. It will do all it can to this end, to the utmost of its own resources and, where appropriate, with any international assistance and cooperation, in particular, financial, artistic, scientific and technical, which it may be able to obtain.

Article 5 states:

> To ensure that effective and active measures are taken for the protection, conservation and presentation of the cultural and natural heritage situated on its territory, each State Party to this Convention shall endeavour, in so far as possible, and as appropriate for each country:
> a) to adopt a general policy which aims to give the cultural and natural heritage a function in the life of the community and to integrate the protection of that heritage into comprehensive planning programmes;
> b) to set up within its territories, where such services do not exist, one or more services for the protection, conservation and presentation of the cultural and natural heritage with an appropriate staff and possessing the means to discharge their functions;
> c) to develop scientific and technical studies and research and to work out such operating methods as will make the State capable of

---

[49] Operational Guidelines, note 7 above, paras. 49-50.

counteracting the dangers that threaten its cultural or natural heritage;
d) to take the appropriate legal, scientific, technical, administrative and
financial measures necessary for the identification, protection,
conservation, presentation and rehabilitation of this heritage; and
e) to foster the establishment or development of national or regional
centres for training in the protection, conservation and presentation of
the cultural and natural heritage and to encourage scientific research in
this field.

The only Court to have considered the nature of the obligations
imposed on Parties by Articles 4 and 5 is the High Court of Australia
in the recent case of *The Commonwealth of Australia v. The State of
Tasmania.*[50] The case arose because of plans by the State of
Tasmania to construct a dam on the Gordon River, downstream of
its junction with the Franklin River, in an area known as the
Western Tasmania Wilderness National Parks which the
Commonwealth of Australia (i.e. the federal Australian government)
nominated for inclusion in the World Heritage List on 13 November
1981. The World Heritage Committee accepted the nomination in
December 1982 although, aware of Tasmania's plans, it expressed
"serious concern" at the likely effect of the proposed dam and
recommended that "the Australian authorities take all possible
measures to protect the integrity of the property." The
Commonwealth of Australia then took two steps to protect the site.
The Governor-General, exercising his authority under section 69 of
the National Parks and Wildlife Conservation Act of 1975, issued the
World Heritage (Western Tasmania Wilderness) Regulations (S.R.
Nos. 31 and 66 of 1983), and the Australian Parliament adopted the
World Heritage Properties Conservation Act of 1983. Both the
Regulations and the Act made construction of the dam illegal. The
State of Tasmania challenged the constitutional authority of the
Commonwealth of Australia to make a law or to adopt regulations
prohibiting construction of the dam, and the Commonwealth
sought a ruling from the High Court that the measures taken to
protect the Western Tasmania Wilderness National Parks were
valid. A key question in the argument before the Court was whether
the World Heritage Convention imposes a legal duty on each Party
to protect a site in the World Heritage List which is situated on its
territory. The Commonwealth of Australia contended that the
Convention does impose such a duty, while the State of Tasmania
argued that the Convention imposes no real obligation but is merely
a statement of aspiration or political accord.

[50] No. C6 of 1983. *The Commonwealth of Australia v. The State of Tasmania,* 46 A.L.R. 625; 68
I.L.R. 266.

Since it is the only case in which this issue has been considered, the findings of the Court bear consideration in some detail. By a 4-3 majority decision the Court upheld the authority of the Commonwealth to stop the dam, and the opinions of the four Justices who formed the majority all state categorically that the Convention imposes a legal duty on Australia to protect Western Tasmania Wilderness National Parks. The Court recognised that the key sections of the Convention are Articles 4 and 5. Asking himself the question "does the Convention impose an obligation on Australia to protect the area which has been entered on the World Heritage List and, if so, what kind of obligation?", Mason J. stated in *The Commonwealth of Australia v. The State of Tasmania* that Article 5

> ...imposes obligations on each State with the object set out in the opening words of the article "To ensure that effective and active measures are taken for the protection, conservation" etc. of the heritage in the discharge of the responsibility acknowledged by Art. 4. Article 5 cannot be read as a mere statement of intention. It is expressed in the form of a command...Indeed, there would be little point in adding the qualifications "in so far as possible" and "as appropriate for each country" unless the Article imposed an obligation. The first qualification means "in so far as is practicable" and the second takes account of the difference in legal systems. Neither of these qualifications nor the existence of an element of discretion is inconsistent with the existence of an obligation. There is a distinction between a discretion as to the manner of performance and a discretion as to performance or non-performance. The latter, but not the former, is inconsistent with a binding obligation to perform (see *Thorby v. Goldberg* (1964) 112 C.L.R. 597, at pp. 604-605, 613, 614-615).

Brennan J. stated that the last part of Article 4 and the first part and (d) of Article 5 are critical. In considering whether the want of specificity in Articles 4 and 5 and the discretion they leave to each Party as to how it will protect World Heritage sites makes them merely hortatory, he concluded that the Articles are not merely hortatory and that

> there is a clear obligation on Australia to act under Articles 4 and 5, though the extent of that obligation may be affected by decisions taken by Australia in good faith.

Brennan J. went on to say that

> the obligation under Art. 4 of the Convention leaves no discretion in a Party as to whether it will abstain from taking steps in discharge of the 'duty' referred to in that Article. Each Party is bound to 'do all it can...to

the utmost of its own resources' and the question whether it is unable to take a particular step within the limits of its resources is a justiciable question. No doubt the allocation of resources is a matter for each Party to decide and the allocation of resources for the discharge of the obligation may thus be said to be discretionary, but the discretion is not large. It must be exercised 'in good faith', as Art. 26 of the Vienna Convention requires. If a Party sought exemption from the obligation on the ground that it had allocated its available resources to other purposes, the question whether it had done so in good faith would be justiciable.

In a strongly worded dissenting opinion the Chief Justice, Sir Harry Gibbs, disagreed with the court's decision, stating that

it is unnecessary to consider whether if the words of Arts. 4 and 5 which purport to impose an obligation had appeared in, for example, a commercial contract, they would in an appropriate context have imposed a duty to do what was reasonably possible and fitting in the circumstances. It is however impossible to conclude that Arts. 4 and 5 were intended to impose a legal duty of that kind on the States Parties to the Convention. If the conduct which those articles purport to prescribe was intended to be legally enforceable, the obligations thereby created would be of the most onerous and far reaching kind. The obligations would extend to any property which might reasonably be regarded as cultural or natural heritage within the meaning of Arts. 1 and 2 of the Convention, whether or not it was included on the World Heritage List, and would require a State Party to the Convention to take all legal measures within its constitutional power that might reasonably be regarded as appropriate for the identification and protection of such property, and to apply all of its financial resources that it could possibly make available for the same purpose; there would of course be further obligations, but what I have said suffices to indicate the nature of the burden which the articles would impose. The very nature of these obligations is such as to indicate that the State Parties to the Convention did not intend to assume a legal obligation to perform them.

The Commonwealth of Australia v. The State of Tasmania is a landmark decision both because it is the first test of the scope of the Convention in a court of law and because the majority of judges stated so clearly that each Party has a legal duty to do all it can to protect sites in the World Heritage List which are situated within its own territorial boundaries. Although decisions of the High Court of Australia are not binding on other Parties, the case is certain to be of considerable influence as and when other Parties to the Convention are faced with a similar problem.

b)   *Conservation of sites not in the World Heritage List but which are part of the cultural and natural heritage referred to in Articles 1 and 2*

The conservation obligations imposed on Parties by Articles 4 and 5 are not limited to sites in the World Heritage List. Also included are sites which are part of the cultural and natural heritage as defined by Articles 1 and 2 of the Convention.

Article 4 states that

> [e]ach State Party to this Convention recognizes that the duty of ensuring the identification, protection, conservation, presentation and transmission to future generations of *the cultural and natural heritage referred to in Articles 1 and 2 and situated on its territory*, belongs primarily to that State... (emphasis added).

Article 5 starts with the words

> [t]o ensure that effective and active measures are taken for the protection, conservation and presentation of *the cultural and natural heritage situated on its territory*, each State Party shall endeavour... (emphasis added).

This is an important point since the cultural and natural heritage within the meaning of Articles 1 and 2 may include substantially more sites than those in the World Heritage List. As was pointed out earlier in this chapter, it is up to each Party to identify sites on its territory which it deems to be part of the cultural and natural heritage within the meaning of Articles 1 and 2, while the compilation of the World Heritage List is the responsibility of the World Heritage Committee.[51] It is quite conceivable, therefore, that a Party might decide that a site on its territory is part of the cultural and natural heritage as defined by Articles 1 and 2, notwithstanding that it is not in the World Heritage List. Australia, for example, has declared a 780 hectare area and numerous cultural sites in Tasmania, which are outside the Western Tasmania Wilderness National Parks and not in the World Heritage List, to be part of the natural and cultural heritage as defined by Articles 1 and 2 of the Convention. Furthermore, section 3(2) of Australia's World Heritage Properties Conservation Act states that the provisions of the Act apply to sites submitted to the World Heritage Committee for listing and to sites "declared by the regulations to form part of the cultural or natural heritage" as well as to sites that the World Heritage Committee has actually agreed to include in the World Heritage List.

[51] See pp. 212-213 above.

However, the fact that Articles 4 and 5 apply to parts of the cultural and natural heritage within the meaning of Articles 1 and 2 as well as to sites in the World Heritage List does not give a Party (or the World Heritage Committee) the right to say to another Party "X site on your territory is obviously part of the cultural or natural heritage as defined by Articles 1 and 2, and you are therefore obliged by Articles 4 and 5 to protect it even though it is not in the World Heritage List". Article 3's pronouncement that "it is for each State Party to this Convention to identify and delineate the different properties on its territory mentioned in Articles 1 and 2 above" makes it quite clear that only Parties on whose territory a property is situated can decide whether or not it is part of the cultural and natural heritage within the meaning of Articles 1 and 2. Therefore, unless a Party decides that a site on its territory is part of the cultural and natural heritage as defined by Articles 1 and 2 , Articles 4 and 5 will not apply to that site.

c) *Conservation of sites situated outside their territories*

Article 6 of the Convention imposes two obligations on Parties with respect to sites situated outside their own territories. The first requires each Party to help other Parties, on whose territory a property in the World Heritage List or the List of World Heritage in Danger is situated, if the latter request assistance. Article 6(2) states:

> The States Parties undertake, in accordance with the provisions of this Convention, to give their help in the identification, protection, conservation and preservation of the cultural and natural heritage referred to in paragraphs 2 and 4 of Article 11 [i.e. the World Heritage List and the List of World Heritage in Danger] if the States on whose territory it is situated so request.

The second obligation imposed by Article 6 is more far-reaching. Article 6(3) requires each Party not to do anything that will directly or indirectly damage a site situated outside its territory which is deemed to be part of the cultural or natural heritage as defined by Articles 1 and 2. Article 6(3) states:

> Each State Party to this Convention undertakes not to take any deliberate measures which might damage directly or indirectly the cultural and natural heritage referred to in Articles 1 and 2 situated on the territory of other States Parties to this Convention.

This means that Parties must not harm sites outside their territories which are in the World Heritage List or sites outside their territories which are considered by the State in whose territory they are situated to be part of the cultural or natural heritage — even if they are not in the World Heritage List. The scope of Article 6(3) is extremely broad since it prohibits Parties from taking *any* deliberate measure which might harm, directly or indirectly, such sites. Article 6(3) therefore prohibits Parties from deliberately discharging pollutants whose effect is to damage a World Heritage site situated on the territory of another Party. It also prohibits Parties from granting financial or technical assistance to a development project in the territory of another Party which will harm a World Heritage site. If a site has been included in the World Heritage List because of its value as a wintering or breeding area for migratory birds, but its importance is threatened by excessive shooting or trapping along the birds' migratory route, Article 6(3) would require Parties situated on the migratory route to restrict shooting or trapping accordingly. The latter two examples are directly relevant to two sites in the World Heritage List — Djoudj National Bird Sanctuary in Senegal and Ichkeul National Park in Tunisia. Both are outstandingly valuable wildlife habitats, particularly as wintering areas for migratory waterfowl, and the value of both is threatened by dams constructed with the financial assistance of other countries and by excessive shooting of waterfowl along the European section of their migratory route.[52]

6.   *Other Responsibilities of the Parties*

a)   *Presentation and education*

Several Articles of the World Heritage Convention make it clear that Parties should not "lock up" their World Heritage sites but should do their utmost to encourage appreciation and respect for them and, so far as possible, give them an active role in the life of the local community.

Article 4, for example, requires the Parties to do all they can to promote the "presentation" of the cultural and natural heritage. The Convention does not define "presentation", but in the context of Article 5 which expresses the need to give the cultural and natural heritage "a function in the life of the community" and to establish centres for training in its presentation, it is clearly intended that Parties should encourage people to appreciate and make use of them provided that such usage does not damage their cultural or natural values. Article 27(1) of the Convention urges Parties "to strengthen appreciation and respect" for heritage sites "by educational and

[52] See Chapter 10 above at pp. 195 and 199.

information programmes," and Article 27(2) requires them "to keep the public broadly informed of the dangers threatening this heritage and of activities carried on in pursuance of this Convention". Article 28 obliges Parties receiving international assistance under the Convention to "take appropriate measures to make known the importance of the property for which assistance has been received and the role played by such assistance."

Recognising the importance of publicising the Convention, the World Heritage Committee and UNESCO have made a special effort in recent years to make it better known. Among other things, they have published a booklet on the objectives of the Convention, produced a calendar in the form of a poster on the Convention and organised a number of slide programmes on World Heritage sites at several international conferences.[53]

b) *Reports*

In the report which Parties submit biennially to the General Conference of UNESCO, they are required to "give information on the legislative and administrative provisions which they have adopted and other action which they have taken for the application of this Convention, together with details of the experience acquired in this field."[54] The reports are submitted to the Committee,[55] which itself submits a report on its activities at the biennial ordinary sessions of the General Conference of UNESCO.[56]

7. *The World Heritage Fund*

The World Heritage Fund is the most distinctive feature of the World Heritage Convention in relation to other conservation treaties. It is a trust fund to which Parties must contribute according to the scale of their contributions to the regular budget of UNESCO. This is an important "carrot" for States whose contributions to UNESCO are small and involves a significant commitment for the wealthy industrialised States — particularly the U.S.A. whose share amounts to 25% of all contributions.

a) *System of contribution*

The Convention allows Parties to choose between a compulsory system of contribution whereby they undertake to pay to the Fund

---

[53] See World Heritage Committee, Sixth Session, UNESCO Doc. CLT-82/CONF.015/7, pp. 9-10.
[54] World Heritage Convention, Article 29(1).
[55] *Ibid.*, Article 29(2).
[56] *Ibid.*, Article 29(3).

one percent of their contribution to the regular budget of UNESCO every two years[57] and a theoretically "voluntary" system whereby their contributions "shall be paid on a regular basis, at least every two years, and should not be less than the contributions which they should have paid if they had been bound by" the compulsory system.[58] In effect, therefore, both systems are compulsory. The reason for having the "voluntary" system was not so much because some Parties wished to avoid making a financial contribution to the Fund as because it was felt that internal ratification procedures would be simpler in some States if contributions were theoretically voluntary.[59] A Party in arrears with the payment of "its compulsory or voluntary contribution for the current year and the calendar year immediately preceding it shall not be eligible as a Member of the World Heritage Committee, although this provision shall not apply to the first election".[60]

Parties may, of course, make contributions to the Fund over and above the one percent level, and they are required by the Convention to assist wherever possible in other money-raising efforts which will benefit either the Fund or World Heritage sites. In particular, Parties "shall give their assistance to international fund-raising campaigns organised for the World Heritage Fund under the auspices of UNESCO"[61] and "shall consider or encourage the establishment of national, public and private foundations or associations whose purpose is to invite donations for the protection of the cultural and natural heritage".[62] Contributions to the Fund may also be made by non-Parties or by any public or private body or individual.[63] Austria and the Netherlands, which are both non-Parties, have already contributed U.S.$23,590 and U.S.$30,711 respectively.[64] Political conditions may not be attached to contributions, although earmarking for a certain programme or project is permissible provided that the Committee has decided to implement that particular programme or project.[65]

---

[57] *Ibid.*, Article 16(1). Under this Article, the amount of the Parties' contributions can be any amount which is determined by the General Assembly of Parties to the Convention meeting during the sessions of the General Conference of UNESCO provided that it does not exceed one percent of Parties' contributions to the regular budget of UNESCO. It has in fact been set at the one percent level since the Convention came into force.

[58] World Heritage Convention, Article 16(4).

[59] See Meyer, note 4 above, p. 58.

[60] World Heritage Convention, Article 16(5).

[61] *Ibid.*, Article 18.

[62] *Ibid.*, Article 17.

[63] *Ibid.*, Article 15(3)(b).

[64] See World Heritage Committee, Sixth Session, UNESCO Doc. CLT-82/CONF.015.4 (Paris, 7 December 1982), p. 2.

[65] World Heritage Convention, Article 15(4).

b)   Operating budget

The World Heritage Committee approved a budget of U.S.$741,000 for 1984.[66] Although not sufficient to finance massive conservation programmes, the operating budget provides plenty of scope for assistance to relatively low-cost projects.

c)   Use of the resources of the Fund

Parties may apply to the World Heritage Committee for assistance, to be paid for out of the resources of the Fund, in order to secure the protection, conservation, presentation or rehabilitation of sites situated within their territories which have been included in, or are potentially suitable for inclusion in, either the World Heritage List or the List of World Heritage in Danger.[67] They may also apply for assistance "with identification of cultural or natural [heritage sites]...when preliminary investigations have shown that further inquiries would be justified."[68] The Operational Guidelines specify the types of assistance that are available and lay down an order of priorities for the granting of assistance. The Convention requires that, as a general rule, the international community should bear "only part of the cost of the work necessary" and that the Party benefiting from assistance should contribute "a substantial share of the resources devoted to each programme or project unless its resources do not permit this."[69]

Requests for assistance should be submitted to the Secretariat. They are decided upon by the World Heritage Committee, although the Chairman of the Committee is authorised to approve requests for assistance costing less than U.S.$20,000 without obtaining the approval of the whole Committee.[70]

d)   Types of available assistance

The Operational Guidelines divide the types of available assistance into four categories:

(i)   Preparatory assistance

Assistance is available for the preparation of inventories of sites suitable for inclusion in the World Heritage List, for the preparation of nominations of sites for the List and for the preparation of requests

[66] World Heritage Committee, Seventh Session, UNESCO Doc. SC/83/CONF.009/8.
[67] World Heritage Convention, Article 13(1).
[68] Ibid., Article 13(2).
[69] Ibid., Article 25.
[70] Operational Guidelines, note 7 above, para. 71.

for technical cooperation.[71] In 1978 and 1979, the first two years in which expenditures from the Fund were authorised, fourteen requests for preparatory assistance were granted.[72] Recently there have been fewer such requests and fewer grants, but since so few inventories of sites suitable for inclusion in the List have been submitted[73] and since some Parties may have technical and financial difficulties in drawing up such inventories, the need for preparatory assistance may still be very real in some instances. The budgetary ceiling for each project is fixed at U.S.$15,000, and assistance may take the form of "consultant services, equipment or, in exceptional cases, financial grants."[74] Requests for preparatory assistance should be sent to the Secretariat which will transmit them to the Chairman, who will decide in consultation with the Director General on the type and extent of assistance to be granted.[75]

(ii)   *Emergency assistance*

Parties may request emergency assistance for work in connection with properties "included or suitable for inclusion in the World Heritage List and which have suffered severe damage due to sudden, unexpected phenomena (such as sudden land subsidence, serious fires or explosions, flooding) or are in imminent danger of severe damage." Such assistance may be granted to prepare a nomination of a site for the List or to draw up an emergency plan or to undertake emergency measures to safeguard the site.[76] Emergency assistance may be made available in the same form as preparatory assistance, and requests are processed in the same way as requests for preparatory assistance.[77] The amounts spent on emergency assistance have varied considerably from year to year — in 1981 U.S.$174,000 was authorised for emergency measures, about one quarter of the total amount spent or authorised out of the World Heritage Fund in that year, but in 1982 a U.S.$20,000 grant to establish a waste water drainage system for Shibam in Democratic Yemen was the only emergency assistance provided.[78] Until 1983 only cultural heritage sites had received emergency assistance, but in that year Zaire was awarded an emergency grant of U.S.$40,000 to

[71]   *Ibid.*, para. 60.
[72]   See World Heritage Committee, Fifth Session, UNESCO Doc. CC-81/CONF.003/ INF.2, pp. 1-3.
[73]   See p. 218 above.
[74]   Operational Guidelines, note 7 above, para. 60.
[75]   *Ibid.*, para. 61.
[76]   *Ibid.*, para. 62.
[77]   *Ibid.*, para. 63.
[78]   See World Heritage Committee, Sixth Session, UNESCO Doc. CLT-82/CH/ CONF.015/INF.1, p. 7.

make improvements to Garamba National Park. Garamba is particularly noteworthy because it has the last known remnant population of northern white rhinoceros (*Ceratotherium simum cottoni*), consisting of less than 20 animals.

(iii)   *Training*

Parties may request fellowships for the training of specialised staff at all levels in the field of identification, protection, conservation, and presentation of World Heritage sites.[79] Requests should be submitted on the standard "Application for Fellowship" form used for all fellowships administered by UNESCO and should indicate the relationship of the proposed study plan to the implementation of the Convention.[80] In 1981 and 1982, 60 fellowships were granted to nationals of 23 Parties at a cost to the World Heritage Fund of over U.S.$600,000. Many of these, such as a nine month fellowship for two Egyptian specialists at the College of African Wildlife Management in Mweka, Tanzania, were for the benefit of natural sites. The Fund also financed the organisation of nine training courses at a cost of over U.S.$160,000, including a contribution of U.S.$10,000 to a course managed by the Charles Darwin Foundation in the Galapagos Islands and U.S.$60,000 to courses run by the College of African Wildlife Management in Mweka.[81] Although the majority of requests approved by the World Heritage Committee are from poorer countries, this is not always the case — requests from Canada and the U.S.A. for small grants in order to send two people on a course on the conservation of historic buildings were both approved in 1980.[82]

(iv)   *Technical cooperation*

Parties may request technical cooperation for "work foreseen in safeguarding projects for properties in the World Heritage List" and for "support for the training of specialised staff at the national or regional level".[83] Technical cooperation can take a number of different forms[84] but normally involves financial contributions to protection programmes or the supply of equipment or experts.[85]

---

[79] Operational Guidelines, note 7 above, para. 64.

[80] *Ibid.*, para. 66.

[81] See World Heritage Committee, Sixth Session, UNESCO Doc. CLT-82/CH/CONF.015/7, p. 7.

[82] See World Heritage Committee, Fifth Session, UNESCO Doc. CC-81/CONF.003/INF.2, p. 6.

[83] Operational Guidelines, note 7 above, para. 69.

[84] *Ibid.*, para. 72. See also Article 22 of the World Heritage Convention.

[85] See World Heritage Committee, Fifth Session, UNESCO Doc. CC-81/CONF.003/INF.2, pp. 12-13.

Most of the large expenditures authorised by the World Heritage Committee have been in response to requests for technical cooperation. In 1980, the Committee authorised U.S.$435,000 to be spent on technical cooperation for the benefit of eight sites in six countries, including U.S.$118,000 to pay for consultants and equipment necessary for the preservation of Carthage in Tunisia, and in 1981 U.S.$113,450 was spent on equipment for Simien National Park in Ethiopia.[86] In 1983 the World Heritage Committee spent some U.S.$200,000 on technical cooperation, rather less than in previous years, but more than half of this was spent on natural heritage sites.[87]

Requests for technical assistance are decided upon by the World Heritage Committee and must reach the Secretariat before 1 March in order to be considered in the same year.[88] This schedule does not apply, however, to projects costing less than U.S.$20,000. The Chairman is authorised to take decisions on the financing of such projects up to the total amount set aside annually by the World Heritage Committee for this purpose, although he must receive the advice of IUCN before so doing in the case of projects benefiting natural heritage sites.[89] The Operational Guidelines set out the information which Parties should provide in requests for technical assistance.[90]

e) Order of priorities for the granting of assistance

The Operational Guidelines stipulate that top priority will be given to requests for emergency measures to save a site included in, or nominated for inclusion in, the World Heritage List. Requests for preparatory assistance in drawing up nominations to the List and requests for technical cooperation will receive second priority, whilst projects likely to have a "multiplier effect" — such as the training of specialised personnel — will receive third priority.[91]

f) The conclusion of agreements with Parties receiving assistance

When the World Heritage Committee decides to give assistance to a Party for a certain project, the Convention stipulates that the

[86] See World Heritage Committee, Sixth Session, UNESCO Doc.CLT-82/CH/CONF.015/INF.1, pp. 19-20.
[87] See World Heritage Committee, Seventh Session, UNESCO Doc. SC/83/CONF.009/8, paras. 36-7.
[88] Operational Guidelines, note 7 above, para. 70.
[89] Ibid., para. 71.
[90] Ibid., para. 78.
[91] Ibid., para. 80. Factors relating to the urgency of the work, the cost of the project etc. will also be taken into account (para. 81 of the Operational Guidelines).

Committee and the Party concerned must formalise their arrangement in an agreement. Article 26 of the Convention states that

> [t]he World Heritage Committee and the recipient State shall define in the agreement they conclude the conditions in which a programme or project for which international assistance under the terms of this Convention is provided, shall be carried out. It shall be the responsibility of the State receiving such international assistance to continue to protect, conserve and present the property so safeguarded, in observance of the conditions laid down by the agreement.

In circumstances where technical cooperation is granted "on a large scale", the Operational Guidelines stipulate that the Committee and the recipient Party shall conclude a written agreement setting out:

a) the scope and nature of the technical cooperation granted;
b) the obligations of the Government; and
c) the facilities, privileges and immunities to be applied by the Government to the Committee and/or UNESCO, to the property, funds and assets allocated to the project as well as to the officials and other persons performing services on behalf of the Committee and/or UNESCO in connection with the project.[92]

g)   *Implementation of projects*

In order to ensure that technical cooperation projects are efficiently implemented, the Operational Guidelines provide that "a single body — whether national, regional, local, public or private — should be entrusted with the responsibility of executing the project in the state Party concerned."[93]

8.   *The World Heritage Committee*

a)   *Structure*

The World Heritage Committee is made up of representatives of 21 Parties.[94] The term of office of each member of the Committee is six years, and a system of rotation exists whereby one third of the members are replaced every two years.[95] Members are elected by all Parties meeting during the ordinary session of the General

---

[92] Operational Guidelines, note 7 above, para. 83.

[93] *Ibid.*, para. 86.

[94] World Heritage Convention, Article 8(1). Originally composed of representatives of 15 Parties, the membership of the Committee increased to 21 after 40 countries had become Parties to the Convention.

[95] World Heritage Convention, Articles 9(1) and (2).

Conference of UNESCO which is held every two years,[96] and the Convention stipulates that the "election of members of the Committee shall ensure an equitable representation of the different regions and cultures of the world". So far this has been successfully implemented — in 1983, for example, the members of the Committee consisted of representatives of one Australasian, four Asian, seven African, five European, one North American and three South American countries. Decisions of the Committee are taken by a majority of two-thirds of its members present and voting, and a majority of the members constitutes a quorum.[97]

b)   *Operation of the Committee*

The Operational Guidelines require the Committee to meet at least once a year in order to consider nominations for the World Heritage Lists and applications for assistance from the World Heritage Fund, and they also establish a system whereby such nominations and applications are the subject of continuing consultation between individual Parties and the Committee or its appointed sub-committees or consultants throughout the year.[98] These frequent meetings and consultations ensure that the Convention is regularly at the forefront of the Parties' attention. The importance of this cannot be over-emphasised. Chapters 6 and 7 of this book have already shown how the Western Hemisphere and African Conventions have become largely forgotten "sleeping treaties" primarily because they have no mechanism requiring their Parties to meet regularly to review their practical implementation. Regular meetings of the Committee will not of themselves ensure that the objectives of the World Heritage Convention are achieved, but they will provide the Parties with good opportunities to achieve them.

To assist it in its tasks, the Committee "may create such consultative bodies as it deems necessary"[99] and may invite "public or private organisations or individuals to participate in its meetings for consultation on particular problems".[100] In addition, the Convention requires UNESCO to appoint a Secretariat to assist the Committee, to prepare the Committee's documentation and the agenda for its meetings and to be responsible for implementing the decisions of the meetings.[101] The Convention entitles an IUCN

[96] *Ibid.*, Article 8(1) and(2).
[97] *Ibid.*, Article 13(8).
[98] Operational Guidelines, note 7 above, paras. 41-59.
[99] World Heritage Convention, Article 10(3).
[100] *Ibid.*, Article 10(2).
[101] *Ibid.*, Article 14(1)-(2).

representative to attend Committee meetings as an adviser,[102] UNESCO is required to use the services of IUCN "to the fullest extent possible" in areas within its competence,[103] the Operational Guidelines make IUCN responsible for evaluating each nomination of a natural heritage site for the World Heritage List,[104] and IUCN also evaluates requests for assistance for natural areas to be paid out of the World Heritage Fund.

9. *Final Provisions*

The final provisions of the Convention are unexceptional. The text is drawn up in Arabic, English, French, Russian and Spanish, and each version is equally authoritative.[105] The Convention is open to ratification or acceptance by States which are members of UNESCO[106] and to accession by States that are not members provided that they are invited to accede by the General Conference of UNESCO.[107] Instruments of ratification, acceptance or accession should be deposited with the Director General of UNESCO.[108] Each Party has the right to denounce the Convention,[109] which may be amended by the General Conference of UNESCO. Amendments only bind States which become Parties to the amended Convention.[110] Unlike CITES and the Bonn Convention, the World Heritage Convention does not allow its Parties to take reservations with respect to any of its provisions.

10. *Conclusion*

The World Heritage Convention does not have a very broad scope as far as wildlife conservation is concerned, but it does offer a tremendous opportunity to protect unique wildlife habitats and representative examples of the most important ecosystems. Although Ramsar's List of Wetlands of International Importance and the World Heritage Lists both provide international prestige for listed sites, the World Heritage Convention goes far beyond Ramsar in two important respects. It offers the opportunity of financial and

---

[102] *Ibid.*, Article 8(3). Article 8(3) also provides that "representatives of other inter-governmental or non-governmental organisations with similar objectives" may attend in a similar capacity if so requested by Parties meeting in general assembly during the ordinary session of the General Conference of UNESCO.

[103] World Heritage Convention, Article 14(2).

[104] Operational Guidelines, note 7 above, para. 43.

[105] World Heritage Convention, Article 30.

[106] *Ibid.*, Article 31(1).

[107] *Ibid.*, Article 32(1).

[108] *Ibid.*, Article 31(2) and 32(2).

[109] *Ibid.*, Article 35.

[110] *Ibid.*, Article 37(1).

technical assistance for the protection of sites in the World Heritage List, and it imposes far stricter obligations on its Parties to conserve listed sites than does Ramsar.

In the few years that it has been in force, a number of important wildlife habitats have already benefited from the patronage of the World Heritage Convention and, as more States become Parties and as more sites are included in the World Heritage Lists, its contribution to wildlife conservation is certain to become increasingly significant.

CHAPTER 12

THE CONVENTION ON INTERNATIONAL TRADE IN ENDANGERED SPECIES OF WILD FAUNA AND FLORA ("CITES")

"Wild fauna and flora are at greater risk today than ever before. In such a situation, CITES has a role of the greatest importance to perform."
(Samar Singh, Chairman of the Standing Committee to CITES, 1983)

1. *Background*

International trade in wildlife is big business. In 1981 the U.S.A. imported and exported wildlife and wildlife products worth over U.S.$962 million.[1] A fur coat made from South American ocelots fetches up to U.S.$40,000 in the Federal Republic of Germany, a single orchid or macaw may sell for over U.S.$5,000 and an ounce of rhinoceros horn in an eastern medicine shop can cost more than an ounce of gold. The trade goes back for centuries, but there was a dramatic increase in its volume 15-20 years ago. By the late 1960s a staggering 5-10 million crocodilian skins were entering international trade each year. In 1968 the U.S.A. alone imported the skins of 1,300 cheetah (*Acinonyx jubatus*), 9,600 leopard (*Panthera pardus*), 13,500 jaguar (*Panthera onca*) and 129,000 ocelot (*Felis pardalis*), and in 1972 Kenya's ivory exports reached their highest recorded annual level of 150 tonnes.[2]

The first demand for controls on the international wildlife trade was made as early as 1911 when Paul Sarasin, a Swiss conservationist, called for restrictions on the import and export of bird feathers because of the effect of the vogue for plumed hats on bird populations. Sarasin's pleas came to nothing, but in 1963, aware of the increasing levels of trade, the General Assembly of the International Union for Conservation of Nature and Natural Resources ("IUCN") called for "an international convention on regulations of export, transit and import of rare or threatened wildlife species or their skins and trophies." The IUCN initiative was more successful and ten years later, on 6 March 1973, the Convention on International Trade in Endangered Species of Wild

---

[1] 12 *I.L.M.* 1085; *T.I.A.S.* no. 8249; *U.K.T.S.* 101 (1976), Cmd. 6647; 27 *U.S.T.* 1087.
[2] See *International Trade in Animal Products Threatens Wildlife* (U.S. Fish and Wildlife Service, Washington, D.C., 1982).

Fauna and Flora ("CITES")[3] was finally concluded in Washington, D.C. CITES was originally signed by 21 States but it did not enter into force until 1 July 1975, being ninety days after the tenth signatory had deposited an instrument of ratification.[4] Since then the Convention has expanded at an astonishing rate, and at the time of writing 87 States are Parties to it.[5]

CITES is perhaps the most successful of all international treaties concerned with the conservation of wildlife. Its success is explained primarily by its basic principles, which most States have proved willing to accept, and by the way in which it operates, which ensures that on the whole it is better enforced than many other treaties.

The basic principles of CITES are quite straightforward. It regulates international trade in wild animals and plants which are listed in the three Appendices to the Convention. It is a protectionist treaty in the sense that it prohibits, with a few exceptions, international commercial trade in species that are threatened with extinction (they are listed in Appendix I). It is also a trading treaty in the sense that it allows a controlled international trade in species whose survival is not yet threatened but may become so (they are listed in Appendix II). CITES limits exports of Appendix II species to a level which will not be detrimental to their survival. Appendix III provides a mechanism whereby a Party which has domestic legislation regulating the export of species not in Appendix I or II can seek the support of other Parties in enforcing its own domestic legislation.

The Convention operates by means of a permit system. With a few exceptions it prohibits international trade in specimens of species included in any of the Appendices without the prior grant of a CITES permit. It lays down strict conditions that must be satisfied before a permit is granted, and it requires each Party to establish one or more Management Authorities and Scientific Authorities which, between them, are responsible for ensuring that the conditions have

---

[3] For a detailed analysis of the extent and nature of international trade in wildlife, see T. Inskipp and S. Wells, *International Trade in Wildlife* (Earthscan, London, 1979).

[4] As required by Article XXII(1) of the Convention.

[5] They are: Algeria, Argentina, Australia, Austria, Bahamas, Bangladesh, Belgium, Benin, Bolivia, Botswana, Brazil, Cameroon, Canada, Central African Republic, Chile, China, Colombia, Congo, Costa Rica, Cyprus, Denmark, Ecuador, Egypt, Finland, France, Gambia, German Democratic Republic, Federal Republic of Germany, Ghana, Guatemala, Guinea, Guyana, India, Indonesia, Iran, Israel, Italy, Japan, Jordan, Kenya, Liberia, Liechtenstein, Luxembourg, Madagascar, Malawi, Malaysia, Mauritius, Monaco, Morocco, Mozambique, Nepal, Netherlands, Nicaragua, Niger, Nigeria, Pakistan, Panama, Papua New Guinea, Paraguay, Peru, Philippines, Portugal, Rwanda, Senegal, Seychelles, South Africa, Sri Lanka, St. Lucia, Sudan, Suriname, Sweden, Switzerland, Tanzania, Thailand, Togo, Trinidad and Tobago, Tunisia, U.K., United Arab Emirates, Uruguay, U.S.A., U.S.S.R., Venezuela, Zaire, Zambia, and Zimbabwe.

been satisfied and, if they have been, for granting a permit. It would be misleading to suggest that the permit system always works perfectly, but on the whole it has proved to be relatively effective. Much of the credit for this is due to the administrative structure of the Convention. In addition to the Management and Scientific Authorities operating on a national level, there is a Secretariat in Switzerland whose function is to oversee the permit system on an international level, and the Parties are required to meet every two years in order to review implementation of CITES and to make appropriate recommendations on how to improve it. Thus there are regular opportunities for the Parties to take the necessary measures to solve any problems that may arise. There have now been four of these biennial meetings known as ordinary meetings of the Conference of the Parties: in 1976 in Switzerland (the "Berne Conference"), in 1979 in Costa Rica (the "San José Conference"), in 1981 in India (the "New Delhi Conference") and in 1983 in Botswana (the "Gaborone Conference"). The Parties have also held two extraordinary meetings — one in Bonn in 1979 and the other in Gaborone in 1983 — and they held a "special working session" in Geneva in 1977.

The fact that 87 States are now Parties to CITES demonstrates the widespread appeal of a treaty which strictly limits international trade in species in genuine need of protection, allows a controlled trade in those able to sustain some exploitation and sets up a system of international cooperation to help it achieve its objectives. The Convention is attractive to the "producer" nations who see controls at the place of import as well as the place of export as essential weapons in their fight to protect their valuable wildlife resources from poachers and illegal traders. The "consumer" nations support it because without controls their legitimate dealers might have no raw material in which to trade in the generations to come.

This chapter starts by looking at the Convention's definition of "specimens" and "species". It goes on to consider the criteria for adding species to or removing them from the Appendices, the procedures for amending the Appendices, the rules governing international trade in species listed in the Appendices, the exceptional circumstances where these rules do not apply, the measures which Parties are required to take to enforce CITES, the Convention's system of administration, its relationship to other treaties, and the recent amendment to the Convention designed to allow the European Economic Community to become a Party in its own right.

2. Definitions

CITES applies to "specimens of species" listed in the Appendices to the Convention. It defines the terms "specimens" and "species" as follows:

a) "Specimens"

Article I(b) of CITES stipulates that "specimens" may be living or dead and include "any readily recognisable part or derivative thereof." The latter is important because it means that the Convention covers international trade in products such as ivory, skins and horns which form the bulk of the wildlife trade. The Convention does not define "readily recognisable" with the result that trade in certain parts and derivatives is regulated by some Parties but not others. The U.K., for example, has compiled a list of items which it deems to be readily recognisable while other Parties treat parts and derivatives on a case by case basis, regulating trade in those which they can actually identify. Because of the confusion arising from different Parties adopting different practices, Switzerland, the U.K. and the Federal Republic of Germany proposed at the San José Conference that a "minimum list" of readily recognisable parts and derivatives be adopted by all Parties. The proposal was defeated on the grounds that a "minimum list" would soon become a "maximum list" and that products such as turtle soup and ground rhinoceros horn, which might be deemed readily recognisable by some Parties but not by others, would be freely traded everywhere.[6]

b) "Species"

Article I(a) defines "species" to include "any species, subspecies or geographically separate population thereof". This allows different populations of the same species to be considered independently for listing purposes. All populations of saltwater crocodile (*Crocodylus porosus*), for example, are in Appendix I except for the Papua New Guinea population which is in Appendix II, and there are nearly thirty other similar "split listings" in the Appendices. The fact that CITES allows these split listings is important because it enables a Party with a non-endangered, well managed population of a species, that is endangered in other parts of its range, to include its own population in Appendix II and thus allow a limited commercial trade which would be prohibited if the population was in

---

[6] See M. Hornblower, "Noble Sentiments, Sharp Disagreements", *Audubon*, Vol. 81, No. 4 (1979), p. 111.

Appendix I. Conversely, it also enables Parties to list an endangered population of a species in Appendix I and thus protect it from commercial trade in situations where the species is not endangered in other parts of its range.

3.   *Criteria for including species in, or removing them from, the Appendices*

The text of CITES lays down the basic conditions for the inclusion of a species in Appendix I, II or III. However, it was generally agreed at the Berne Conference, held just one year after the Convention's entry into force, that more detailed guidelines on the listing of species in, and removing them from, Appendices I and II would be useful. The Berne Conference therefore adopted the controversial "Berne criteria" which now guide proposals to list or de-list species in or from Appendices I and II.[7] The Berne criteria are controversial not so much because of what they say with respect to the listing of species but because they make it difficult to remove a species from Appendix I or II or to transfer a species from Appendix I to II. This section looks at the listing criteria established by the Convention and at the amplifications thereto made by the Berne criteria.

a)   *Inclusion of species in Appendix I*

Article II(1) of CITES stipulates that Appendix I shall include "all species threatened with extinction which are or may be affected by trade". The Berne criteria state that "to qualify for Appendix I, a species must be currently threatened with extinction". Neither the Convention nor the Berne criteria define what is meant by "threatened with extinction", although the Berne criteria outline the types of information required in order to make that judgment. These include reports on population size, geographic range and potential causes of extinction. The Berne criteria also provide that a species should be included in Appendix I if it is seriously declining even if there is only a probability of trade, and that whole genera should be listed "if most of their species are threatened with extinction and if identification of individual species within the genus is difficult." The objective behind this latter provision is to control trade in species, even if they are widespread and common, which look like and could be confused with a threatened species. Without this safeguard unscrupulous traders might hoodwink customs officers and other enforcement agents into believing that a specimen of a threatened species was in fact a specimen of a common one and thereby escape

---

[7] See *Proceedings of the First Meeting of the Conference of the Parties*, Conf. 1.1, p. 31. Copies of the Proceedings of all meetings of the Conference of the Parties are available from the CITES Secretariat, 6 Rue du Maupas, P.O. Box 78, 1000 Lausanne 9, Switzerland.

CITES controls. The Berne criteria specify that any Appendix I species listed purely as a "look-alike" should be specially annotated as such.

When the Convention first came into force, Appendix I contained approximately 450 species, the majority being well-known endangered animals such as tiger (*Panthera tigris*), cheetah (*Acinonyx jubatus*), humpback whale (*Megaptera novaeangliae*) and peregrine falcon (*Falco peregrinus*). Since then, the number of Appendix I species has almost doubled and includes a much greater variety of wildlife, particularly endangered plants.

b) *Inclusion of species in Appendix II*

Article II(2) states that Appendix II shall include

(a) all species which although not necessarily now threatened with extinction may become so unless trade in specimens of such species is subject to strict regulation in order to avoid utilization incompatible with their survival; and (b) other species which must be subject to regulation in order that trade in specimens of certain species referred to in sub-paragraph (a) of this paragraph may be brought under effective control.

The purpose behind Article II(2)(a) is to regulate international trade in species which are not sufficiently endangered to warrant inclusion in Appendix I but which may become so unless trade is controlled. Species in this category range from heavily traded species whose populations are still relatively secure to those which are not yet in trade but could be vulnerable if, as frequently happens, traders suddenly switch from one target species to another. The purpose behind Article II(2)(b) is to control trade in species which are similar in appearance to and could be confused with those listed under Article II(2)(a). Although the reasons for listing a species in Appendix II may be quite different — either because it is potentially threatened (Article II(2)(a)) or because it looks like a potentially threatened species (Article II(2)(b)) — all species are treated equally once they are in Appendix II, and the Convention regulates trade in a species listed for II(2)(a) reasons in exactly the same way as a species listed for II(2)(b) reasons.[8]

In order to qualify for Appendix II under Article II(2)(a), the Berne criteria state that species need not currently be threatened with extinction but that "there should be some indication that they might become so." If there is such an indication, species should be listed "if they presently are subject to trade or are likely to become

---

[8] See pp. 253-255 below.

subject to trade." Regarding the listing of species as look-alikes under Article II(2)(b), the Berne criteria state that "genera should be listed if some of their species are threatened and identification of individual species within the genus is difficult. The same should apply to listing any smaller taxa within larger ones." In contrast to Appendix I which does not contain any species solely for reasons of similarity of appearance, numerous species have been listed in Appendix II under Article II(2)(b). At the New Delhi Conference, for example, the Parties listed the entire Order Psittaciformes (parrots and parrot-like birds) in Appendix II except for three species that were deemed to be easily recognisable and some thirty species that were already in Appendix I. The Order contains some 330 species most of which were included under Article II(2)(a), but over a hundred were listed under Article II(2)(b) because of the general similarity in appearance of psittacines.[9]

Appendix II is much larger than Appendix I, containing tens of thousands of species varying from the African elephant (*Loxodonta africana*) to the entire Order Cactaceae. The larger size of Appendix II is a consequence of the Parties' tendency to list individual species in Appendix I and whole families in Appendix II. For example, there are over 30,000 species of orchids and, except for a few in Appendix I, all of them are in Appendix II.

c)   *Removal of species from Appendix I or II*

The text of CITES makes no mention of the kind of information needed before a species can be removed from Appendix I or II or downgraded from Appendix I to II. The Berne Conference considered the problem and decided that any proposed decrease in protection for a species should be treated cautiously and that it was preferable to err on the side of protection than over-exploitation. The Conference resolved that

the deletion of a plant or animal taxon from Appendix I or II or the reduction of protection given to this taxon by transfer from Appendix I to Appendix II is a serious matter that should be approached with caution,

and that if a Conference of the Parties

errs in prematurely removing a plant or animal from protection, or lowering the level of protection afforded, the result can be the permanent loss of the resource. If it errs it should therefore be toward protection of the resource.[10]

[9] See *Proceedings of the Third Meeting of the Conference of the Parties*, Doc. 3.32, pp. 920-946.
[10] See *Proceedings of the First Meeting of the Conference of the Parties*, Conf. 1.2, p. 33.

The Berne Conference then established very strict conditions which must be satisfied before a species can be deleted from Appendix I or II or transferred from Appendix I to Appendix II. To do any of these things, the Berne criteria require

> positive scientific evidence that the plant or animal can withstand the exploitation resulting from the removal of protection...[this] evidence should include at least a well documented population survey, an indication of the population trend of the species, showing recovery sufficient to justify deletion, and an analysis of the potential for commercial trade in the species or population.

A proposal modifying the Berne criteria will be considered at the Fifth Meeting of the Conference of the Parties to CITES in April 1985. The proposal suggests that in the case of species listed in Appendix I before the Berne criteria were adopted (about 80% of all Appendix I species), the Berne criteria should not be applied to proposals to transfer them to Appendix II where (1) it is virtually impossible to supply the data required by the Berne criteria within reasonable time or with reasonable effort, but where one can take for granted that the populations concerned can withstand a certain level of exploitation for commercial trade and (2) the countries of origin agree to introduce a quota system which is deemed by the Conference of the Parties to be sufficiently safe so as not to endanger the survival of the species in the wild.

d) *Inclusion of species in Appendix III*

Article II(3) stipulates that Appendix III shall include "all species which any Party identifies as being subject to regulation within its jurisdiction for the purpose of preventing or restricting exploitation, and as needing the co-operation of other Parties in the control of trade."

The objective of Appendix III is to provide a mechanism whereby a Party with domestic legislation regulating the export of species not listed in Appendix I or II can seek international help in enforcing its legislation. For example, Canada listed the walrus (*Odobenus rosmarus*) in Appendix III (it is not in Appendix I or II) to inform the appropriate authorities in other States that trade in walrus is regulated in Canada and that imports of walrus, or its parts and derivatives, from Canada are illegal without a CITES export permit issued by the Canadian Management Authority. In spite of its potential value as an international aid to enforcement of national legislation, only ten Parties have so far listed a total of some 150 species in Appendix III.

4. *Procedures for amending the Appendices*

Each Party has the right to propose an amendment to Appendix I or II. There is a procedure which enables proposed amendments to be considered by postal vote,[11] but they are normally considered at the biennial meetings of the Conference of the Parties. Parties must submit proposed amendments to the Secretariat at least 150 days prior to the meeting at which they will be considered.[12] Proposals are adopted if approved by a two-thirds majority of Parties present and voting. If approved, they take effect 90 days thereafter.[13]

In contrast, any Party can unilaterally amend Appendix III at any time simply by notifying the Secretariat.[14] Additions to Appendix III take effect 90 days after the Secretariat has notified all the Parties, while withdrawals take effect just 30 days after such notification.[15]

5. *Rules governing international trade in specimens of species listed in the Appendices*

a) *Appendix I species*

The strictest rules apply to trade in Appendix I species. Article II(1) of CITES states that international trade in these species shall only be authorised in "exceptional circumstances", and Article III imposes such strict conditions on the grant of trading permits that legal trade among Parties is only possible if it is for non-commercial purposes. In practice this limits the legal trade in Appendix I species to a few hundred specimens each year.

(i) *Export*

Article III prohibits the export of specimens of Appendix I species without the prior grant and presentation of an export permit. A permit will be granted only if a Scientific Authority of the State of export determines that the "export will not be detrimental to the survival of that species" and if a Management Authority of the State of export is satisfied that the specimen was acquired legally and, if

---

[11] On receiving a proposal to amend the Appendices by means of the postal voting procedures, the Secretariat circulates a copy, together with its own recommendations, to the Parties and re-circulates any comments it receives on the proposal. If no objection is received within 30 days of this second circulation, the amendment will take effect 90 days thereafter. If a single objection is received, the Secretariat will notify the Parties and unless half the Parties vote within 60 days the proposed amendment will be referred to the next meeting of the Conference of the Parties. If half the Parties vote, the amendment will be passed by a two-thirds majority of those casting an affirmative or negative vote.

[12] CITES, Article XV(1)(a). It should be noted that Parties are not limited to making proposals concerning species which are native to their own territory.

[13] CITES, Article XV(1)(b) and (c).

[14] *Ibid.*, Article XVI(1).

[15] *Ibid.*, Article XVI(2) and (3).

alive, is "so prepared and shipped as to minimise the risk of injury, damage to health or cruel treatment".[16] The Management Authority must also be satisfied that the State of import has already granted an import permit for the specimen.[17] In any international trading of Appendix I species, therefore, the import permit must come first.

(ii)   Re-export

CITES prohibits the re-export of Appendix I species without a re-export certificate. This will only be granted after a Management Authority of the State of re-export is satisfied that the specimen was imported into that State in accordance with the provisions of CITES and, if alive, will be shipped with a minimum of risk to injury, damage to health or cruel treatment. In the case of living specimens, the Management Authority must also be satisfied that an import permit has been granted by the State of destination.[18]

(iii)   Import

Article III of the Convention prohibits the import of Appendix I species without the prior grant and presentation of an import permit and either an export permit or re-export certificate. Although there are strict controls on the grant of export permits, it is the tight restrictions on the grant of import permits which limit the trade so severely. An import permit may not be granted unless a Scientific Authority of the State of import has advised that the import is for purposes which are not detrimental to the survival of the species and that, if the specimen is alive, the proposed recipient is suitably equipped to house and care for it. More important still, an import permit may not be granted unless a Management Authority of the State of import is satisfied that the specimen will not be used for primarily commercial purposes.[19] This latter provision effectively prohibits international commercial trade in Appendix I species and limits legal trade among the Parties to specimens required for scientific and educational purposes and, in limited circumstances, to hunting trophies.[20]

However, a resolution adopted by the Gaborone Conference concerning the leopard, an Appendix I species, may set a precedent for broadening the circumstances in which Appendix I species may

---

[16]   Ibid., Article III(2)(a)-(c). See pp. 271-273 below for further discussion of Management and Scientific Authorities.

[17]   CITES, Article III(2)(d).

[18]   Ibid., Article III(4).

[19]   Ibid., Article III(3).

[20]   See Proceedings of the Second Meeting of the Conference of the Parties, Conf. 2.11, p. 48, for details of the restrictions recommended on the import of hunting trophies.

be traded. The Gaborone Conference rejected a proposal to transfer southern and eastern African populations of leopard from Appendix I to II on the grounds that a re-opening of commercial markets for leopard skins could prejudice threatened populations of leopard in other parts of its range. But the Conference also recognised that the leopard is not endangered in Botswana, Kenya, Malawi, Mozambique, Tanzania, Zambia and Zimbabwe and agreed that these States should be allowed to utilise the skins of leopards killed each year in defense of life or property. The Conference allotted an annual quota for each of the seven States, ranging from 20-80 skins, and recommended that other Parties should issue import permits for tagged leopard skins exported in accordance with the quotas, provided that they are satisfied that the owner of the skin will import no more than one skin in any calendar year and is importing the skin as a personal item which is not intended for re-sale. The system is subject to review by future meetings of the Conference of the Parties.[21]

(iv) *Introduction from the sea*

Finally, CITES prohibits the introduction of Appendix I species from the sea without a permit. The Convention deems a specimen to be introduced from the sea if it is "taken in the marine environment not under the jurisdiction of any State" and is imported into that State.[22] A permit will only be granted if a Scientific Authority of the State of introduction advises that it will not be detrimental to the survival of the species and if a Management Authority is satisfied that the other conditions for imports of Appendix I species have been met.[23] The objective of these requirements is to ensure that whales, sea turtles and other threatened marine animals are not taken on the high seas and then brought into the territory of a Party for commercial purposes. The annual reports submitted by the Parties give no indication that a permit for introducing Appendix I species from the sea has ever been granted, although it is conceivable that dolphinariums or other exhibitions which display marine animals might apply for one.

b) *Appendix II species*

Controls imposed on the export or re-export of Appendix II species are similar to those which apply to Appendix I species, but the rules for imports are much less stringent.

---

[21] See *Proceedings of the Fourth Meeting of the Conference of the Parties*, Conf. 4.13, pp. 59-60.
[22] CITES, Article I(e).
[23] *Ibid.*, Article III(5).

(i) *Export*

CITES prohibits the export of specimens of Appendix II species without a permit. To obtain a permit, a Scientific Authority and Management Authority of the State of export must make determinations similar to those required for the export of Appendix I species. Article IV(2) states that an export permit shall be granted only if a) a Management Authority of the State of export is satisfied that the specimen was acquired legally and, if alive, is "so prepared and shipped as to minimise the risk of injury, damage to health or cruel treatment" and b) a Scientific Authority of the State of export determines that the "export will not be detrimental to the survival of that species".

Article IV(3) requires a Scientific Authority in each Party to monitor export permits granted and actual exports made. Whenever a Scientific Authority determines that the export of any Appendix II species should be limited "in order to maintain that species throughout its range at a level consistent with its role in the ecosystems in which it occurs and well above the level at which that species might become eligible for inclusion in Appendix I", Article IV(3) requires it to advise the appropriate Management Authority of suitable measures to be taken to limit the grant of export permits.

(ii) *Re-export and introduction from the sea*

CITES prohibits the re-export of specimens of Appendix II species without a re-export certificate. A re-export certificate will be granted only after a Management Authority of the State of re-export is satisfied that the specimen was imported in accordance with the provisions of CITES and that, if alive, it will be shipped with a minimum of risk to injury, damage to health or cruel treatment.[24] The Convention also prohibits the introduction of Appendix II species from the sea without a certificate, and a certificate will only be granted if a Scientific Authority of the State of introduction determines that it will not be detrimental to the survival of the species and if a Management Authority of that State is satisfied that any living specimen will be handled so as to minimise the risk of injury, damage to health or cruel treatment.[25]

(iii) *Import*

CITES prohibits the import of specimens of Appendix II species unless they are accompanied by a valid export permit or re-export

---

[24] CITES, Article IV(5).
[25] *Ibid.*, Article IV(6).

certificate.[26] However, an import permit is not required, and imports for commercial purposes are permissible. As a result, international trade in tens of thousands of specimens of a single Appendix II species for which there is a large commercial demand may be carried on quite legally each year provided that the State of export has been advised by its Scientific Authority that the export of such quantities will not be detrimental to the survival of the species and provided that the other requirements with respect to export, re-export or introduction from the sea have been met.

(iv)   *Size of the trade*

Although the export of tens of thousands of specimens of an Appendix II species in one year is not necessarily illegal, the Gaborone Conference recognised that there are some heavily traded Appendix II species about which there is insufficient information on their ability to withstand such levels of trade. The Conference also acknowledged that Parties are not always able to comply with the requirement of Article IV of CITES that exports of Appendix II species shall be limited to a level which is not detrimental to their survival and which will maintain these species throughout their range at levels consistent with their roles in the ecosystems in which they occur. Worried about the possible adverse effects of excessive trade in some species, the Gaborone Conference recommended that the CITES Technical Committee[27] should identify those Appendix II species that are subject to "significant" international trade and for which scientific information on their capacity to withstand such levels of trade is insufficient to comply with the requirements of the Convention, as determined by the range States of the species. The Gaborone Conference also recommended that the Technical Committee should 1) at the request of the States involved, develop and negotiate measures necessary to ensure that trade in these species meets the requirements of the Convention and 2) encourage Parties to develop agreements for the cooperative implementation of these measures.[28]

(v)   *Evidence required for a "no-detriment" finding*

The CITES permit system raises an interesting question as to the amount of evidence a Scientific Authority of a State of export requires in order to determine whether or not a proposed export of a specimen of a species in Appendix I or II will be detrimental to the

[26] *Ibid.*, Article IV(4).
[27] See p. 274 below for further discussion of the Technical Committee.
[28] See *Proceedings of the Fourth Meeting of the Conference of the Parties*, Conf. 4.7, pp. 49-50.

survival of that species. This has never been considered by a meeting of the Conference of the Parties to CITES but it has been the subject of litigation in the U.S.A. In *Defenders of Wildlife, Inc. v. Endangered Species Scientific Authority*, the plaintiff, a private conservation organisation, contended that the U.S. Scientific Authority did not have adequate scientific data to support its finding that the proposed level of export of bobcat (*Felis rufus*) pelts for the 1979-80 season would not be detrimental to the survival of the species. The bobcat is listed in Appendix II. The United States Court of Appeals for the District of Columbia Circuit ruled in favour of the plaintiff, holding the export quotas set by the Scientific Authority invalid, on the basis that

> the Scientific Authority cannot make a valid no-detriment finding without (1) a reliable estimate of the number of bobcats and (2) information concerning the number of animals to be killed in the particular season. If that material is not presently available, the Scientific Authority must await its development before it authorises the export of bobcats.

The Appeals Court recognised that

> ...because of the secretive nature of the bobcat's life and behaviour, it is difficult to obtain accurate information about the size of the bobcat population. There are indications that techniques for making more accurate population estimates can and may be developed. We do not suggest that the Scientific Authority may base a no-detriment finding only upon some kind of head count of the animals or some other method of measurement that, as a practical matter, would be virtually impossible to make. All the Scientific Authority is required to do is to have a reasonably accurate estimate of the bobcat population before it makes a no-detriment finding. The Scientific Authority has considerable discretion to determine the method by which that estimate may be made and in evaluating its reliability.

The Court went on to say that

> any doubt whether the killing of a particular number of bobcats will adversely affect the survival of the species must be resolved in favor of protecting the animals and not in favor of approving the export of their pelts...The approach of the Scientific Authority often seemed primarily concerned with an acceptable basis for authorizing bobcat exports despite the absence of convincing factual grounds for making no-detriment findings.[29]

[29] 659 F.2d 168, (D.C. Cir.), *cert denied*, 454 U.S. 963 (1981).

The effect of the Appeals Court decision was overturned in 1982 by an amendment to the Endangered Species Act of 1973, which implements CITES in the U.S.A.[30] The amendment puts the duties of the U.S. Management and Scientific Authorities into the hands of the U.S. Secretary of the Interior and states that

> the Secretary shall base the determinations and advice given by him under Article IV of the [CITES] Convention with respect to wildlife upon the best available biological information derived from professionally accepted wildlife management practices; but is not required to make, or require any State to make, estimates of population size in making such determinations or giving such advice.[31]

Neither the views of the U.S. Appeals Court nor those of the U.S. Congress on the evidence required for a "no-detriment" finding are binding on other Parties to CITES. However, the Appeals Court decision should carry greater weight in the eyes of other Parties faced with a similar dilemma since it was a non-biased judicial interpretation of the provisions of CITES, while the amendment to the Endangered Species Act was a politically motivated action designed to bring about a resumption in the export of bobcat pelts.

(vi) *Export of species listed under Article II(2)(b)*

The U.S.A. has taken the view that if a species is listed in Appendix II for look-alike reasons only (i.e. under Article II (2)(b) — see page 244 above) the State of export need not determine whether proposed exports of the species will be detrimental to the survival of *that* species but need only consider whether proposed exports will be detrimental to the survival of *other* species that it looks like and was listed to protect. The bobcat, an apparently incurable source of controversy in the U.S.A., is once again the species most seriously affected. In August 1983, the U.S. Government announced that it now considered the bobcat to be listed in Appendix II purely as a look-alike under Article II(2)(b) rather than as a potentially threatened species under Article II(2)(a) (again see page 244 above for an explanation of the difference between Articles II(2)(b) and II(2)(a)). It would therefore be inappropriate, the U.S. Government stated, to consider whether proposed export levels of bobcat pelts would be detrimental to the survival of bobcats, and it would only be appropriate to consider whether proposed export levels would be detrimental to the survival of other spotted cats which the bobcat looks like and was listed to protect.[32]

While not denying the right of the U.S.A. to consider an Appendix II species to be listed as a look-alike only, other Parties have disagreed with the U.S. interpretation of how they should treat proposed exports of such a species. In the view of these other Parties, Article IV(2) of CITES makes it quite clear that Scientific Authorities of exporting States must be satisfied that a proposed export of a specimen of any Appendix II species will not be detrimental to the survival of *that* species before granting a permit for its export, irrespective of whether the species was listed under Article II(2)(a) or II(2)(b). Article IV(2) states that "the export of *any* specimen of a species included in Appendix II shall require the prior grant and presentation of an export permit" and that a permit shall only be given "if the Scientific Authority of the State of export has advised that the export will not be detrimental to the survival of *that* species" (emphasis added). During discussions on the matter at the Gaborone Conference,

> the delegation of Australia stated that once a species is listed on Appendix II, no distinction can be made as to whether it is listed under Article II(2)(a) or II(2)(b). In particular, Article IV paragraph (2) of the Convention makes no distinction as to the findings required of exporting countries in relation to the export of any specimen of a species included in Appendix II. The delegation of Australia stated that such an application of Article IV paragraph 2 was essential for the protection of Appendix II species.[33]

The Australian view was echoed by the Norwegian and U.K. delegations and by the IUCN observer at the Gaborone Conference, and has since been supported by the CITES Secretariat.[34] The author shares the view that Parties should not grant a permit for the export of a specimen of any Appendix II species without first being advised by their Scientific Authority that the export will not be detrimental to the survival of the species. Article IV(2) imposes such an obligation in clear and unambiguous terms, the objective of the Convention is to prevent populations of Appendix II species from being jeopardised by international trade, and the rules of international law require that

[32] See U.S. Federal Register, Vol. 48, No. 161, pp. 37494-8 (18 August 1983).

[33] See *Proceedings of the Fourth Meeting of the Conference of the Parties*, Plen. 4.11, pp. 139-40.

[34] *Ibid.* In a letter to the author dated 13 June 1983, the Assistant Secretary General of the CITES Secretariat stated that "it is equally clear that when a species is listed in Appendix II, the Convention does not make any distinction as to whether the species is listed under Article II(2)(a) or II(2)(b)." He went on to say that Article IV(2) "should be implemented on the basis of the biological status of the species concerned in the country of export."

a treaty shall be interpreted in good faith in accordance with the ordinary meaning to be given to the terms of the treaty in their context and in the light of its object and purpose.[35]

c) *Appendix III species*

Restrictions on trade in Appendix III species are limited to specimens originating from the State which listed them. To export specimens from that State, Article V(2) of CITES requires the prior grant and presentation of an export permit, and to import specimens from that State the importer must present a certificate of origin and an export permit. If the import is from any other State, a certificate of origin is sufficient.[36] Re-export is permissible from any State without restriction provided a Management Authority of that State certifies that the specimen is being re-exported.[37]

d) *Permits*

CITES requires that a separate permit or certificate be obtained for each consignment of specimens and that an export permit be considered valid for six months from the date it was granted.[38] In order to standardise permits and make them more difficult to forge, the New Delhi Conference recommended that Parties should adapt their permits as closely as possible to a standard model approved at the Conference and should use security paper or serially numbered adhesive security stamps.[39] The Conference commissioned a study to evaluate the implementation and effectiveness of these recommendations.[40] In September 1982, coinciding with the entry into force of new regulations to implement CITES, the Zimbabwean Management Authority initiated the use of a security stamp on all CITES export documents, making Zimbabwe the first Party to adopt this procedure.[41] Because of the particularly serious problem of illegal trade in African elephant ivory, the New Delhi Conference approved a special marking system for ivory using punch-dies.[42] CITES security stamps were supplied to all interested Parties in June 1984.

[35] Vienna Convention on the Law of Treaties, Article 31(1). See Chapter 1, p. 7 above.

[36] CITES, Article V(3).

[37] *Ibid.*, Article V(4).

[38] *Ibid.*, Article VI(2) and (5). The Gaborone Conference resolved that export permits and re-export certificates, when required for import permits, must be presented within six months of the date on which granted. If the transaction is not completed within the six month period, the export permit should be considered void (Conf. 4.9).

[39] See *Proceedings of the Third Meeting of the Conference of the Parties*, Conf. 3.6 and 3.7, pp. 46-52.

[40] See *Proceedings of the Third Meeting of the Conference of the Parties*, Conf. 3.6, p. 47.

[41] See Zimbabwe's Control of Goods (Import and Export) (Wildlife) Regulations of 1982.

[42] See *Proceedings of the Third Meeting of the Conference of the Parties*, Conf. 3.12, pp. 60-1.

e)   *Trade with non-Parties*

CITES cannot prevent free trade between non-Parties, but it can and does regulate trade between Parties and non-Parties. It prohibits Parties from trading with non-Parties unless the latter produce documentation comparable to that required of Parties,[43] and the New Delhi Conference agreed on strict standards for assessing comparability.[44] The tough line taken in this respect may have contributed to the steadily increasing membership of the Convention since non-Parties may feel that the advantages of being a Party, and therefore in a position to influence the development of the Convention, outweigh those of remaining outside where there are ever fewer States with which they can freely trade.

f)   *Non-customs zones*

Each Party is deemed to have sovereignty over the whole of its territory, and CITES makes no special provision for airport lounges (including duty free shops), free ports or other non-customs zones. Aware that some Parties were allowing specimens of species in the Appendices to be exported from non-customs zones without CITES permits, the Gaborone Conference urged the Parties to apply the Convention to all parts of their territory including non-customs zones.[45]

6.   *Exemptions*

There are a number of circumstances where international trade in specimens of species in the Appendices does not require a CITES permit. They are:

a)   *Transit*

CITES permits are not required for "the transit or trans-shipment of specimens through or in the territory of a Party while the specimens remain in customs control".[46] The intention behind the exemption was to avoid imposing an unreasonable burden on shipments that stop in a State on the way to their ultimate destination merely to change planes or to continue their journey by other means of transport. It was felt that stoppages for these

---

[43] CITES, Article X. It should also be emphasised that Parties must comply with the permit requirements of CITES when trading with non-Parties. Thus, for example, the requirements of the Convention with respect to import permits for Appendix I species apply to Parties whether or not the specimen concerned originated in a non-Party country.

[44] See *Proceedings of the Third Meeting of the Conference of the Parties*, Conf. 3.8, pp. 53-4.

[45] See *Proceedings of the Fourth Meeting of the Conference of the Parties*, Conf. 4.10(b), p. 53.

[46] CITES, Article VII(1).

purposes did not constitute a genuine import into the State concerned and that it would be unreasonable for that State to require valid CITES documentation before allowing the shipment to continue.

In 1980 the U.K. government received reports that middle men were importing Appendix I species from non-Parties without a permit and were holding them theoretically "in transit", which meant they did not have to obtain a CITES permit, while they were in fact looking for a buyer in other non-Parties. Once they had located a buyer, they simply sent the specimen on to him without a permit. In order to prevent traders in Party countries from abusing the transit exemption in this way, the Gaborone Conference recommended that the exemption should apply only to situations where a specimen was in the process of shipment to a named consignee and where the shipment was interrupted only by the necessity implicit in those arrangements.[47]

b) *Pre-Convention specimens*

CITES also waives permit requirements for international trade in specimens of listed species acquired before the Convention applied to them. In order to qualify for the exemption, the Management Authority of the State of export or re-export must certify that the specimen is pre-Convention.[48]

The objective of this exemption was to allow traders to clear their existing stocks when the Convention first came into force and to permit them to continue to trade in items such as old leopard skin coats. However, there has been a considerable amount of argument as to the date on which the Convention "applies" to a specimen for the purposes of the exemption. If X species was listed in Appendix I in 1977 and Y State acceded to CITES in 1982, does the Convention apply to a specimen of X species which was acquired in Y State in 1980? It has been argued that the Convention only applies to the specimen from the date that Y State became a Party and therefore that the specimen can be traded without a CITES permit by virtue of the pre-Convention exemption. However, it has also been argued that CITES applies to all specimens of a species, whether or not they are located in a State that is a Party to the Convention, from the date that the species is first included in the Appendices. If this argument is accepted, CITES does apply to the specimen acquired in 1980 which cannot therefore qualify for the pre-Convention exemption. Proponents of this latter argument point to the provisions dealing

[47] See *Proceedings of the Fourth Meeting of the Conference of the Parties*, Conf. 4.10(a), p. 53.
[48] CITES, Article VII(2).

with trade with non-Parties — i.e. Parties cannot accept a specimen of a listed species from a non-Party unless the latter produces comparable documentation to that required of a Party[49] — in support of their contention because it demonstrates that CITES can apply to a specimen of a listed species before the State in which it is situated becomes a Party to the Convention. After lengthy debate on this point, the Gaborone Conference decided not to recommend either interpretation as the correct one but left it up to each Party to make its own determination.[50]

There has also been some argument regarding the date that a specimen is "acquired" for purposes of the pre-Convention exemption. It has been asserted that a tree is acquired when the land on which it stands comes into ownership and that if this happens earlier than the date on which the Convention came into force the landowner is entitled to export timber from the tree without a CITES permit on the basis that it is a pre-Convention specimen. In order to close this potentially serious loophole, the Gaborone Conference recommended that the word "acquired" meant "the initial removal of whole live or dead specimens from their habitat or the introduction to personal possession of any part or derivative" in this context.[51]

c)   *Personal effects*

"Personal or household effects" may also be traded without a CITES permit.[52] They are not defined by the Convention and, consequently, some Parties apply the exemption liberally — the U.S.A., for example, considers any items of personal baggage to be personal or household effects, with a limit of twelve items for plants — while other Parties are more strict. Canada will not grant an exemption unless the specimen has been in the possession of the person concerned for at least two years, and Switzerland will not grant an exemption for live animals.[53]

The objective of the exemption is not to put an undue burden on, say, someone with a crocodile skin wristwatch strap whose business involves a lot of international travel or a holidaymaker who takes his pet parrot abroad for a couple of weeks. However, in order to prevent the personal effects exemption from being seriously abused, the Convention specifies two circumstances where it shall not apply.

[49] See p. 256 above.
[50] See *Proceedings of the Fourth Meeting of the Conference of the Parties*, Conf. 4.11, pp. 55-6.
[51] *Ibid.*
[52] CITES, Article VII(3).
[53] See *Proceedings of the Third Meeting of the Conference of the Parties*, Doc. 3.17, section 3.1, p. 581.

The first is where specimens of Appendix I species "were acquired by the owner outside his State of usual residence, and are being imported into that State".[54] It is not permissible, therefore, for an Australian who acquires the skin of a cheetah, an Appendix I species, in Africa to take it back into Australia without a CITES permit even if it is a genuine personal effect. It is interesting to note that the Convention does not prevent him from taking the skin to any other State without a CITES permit provided he can convince that State's customs officers that it is a genuine personal effect. The negotiators of CITES may have felt that the chances of someone buying a specimen of an Appendix I species outside his own State and then taking it to another State as a personal effect without then bringing it back to his own State were sufficiently small so as not to jeopardise the species concerned.

The second circumstance where the personal effects exemption does not apply is where specimens of Appendix II species:

(i) were acquired by the owner outside his State of usual residence and in a State where removal from the wild occurred;

(ii) are being imported into the owner's State of usual residence; and

(iii) the State where removal from the wild occurred requires the prior grant of export permits before any export of such specimens.[55]

To give an example of what this means in practice, a resident of a Party will not need a CITES permit to take home from Hong Kong as many items of African elephant ivory as he can prove are personal effects (assuming that the State of import does not have stricter domestic legislation than is required by the Convention) because the African elephant is in Appendix II and Hong Kong has no wild elephant populations. However, he will need to present a CITES export permit in order to import the same items from the African State where removal from the wild occurred if that State requires the prior grant of a permit before ivory can legally be exported.

The exemption for personal or household effects is clearly open to abuse because few Parties limit the quantity or monetary value of the personal effects that a person may export or import and few Parties impose restrictions on re-sale once these items have been imported.[56] Whether the exemption is in fact seriously abused is difficult to assess because of the lack of available information. Most Parties do not even keep a record of the number of personal effects that they allow to be exported or imported without a CITES permit.

---

[54] CITES, Article, VII(3)(a).

[55] *Ibid.*, Article VII(3)(b).

[56] See *Proceedings of the Third Meeting of the Conference of the Parties*, Doc. 3.17, section 3.5., p. 583.

d)   *Captive breeding and artificial propagation*

Article VII(4) of CITES states that specimens of Appendix I animals "bred in captivity" for commercial purposes and specimens of Appendix I plants "artificially propagated" for commercial purposes shall be deemed to be in Appendix II. The San José Conference adopted detailed criteria which must be satisfied before a species may be considered to be "bred in captivity", the essence of which are that the breeding stock must be established in a manner not detrimental to the survival of the species in the wild and that it must be managed in a manner "capable of reliably producing second generation offspring in a controlled environment" and in a manner "designed to maintain the breeding stock indefinitely." Augmentation from the wild is only permitted for the purpose of adding occasional specimens to prevent inbreeding. The Conference established similar criteria which must be satisfied before plants can be considered "artificially propagated".[57]

The criteria make good sense because they require a captive stock of Appendix I species to be capable of sustaining itself without significant replenishment from the wild before any international trade for commercial purposes is allowed. However, they have been the source of considerable controversy, particularly in relation to the Cayman Turtle Farm, an operation established in the Cayman Islands in 1968 in order to breed green turtles (*Chelonia mydas*), an Appendix I species, in captivity for commercial purposes. Slow maturing species such as sea turtles take many years to produce second generation specimens, and in 1979 the U.S.A. — the prime intended market for the products of the Farm — banned imports of Cayman turtle products because the Farm did not yet qualify for the captive bred exemption. The U.K. has always been sympathetic to the problems faced by Cayman Turtle Farm (the Cayman Islands are a former British colony), and in 1982, backed by the U.S.A., the U.K. government urged the CITES Technical Committee to draft an amendment to the San José criteria which would allow commercial trade in specimens of slow maturing species in certain circumstances even if they were not yet "capable of reliably producing second generation offspring in a controlled environment". The proposed amendment was considered by the Gaborone Conference but was referred back to the Technical Committee after numerous Parties had spoken of the importance of maintaining the integrity of the San José definition.[58] A U.K. proposal to make the Cayman Turtle Farm a special case and to

---

[57] See *Proceedings of the Second Meeting of the Conference of the Parties*, Conf. 2.12, pp. 49-50.

[58] See *Proceedings of the Fourth Meeting of the Conference of the Parties*, Doc. 4.45, pp. 1092-3.

deem its products to be specimens of species in Appendix II will be considered by the Fifth Meeting of the Conference of the Parties in April 1985.

e) *Ranching*

Although not strictly an exemption to the Convention, the question of "ranching" Appendix I species has received special treatment from the Parties and merits brief consideration here. A ranching operation is not closed cycle like captive breeding but involves the rearing of wildlife, usually from wild caught eggs or young, in a controlled environment.

Since they do not qualify for the captive bred exemption, specimens of Appendix I species cannot be ranched and then traded internationally for commercial purposes without violating CITES. At the San José Conference, however, delegates from several Parties argued that they could only justify protecting habitats of endangered species from agricultural and industrial development if they could derive some economic benefit from the species. They stated that they could not realistically be expected to achieve closed cycle captive breeding operations, but that ranching might be a viable proposition for some species. In response to these concerns, the New Delhi Conference developed and agreed on "ranching criteria" which allow Parties to transfer a population of an Appendix I species to Appendix II for ranching purposes in certain circumstances.[59] The basic requirements of these criteria are that the population is no longer endangered and that the ranching operation will benefit the conservation of the population. Four ranching proposals were submitted to the Gaborone Conference, but only one — a proposal to transfer the Zimbabwean population of Nile crocodile (*Crocodylus niloticus*) to Appendix II for ranching purposes — was approved unconditionally. A proposal to transfer the Suriname population of green turtle to Appendix II for ranching purposes was rejected pending submission to the Technical Committee of further details by Suriname of a system of marking and certification of products to ensure that turtles ranched by Suriname could not be confused with, and therefore lead to illegal trade in, other populations of turtles. Proposals to transfer the Australian population of saltwater crocodile (*Crocodylus porosus*) and the Tromelin and Europa Islands populations of green turtle from Appendix I to Appendix II for ranching purposes were withdrawn at the Gaborone Conference.[60]

[59] See *Proceedings of the Third Meeting of the Conference of the Parties*, Conf. 3.15, pp. 65-6, for full details of the ranching criteria.
[60] See *Proceedings of the Fourth Meeting of the Conference of the Parties*, Plen. 4.10 (Rev.), pp. 128-30.

However, they will be reconsidered, together with several new ranching proposals, at the Fifth Meeting of the Conference of the Parties in April 1985.

f) Science and exhibition

Article VII(6) of CITES exempts the non-commercial exchange of specimens between scientists or scientific institutions from permit requirements provided that the scientists or scientific institutions have been registered for these purposes by a Management Authority of the State in which they are situated. Article VII(7) gives Management Authorities the discretion to allow specimens which are part of travelling zoos, circuses or other travelling exhibitions to move without a permit.[61]

g) Reservations

Like many treaties concerned with the conservation of wildlife, CITES allows Parties to exempt themselves from the requirements of the Convention in relation to species whose inclusion in the Appendices they find objectionable by taking a "reservation". Reservations must be specific as to the species that they cover and must be taken at the time a Party deposits its instrument of ratification, acceptance, approval or accession to the Convention.[62] Parties may also reserve on any subsequent amendment to the Appendices provided that the reservation is registered with the Swiss government within 90 days of the adoption of the amendment.[63] Reservations may be withdrawn at any time.

Fifteen Parties have reservations in effect at the time of writing. Some have reservations on just one species while others have reserved on a wide variety of wildlife. Reasons for taking reservations need not be given, although they are normally taken by Parties objecting to increased protection for species in which they have an established trade.[64] France and Italy, for example, took reservations

---

[61] See Proceedings of the Second Meeting of the Conference of the Parties, Conf. 2.14, for details of guidelines for the non-commercial loan, donation or exchange of museum and herbarium specimens.

[62] CITES, Article XXIII(2).

[63] Ibid., Articles XV(3) and XVI(2).

[64] See Proceedings of the Third Meeting of the Conference of the Parties, Doc. 3.22, pp. 716-725. See also Proceedings of the Fourth Meeting of the Conference of the Parties, Doc. 4.19, Annex 1, pp. 450-53. In a letter to the author dated 13 September 1982, Dr. Peter Dollinger of the Swiss Management Authority gave the reasons for Swiss reservations as "inadequate supporting statements (proposals from India at the San José meeting) and implementation problems (e.g. national legislation insufficient for plants)".

on species of reptiles important to their luxury leather trade,[65] and Japan took reservations on whales, sea turtles and monitor lizards, products of which are all in great demand in Japanese markets.

Article XXIII(3) of CITES requires that Parties be treated as non-Parties in relation to trade in species on which they have taken reservations. This should mean that the effect of reservations in relation to trade between reserving and non-reserving Parties is minimal because non-Parties must produce documentation comparable to that required of Parties.[66] In practice, however, reservations can be very damaging. Not only can reserving Parties trade freely with non-Parties, but reservations sometimes encourage trade to continue, albeit illegally, with other Parties. For example, Japan has taken a reservation on green, hawksbill and olive ridley turtles (*Chelonia mydas*, *Eretmochelys imbricata* and *Lepidochelys olivacea*), all of which are in Appendix I. In 1981 Japan imported over 25,000 kilogrammes of turtle skin and over 10,000 kilogrammes of turtle leather (mostly green and olive ridley turtles). Japan also imported over 50,000 kilogrammes of raw and worked tortoiseshell (mostly hawksbill turtles). Almost all these imports of turtle leather came from Mexico, a non-Party, but almost all imports of worked tortoiseshell came from Indonesia which is a Party. Ecuador, Philippines, Kenya, Tanzania, Seychelles, Pakistan, Nicaragua and Panama are other Parties which exported wild caught Appendix I sea turtles to Japan in significant quantities in 1981 notwithstanding that international commercial trade in Appendix I species is prohibited.[67] Another damaging effect of reservations is that Parties are under no obligation to provide the Secretariat with data on trade in species on which they have taken reservations because they are deemed to be non-Parties with respect to those species. Valuable statistical material for the purposes of monitoring trade may therefore be lost. Recognising this, the Gaborone Conference called on Parties to maintain and report trading statistics for species on which they have reservations.[68]

The Gaborone Conference also recommended that Parties which take reservations on the transfer of a species from Appendix II to Appendix I should continue to treat the species as if it was still in Appendix II and that Parties which take reservations on the inclusion of an unlisted species in Appendix I should at least treat it

[65] France and Italy have now withdrawn their reservations. On 1 January 1984 all Member States of the EEC were obliged to withdraw their reservations by a Regulation (No. 3626/82, *O.J. Eur. Comm.* No. L 384, 31 December 1982, p. 1) implementing CITES in the EEC.

[66] See p. 256 above.

[67] See *Sea Turtles in Trade* (Center for Environmental Education, 1983), pp. 1-14.

[68] See *Proceedings of the Fourth Meeting of the Conference of the Parties*, Conf. 4.25, p. 81.

as an Appendix II species.[69] These recommendations were made because of the Convention's provision that a Party with a reservation on a species shall be treated as a non-Party with respect to trade in that species. Literally interpreted, this means that a Party taking a reservation on the transfer of a species from Appendix II to Appendix I would not even be required to treat the species as if it was still in Appendix II. France adopted this position after taking a reservation on the transfer in 1979 of all populations of saltwater crocodile from Appendix II to Appendix I except for the Papua New Guinea population which remained in Appendix II. France notified the Secretariat that although it would treat the Papua New Guinea population as still in Appendix II, it considered French trade in all other populations totally outside the scope of the Convention.[70] The consequence of this interpretation was that trade in the less endangered Papua New Guinea population was subject to CITES permit requirements in France while trade in other more endangered populations was not. The recommendations made by the Gaborone Conference should ensure that such an absurd situation does not re-occur.

7. Enforcement measures

Article VIII of CITES requires the Parties to take a number of different measures that are designed to improve the Convention's level of enforcement. These include penalising trade which violates the terms of the Convention, confiscating illegally traded specimens, designating special ports of exit and entry for wildlife, maintaining records of exports and imports of specimens of listed species and submitting annual reports to the Secretariat summarising this information.

a) Penalties

Article VIII requires each Party to take measures to penalise trade which violates the terms of the Convention and to penalise possession of specimens which have been so traded.[71]

CITES gives no guidance as to the level of penalties which should be imposed on persons convicted of illegal trade or possession with the result that there has been a considerable variation in the punishments inflicted. For example, Hong Kong made some 350 prosecutions under its Animals and Plants (Protection of

[69] Ibid.
[70] See Proceedings of the Third Meeting of the Conference of the Parties, Doc. 3.22, p. 723 and Proceedings of the Fourth Meeting of the Conference of the Parties, Doc. 4.19, Annex 1, pp. 450-53.
[71] CITES, Article VIII(1)(a).

Endangered Species) Ordinance between June 1978 and November 1981,[72] but a fine of approximately U.S.$1,000 was the highest penalty levied because it was the maximum allowed under the Ordinance.[73] Thus, although a trader who had illegally imported 319 cheetah skins into Hong Kong in 1979 was fined the maximum amount, the fine bore no relation to the value of the shipment. On the other hand, penalties in the U.S.A. have been much heavier. In an 18 month period between January 1980 and July 1981, 23 offenders were imprisoned with sentences ranging from 6 months to 5 years.[74]

b)   *Confiscation*

Article VIII also requires each Party to provide for the confiscation of live or dead specimens which have been illegally traded or possessed.[75] In States where penalties imposed by the courts have been relatively light, confiscation can be a very effective deterrent because the loss of a valuable consignment may inflict a serious financial blow on the offender. In Hong Kong, for example, confiscation is mandatory on conviction under the Animals and Plants (Protection of Endangered Species) Ordinance,[76] so that even a technical offender whose fine is light may suffer a considerable loss. A trader who imported 17 Cape fur seal skins into Hong Kong without an import licence in 1979, notwithstanding that he had an export permit from the U.K., was convicted under the Ordinance and fined a nominal U.S.$100 because of the technical nature of the offence but his entire shipment, worth approximately U.S.$1,500, was confiscated and lost to him forever.[77] Similarly, a Canadian who illegally imported worked ivory worth about U.S.$150,000 into Canada in 1978 suffered a relatively small fine but a huge financial loss because the ivory was confiscated.[78]

Although it may be a valuable deterrent to illegal trade, confiscation creates its own problems particularly with respect to the disposal of confiscated stock. CITES requires that confiscated live specimens are either returned to their State of export or sent to a

[72] Comment made to the author by C. Huxley, ex-Enforcement Officer, Hong Kong Management Authority.
[73] Animals and Plants (Protection of Endangered Species) Ordinance, Cap. 187.
[74] See "Busted: America's Snake Smugglers", *New Scientist* (August 1981).
[75] CITES, Article VIII(1)(b).
[76] Animals and Plants (Protection of Endangered Species) Ordinance, Cap. 187, Section 13(1).
[77] Comment made to the author by C. Huxley, see note 72 above.
[78] Comment made to the author by E. Lapointe, Secretary General of the CITES Secretariat and ex-Enforcement Officer of Canadian Management Authority.

rescue centre or other appropriate place.[79] There have been a few cases of live specimens being returned to their State of export. Eight chimpanzees, three pythons and two crocodiles illegally shipped to France in 1979 were seized by French authorities and returned to West Africa. Thirty crocodiles illegally imported into Hong Kong from Singapore in 1980 were returned to Indonesia, which was believed to be the true country of origin. The Federal Republic of Germany returned two chimpanzees to the Gambia in 1981 where they were prepared for reintroduction to the wild at the Gambian Chimpanzee Rehabilitation Centre. Practical difficulties, notably the cost and problems involved in reintroducing animals to the wild, inevitably make such cases relatively rare particularly since the Convention stipulates that the expenses involved should be met by the State of export[80] which is normally a developing country and hard pressed for cash. However, Australia and the U.K. have recently enacted legislation authorising customs officials to recover from the importer any expenses incurred in returning confiscated live specimens to their country of origin,[81] and the Gaborone Conference recommended that all Parties take such legislative measures.[82] Reintroduction to the wild may, therefore, become more feasible in some instances.

In cases where return to the wild is not practicable and where adequate rescue centres are not available, the problem of disposal of Appendix I specimens is particularly serious because re-entry into commercial trade is prohibited. In an attempt to ease this problem, the New Delhi Conference recommended a system whereby lists of each Party's confiscated living specimens and appropriate institutions to house them would be made available to the Secretariat and all other Parties in order to promote international exchange. The Conference recommended that institutions with facilities to promote reproduction of the species in question, such as zoos, should be given priority in receiving specimens.[83]

The problem of disposal is equally acute with respect to dead specimens. In 1979, the U.S. government reported that the value of skins, horns, ivory and other confiscated stock in its possession was approximately U.S.$2.5 million, that it cost U.S.$51,000 annually merely to rent storage space for the stock and that some specimens were being stolen.[84] Conscious of the expense and security risks

[79] CITES, Article VIII(4)(b).
[80] Ibid.
[81] Wildlife and Countryside Act, 1981, Schedule 10(2).
[82] See Proceedings of the Fourth Meeting of the Conference of the Parties, Conf 4. 18, pp. 68-9.
[83] See Proceedings of the Third Meeting of the Conference of the Parties, Conf. 3.14, pp. 63-4.
[84] News Release, U.S. Department of the Interior (21 September 1981).

involved with such stockpiles and aware of the need to prevent specimens of Appendix I species from re-entering commercial trade, the New Delhi Conference recommended the establishment of a system of international exchange for non-commercial scientific and educational purposes similar to that recommended for live specimens. This would allow specimens to be sent to other Parties for display in museums or to train enforcement officers in the identification of species. If international exchange should prove not to be practicable, the New Delhi Conference recommended that Parties "save in storage or destroy" excess stock of Appendix I specimens.[85] The action taken at the Conference could be especially significant for valuable items such as rhinoceros horn which it may be preferable to destroy rather than risk theft and consequent re-entry into illegal trade. The government of Bophuthatswana publicly burned its confiscated stock of rhinoceros horns in 1980 in order to ensure that they would not find their way back on to the market. In 1981 Switzerland also destroyed a number of confiscated skins, and in 1982 the U.S. government promulgated regulations authorising the destruction of confiscated stock in certain circumstances.[86]

c)   *Ports of exit and entry*

Article VIII(3) urges each Party to designate special ports of exit and entry through which all exports and imports of wildlife must pass. Recognising that identification of wildlife, especially parts and derivatives, is very difficult and that enforcement of CITES is a complex matter, Article VIII(3) was intended to encourage Parties to build up expertise among their enforcement officers in a few ports and then to channel all trade through those ports. It was hoped that this would minimise the delay for legal traders and would help reduce smuggling because it would enable a few experts in species identification to inspect the bulk of the trade. Only a few Parties have so far adopted the system of restricted ports of exit and entry for wildlife, but in the U.S.A., where the system has been adopted and just 9 ports are authorised to handle wildlife exports and imports, the evidence suggests that it has helped combat illegal trade.[87]

---

[85] See *Proceedings of the Third Meeting of the Conference of the Parties*, Conf. 3.14, p. 64.
[86] 50 C.F.R. Part 12.3 and Part 12.30-39.
[87] See U.S. Federal Register, Vol. 46, No. 169, p. 43834 (1 September 1981).

d)   *Records and reports*

Article VIII obliges each Party to maintain detailed records of trade in specimens of species included in the Appendices[88] and to submit annual reports to the Secretariat summarising the trade.[89] The Secretariat is responsible for reviewing these reports[90] and has arranged for the Wildlife Trade Monitoring Unit of IUCN's Conservation Monitoring Centre to computerise the statistics so that a detailed analysis of international trade can be produced on a species by species level. The Parties are also required to submit biennial reports on the legislative, regulatory and administrative measures they have taken to enforce the provisions of CITES.[91] Unless it would be inconsistent with their domestic legislation, Parties are obliged to make both sets of reports available to the public.[92]

The primary function of the annual reports is to monitor international trade in wildlife covered by CITES, and numerous recommendations have been made with a view to making the annual reports more effective as a monitoring instrument. The Berne Conference recommended that all Parties should adopt the calendar year beginning 1 January as the period covered by annual reports.[93] The San José Conference recommended that reports should follow a uniform format in order to make statistics more easily comparable, that the reports should indicate whether they are based on permits issued or on actual exports and imports, and that they should be submitted not later than 31 October of the year following the period covered.[94] The New Delhi Conference recommended that the mandate of the Technical Committee should be expanded to review annual reports and requested the Secretariat to continue its comparative tabulation of annual reports with a view to publishing a Yearbook of International Wildlife Trade.[95]

In some respects, statistical material gathered from Parties' annual reports has been useful. It has provided a general picture of the extent of trade in many species and of the countries involved in

---

[88] CITES, Article VIII(6). These records shall cover "(a) the names and addresses of exporters and importers; and (b) the number and type of permits and certificates granted; the States with which such trade occured; the numbers or quantities and types of specimens, names of species as included in Appendices I, II and III and, where applicable, the size and sex of the specimens in question."

[89] CITES, Article VIII(7)(a).

[90] *Ibid.*, Article XII(2)(d).

[91] *Ibid.*, Article VIII(7)(b).

[92] *Ibid.*, Article VIII(8).

[93] See *Proceedings of the First Meeting of the Conference of the Parties*, Conf. 1.5, p. 38.

[94] See *Proceedings of the Second Meeting of the Conference of the Parties*, Conf. 2.16, p. 57.

[95] See *Proceedings of the Third Meeting of the Conference of the Parties*, Conf. 3.10, pp. 57-8.

the trade, and it has revealed instances of illegal trade. For example, an analysis of Parties' annual reports led the Secretariat to notice a marked increase of wildlife exports originating in Paraguay in 1978, and further investigation revealed that large quantities of wildlife were being smuggled into Paraguay from neighbouring countries and then exported to Europe with forged permits.[96]

On the other hand, information received from annual reports has not been as useful as it should have been. About one third of the Parties have never submitted a report at all, and those that have submitted reports have almost all been appallingly late in so doing. At the time of writing just 33 of the 55 Parties due to submit reports for the year 1979 and 32 of the 61 Parties due to submit reports for the year 1980 had actually done so. By 31 October 1982, the date by which all reports for the year 1981 should have been submitted, the Secretariat had received just 8, although this had increased to 39 at the time of writing. This is a dismal record, and it means that the information derived from national reports reveals a very limited picture of the true extent of international trade in wildlife.

Furthermore, an analysis prepared for the CITES Secretariat by the Wildlife Trade Monitoring Unit and submitted to the Gaborone Conference reveals that the content of annual reports has generally been so inadequate that the value of those reports which are submitted is highly dubious. The analysis found that at least 45% of all CITES transactions involving animals and 79% of those involving plants go unreported even when the transactions are between Parties which have submitted annual reports. It also found that of transactions that might be expected to correlate (i.e. reported transactions involving Parties that have submitted annual reports) less than 5% involving animals and about 1% involving plants correlated perfectly. These discrepancies were primarily due to faults such as one Party failing to record a transaction or to errors in reporting the number, identity or State of origin of the specimens involved.[97]

In March 1982 the Secretariat circulated "Guidelines for the Preparation of CITES Annual Reports" to all Parties with a view to increasing the number of reports submitted and to make them more uniform. The guidelines recommend a standardised format for reports to follow and provide specific instructions as to how information should be presented.

[96] See *Proceedings of the Third Meeting of the Conference of the Parties*, Doc. 3.6, Annex 3, pp. 297-303. See also *Proceedings of the Fourth Meeting of the Conference of the Parties*, Doc. 4.8, para. 12.2, pp. 307-9.

[97] See *Proceedings of the Fourth Meeting of the Conference of the Parties*, Doc. 4.18, pp. 435-48.

8. Administration

The administrative structure established by CITES consists of a Secretariat, Management and Scientific Authorities and the Conference of the Parties, all of which have different functions and responsibilities. In practice, this structure is probably as important to enforcement of the Convention as the measures described in section 7 above because it ensures that there are official bodies continually watching over the operation of the Convention on both a national and international level.

a) The Secretariat

Established by Article XII of CITES, the Secretariat consists of a Secretary General, three full-time professionals and three full-time secretaries. Part-time staff and consultants are also employed, and the Secretariat has an annual budget of approximately U.S.$500,000. The Secretariat was initially funded by the United Nations Environment Programme but is now financed by the contributions of the Parties themselves.[98]

The Secretariat performs many different functions. It arranges and services meetings of the Parties and prepares numerous reports and draft resolutions on items to be considered at those meetings. It prepares an annual report on its work and on the implementation of the Convention. After each meeting of the Parties, it publishes and distributes reports of the proceedings to all Party governments. It also issues approximately thirty five official notices to the Parties each year (simultaneously in English, French and Spanish) on matters ranging from the names of national scientific institutions entitled to receive specimens for scientific or educational purposes under the Article VII exemption, to notification that Zaire has banned the commercial export of ivory or that Brazil has banned the export of all wildlife. The latter type of notices are particularly valuable because they alert Management Authorities to the fact that certain transactions, such as imports of ivory from Zaire or of any wildlife product from Brazil, will almost certainly be illegal.[99]

When the Secretariat is satisfied that a listed species is being affected adversely by trade or that the provisions of the treaty are not being effectively implemented, it is required to "communicate such

---

[98] See p. 273 below.

[99] CITES, Article XII(2) sets out the functions of the Secretariat in detail. See also "The Secretariat and its Duties, 1978 Annual Report on the Work of the Secretariat", *Proceedings of the Second Meeting of the Conference of the Parties*, Doc. 2.5, pp. 231-247; "Report of the Secretariat", *Proceedings of the Third Meeting of the Conference of the Parties*, Doc. 3.6, pp. 283-303 and "Report of the Secretariat", *Proceedings of the Fourth Meeting of the Conference of the Parties*, Doc. 4.8, Annex 1, pp. 314-5.

information to the authorised Management Authority of the Party or Parties concerned".[100] The Secretariat has implemented this requirement vigorously, drawing the attention of a total of 39 Parties to a total of 274 cases of alleged violations of the Convention during 1979 and 1980 and maintaining a similar level in 1981-2.[101] Its efforts in this area have proved very effective. For example, in 1979 the Secretariat notified South Africa that although it had reported exporting a total of 300 kilogrammes of ivory to Hong Kong in the last six months of 1978, Hong Kong had reported imports of 16,300 kilogrammes from South Africa over the same period. South Africa, which was being used to "launder" ivory obtained elsewhere, subsequently tightened up its controls. By cross-checking dubious trading documents with the issuing Management Authority, the Secretariat was able to verify fifteen cases of forgeries in 1980 alone, and information supplied by the Secretariat to Management Authorities has led to the initiation of criminal proceedings against the offending trader in several instances.[102] Secretariat staff have also undertaken missions to Congo, Zaire, Togo, Paraguay, Bolivia, Uruguay, Argentina and several other Parties to help solve enforcement problems.

b) *Management and Scientific Authorities*

Each Party is required to designate one or more Management Authorities competent to grant permits or certificates on behalf of that Party and one or more Scientific Authorities.[103] The role played by each Authority with respect to the granting of CITES permits has already been described.[104] In order to fulfil their responsibilities, Management Authorities in importing countries frequently have to correspond with Management Authorities in exporting countries. In 1981, for example, the U.K. seized a consignment of 45 royal pythons which arrived from Ghana without an export permit and informed the Ghanean Management Authority of the seizure. The latter confirmed that the shipment was illegal, and the pythons were subsequently returned to Ghana and released into a national park.[105] To facilitate such communication, CITES requires each Party to inform the Depositary government (the Swiss government)

[100] CITES, Article XIII(1).
[101] See *Proceedings of the Third Meeting of the Conference of the Parties*, Doc. 3.6, p. 289 and *Proceedings of the Fourth Meeting of the Conference of the Parties*, Doc. 4.8, para 9.2, pp. 300-1.
[102] See *Proceedings of the Third Meeting of the Conference of the Parties*, Doc. 3.6, pp. 289-290.
[103] CITES, Article IX(1)
[104] See pp. 247-255 above.
[105] See *TRAFFIC Bulletin*, Vol. III, Nos. 3/4 (Wildlife Trade Monitoring Unit, May – August 1981).

of the name and address of its Management Authority and to inform the Secretariat of any changes thereto.[106] The Secretariat has compiled and regularly updates a "CITES Directory" containing the addresses, telephone and telex numbers of Management and Scientific Authorities; each Party is supplied with a copy.

CITES is unique in requiring its Parties to establish specific national authorities to administer the provisions of the Convention and in establishing a global network of institutions which co-operate directly with their counterparts in other States unfettered by the constraints of formal diplomatic channels. Their establishment is particularly significant for two reasons. Firstly, the mere fact that each Party has two permanent bodies responsible for implementing CITES goes a long way towards ensuring that each Party makes at least some effort to enforce the Convention. Secondly, although their mandate under CITES is limited to international trade, some Parties have given Management and Scientific Authorities additional responsibilities relating to wildlife conservation. As a result, their establishment has not only helped regulate international trade but has also contributed to an organised and rational approach to the overall management of wildlife resources in those States.

Recognising that more than two thirds of the Parties are developing countries with special difficulties in staffing, training and equipping their Management and Scientific Authorities, the New Delhi Conference urged Parties to make appropriate technical assistance available to developing countries and requested the Secretariat to seek external funding for this purpose.[107] In 1981 the World Wildlife Fund paid for two consultants to visit sixteen African States in order to provide technical advice on the establishment of Management and Scientific Authorities, and the Swiss General Direction of Customs and the Swiss Department of Foreign Affairs organised a ten week course, including lectures on CITES, for customs officers from twelve African States.[108] In 1982 the World Wildlife Fund paid for representatives from Botswana, Cameroon, the Central African Republic and Tanzania to attend a two week training course in Switzerland run by the Swiss Management Authority and the CITES Secretariat. In 1983 the Secretariat, in conjunction with the U.S. and Canadian Governments, World Wildlife life Fund — U.S. and the United Nations Environment Pro-

[106] CITES, Article IX(2)-(3).

[107] See *Proceedings of the Third Meeting of the Conference of the Parties*, Conf. 3.4, p. 43.

[108] See *Annual Report of Switzerland and Liechtenstein for 1981*, p. 7 (available from CITES Secretariat, 6 Rue du Maupas, P.O. Box 78, 1000 Lausanne 9, Switzerland).

gramme, organised a two week seminar in Washington D.C. for the benefit of States in North, Central and South America. In 1984 similar seminars were held in Brussels for the benefit of African States and in Kuala Lumpur for Asian States.

c)   *The Conference of the Parties*

The Conference of the Parties, the official title given to a meeting of the Parties, is the decision-making body on all matters related to CITES. It meets regularly every two years and may hold extraordinary meetings on the written request of at least one third of the Parties.[109]

The scope of the activities of the Conference of the Parties is wide. It must approve a budget for the Secretariat, and when it became evident that the United Nations Environment Programme would phase out its financial support for the Secretariat, the Conference of the Parties amended the text of the Convention in order to make financial contributions from the Parties compulsory.[110] It is also responsible for making appropriate recommendations in order to improve the effectiveness of the Convention.[111] To give two examples, the New Delhi Conference recommended that the Parties should use a standardised CITES permit form in order to simplify the task of customs and other enforcement officers who are responsible for checking the validity of permits.[112] The New Delhi Conference also recommended that the Secretariat should approach all non-Party governments known to be trading in rhinoceros horn and request them, on behalf of the Parties to the Convention, to halt the trade.[113] This rather extraordinary measure was taken because of

[109] CITES, Article XI(2).

[110] The amendment was adopted at an extraordinary meeting of the Parties held in Bonn in June 1979, but it is not yet in force because only 26 of the 51 States which were Parties in June 1979 have deposited instruments of acceptance. The amendment will come into force when 34 of those Parties have accepted it. Amendments to the text of the Convention, as opposed to amendments to the Appendices, can only be considered at extraordinary meetings of the Parties and are adopted if approved by a two-thirds majority of the Parties present and voting. An amendment enters into force, for those Parties which have accepted it, 60 days after two-thirds of the Parties (i.e. two thirds of the Parties at the time the amendment was adopted rather than two thirds of the current number of Parties — see *Proceedings of the Fourth Meeting of the Conference of the Parties*, Conf. 4.27, p. 83) have deposited an instrument of acceptance with the Depositary government (Switzerland). It will enter into force for any other Party 60 days after that Party deposits an instrument of acceptance. Until the amendment enters into force the Secretariat is dependant upon the goodwill of the Parties to contribute their share (worked out according to the U.N. scale) of the Secretariat budget. The financial report to the Gaborone Conference revealed that unpaid contributions to the Trust Fund (out of which Secretariat expenses are paid) for 1982 and prior years involved 25 Parties and amounted to about U.S.$200,000.

[111] CITES, Article XI(3).

[112] See *Proceedings of the Third Meeting of the Conference of the Parties*, Conf. 3.6, pp. 46-50.

[113] See *Proceedings of the Third Meeting of the Conference of the Parties*, Conf. 3.11, p. 59.

the particularly precarious status of four of the five species of rhinoceros and the continuing demand for their horns in North Yemen, Singapore, South Korea, Taiwan and other non-Party States.[114]

Another major responsibility of the Conference of the Parties is to review the list of species included in the Appendices. Large numbers of amendments, affecting hundreds of species, have been made at all four of its biennial meetings. The vast majority of proposals have been to add species to the Appendices or to transfer them from Appendix II to I. However, CITES is a flexible instrument and each Conference has also decreased protection for species, or populations thereof, after being satisfied that the Berne criteria have been met.[115] The New Delhi Conference, for example, transferred the North American population of gyrfalcons from Appendix I to Appendix II on the basis that it was not threatened with extinction, that it could withstand some exploitation and that safeguards would be made to prevent any consequent damage to more vulnerable populations of the species in other parts of the world.[116] The Gaborone Conference agreed to reduce protection for the Zimbabwean population of Nile crocodile (*Crocodylus niloticus*), a coastal population of Chilean false larch (*Fitzroya cupressoides*) and numerous Australian plants.

To assist it in its task, the Conference of the Parties has established several committees. Some, such as the Nomenclature Committee and the Identification Manual Committee are limited to a particular field of responsibility while others such as the Technical Committee and the Standing Committee have a broader role. The Technical Committee was established by the San José Conference to standardise permit forms and procedures, but the New Delhi Conference changed it to a permanent committee of experts from all interested Parties which would meet periodically to discuss problems relating to implementation and enforcement of CITES and to draft appropriate recommendations for consideration by the Conference of the Parties.[117] The Standing Committee is a permanent advisory committee with a rotating membership of nine Parties from different geographical regions and with responsibilities that are mainly administrative. It has become something of an "Inner Cabinet" which performs such functions on behalf of the

[114] In November 1982, the government of North Yemen banned the import of rhinoceros horn.
[115] See pp. 243-246 above for an explanation of the Berne criteria.
[116] See *Proceedings of the Third Meeting of the Conference of the Parties*, Plen. 3.10 and Plen. 3.11, pp. 138-142.
[117] See *Proceedings of the Third Meeting of the Conference of the Parties*, Conf. 3.5, pp. 44-5. The Technical Committee was initially known as the Technical Expert Committee, but the Gaborone Conference changed its name to the Technical Committee.

Parties as may be necessary between ordinary meetings of the Parties. In particular, the Standing Committee is responsible for overseeing execution of the Secretariat's budget and for giving advice on matters brought to it by the Secretariat. It is required to submit a report on its activities to the Conference of the Parties.[118]

Non-Party governments, the International Atomic Energy Authority and the United Nations and its specialised agencies have a right to be represented as observers at meetings of the Conference of the Parties but may not vote.[119] International, national, governmental and non-governmental bodies or agencies which are technically qualified in the protection, conservation or management of wildlife may also attend as observers unless at least one third of the Parties present object.[120] Observers other than the United Nations and its specialised agencies have to pay a U.S.$50 participation charge to attend meetings although the Standing Committee has a discretionary power to reduce the charge if appropriate.[121] Non-governmental organisations have been particularly quick to seize the opportunity to participate in meetings. Relatively few attended the Berne Conference, but fifty six were registered in San José, there were eighty in New Delhi and sixty nine in Gaborone. Although many have represented conservationist and trading constituencies in the U.S.A., the large number of non-governmental organisations from other countries demonstrates the considerable worldwide interest in trade in threatened and potentially threatened wildlife.

9.   *Effect on national law and other international treaties*

Article XIV(1) expressly states that the provisions of CITES do not affect the right of each Party to introduce stricter trading measures than are required by the Convention, and several Parties have exercised this right. Venezuela, for example, has outlawed the export of all crocodile hides, and the U.K. prohibits the import of Appendix II species without an import permit notwithstanding that CITES insists only on permits from the State of export.

Article XIV also states that CITES is not intended to affect the provisions of other international treaties, including those pertaining to "Customs, public health, veterinary or plant quarantine" and those creating regional trade agreements affecting customs control such as the Treaty of Rome. In a clear reference to the International Convention for the Regulation of Whaling and the Interim

[118] See *Proceedings of the Third Meeting of the Conference of the Parties*, Conf. 3.1, pp. 33-4.
[119] CITES, Article XI(6).
[120] *Ibid.*, Article XI(7).
[121] See *Proceedings of the Third Meeting of the Conference of the Parties*, Conf. 3.2, p. 36.

Convention for the Conservation of North Pacific Fur Seals, Article XIV (4) relieves Parties, which are also Party to any other treaty affording protection "to marine species", of obligations imposed by CITES with respect to trade in species in Appendix II which are taken in accordance with the provisions of such other treaty.

10.   Regional economic integration organisations

The second extraordinary meeting of the Conference of the Parties, held in Gaborone immediately following the conclusion of the Gaborone Conference, agreed to amend Article XXI of CITES in order to allow "regional economic integration organisations constituted by sovereign States which have competence in respect of the negotiation, conclusion and implementation of international agreements in matters transferred to them by their Member States and covered by this Convention" to accede to the Convention. The amendment was adopted at the instigation of the European Economic Community which is anxious to become a Party to CITES. In their instruments of accession, regional economic integration organisations must declare "the extent of their competence with respect to the matters governed by the Convention" and inform the Depositary government of any subsequent modifications thereof. In fields within their competence, these organisations "shall exercise their right to vote with a number of votes equal to the number of their Member States which are Parties to the Convention. Such organisations shall not exercise their right to vote if their Member States exercise theirs, and *vice versa*."[122]

11.   Conclusion

During the few years that CITES has been in force, real progress has been made. Most of the major wildlife trading nations are now Parties and the level of enforcement is improving. There is no doubt that serious instances of non-compliance with the Convention do still occur — the ivory trade is a notable example — but international trade in most Appendix II species is more carefully regulated than it was fifteen years ago, and international trade in Appendix I species is by and large very sporadic. These are no mean achievements, and CITES can justifiably claim much of the credit.

On the other hand, growing pains still persist. The staff of Management and Scientific Authorities is often too small and inadequately trained, communication between Management Authorities is not always as good as it might be, the rate of

[122] See *Second Extraordinary Meeting of the Conference of the Parties*, Doc. E.2.3.

submission of annual reports and the quality of statistics contained in the reports is still extremely poor, and the length and complexity of the Appendices makes the already difficult task of enforcement officers that much harder. Resolutions passed in New Delhi and Gaborone in relation to the standardisation of permits, the submission of annual reports, the publication of identification manuals, the use of security paper and the granting of technical assistance to Management Authorities show how anxious the Parties are to try and improve the level of enforcement of the Convention, and future meetings of the Conference of the Parties are likely to continue to concentrate on improving enforcement.

Of all the reasons for the relative success of CITES, it is its administrative system which stands out. The existence of a permanent Secretariat and the numerous administrative obligations imposed on the Parties — to set up at least two bodies to enforce the Convention, to communicate regularly with other Parties, to communicate regularly with the Secretariat and to meet regularly to review implementation of the Convention — are all critical factors. In simple terms, there is no chance of CITES becoming a "sleeping treaty" which its Parties can safely ignore. By demonstrating how to keep its Parties constantly on their toes, CITES has taught a lesson which other treaties concerned with the conservation of wildlife badly need to learn.

CHAPTER 13

THE CONVENTION ON THE CONSERVATION OF MIGRATORY SPECIES OF WILD ANIMALS
(THE "BONN CONVENTION")

"Migration is one of the most fascinating natural phenomena, and it is still a highly mysterious one."
(Dr. Klaus Schmidt-Koenig, *Avian Orientation and Navigation*, 1979)

1. *Background*

The United Nations Conference on the Human Environment, held in Stockholm in 1972, made a number of recommendations regarding international treaties. One of these, Recommendation 32 of the Action Plan, was that governments should consider the need to enact international conventions and treaties in order to protect species which inhabit international waters or migrate from one territory to another. Recommendation 32 arose out of the realisation that failure to protect a migratory species throughout every stage of its migration can severely damage efforts to maintain or restore its population. The endangered Siberian crane (*Grus leucogeranus*), for example, is relatively secure in its Russian breeding sites and Indian wintering grounds, but its numbers have steadily declined in recent years primarily because it is hunted on its migratory route through Pakistan and Afghanistan. Many species of North American breeding birds are thought to be declining because of deforestation and the continuing use of DDT and other pesticides in their Central and South American wintering habitats. Passerines breeding in Northern Europe run a biannual gauntlet through the Mediterranean region where they are shot and trapped in their thousands as they make their way to and from their African wintering areas.

As a direct result of Recommendation 32,[1] the Federal Republic of

---

[1] It was also felt that the provisions of existing agreements for the conservation and management of migratory animals lacked uniformity and covered only a portion of migratory species which could benefit from international treaties. The Bonn Convention is intended to provide such uniformity and covers the whole spectrum of migratory animals. See *Convention on the Conservation of Migratory Species of Wild Animals* (Federal Ministry of Food, Agriculture and Forestry of the Federal Republic of Germany, 1979), p. 95. This publication prints the text of the Convention on the Conservation of Migratory Species of Wild Animals, the names of species included in Appendices I and II, the Final Act of the Conference held in 1979 to conclude the Convention, the Summary Record of the Conference, the Second Revised Draft Convention which had been submitted by the Federal Republic of Germany in December 1978, the Rules of Procedure of the Conference and a number of letters and declarations made by various individuals and organisations.

Germany agreed in 1974 to take the initiative in preparing a draft convention for the conservation of migratory animals and, after several years of negotiation, the Convention on the Conservation of Migratory Species of Wild Animals (the "Bonn Convention")[2] was finally concluded on 23 June 1979. Twenty eight States signed, but the Convention did not enter into force until 1 November 1983, being the first day of the third month after the Depositary (the government of the Federal Republic of Germany) had received the fifteenth instrument of ratification, approval, acceptance or accession.[3] At the time of writing there are still only 15 Parties. Because it has so recently come into force, considerations of the practical effect of the Convention are still rather theoretical. However, a meeting of the Parties must be held within two years of the Convention coming into force,[4] and one of the first tasks of this meeting will be to set up a machinery for implementing the Convention.

This chapter examines the objectives of the Bonn Convention, the definitions of its most important terms, the criteria for including species in Appendix I or II of the Convention, the nature of the obligations imposed on Parties to protect species in the Appendices and the system of administration established by the Convention.

2. *Objectives*

The fundamental objective of the Bonn Convention is to protect migratory species. In order to achieve its goal, the Convention has two quite distinct sub-objectives.

The first of these is to provide strict protection for species listed in Appendix I, which consists of migratory species in danger of extinction throughout all or a significant portion of their range. The Convention seeks to protect Appendix I species by imposing strict conservation obligations on Parties that are "Range States". "Range States" and other important words and phrases used by the Convention are defined in section 3 below.

The second sub-objective is to persuade Range States to conclude "AGREEMENTS" for the conservation and management of Appendix II species. Migratory species are eligible for Appendix II either if they have an unfavourable conservation status and require

---

[2] 19 *I.L.M.* 15.

[3] As required by Article XVIII(1) of the Convention. Cameroon, Chile, Denmark, Egypt, the European Economic Community, Hungary, India, Ireland, Israel, Italy, Luxembourg, the Netherlands, Niger, Portugal and Sweden are full Parties. Central African Republic, Chad, Federal Republic of Germany, France, Greece, Ireland, Ivory Coast, Jamaica, Madagascar, Malawi, Morocco, Norway, Paraguay, Philippines, Somalia, Spain, Sri Lanka, Togo, Uganda and U.K. have signed but not yet ratified.

[4] Bonn Convention, Article VII(2).

international agreements for their conservation or if they have a conservation status which would significantly benefit from international cooperation. Two elements of this sub-objective are noteworthy. Firstly, the Convention does not impose direct obligations on Range States to protect Appendix II species — it merely requires Range States to conclude further AGREEMENTS for their protection and establishes guidelines as to what these AGREEMENTS should contain. Secondly, a species does not need to be, although it may be, threatened or even potentially threatened with extinction in order to qualify for Appendix II. The important criterion is whether or not the species would benefit from the international cooperation that an AGREEMENT would bring. Thus the Bonn Convention does not follow the pattern adopted by CITES whereby species are listed in Appendix I or II depending, among other things, upon their level of endangerment.

3. *Definitions*

a) *Range States*

Article I(1)(h) of the Convention defines a Range State of a migratory species as "any State...that exercises jurisdiction over any part of the range of that migratory species, or a State, flag vessels of which are engaged outside national jurisdictional limits in taking that migratory species."

b) *Migratory Species*

Article I(1)(a) defines a "migratory species" as

the entire population or any geographically separate part of the population of any species or lower taxon of wild animals, a significant proportion of whose members cyclically and predictably cross one or more national jurisdictional boundaries.

Four points about this definition are noteworthy:

(i) By allowing geographically separate populations of a species to be considered independently, the Bonn Convention is following a precedent set by CITES. In the context of CITES the concept has proved extremely useful in enabling a State with a non-endangered, well managed population of a species which is endangered in other States to allow limited exploitation of its population and, conversely, in enabling States to single out endangered populations of a species for special protection when populations elsewhere are not endangered. Early indications are that the concept will continue to prove useful in the context of the Bonn Convention since four of the forty original listings in Appendix I consist of geographically separate populations of species rather than the species as a whole. They are the North-west African populations of dorcas gazelle (*Gazella dorcas*) and houbara bustard (*Chlamydotis undulata*), Upper Amazon populations of giant river turtles (*Podocnemis expansa*) and non-Peruvian populations of vicuna (*Vicugna vicugna*).

(ii) Defining a species as migratory if a "significant portion" of its members migrate allows the inclusion of relatively sedentary species in the Appendices. For example, adults of the Mediterranean monk seal (*Monachus monachus*) are not migratory, but the species is in Appendix I because it is in danger of extinction and "post breeding dispersal of young must regularly involve crossing of national frontiers".[5]

(iii) The Second Revised Draft Convention, which was prepared by the Federal Republic of Germany in December 1978 and was the last formal draft to be considered prior to Final Conference in June 1979 at which the Convention was signed, defined migratory species as those whose members "periodically" cross national jurisdictional boundaries.[6] The intention behind the word "periodically" was to include species living in border areas which might be relatively sedentary but which nevertheless wandered back and forth across national frontiers on a regular basis.[7] "Periodically" was replaced by the words "cyclically and predictably" in the final version of the Convention, and the report of the United States delegation to the Final Conference suggests that species living in border areas are now not to be considered migratory for the purposes of the Convention unless their trans-boundary movement is in response to seasonal or longer term environmental influences.[8] However, the fact that the Final Conference decided to include the mountain gorilla (*Gorilla gorilla beringei*) in Appendix I (mountain gorillas live in the border areas of Rwanda, Uganda, and Zaire and regularly cross national boundaries, although it is not certain whether their crossings are

---

[5] See "Explanatory Notes on Second Revised Draft Convention on the Conservation of Migratory Species of Wild Animals" (hereinafter referred to as 'Explanatory Notes'), reprinted in *Convention on the Conservation of Migratory Species of Wild Animals*, note 1 above, para. 16, p. 99.

[6] Second Revised Draft Convention, Article I(1)(a); reprinted in *Convention on the Conservation of Migratory Species of Wild Animals*, note 1 above, p. 87.

[7] See 'Explanatory Notes', note 5 above, para. 2, p. 95.

[8] See *Report of the U.S. Delegation to the Conference to Conclude a Convention on the Conservation of Migratory Species of Wild Animals* (17 October 1979), pp. 2-4; (available from the Department of State, Washington D.C. and hereinafter referred to as *Report of the U.S. Delegation*).

cyclical and predictable)[9] suggests that most Parties do not agree
with the U.S.A.'s restrictive interpretation of what is migratory.

(iv) The definition adopted by the Final Conference includes *all*
species of migratory animals notwithstanding attempts during the
course of negotiations by several countries, including Australia,
Canada, Japan, New Zealand, the U.S.A. and the U.S.S.R., to
exclude certain marine species, particularly finfish and shellfish, on
the grounds that their inclusion could undermine existing and
pending international agreements and negotiations.[10]

c) *"Unfavourable" conservation status*

Article I(1)(d) states that the conservation status of a migratory
species will be considered "unfavourable" if any of the following
conditions set out in Article I(1)(c) are *not* met:

(1) population dynamics data indicate that the migratory species is
maintaining itself on a long-term basis as a viable component of its
ecosystems;
(2) the range of the migratory species is neither currently being reduced,
nor is likely to be reduced, on a long-term basis;
(3) there is, and will be in the foreseeable future, sufficient habitat to
maintain the population of the migratory species on a long-term basis;
and
(4) the distribution and abundance of the migratory species approach
historic coverage and levels to the extent that potentially suitable
ecosystems exist and to the extent consistent with wise wildlife
management.

d) *AGREEMENTS*

Article I(1)(j) defines an AGREEMENT as "an international
agreement relating to the conservation of one or more migratory
species as provided for in Articles IV and V of this Convention."
Articles IV and V, which are discussed in more detail later in this
chapter,[11] set out the circumstances in which AGREEMENTS
should be concluded and establish guidelines as to what each
AGREEMENT should contain.

[9] *Ibid.*, p. 10.
[10] *Ibid.*, pp. 3, 8 and 9. The alliance of Pacific powers on this question provides an
interesting illustration of how issues of protection and utilisation of natural resources can
transcend normal political allegiances. On one working group, the U.S.A. specifically
represented the views of the U.S.S.R.!
[11] See pp. 288-291 below.

4. *Appendix I Species*

a) *Listing criteria*

Article III(1) of the Bonn Convention requires that a species be "migratory" and "endangered" as defined by the Convention in order to merit inclusion in Appendix I. The Convention stipulates that a species shall be considered endangered if "reliable evidence, including the best scientific evidence available,"[12] indicates that it is "in danger of extinction throughout all or a significant portion of its range."[13] The fact that a species is still relatively abundant in some areas will not therefore preclude it from being considered "endangered" if it is in danger of extinction elsewhere, provided that the areas where it is endangered are large enough to form a "significant portion of its range". The latter qualification is important because even a very common species may be in danger of extinction on the fringes of its range, and the Parties clearly did not intend that such a species should be eligible for Appendix I.

There was considerable debate at the Final Conference as to whether to include any species in Appendix I at that stage since there had been no opportunity to evaluate "the best scientific evidence available".[14] It was eventually agreed to list a representative sample of forty species, consisting of fifteen mammals, twenty birds, four reptiles and one freshwater fish, in order to ensure that the Convention had some practical impact as soon as it entered into force.

A species may be removed from Appendix I if the Conference of the Parties decides that

> reliable evidence, including the best scientific evidence available, indicates that the species is no longer endangered, and the species is not likely to become endangered again because of loss of protection due to its removal from Appendix I.[15]

b) *Conservation obligations*

(i) *Regulation of threats, other than "taking", to Appendix I species*

Article III(4) states that Parties which are Range States of Appendix I species shall endeavour:

> a) to conserve and, where feasible and appropriate, restore those habitats of the species which are of importance in removing the species from danger of extinction;

[12] Bonn Convention, Article III(2).
[13] *Ibid.*, Article I(1)(e).
[14] See *Report of the U.S. Delegation*, note 8 above, pp. 3 and 10.
[15] Bonn Convention, Article III(3).

b) to prevent, remove, compensate for or minimize, as appropriate, the adverse effects of activities or obstacles that seriously impede or prevent the migration of the species; and

c) to the extent feasible and appropriate, to prevent, reduce or control factors that are endangering or are likely to further endanger the species, including strictly controlling the introduction of, or controlling or eliminating, already introduced species.

The scope of Article III(4) is extraordinarily broad. Although it emphasises loss of habitat, impediments to migration and the introduction of exotic species as threats to Appendix I species which Parties should make special efforts to counteract, Article III(4)(c) extends to "factors" that are dangerous or potentially dangerous to Appendix I species — which effectively covers every possible threat.

In order to illustrate what Article III(4) actually requires of the Parties, the following describes how some Appendix I species will be affected by Article III(4): The status of the kouprey (*Bos sauveli*), a species of wild cow listed in Appendix I, is unknown because of years of warfare in the areas of Kampuchea, Laos and Thailand where it occurs, but it is believed to be critically endangered by loss of its forest habitat and to be likely to survive only if effective sanctuaries are maintained in all three States.[16] If any of the three accede to the Convention, Article III(4) will oblige them to endeavour to take the appropriate measures to set up effective protected areas for this mammal. The survival of two Appendix I birds, the cahow (*Pterodroma cahow*) and bald ibis (*Geranticus eremita*), is threatened primarily by use of pesticides,[17] and Article III(4) obliges Parties that are Range States to endeavour to control this threat. The blue whale (*Balaenoptera musculus*), another species listed in Appendix I, is protected from exploitation by the International Whaling Commission, but its recovery may be threatened by over-exploitation of krill (its principal food supply) in the Antarctic.[18] Article III(4) obliges Parties with flag vessels engaged in fishing in the Antarctic to limit their exploitation of krill to a level which will not be detrimental to the blue whale's recovery. The dark-rumped petrel (*Pterodroma phaeopygia*) is also in Appendix I, but it is threatened by the introduction of predators on its breeding grounds in the Galapagos Islands. Consequently, if Ecuador becomes a Party to the Bonn Convention, it will be under a legal duty to endeavour to eradicate these predators.[19]

---

[16] See 'Explanatory Notes', note 5 above, para. 16, p. 99.

[17] *Ibid.*, p. 100.

[18] *Ibid.*, p. 99.

[19] *Ibid.*, p. 100. Ecuador has in fact already taken steps to eradicate introduced predators from many of the Galapagos Islands.

Although its scope is exceptionally broad, Article III(4) qualifies the obligations it imposes by requiring Parties to "endeavour" to protect habitats, control the introduction of exotic species etc. The legal implications of the word "endeavour" are not totally clear. J.E.S. Fawcett, a distinguished legal commentator, stated in an article entitled "The Legal Character of International Agreements"[20] that

> it is doubtful whether undertakings 'to use best endeavours' or 'to take all possible measures' can in most cases amount to more than declarations of policy, or of goodwill towards the objects of the agreement.

Some of the negotiators of the Convention may also have felt that the word "endeavour" gave them a discretion as to whether or not they complied with Article III(4). The Second Revised Draft Convention stated that Parties that are Range States of Appendix I species *shall* protect habitats etc., and the U.S.A. and others fought hard and successfully at the Final Conference to change the text so that it obliged them only to "endeavour" to do these things.[21]

However, in a recent case concerning the World Heritage Convention brought before the High Court of Australia, *The Commonwealth of Australia v. The State of Tasmania*,[22] very similar issues were argued, and the Court held by a majority of 4-3 that Australia was under a legal obligation to comply with the conservation provisions of the Convention notwithstanding that they are prefaced by qualifying words such as "endeavour". Article 5 of the World Heritage Convention requires Parties to "endeavour, in so far as possible, and as appropriate for each country" to do certain things to protect sites that are part of the world's cultural and natural heritage. Referring to the word "endeavour" and the other qualifying words in Article 5, Mason J., one of the four Justices who formed the majority in *The Commonwealth of Australia v. The State of Tasmania*, stated that

> Article 5 cannot be read as a mere statement of intention. It is expressed in the form of a command requiring each party to endeavour to bring about the matters dealt with in the lettered paragraphs...Neither of these qualifications nor the existence of an element of discretion and value judgment in par.(d) is inconsistent with the existence of an obligation. There is a distinction between a discretion as to the manner

[20] *British Year Book of International Law* 30 (1953), p. 391.

[21] See *Report of the U.S. Delegation*, note 8 above, pp. 2 and 5.

[22] 46 *A.L.R. 625;* 68 *I.L.R.* 266. The background of the case and the ruling of the court are described in more detail in Chapter 11, pp. 223-225.

of performance and a discretion as to performance or non-performance. The latter, but not the former, is inconsistent with a binding obligation to perform (see *Thorby v. Goldberg* (1964) 112 C.L.R. 597, at pp. 604-605, 613, 614-615). And it is only natural that in framing a command to States to take measures of the kind described in par.(d) in relation to their heritage the command will be expressed in terms of endeavour, subject to the qualifications mentioned.

Brennan J. agreed with Mason J. that Australia was under a legal obligation to perform the measures laid down in Article 5 but looked at the issue in a rather different light. In considering whether Australian relations with other nations would be affected if Australia failed to carry out its duty to endeavour to comply with the Convention, he said

> unless Australia were to attribute hypocrisy and cynicism to the international community, only an affirmative answer is possible. There is a clear obligation upon Australia to act under Arts. 4 and 5, though the extent of that obligation may be affected by decisions taken by Australia in good faith.

Neither the Australian decision, nor the comments of individual judges in that case, are in any way binding on other Parties to the Bonn Convention, and an obligation to endeavour to perform an act is clearly less strict than a straight undertaking to do it. Nevertheless, the views of Brennan J. and Mason J. do lend some weight to the view that an undertaking to endeavour to perform does impose an obligation to perform with the understanding that there may be circumstances in which non-performance is excusable provided that the State concerned has made a genuine attempt.

(ii)   *Regulation of "taking" of Appendix I species*

In contrast to Article III(4), Article III(5), which regulates the "taking" of Appendix I species, does not preface its provisions with the word "endeavour" or any other such qualifying term but imposes an unequivocal obligation on Parties that are Range States to prohibit "taking" except in a few limited circumstances. It states that

> Parties that are Range States of a migratory species listed in Appendix I shall prohibit the taking of animals belonging to such species. Exceptions may be made to this prohibition only if:
> a) the taking is for scientific purposes;
> b) the taking is for the purpose of enhancing the propagation or survival of the affected species;

c) the taking is to accommodate the needs of traditional subsistence users of such species; or

d) extraordinary circumstances so require.

Article III(5) goes on to state that exceptions can be made only if they are "precise as to content and limited in space and time" and that taking pursuant to one of the exceptions "should not operate to the disadvantage of the species." Parties must inform the Secretariat "as soon as possible" of every exception that they allow.[23]

That the negotiators of the Convention were more willing to undertake clear and unequivocal obligations with respect to taking than with respect to habitat protection might be expected since the former do not have such far-reaching implications for agricultural and industrial development as the latter. In addition, many States already have national legislation prohibiting the taking of endangered species (and may therefore feel that Article III(5) will not require them to revise their existing legislation), while national legislation providing strict protection for the habitat of endangered species is still relatively rare. Nevertheless, the fact that the Convention imposes such a strict duty on Parties to prohibit taking is surprising in view of the Convention's definition of "taking" which is deemed to include "hunting, fishing, capturing, harassing, deliberate killing, or attempting to engage in any such conduct".[24] This very broad definition could have far-reaching implications for Parties.

The circumstances surrounding the decline of the Atlantic ridley turtle (*Lepidochelys kempii*), an Appendix I species, provide a good example of just how far-reaching Article III(5) might be. The Atlantic ridley, like other species of sea turtle, has a propensity to become entangled in fishermen's nets, and The IUCN Amphibia-Reptilia Red Data Book states that the accidental catch of Atlantic ridleys in shrimp trawls in the Gulf of Mexico "now appears to be the major direct threat to the species with probably several hundred individuals being accidentally caught annually, and drowned or killed aboard trawlers".[25] Since the entanglement of turtles in the trawls clearly constitutes "capturing" or "harassing", even if the killing of turtles is deemed not to be "deliberate", it is probably fair to conclude that Article III(5) imposes a legal duty on Parties that are Range States of the Atlantic ridley to prohibit the use of shrimp trawls in areas where the turtle occurs unless the trawls are fitted

---

[23] Bonn Convention, Article III(7).

[24] *Ibid.*, Article I(1)(i).

[25] *The IUCN Amphibia-Reptilia Red Data Book, Part I* (IUCN, 1982), pp. 201 and 204.

with "Trawling Efficiency Devices".[26] These Devices, which are now being used in the U.S.A. and elsewhere, release inadvertently captured sea turtles and other large animals through a trap door, while shrimps pass into the end of the trawl.

(iii)   *Further measures to benefit Appendix I species*

The Convention expressly authorises the Conference of the Parties to recommend to Range States of an Appendix I species "that they take further measures considered appropriate to benefit the species".[27] Although it is commonplace for a Conference of the Parties to make recommendations which are applicable to all Parties to a treaty, it is unusual for such a body to point a finger in public at an individual Party or a group of Parties and recommend that it, or they, should take certain specific actions. The provision illustrates, at least theoretically, an interesting willingness by the Parties to accept an unusual degree of outside interference in their domestic activities in order to promote the conservation of an endangered species.

5.   *Appendix II Species*

a)   *Listing criteria*

To merit inclusion in Appendix II, a species must either have an "unfavourable conservation status" and require "an international agreement for its conservation and management" or have "a conservation status which would significantly benefit from the international cooperation that could be achieved by an international agreement."[28] Therefore, the most important criterion for listing a species in Appendix II is whether or not it will benefit from international cooperation rather than whether or nor it is currently or potentially in danger of extinction. All phalaropes (*Phalaropodidae* spp.,) for example, are in Appendix II because they have exceptionally long migratory routes and would obviously benefit from international cooperation in their conservation — notwithstanding that the survival of most species of phalarope is neither currently nor even potentially in danger.

Since Appendix II is so different in outlook to Appendix I, the same species may be listed in both Appendices for entirely different reasons. The Atlantic ridley turtle, for example, is in Appendix I because it is migratory and in danger of extinction. It is also in Appendix II because its conservation status would benefit from

---

[26] *Ibid.*
[27] Bonn Convention, Article III(6).
[28] *Ibid.*, Article IV(I).

international cooperation. However, not all Appendix I species will qualify for Appendix II. The dark-rumped petrel is in Appendix I because it is an endangered migratory species, but it will not qualify for Appendix II because its threatened status is due to introduced predators and loss of suitable breeding habitat in the Galapagos Islands.[29] This is purely a local problem, and an international agreement to protect the petrel along all stages of its migratory route would do nothing to enhance its prospects of survival.

The Final Conference agreed to include a representative sample of species in Appendix II. Only seven mammals, one freshwater fish and one insect were chosen, but all sea turtles, falcons, accipiters and cranes, together with numerous other reptiles and birds, were listed. The Convention provides no criteria for removing species from Appendix II, presumably because the capacity of a species to benefit from international cooperation is unlikely to change even if its conservation status improves.

b)   Obligations to conclude AGREEMENTS

The Convention's approach to the protection of species in the two Appendices varies enormously. In contrast to the direct conservation obligations imposed on Parties which are Range States of Appendix I species, the Convention requires Parties which are Range States of Appendix II species to endeavour to conclude "AGREEMENTS" amongst themselves where this would benefit the species and to give priority to Appendix II species in an unfavourable conservation status[30].

There are a number of mandatory conditions which each AGREEMENT must fulfil. The object of each AGREEMENT "shall be to restore the migratory species concerned to a favourable conservation status or to maintain it in such a status," and each AGREEMENT "should deal with those aspects of the conservation and management of the migratory species concerned which serve to achieve that object."[31] Each AGREEMENT should cover the whole range of the species concerned, be open to accession by all Range States whether or not they are Parties to the Convention[32] and deal wherever possible with more than one migratory species.[33] Each AGREEMENT should also identify the species covered,[34] describe

---

[29] See 'Explanatory Notes', note 5 above, para. 16, p. 100.
[30] Bonn Convention, Article IV(3).
[31] Ibid., Article V(1).
[32] Ibid., Article V(2).
[33] Ibid., Article V(3).
[34] Ibid., Article V(4)(a).

the range and migratory route of the species,[35] require each Party to designate a national authority with responsibility for implementing the AGREEMENT,[36] set up an administrative machinery to monitor the effectiveness of the AGREEMENT[37] and establish procedures for the settlement of disputes.[38] AGREEMENTS concerning the Order Cetacea should prohibit any taking that is not permitted under other multilateral agreements, notably the International Convention for the Regulation of Whaling, and should be open to accession by States other than Range States.[39] The latter are not normally permitted to accede to AGREEMENTS, and the reason for the exception in the case of whales was probably to bring the Bonn Convention into line with the International Convention for the Regulation of Whaling which is open to landlocked non-whaling States.[40] The Secretariat must be provided with a copy of each AGREEMENT.[41]

In addition to the above requirements, Article V(5) of the Bonn Convention suggests fourteen different aspects of conservation and management which should be covered by each AGREEMENT "where appropriate and feasible". These include a periodic review of the conservation status of the species concerned, the identification of factors which might be harmful to that status, the taking of appropriate action against harmful factors, the maintenance of a network of suitable habitats along migration routes, the exchange of information and the education of the public on the contents and objectives of the AGREEMENT.

The system of AGREEMENTS established by the Convention is an interesting one, but it faces two potentially serious problems. The first is time. Parties were obliged to protect Appendix I species as soon as the Convention entered into force, but Appendix II species will receive no protection under the Convention until further AGREEMENTS are concluded and themselves come into force — a process which could take several years. The second problem is to persuade the Range States of an Appendix II species to accede to an AGREEMENT which is tough enough to ensure that they take the measures needed to counteract the threats to that species. If an AGREEMENT is negotiated so as to be acceptable to all Range States, its provisions will inevitably be diluted to a level which the

---

[35] *Ibid.*, Article V(4)(b).
[36] *Ibid.*, Article V(4)(c).
[37] *Ibid.*, Article V(4)(d).
[38] *Ibid.*, Article V(4)(e).
[39] *Ibid.*, Article V(4)(f).
[40] See Chapter 2 above, p. 20.
[41] Bonn Convention, Article IV(5).

least conservation-oriented Range State is willing to accept. Yet if the most conservation-oriented Range States conclude an AGREEMENT with strongly protectionist provisions, other Range States may decide not to accede and portions of the relevant migratory route will therefore remain outside the scope of the AGREEMENT.

c) *Obligations to conclude agreements*

In addition to the provisions of the Convention concerning AGREEMENTS, Article IV(4) encourages Parties to conclude "agreements" (spelled in ordinary letters to differentiate them from AGREEMENTS)[42] "for any population or any geographically separate part of the population of any species or lower taxon of wild animals, members of which periodically cross one or more national jurisdictional boundaries." At first sight Article IV(4) is rather confusing because its provisions appear so similar to those relating to AGREEMENTS, but there are some differences. "Agreements" under Article IV(4) cover a wider variety of species than AGREEMENTS since they encompass any population of any species whose members periodically cross one or more national boundaries. This might include species not listed in Appendix II or even species that are not considered "migratory" as defined by the Convention.[43] The purpose of Article IV(4) is to encourage Parties to conclude agreements to protect species which would benefit from international cooperation in situations where for some reason the species has not yet been listed in Appendix II or does not technically qualify for Appendix II.

6. *Range States*

The Convention requires the Parties to inform the Secretariat as to which species in the Appendices they consider themselves to be Range States, and they must also provide the Secretariat with information on any of their flag vessels which are taking or planning to take specimens of species in the Appendices outside national jurisdictional limits.[44] At least six months prior to each ordinary meeting of the Conference of the Parties, Parties should inform the Secretariat of measures that they are taking to implement the

[42] The published text of the Bonn Convention contains an important misprint because it prints "agreements" in Article IV(4) as "AGREEMENTS". This misprint was acknowledged in a Note Verbale from the Ministry of Foreign Affairs of the Federal Republic of Germany to signatory governments dated 28 January 1982.

[43] The wider application of the word "periodically" compared to the words "cyclically and predictably" is discussed on pp. 281-282 above.

[44] Bonn Convention, Article VI(2).

Convention in relation to species of which they are Range States,[45] and the Secretariat is required to maintain an up-to-date list of Range States.[46]

7. Administration

a) The Conference of the Parties

Article VII establishes the Conference of the Parties as the decision-making body of the Convention and sets out its powers and functions. It is modelled closely on the corresponding provisions under CITES.[47]

The Conference of the Parties is required to meet not later than two years after the Convention comes into force (i.e. by November 1985) and at least every three years thereafter.[48] Its responsibilities include the establishment and review of the financial regulations of the Convention and the adoption of a budget for the following financial period at each of its ordinary meetings.[49] Its decisions will normally be arrived at by a two-thirds majority of Parties present and voting[50] but in relation to financial regulations, including the scale of each Party's contribution to the budget, they must be unanimous.[51] The Conference of the Parties will also be responsible for reviewing implementation of the Convention at each of its meetings. The exact nature of the review is flexible, but Article VII recommends that matters under review should include the status of listed and unlisted migratory species, the progress made towards their conservation particularly under any AGREEMENTS, and reports submitted by the Parties, the Scientific Council, the Secretariat or any other such body. Article VII also suggests that the Conference of the Parties should make recommendations on ways of improving the conservation status of listed and unlisted migratory species and the effectiveness of the Convention in any other respect.[52] Each meeting of the Conference of the Parties is responsible for determining its own rules of procedure.[53]

Like CITES, the Bonn Convention allows representatives of a wide variety of organisations to attend meetings of the Conference of

[45] Ibid., Article VI(3).
[46] Ibid., Article VI(1).
[47] See Chapter 12 above, pp. 273-275.
[48] Bonn Convention, Article VII(2) and (3). Article VII(3) authorises extraordinary meetings to be held at any time on the written request of at least one third of the Parties.
[49] Bonn Convention, Article VII(4).
[50] Ibid., Article VII(7).
[51] Ibid., Article VII(4).
[52] Ibid., Article VII(5).
[53] Ibid., Article VII(7).

the Parties as observers who may participate in the proceedings but
may not vote. The United Nations, its Specialised Agencies, the
International Atomic Energy Authority and non-Party States are
automatically entitled to be represented in this capacity.[54]
International agencies or bodies, national governmental agencies or
bodies and "national non-governmental agencies or bodies which
have been approved for this purpose by the State in which they are
located" may also be represented by observers provided that they
have informed the Secretariat of their desire to be so represented and
that they are "technically qualified in protection, conservation and
management of migratory species", unless at least one third of the
Parties present at the meeting object.[55] If the experience of CITES
and the Final Conference to conclude the Bonn Convention is
repeated, meetings of the Conference of the Parties will be attended
by large numbers of non-governmental organisations from all over
the world. Representing commercial and conservation interests,
these organisations have consistently played a significant role in the
development of the two Conventions both as a source of information
and as lobbyists for the causes that they espouse.[56] Over twenty were
accredited at the Final Conference, and a letter signed on behalf of
three hundred of them was included in the Conference Documents
and published in at least one official governmental report on the
negotiation and adoption of the Convention.[57]

b)   *The Scientific Council*

Article VIII(1) requires the first meeting of the Conference of the
Parties to establish a Scientific Council in order to provide advice on
scientific matters. Each Party may appoint a qualified expert to be a
member of the Council, and the Conference of the Parties may itself
add others. The number of experts, the criteria for their selection
and their terms of appointment will be decided by the Conference of
the Parties.[58]

The Second Revised Draft Convention envisaged the Scientific
Council as a largely autonomous body.[59] However, the final version
of the Convention places the Council firmly under the control of the
Conference of the Parties, which has absolute power to determine

[54]   *Ibid.*, Article VII(8).
[55]   *Ibid.*, Article VII(9).
[56]   See Chapter 12 above p. 275.
[57]   See *Convention on the Conservation of Migratory Species of Wild Animals*, note 1 above, p. 163.
[58]   Bonn Convention, Article VIII(2).
[59]   See Second Revised Draft Convention, Article VIII(7), reprinted in *Convention on the Conservation of Migratory Species of Wild Animals*, note 1 above.

when the Council meets[60] and precisely what its functions will be,[61] although the Convention does make some suggestions as to what these functions might be. They include providing scientific advice to the Conference of the Parties; recommending, coordinating and evaluating research into the conservation status of migratory species and reporting the results to the Conference of the Parties; recommending additions to Appendices I and II; recommending specific conservation and management measures to be included in AGREEMENTS; and recommending "solutions to problems relating to the scientific aspects of the implementation of this Convention, in particular with regard to the habitats of migratory species."[62] The advisory nature of the Scientific Council is not unusual, but the decision to prevent the Council from taking any initiative with respect to its own activities indicates that some States were concerned lest it might become involved in issues which are scientifically interesting but politically undesirable.[63]

c)   *The Secretariat*

Article IX establishes a Secretariat whose funding arrangements and functions are very similar to those of the CITES Secretariat.

The United Nations Environment Programme originally financed the CITES Secretariat and it will do the same for the Secretariat of the Bonn Convention,[64] although on the understanding that the Parties will take over this responsibility four years after the Convention enters into force.[65] A resolution attached to the Final Act of the Final Conference requested the Depositary (the government of the Federal Republic of Germany) to carry out interim Secretariat functions until the Convention enters into force.[66] Article IX(4) sets out twelve specific duties of the Secretariat which include arranging and servicing meetings of the Conference of the Parties and of the Scientific Council, acting as a liaison between the Parties, disseminating relevant information received from the Council and other such bodies, publishing lists of Range States of species in Appendices I and II, promoting the conclusion of AGREEMENTS and maintaining a list of those in force, preparing reports for meetings of the Conference of the Parties and publishing

---

[60] Bonn Convention, Article VIII(3).
[61] *Ibid.*, Article VIII(5).
[62] *Ibid.*
[63] The U.S.A. was one such country. See *Report of the U.S. Delegation*, note 8 above, p. 6.
[64] Bonn Convention, Article IX(2).
[65] See "Address by the Executive Director of UNEP to the Final Conference", *Convention on the Conservation of Migratory Species of Wild Animals*, note 1 above, pp. 158-9.
[66] See *Convention on the Conservation of Migratory Species of Wild Animals*, note 1 above, p. 36.

their recommendations, providing the public with information on the Convention and performing "any other function" entrusted to it by the Conference of the Parties. Since the functions of the CITES and Bonn Convention Secretariats are so similar and since both will clearly benefit from mutual cooperation, it has been suggested that they should share office accommodation although they would, of course, remain as two separate legal entities.

8. *Final Clauses*

Most of the final clauses of the Bonn Convention are standard, and many are similar to their counterparts under CITES. Procedures for amending the Appendices, for example, are almost identical to the amendment procedures under CITES. Proposals for amendment may be made by any Party,[67] must be submitted to the Secretariat for circulation to the Parties at least 150 days before the meeting of the Conference of the Parties at which they will be considered,[68] require a two-thirds majority of Parties present and voting to be adopted,[69] and will enter into force ninety days after the meeting for all Parties except those that notify the Depositary in writing that they are making a reservation.[70] Proposed amendments to other parts of the Convention must undergo similar procedures except that they will only enter into force for those Parties who specifically accept them.[71] As with CITES, the Bonn Convention does not allow Parties to make general reservations to its provisions,[72] but they may make a specific reservation with respect to the inclusion of a species in Appendix I or II, provided that the reservation is made at the time of the Party's ratification, acceptance, approval or accession or within ninety days of the species being added to or deleted from either Appendix.[73] Reservations may be withdrawn by written notice to the Depositary at any time.[74]

The procedures of the Convention for the settlement of disputes are absolutely identical to those under CITES, requiring that disputes be settled by negotiation or, if negotiation fails and the disputing Parties consent, by arbitration.[75] The Second Revised Draft Convention would have allowed a Party to a dispute to force all

[67] Bonn Convention, Article XI(2).
[68] Bonn Convention, Article XI(3).
[69] *Ibid.*, Article XI(4).
[70] *Ibid.*, Article XI(5).
[71] *Ibid.*, Article X(5).
[72] *Ibid.*, Article XIV(1).
[73] *Ibid.*, Article XIV(2).
[74] *Ibid.*, Article XI(6).
[75] *Ibid.*, Article XIII(3).

Parties to the dispute to accept arbitration[76] but this was changed at the Final Conference. The Convention is subject to ratification, acceptance, or approval by the twenty two states who signed before 22 June, 1980 and to accession by those who did not.[77] It is also subject to accession by "any regional economic integration organization" such as the European Economic Community.[78]

Article XII deals with a number of points concerning other treaties and national legislation. Article XII(1) provides that nothing in the Bonn Convention shall prejudice the development of the law of the sea or the nature and extent of coastal and flag State jurisdiction. This disclaimer, also found in CITES, was particularly important to maritime powers which were anxious that nothing should prejudice their positions in the long and complex negotiations for an international agreement on exploitation of the living and non-living resources of the sea.[79] Article XII(2) provides that the Convention "shall in no way affect the rights or obligations of any Party deriving from any existing treaty, convention or agreement." This kind of clause is not uncommon in conservation conventions, but it represents a considerable change from the Second Revised Draft Convention which would have encouraged the Conference of the Parties to review existing agreements relevant to migratory species to see if their provisions conformed with the standards required for an AGREEMENT under the Bonn Convention and to indicate the appropriate action to be taken if they did not so conform.[80] Article XII(2) is significant because it should allay any fears that a non-Party may have that its accession to the Bonn Convention will require it to re-open existing agreements for further negotiation. Under the text of the Convention that was finally adopted, such fears are no longer valid.

Finally, Article XII(3) permits the Parties to adopt stricter domestic measures for the conservation of migratory species than are required by the Convention, a provision which is also found in CITES and several other treaties concerned with the conservation of wildlife.

[76] Second Revised Draft Convention, Article XII(2), reprinted in *Convention on the Conservation of Migratory Species of Wild Animals*, note 1 above.

[77] Bonn Convention, Articles XVI and XVII.

[78] *Ibid.*, Article XVII. The EEC has already acceded to the Convention.

[79] The Law of the Sea Convention (1982) was finally signed by 119 States in December 1982, although a number of the wealthier maritime States were not among the signatories.

[80] Second Revised Draft Convention, Article XI(2), reprinted in *Convention on the Conservation of Migratory Species of Wild Animals*, note 1 above.

9. *Conclusion*

The Bonn Convention is particularly interesting for three reasons. It covers an unusually broad range of threats to the survival of Appendix I species, its provisions are unusually rigorous in their restrictions on the taking of Appendix I species, and there is no precedent in international wildlife law for the system of AGREEMENTS set up to help migratory species which would benefit from international cooperation in their conservation and management.

At the time of writing, it is too early to judge what the practical effect of the Convention will be, but there is no doubt that it has the potential to be of considerable value to a large number of species which arc not adequately protected by existing international agreements. Sea turtles are just one example of migratory species which are gravely threatened by over-exploitation and disturbance of their nesting sites, which receive only limited protection from other wildlife treaties, and which could benefit significantly from the international cooperation with respect to their conservation and management that an AGREEMENT might stimulate. Migratory birds in South America, Africa and Southern Asia also badly need this kind of international cooperation in order to close the gap in the existing network of migratory bird treaties.[81]

However, before the Bonn Convention has any significant practical effect it is essential that a large number of States accede to it. Appendix I species will gain nothing from being listed under the Convention unless their Range States become Parties, and although AGREEMENTS are open to Range States that are non-Parties, there is little likelihood of an effective AGREEMENT being concluded for the benefit of an Appendix II species unless a large portion of its Range States are Parties. In addition, implementation of the provisions of the Convention will require money and technical expertise, and the problems which have arisen under the Convention on Wetlands of International Importance Especially as Waterfowl Habitat in this respect[82] are certain to reappear here. Recognising this, a resolution on assistance to developing countries was appended to the Final Act of the Final Conference.[83] It urges appropriate organisations to give priority to the conservation and management of migratory species and their habitats in developing countries and urges Party governments to "promote" such assistance. The Bonn Convention is not intended to be an "aid"

---

[81] See further Chapter 4 above.
[82] See Chapter 10 above, pp. 202-207.
[83] See *Convention on the Conservation of Migratory Species of Wild Animals*, note 1 above, p. 36.

treaty like the World Heritage Convention, but unless developing nations do receive some outside help they may not be able to make a significant contribution towards the achievement of its objectives.

CHAPTER 14

CONCLUSION

1. *Changing Values*

When the General Assembly of German agriculturalists and foresters passed a resolution in 1868 urging the government of Austria-Hungary to enter into treaties with other countries for the protection of animals useful to agriculture or forestry, their primary concern was to prevent the depletion of insectivorous birds — their vital allies in the perpetual battle against insect pests. The General Assembly was strictly utilitarian in its approach and, at the same time as urging protection for these birds, had no hesitation in condemning grain-eating birds, fish-eating birds and birds of prey which they considered harmful and worthy of destruction. Its members would have been astonished to learn that birds of prey are now among the most strictly protected of all birds and that treaties now demand the conservation of amphibians, reptiles, insects and plants as well as the more obviously beneficial animals. This change in the values attributed to wildlife is perhaps the most striking feature in the development of international wildlife law. Until recently, wildlife treaties concentrated entirely on species of direct value to man, either because they consumed agricultural pests or because they were a source of food, sport, oil or clothing. Now the emphasis is more on the role species play in the ecosystems in which they occur and on the need to prevent any species, however unglamorous or of little apparent importance, from becoming extinct through agencies within man's control.

2. *Changing Threats*

There have also been major changes over the years in the types of threats to wildlife which treaties have attempted to counteract. The early treaties were almost entirely concerned with limiting the killing of animals which either had been, or were in danger of becoming, seriously depleted by human exploitation. At that time wildlife habitats were still relatively unspoiled, and excessive killing was the greatest danger to seals, whales, birds, and other popular target animals. Now the most invidious threat to most species is not excessive killing but disruption of their habitat. In his book *The Sinking Ark*, Dr Norman Myers declares:

> There is no doubt what now constitutes the main form of threat [to wildlife]: habitat disruption...Habitat disruption includes any

significant modification of natural environments and life-support systems. It extends from agriculture and forestry to settlement schemes, highway construction, pollution and a long list of man's activities. Even before the arrival of advanced technology, habitat disruption caused massive loss of living space for wild creatures. Super-sophisticated technology can now inflict as much damage on wildlife habitat in a single year as would have taken a decade in earlier times.[1]

The more modern wildlife treaties have attempted to adapt to this new threat, emphasising the need to protect wildlife habitats and to prevent environmental pollution. There have also been changes in the approach taken by treaties towards habitat protection. The first habitat provisions made by treaties concentrated entirely on the establishment of nature reserves, national parks and other such protected areas. Treaties still encourage the creation of parks and reserves but, recognising that it may be impracticable to set aside large tracts of land from all agricultural or industrial usage for every important breeding or feeding site of every threatened species, they now tend to place more emphasis on specific site protection. Thus, for example, instead of making thousands of acres totally inviolate because they are an important breeding site for a rare bird, there is now a tendency to allow agricultural and industrial activities to continue in the area provided that they do not damage the value of the site for the bird. Article 6(b) of the Berne Convention, which prohibits deliberate damage to, or destruction of, important breeding or resting sites of species listed in Appendix II of the Convention, is a case in point. Parties to the Berne Convention can choose either to set aside important sites for Appendix II species as inviolate parks or reserves or, if they prefer, they can allow existing land usage to continue to the extent that it does not damage the sites in question.

3. *Changing Approach to Exploitation*

Even treaties which are limited to regulating the killing of wildlife are tending towards a new approach in view of the changing values attributed to species. The objective of many of the older treaties was to manage species so that they would produce the greatest harvest year after year. In so doing, these treaties considered only the species being harvested. The modern trend is towards an ecosystem approach which demands that managers look not only at species being harvested but also at other dependent species. The Convention on the Conservation of Antarctic Marine Living

[1] N. Myers, *The Sinking Ark* (Pergamon Press, 1979), pp. 38-9.

Resources ("CCAMLR") embodies this new attitude particularly forcefully, requiring that exploitation of Antarctic marine species should be limited not only to a level that the species being exploited can sustain but also to a level which will not damage other species. The Parties to CCAMLR were especially anxious that krill fishing should not impede the recovery of depleted populations of baleen whales which rely upon krill for food.

4. *Compliance*

An extremely important trend has been the development of techniques to improve the level of compliance with wildlife treaties. The early European migratory bird treaties, the Convention on Nature Protection and Wildlife Preservation in the Western Hemisphere and the African Convention on the Conservation of Nature and Natural Resources have all proved relatively ineffectual because, among other things, none of them established a system of administration to monitor and oversee their enforcement. They have become "sleeping treaties" which have been allowed to drift from the forefront of their Parties' attention and, in consequence, have had nothing like as much practical impact as they might have done if they had been given the proper encouragement. The treaties which have achieved the greatest level of compliance are, by and large, those which keep their Parties active, have a central administrative body to oversee enforcement and have some means of chastising Parties which do not comply with their treaty obligations.

The most widely used means of keeping Parties involved in a treaty are to make them submit regular reports on what they have done to implement the treaty and to hold regular meetings of Party governments to review implementation and to make recommendations for improving it. The Convention on International Trade in Endangered Species of Wild Fauna and Flora ("CITES"), which is more effective than many treaties, does both these things and also requires its Parties to create two domestic bodies with specific responsibilities for implementing the permit system established by the treaty. It is probably fair to say that somebody in government is doing something every working day to implement CITES in every Party to the Convention. CITES still has serious enforcement problems, but as a result of the administrative system it has established it is unlikely ever to become a "sleeping treaty". This is perhaps the most important first step towards proper compliance that any wildlife treaty can take.

CITES is also greatly helped by its well financed Secretariat whose function, among other things, is to monitor compliance with the treaty and to help Parties experiencing problems with illegal trade to stamp it out. The Convention Concerning the Protection of the World Cultural and Natural Heritage is another treaty whose success has been greatly facilitated by the support of a substantial bureaucratic machinery. This Convention has another enormous advantage in that it offers its Parties, especially the poorer ones, the prospect of financial assistance in return for their promise to protect sites in the World Heritage List. It is no surprise that the Convention on Wetlands of International Importance Especially as Waterfowl Habitat, which has been criticised in the past for being ineffective and for having few developing countries as Parties, is progressing towards the establishment of a permanent paid Secretariat and has urged its richer Parties to look favourably on requests for financial assistance from poorer Parties for wetland conservation projects. The intent of these initiatives is both to improve the overall effectiveness of the Convention and to make it more attractive to developing countries. The only drawback to any Secretariat is that it is expensive. The CITES Secretariat has an annual budget of hundreds of thousands of dollars, but the Organization of African Unity, for example, is at an immediate disadvantage as an overseer of the African Convention because that kind of budget is simply not available to it.

Another development which has contributed to the better enforcement of wildlife treaties, particularly in the sense of making non-performing Parties more vulnerable to public chastisement, is the growing tendency to allow meetings of Parties to be attended by non-governmental organisations ("NGOs") as observers. The International Whaling Commission, CITES, the Convention on the Conservation of European Wildlife and Natural Habitats and the Convention on the Conservation of Migratory Species of Wild Animals all allow broad categories of NGOs to attend their meetings, while CCAMLR, the World Heritage Convention, the Agreement on the Conservation of Polar Bears and several other treaties allow attendance by more limited categories of NGOs. The opportunity to participate in these meetings has been seized particularly eagerly by non-governmental conservation organisations. They are an important source of technical expertise on conservation issues, but their presence is also a significant incentive for Parties to comply with their treaty obligations. Parties know that NGOs will be quick to publicise any examples of non-compliance and that they will then face the wrath of the international community at large. Countries generally prefer to implement their treaty obligations than face such adverse publicity, especially in the field of wildlife conservation where public sentiments can run very strong. Japan's image in the international community, for example, has undoubtedly been tarnished by the publicity given to its continuing refusal to abide by conservation measures agreed by the International Whaling Commission.

5. *The Future*

Wildlife treaties have so far evolved on a piecemeal basis, reacting to specific needs in specific areas. They cover many threats to many species and can rightly claim to have achieved some considerable successes.

However, large gaps still remain. The migratory bird treaties considered in Chapter 4 cover North America, parts of Europe, the U.S.S.R., Japan and Australia, but there are no migratory bird treaties covering South America, Africa or the rest of Asia. These are grave omissions because so many birds breed in North America, Northern Europe, the U.S.S.R. and Japan, and then migrate to Central and South America, Africa or southern Asia for the winter. Regional wildlife treaties cover the Americas, Africa, Europe and Antarctica, but an Asian wildlife treaty is badly needed to complete the picture. Member States of the Association of South-East Asian Nations began negotiations for a regional nature conservation treaty in the 1970s, and a draft agreement has been prepared, but it has not yet been signed at the time of writing. Habitat degradation, particularly the loss of tropical forests, is the single most important cause of species extinction, yet there is no worldwide treaty for the protection of habitats of endangered species or of endangered ecosystems. Such a treaty would help fill in gaps left by the regional treaties and, more significantly, would greatly increase cooperation between the developed and developing world. CITES has shown that global cooperation to regulate international trade in wildlife can work, and cooperation to protect habitats is just as important. How much more effective the African Convention, for example, might be if industrialised nations were also Parties to it and were bound to commit their considerable financial and technical resources to helping achieve its objectives.

Although there are important gaps which need to be filled, much could be achieved by more aggressive enforcement of existing treaties. The African and Western Hemisphere Conventions may lack the financial and technical resources available to other treaties, but the fact that they have been allowed to drift in the way that they have also demonstrates a certain lack of political will to promote their implementation. CCAMLR sets an admirable standard for the conservation of Antarctic marine living resources, but fishing in Antarctic waters is still more or less unregulated because the Commission established by the Convention has been unable to agree, with a few exceptions, on how to translate the conservation requirements of the Convention into a system of practical controls. CITES imposes severe restrictions on international trade in wildlife, but smuggling is still widespread. The Convention on the Conservation of European Wildlife and Natural Habitats prohibits deliberate damage to breeding or resting sites of species in Appendix II of the Convention, yet these sites continue to be degraded in many Party countries. This does not mean that wildlife treaties have failed in their objectives — far from it — it simply acknowledges that much could still be done to increase their level of enforcement. The creation of new treaties to fill existing gaps is important, but the ability of governments to improve compliance with treaties already in force is likely to prove a more critical factor for wildlife in the years to come.

APPENDIX

CONVENTION ON NATURE PROTECTION AND WILDLIFE PRESERVATION IN THE WESTERN HEMISPHERE, 1940

PREAMBLE

The Governments of the American Republics, wishing to protect and preserve in their natural habitat representatives of all species and genera of their native flora and fauna, including migratory birds, in sufficient numbers and over areas extensive enough to assure them from becoming extinct through any agency within man's control; and

WISHING to protect and preserve scenery of extraordinary beauty, unusual and striking geologic formations, regions and natural objects of aesthetic, historic or scientific value, and areas characterized by primitive conditions in those cases covered by this Convention; and

WISHING to conclude a convention on the protection of nature and the preservation of flora and fauna to effectuate the foregoing purposes, have agreed upon the following Articles:

Article I

DESCRIPTION OF TERMS USED IN THE WORDING OF THIS CONVENTION

1. The expression *national parks* shall denote:

Areas established for the protection and preservation of superlative scenery, flora and fauna of national significance which the general public may enjoy and from which it may benefit when placed under public control.

2. The expression *national reserves* shall denote:

Regions established for conservation and utilization of natural resources under government control, on which protection of animal and plant life will be afforded in so far as this may be consistent with the primary purpose of such reserves.

3.   The expression *nature monuments* shall denote:

Regions, objects, or living species of flora and fauna of aesthetic, historic or scientific interest to which strict protection is given. The purpose of nature monuments is the protection of a specific object, or a species of flora or fauna, by setting aside an area, an object, or a single species, as an inviolate nature monument, except for duly authorized scientific investigations or government inspection.

4.   The expression *strict wilderness reserves* shall denote:

A region under public control characterized by primitive conditions of flora, fauna, transportation and habitation wherein there is no provision for the passage of motorized transportation and all commercial developments are excluded.

5.   The expression *migratory birds* shall denote:

Birds of those species, all or some of whose individual members, may at any season cross any of the boundaries between the American countries. Some of the species of the following families are examples of birds characterized as migratory: Charadriidae, Scolopacidae, Caprimulgidae, Hirundinidae.

Article II

1.   The Contracting Governments will explore at once the possibility of establishing in their territories national parks, national reserves, nature monuments, and strict wilderness reserves as defined in the preceding article. In all cases where such establishment is feasible, the creation thereof shall be begun as soon as possible after the effective date of the present Convention.

2.   If in any country the establishment of national parks, national reserves, nature monuments, or strict wilderness reserves is found to be impractical at present, suitable areas, objects or living species of fauna or flora, as the case may be, shall be selected as early as possible to be transformed into national parks, national reserves, nature monuments or strict wilderness reserves as soon as, in the opinion of the authorities concerned, circumstances will permit.

3.   The Contracting Governments shall notify the Pan American Union of the establishment of any national parks, national reserves, nature monuments, or strict wilderness reserves, and of the legislation, including the methods of administrative control, adopted in connection therewith.

Article III

The Contracting Governments agree that the boundaries of national parks shall not be altered, or any portion thereof be capable of alienation, except by the competent legislative authority. The resources of these reserves shall not be subject to exploitation for commercial profit.

The Contracting Governments agree to prohibit hunting, killing and capturing of members of the fauna and destruction or collection of representatives of the flora in national parks except by or under the direction or control of the park authorities, or for duly authorized scientific investigations.

The Contracting Governments further agree to provide facilities for public recreation and education in national parks consistent with the purposes of this Convention.

Article IV

The Contracting Governments agree to maintain the strict wilderness reserves inviolate, as far as practicable, except for duly authorized scientific investigations or government inspection, or such uses as are consistent with the purposes for which the area was established.

Article V

1. The Contracting Governments agree to adopt, or to propose such adoption to their respective appropriate law-making bodies, suitable laws and regulations for the protection and preservation of flora and fauna within their national boundaries, but not included in the national parks, national reserves, nature monuments, or strict wilderness reserves referred to in Article II hereof. Such regulations shall contain proper provisions for the taking of the specimens of flora and fauna for scientific study and investigation by properly accredited individuals and agencies.

Article VI

The Contracting Governments agree to co-operate among themselves in promoting the objectives of the present Convention. To this end they will lend proper assistance, consistent with national laws, to scientists of the American Republics engaged in research and field study; they may, when circumstances warrant, enter into agreements with one another or with scientific institutions of the Americas in order to increase the effectiveness of this collaboration;

and they shall make available to all the American Republics equally through publication or otherwise the scientific knowledge resulting from such co-operative effort.

Article VII

The Contracting Governments shall adopt appropriate measures for the protection of migratory birds of economic or aesthetic value or to prevent the threatened extinction of any given species. Adequate measures shall be adopted which will permit, in so far as the respective governments may see fit, a rational utilization of migratory birds for the purpose of sports as well as for food, commerce, and industry, and for scientific study and investigation.

Article VIII

The protection of the species mentioned in the Annex to the present Convention is declared to be of special urgency and importance. Species included therein shall be protected as completely as possible, and their hunting, killing, capturing, or taking, shall be allowed only with the permission of the appropriate government authorities in the country. Such permission shall be granted only under special circumstances, in order to further scientific purposes, or when essential for the administration of the area in which the animal or plant is found.

Article IX

Each Contracting Government shall take the necessary measures to control and regulate the importation, exportation and transit of protected fauna and flora or any part thereof by the following means:

1.   The issuing of certificates authorizing the exportation or transit of protected species of flora or fauna, or parts thereof.

2.   The prohibition of the importation of any species of fauna or flora or any part thereof protected by the country of origin unless accompanied by a certificate of lawful exportation as provided for in Paragraph 1 of this Article.

Article X

1.   The terms of this convention shall in no way be interpreted as replacing international agreements previously entered into by one or more of the High Contracting Powers.

2.   The Pan American Union shall notify the Contracting Parties of any information relevant to the purposes of the present Convention communicated to it by any national museums or by any organizations, national or international, established within their jurisdiction and interested in the purposes of the Convention.

Article XI

1.   The original of the present Convention in Spanish, English, Portuguese and French shall be deposited with the Pan American Union and opened for signature by the American Governments on 12 October 1940.

2.   The present Convention shall remain open for signature by the American Governments. The instruments of ratification shall be deposited with the Pan American Union, which shall notify their receipt and the dates thereof, and the terms of any accompanying declarations or reservations, to all participating Governments.

3.   The present Convention shall come into force three months after the deposit of not less than five ratifications with the Pan American Union.

4.   Any ratification received after the date of the entry into force of the Convention, shall take effect three months after the date of its deposit with the Pan American Union.

Article XII

1.   Any Contracting Government may at any time denounce the present Convention by a notification in writing addressed to the Pan American Union. Such denunciation shall take effect one year after the date of the receipt of the notification by the Pan American Union, provided, however, that no denunciation shall take effect until the expiration of five years from the date of the entry into force of this Convention.

2.   If, as the result of simultaneous or successive denunciations, the number of Contracting Governments is reduced to less than three, the Convention shall cease to be in force from the date on which the last of such denunciations takes effect in accordance with the provisions of the preceding Paragraph.

3.   The Pan American Union shall notify all of the American Governments of any denunciations and the date on which they take effect.

4.   Should the Convention cease to be in force under the provisions of Paragraph 2 of this article, the Pan American Union shall notify all of the American Governments, indicating the date on which this will become effective.

IN WITNESS WHEREOF, the undersigned Plenipotentiaries, having deposited their full powers found to be in due and proper form, sign this Convention at the Pan American Union, Washington, D.C., on behalf of their respective Governments and affix thereto their seals on the dates appearing opposite their signatures.

DONE at Washington, this 12th day of October 1940.

Author's note: The lists of species included in the Annex, which are subject to periodic changes, are not reproduced here but may be obtained from the Organization of American States, Washington, D.C.

INTERNATIONAL CONVENTION FOR THE REGULATION OF WHALING, 1946

The Governments whose duly authorized representatives have subscribed hereto,

RECOGNIZING the interest of the nations of the world in safeguarding for future generations the great natural resources represented by the whale stocks;

CONSIDERING that the history of whaling has seen over-fishing of one area after another and of one species of whale after another to such a degree that it is essential to protect all species of whales from further over-fishing;

RECOGNIZING that the whale stocks are susceptible of natural increases if whaling is properly regulated, and that increases in the size of whale stocks will permit increases in the numbers of whales which may be captured without endangering these natural resources;

RECOGNIZING that it is in the common interest to achieve the optimum level of whale stocks as rapidly as possible without causing widespread economic and nutritional distress;

RECOGNIZING that in the course of achieving these objectives, whaling operations should be confined to those species best able to sustain exploitation in order to give an interval for recovery to certain species of whales now depleted in numbers;

DESIRING to establish a system of international regulation for the whale fisheries to ensure proper and effective conservation and development of whale stocks on the basis of the principles embodied in the provisions of the International Agreement for the Regulation of Whaling signed in London on 8 June 1937, and the protocols to that Agreement signed in London on 24 June 1938, and 26 November 1945; and

HAVING decided to conclude a convention to provide for the proper conservation of whale stocks and thus make possible the orderly development of the whaling industry;

HAVE AGREED as follows:

Article I

1.   This Convention includes the Schedule attached thereto which forms an integral part thereof. All references to "Convention" shall be understood as including the said Schedule either in its present terms or as amended in accordance with the provisions of Article V.

2.   This Convention applies to factory ships, land stations, and whale catchers under the jurisdiction of the Contracting Governments, and to all waters in which whaling is prosecuted by such factory ships, land stations, and whale catchers.

Article II

As used in this Convention:

1.   "factory ship" means a ship in which or on which whales are treated whether wholly or in part;

2.   "land station" means a factory on the land at which whales are treated whether wholly or in part;

3.   "whale catcher" means a ship used for the purpose of hunting, taking, towing, holding on to, or scouting for whales;

4.   "Contracting Government" means any Government which has deposited an instrument of ratification or has given notice of adherence to this Convention.

Article III

1.   The Contracting Governments agree to establish an International Whaling Commission, hereinafter referred to as the Commission, to be composed of one member from each Contracting Government. Each member shall have one vote and may be accompanied by one or more experts and advisers.

2.   The Commission shall elect from its own members a Chairman and Vice-Chairman and shall determine its own Rules of Procedure. Decisions of the Commission shall be taken by a simple majority of those members voting except that a three-fourths majority of those members voting shall be required for action in pursuance of Article V. The Rules of Procedure may provide for decisions otherwise than at meetings of the Commission.

3. The Commission may appoint its own Secretary and staff.

4. The Commission may set up, from among its own members and experts or advisers, such committees as it considers desirable to perform such functions as it may authorize.

5. The expenses of each member of the Commission and of his experts and advisers shall be determined and paid by his own Government.

6. Recognizing that specialized agencies related to the United Nations will be concerned with the conservation and development of whale fisheries and the products arising therefrom and desiring to avoid duplication of functions, the Contracting Governments will consult among themselves within two years after the coming into force of this Convention to decide whether the Commission shall be brought within the framework of a specialized agency related to the United Nations.

7. In the meantime the Government of the United Kingdom of Great Britian and Northern Ireland shall arrange, in consultation with the other Contracting Governments, to convene the first meeting of the Commission, and shall initiate the consultation referred to in paragraph 6 above.

8. Subsequent meetings of the Commission shall be convened as the Commission may determine.

Article IV

1. The Commission may either in collaboration with or through independent agencies of the Contracting Governments or other public or private agencies, establishments, or organizations, or independently

> *a)* encourage, recommend, or if necessary, organize studies and investigations relating to whales and whaling;
>
> *b)* collect and analyze statistical information concerning the current condition and trend of the whale stocks and the effects of whaling activities thereon;
>
> *c)* study, appraise, and disseminate information concerning methods of maintaining and increasing the populations of whale stocks.

2.   The Commission shall arrange for the publication of reports of its activities, and it may publish independently or in collaboration with the International Bureau for Whaling Statistics at Sandefjord in Norway and other organizations and agencies such reports as it deems appropriate, as well as statistical, scientific, and other pertinent information relating to whales and whaling.

Article V

1.   The Commission may amend from time to time the provisions of the Schedule by adopting regulations with respect to the conservation and utilization of whale resources, fixing *(a)* protected and unprotected species; *(b)* open and closed seasons; *(c)* open and closed waters, including the designation of sanctuary areas; *(d)* size limits for each species; *(e)* time, methods, and intensity of whaling (including the maximum catch of whales to be taken in any one season); *(f)* types and specifications of gear and apparatus and appliances which may be used; *(g)* methods of measurement; and *(h)* catch returns and other statistical and biological records.

2.   These amendments of the Schedule *(a)* shall be such as are necessary to carry out the objectives and purposes of this Convention and to provide for the conservation, development, and optimum utilization of the whale resources; *(b)* shall be based on scientific findings; *(c)* shall not involve restrictions on the number or nationality of factory ships or land stations, nor allocate specific quotas to any factory ship or land station or to any group of factory ships or land stations; and *(d)* shall take into consideration the interests of the consumers of whale products and the whaling industry.

3.   Each of such amendments shall become effective with respect to the Contracting Governments ninety days following notification of the amendment by the Commission to each of the Contracting Governments, except that *(a)* if any Government presents to the Commission objection to any amendment prior to the expiration of this ninety-day period, the amendment shall not become effective with respect to any of the Governments for an additional ninety days; *(b)* thereupon, any other Contracting Government may present objection to the amendment at any time prior to the expiration of the additional ninety-day period, or before the expiration of thirty days from the date of receipt of the last objection received during such additional ninety-day period, whichever date shall be the later; and *(c)* thereafter, the amendment shall become

effective with respect to all Contracting Governments which have not presented objection but shall not become effective with respect to any Government which has so objected until such date as the objection is withdrawn. The Commission shall notify each Contracting Government immediately upon receipt of each objection and withdrawal and each Contracting Government shall acknowledge receipt of all notifications of amendments, objections, and withdrawals.

4.   No amendments shall become effective before 1 July 1949.

Article VI

The Commission may from time to time make recommendations to any or all Contracting Governments on any matters which relate to whales or whaling and to the objectives and purposes of this Convention.

Article VII

The Contracting Governments shall ensure prompt transmission to the International Bureau of Whaling Statistics at Sandefjord in Norway, or to such other body as the Commission may designate, of notifications and statistical and other information required by this Convention in such form and manner as may be prescribed by the Commission.

Article VIII

1.   Notwithstanding anything contained in this Convention, any Contracting Government may grant to any of its nationals a special permit authorizing that national to kill, take, and treat whales for purposes of scientific research subject to such restrictions as to number and subject to such other conditions as the Contracting Government thinks fit, and the killing, taking, and treating of whales in accordance with the provisions of this Article shall be exempt from the operation of this Convention. Each Contracting Government shall report at once to the Commission all such authorizations which it has granted. Each Contracting Government may at any time revoke any such special permit which it has granted.

2.   Any whales taken under these special permits shall so far as practicable be processed and the proceeds shall be dealt with in accordance with directions issued by the Government by which the permit was granted.

3.   Each Contracting Government shall transmit to such body as may be designated by the Commission, in so far as practicable, and at intervals of not more than one year, scientific information available to that Government with respect to whales and whaling, including the results of research conducted pursuant to paragraph 1 of this Article and to Article IV.

4.   Recognizing that continuous collection and analysis of biological data in connection with the operations of factory ships and land stations are indispensable to sound and constructive management of the whale fisheries, the Contracting Governments will take all practicable measures to obtain such data.

Article IX

1.   Each Contracting Government shall take appropriate measures to ensure the application of the provisions of this Convention and the punishment of infractions against the said provisions in operations carried out by persons or by vessels under its jurisdiction.

2.   No bonus or other remuneration calculated with relation to the results of their work shall be paid to the gunners and crews of whale catchers in respect of any whales the taking of which is forbidden by this Convention.

3.   Prosecution for infractions against or contraventions of this Convention shall be instituted by the Government having jurisdiction over the offence.

4.   Each Contracting Government shall transmit to the Commission full details of each infraction of the provisions of this Convention by persons or vessels under the jurisdiction of that Government as reported by its inspectors. This information shall include a statement of measures taken for dealing with the infraction and of penalties imposed.

Article X

1.   This Convention shall be ratified and the instruments of ratification shall be deposited with the Government of the United States of America.

2.   Any Government which has not signed this Convention may adhere thereto after it enters into force by a notification in writing to the Government of the United States of America.

3. The Government of the United States of America shall inform all other signatory Governments and all adhering Governments of all ratifications deposited and adherences received.

4. This Convention shall, when instruments of ratification have been deposited by at least six signatory Governments, which shall include the Governments of the Netherlands, Norway, the Union of Soviet Socialist Republics, the United Kingdom of Great Britain and Northern Ireland, and the United States of America, enter into force with respect to those Governments and shall enter into force with respect to each Government which subsequently ratifies or adheres on the date of the deposit of its instrument of ratification or the receipt of its notification of adherence.

5. The provisions of the Schedule shall not apply prior to 1 July 1948. Amendments to the Schedule adopted pursuant to Article V shall not apply prior to 1 July 1949.

Article XI

Any Contracting Government may withdraw from this Convention on June thirtieth of any year by giving notice on or before January first of the same year to the depositary Government, which upon receipt of such a notice shall at once communicate it to the other Contracting Governments. Any other Contracting Government may, in like manner, within one month of the receipt of a copy of such a notice from the depositary Government, give notice of withdrawal, so that the Convention shall cease to be in force on June thirtieth of the same year with respect to the Government giving such notice of withdrawal.

This Convention shall bear the date on which it is opened for signature and shall remain open for signature for a period of fourteen days thereafter.

IN WITNESS WHEREOF the undersigned, being duly authorized, have signed this Convention.

DONE in Washington this second day of December 1946, in the English language, the original of which shall be deposited in the archives of the Government of the United States of America. The Government of the United States of America shall transmit certified copies thereof to all the other signatory and adhering Governments.

PROTOCOL OF AMENDMENT

A Protocol to the International Convention for the Regulation of Whaling was adopted in Washington, D.C. on 19 November 1956. The Protocol provides as follows:-

The Contracting Governments to the International Convention for the Regulation of Whaling signed at Washington under date of December 2, 1946 which Convention is hereinafter referred to as the 1946 Whaling Convention, desiring to extend the application of that Convention to helicopters and other aircraft and to include provisions on methods of inspection among those Schedule provisions which may be amended by the Commission, agree as follows:

Article I

Subparagraph 3 of Article II of the 1946 Whaling Convention shall be amended to read as follows:
"3. 'whale catcher' means a helicopter, or other aircraft, or a ship, used for the purpose of hunting, taking, killing, towing, holding on to, or scouting for whales."

Article II

Paragraph 1 of Article V of the 1946 Whaling Convention shall be amended by deleting the word "and" preceding clause (h), substituting a semicolon for the period at the end of the paragraph, and adding the following language: "and (i) methods of inspection".

Article III

1. This Protocol shall be open for signature and ratification or for adherence on behalf of any Contracting Government to the 1946 Whaling Convention.

2. This Protocol shall enter into force on the date upon which instruments of ratification have been deposited with, or written notifications of adherence have been received by, the Government of the United States of America on behalf of all the Contracting Governments to the 1946 Whaling Convention.

3. The Government of the United States of America shall inform all Governments signatory or adhering to the 1946 Whaling Convention of all ratifications deposited and adherences received.

4. This Protocol shall bear the date on which it is opened for signature and shall remain open for signature for a period of fourteen days thereafter, following which period it shall be open for adherence.

IN WITNESS WHEREOF the undersigned, being duly authorized, have signed this Protocol.

DONE in Washington this nineteenth day of November 1956, in the English language, the original of which shall be deposited in the archives of the Government of the United States of America. The Government of the United States of America shall transmit certified copies thereof to all Governments signatory or adhering to the 1946 Whaling Convention.

Author's note: The Schedule to the 1946 Whaling Convention, which is regularly amended at meetings of the International Whaling Commission, is not reproduced here but may be obtained from the Commission Headquarters at the Red House, Station Road, Histon, Cambridge, England.

INTERIM CONVENTION ON THE CONSERVATION OF NORTH PACIFIC FUR SEALS, 1957, AS AMENDED[1]

The Governments of Canada, Japan, the Union of Soviet Socialist Republics, and the United States of America,

DESIRING to take effective measures towards achieving the maximum sustainable productivity of the fur seal resources of the North Pacific Ocean so that the fur seal populations can be brought to and maintained at the levels which will provide the greatest harvest year after year, with due regard to their relation to the productivity of other living marine resources of the area,

RECOGNIZING that in order to determine such measures it is necessary to conduct adequate scientific research on the said resources, and

DESIRING to provide for international cooperation in achieving these objectives,

AGREE as follows:

Article I

1. The term "pelagic sealing" is hereby defined for the purposes of this Convention as meaning the killing, taking, or hunting in any manner whatsoever of fur seals at sea.

2. The words "each year", "annual" and "annually" as used hereinafter refer to Convention year, that is, the year beginning on the date of entry into force of the Convention.

[1] The Interim Convention on the Conservation of North Pacific Fur Seals, signed in Washington, D.C. on 9 February 1957, has been amended by the Protocol Amending the Interim Convention on the Conservation of North Pacific Fur Seals, signed in Washington, D.C. on 8 October 1963, the Agreement Extending the Interim Convention on the Conservation of North Pacific Fur Seals, effective on 3 September 1969 following an exchange of notes by Contracting Governments, the Protocol Amending and Extending the Interim Convention on the Conservation of North Pacific Fur Seals, signed in Washington, D.C. on 7 May 1976, and the Protocol Amending the Interim Convention on the Conservation of North Pacific Fur Seals, signed in Washington, D.C. on 14 October 1980. An Agreement to extend the Interim Convention for a further four years is being negotiated at the time of writing.
    The text of the Interim Convention, as amended, is reproduced here.

3. Nothing in this Convention shall be deemed to affect in any way the position of the Parties in regard to the limits of territorial waters or to the jurisdiction over fisheries.

Article II

1. In order to realize the objectives of this Convention, the Parties agree to co-ordinate necessary scientific research programs and to cooperate in investigating the fur seal resources of the North Pacific Ocean to determine:

> *a)* what measures may be necessary to make possible the maximum sustainable productivity of the fur seal resources so that the fur seal populations can be brought to and maintained at the levels which will provide the greatest harvest year after year; and

> *b)* what the relationship is between fur seals and other living marine resources and whether fur seals have detrimental effects on other living marine resources substantially exploited by any of the Parties and, if so, to what extent.

2. The research referred to in the preceding paragraph shall include studies of the following subjects:

> *a)* size of each fur seal herd and its age and sex composition;

> *b)* natural mortality of the different age groups and recruitment of young to each age or size class at present and subsequent population levels;

> *c)* with regard to each of the herds, the effect upon the magnitude of recruitment of variations in the size and the age and sex composition of the annual kill;

> *d)* migration routes of fur seals and their wintering areas;

> *e)* numbers of seals from each herd found on the migration routes and in wintering areas and their ages and sexes;

> *f)* relationship between fur seals and other living marine resources, including the extent to which fur seals affect commercial fish catches, the damage fur seals inflict on fishing gear, and the effect of commercial fisheries on the fur seals;

> *g)* effectiveness of each method of sealing from the viewpoint of management and rational utilization of fur seal resources for conservation purposes;

h) quality of sealskins by sex, age, and time and method of sealing;

i) effects of man-caused environmental changes on the fur seal populations; and

j) other subjects involved in achieving the objectives of the Convention, as determined by the Commission established under Article V, paragraph 1.

3.   In furtherance of the research referred to in this Article, the Parties agree:

a)   to continue to mark adequate numbers of pups;

b)   to devote to pelagic research an effort which, to the greatest extent possible, should be similar in extent to that expended in recent years, provided that this shall not involve the annual taking by all the Parties combined of more than 2,500 seals in the Eastern and more than 2,200 seals in the Western Pacific Oceans, unless the Commission, pursuant to Article V, paragraph 3, shall decide otherwise, and

c)   to carry out the determinations made by the Commission pursuant to Article V, paragraph 3.

4.   Each Party agrees to provide the Commission annually with information on:

a)   number of black pups tagged for each breeding area;

b)   number of fur seals, by sex and estimated age, taken at sea and on each breeding area; and

c)   tagged seals recovered on land and at sea;

and, so far as is practicable, other information pertinent to scientific research which the Commission may request.

5.   The Parties further agree to provide for the exchange of scientific personnel; each such exchange shall be subject to mutual consent of the Parties directly concerned.

6.   The Parties agree to use for the scientific pelagic research provided for in this Article only government-owned or government-chartered vessels operating under strict control of their respective authorities. Each Party shall communicate to the other Parties the names and descriptions of vessels which are to be used for pelagic research.

Article III

In order to realize the purposes of the Convention, including the carrying out of the co-ordinated and co-operative research, each Party agrees to prohibit pelagic sealing, except as provided in Article II, paragraph 3, in the Pacific Ocean north of the 30th parallel of north latitude including the seas of Bering, Okhotsk, and Japan by any person or vessel subject to its jurisdiction.

Article IV

Each Party shall bear the expense of its own research. Title to seal skins taken during the research shall vest in the Party conducting such research.

Article V

1. The Parties agree to establish the North Pacific Fur Seal Commission to be composed of one member from each Party.

2. The duties of the Commission shall be to:

   a) formulate and co-ordinate research programs designed to achieve the objectives set forth in Article II, paragraph 1;

   b) recommend these co-ordinated research programs to the respective Parties for implementation;

   c) study the data obtained from the implementation of such co-ordinated research programs;

   d) recommend appropriate measures to the Parties on the basis of the findings obtained from the implementation of such co-ordinated research programs, including measures regarding the size and the sex and age composition of the seasonal commercial kill from a herd and regarding a reduction or suspension of the harvest of seals on any island or group of islands in case the total number of seals on that island or group of islands falls below the level of maximum sustainable productivity; provided, however, that due consideration be given to the subsistence needs of Indians, Ainos, Aleuts, or Eskimos who live on the islands where fur seals breed, when it is not possible to provide sufficient seal meat for such persons from the seasonal commercial harvest or research activities; and *e)* study whether or not pelagic sealing in conjunction with land sealing could be permitted in certain circumstances without adversely affecting achievement of the objectives of the Convention, and make recommendations thereon to the Parties at the end of the twenty-fifth year after entry into force of the Convention.

3. In addition to the duties specified in paragraph 2 of this Article, the Commission shall, subject to Article II, paragraph 3, determine from time to time the number of seals to be marked on the rookery islands, and the total number of seals which shall be taken at sea for research purposes, the times at which such seals shall be taken and the areas in which they shall be taken, as well as the number to be taken by each Party, taking into account any recommendations made pursuant to Article V, paragraph 2(d).

4. Each Party shall have one vote. Decisions and recommendations shall be made by unanimous vote. With respect to any recommendations regarding the size and the sex and age composition of the seasonal commercial kill from a herd, only those Parties sharing in the sealskins from that herd under the provisions of Article IX, paragraph 1 shall vote.

5. The Commission shall elect from its members a Chairman and other necessary officials and shall adopt rules of procedure for the conduct of its work.

6. The Commission shall hold an annual meeting at such time and place as it may decide. Additional meetings shall be held when requested by two or more members of the Commission.

7. The expenses of each member of the Commission shall be paid by his own Government. Such joint expenses as may be incurred by the Commission shall be defrayed by the Parties by equal contributions. Each Party shall also contribute to the Commission annually an amount equivalent to the value of the sealskins it confiscates under the provisions of Article VI, paragraph 5.

8. The Commission shall submit an annual report of its activities to the Parties.

9. The Commission may from time to time make recommendations to the Parties on any matter which relates to the fur seal resources or to the administration of the Commission.

Article VI

In order to implement the provisions of Article III, the Parties agree as follows:

1.   When a duly authorized official of any of the Parties has reasonable cause to believe that any vessel outfitted for the harvesting of living marine resources and subject to the jurisdiction of any of the Parties is offending against the prohibition of pelagic sealing as provided for by Article III, he may, except within the areas in which another State exercises fisheries jurisdiction, board and search such vessel. Such official shall carry a special certificate issued by the competent authorities of his Government and drawn up in the English, Japanese, and Russian languages which shall be exhibited to the master of the vessel upon request.

2.   When the official after searching a vessel continues to have reasonable cause to believe that the vessel or any person on board thereof is offending against the prohibition, he may seize or arrest such vessel or person. In that case, the Party to which the official belongs shall as soon as possible notify the Party having jurisdiction over the vessel or person of such arrest or seizure and shall deliver the vessel or person as promptly as practicable to the authorized officials of the Party having jurisdiction over the vessel or person at a place to be agreed upon by both Parties; provided, however, that when the Party receiving notification cannot immediately accept delivery of the vessel or person, the Party which gives such notification may, upon request of the other Party, keep the vessel or person under surveillance within its own territory, under the conditions agreed upon by both Parties.

3.   The authorities of the Party to which such person or vessel belongs alone shall have jurisdiction to try any case arising under Article III and this Article and to impose penalties in connection therewith.

4.   The witnesses or their testimony and other proofs necessary to establish the offense, so far as they are under the control of any of the Parties, shall be furnished with all reasonable promptness to the authorities of the Party having jurisdiction to try the case.

5.   Sealskins discovered on seized vessels shall be subject to confiscation on the decision of the court or other authorities of the Party under whose jurisdiction the trial of a case takes place.

6.   Full details of punitive measures applied to offenders against the prohibition shall be communicated to the other Parties not later than three months after the application of the penalty.

Article VII

The provisions of this Convention shall not apply to Indians, Ainos, Aleuts, or Eskimos dwelling on the coast of the waters mentioned in Article III, who carry on pelagic sealing in canoes not transported by or used in connection with other vessels, and propelled entirely by oars, paddles, or sails, and manned by not more than five persons each, in the way hitherto practiced and without the use of firearms; provided that such hunters are not in the employment of other persons or under contract to deliver the skins to any person.

Article VIII

1.   Each Party agrees that no person or vessel shall be permitted to use any of its ports or harbors or any part of its territory for any purpose designed to violate the prohibition set forth in Article III.

2.   Each Party also agrees to prohibit the importation and delivery into and the traffic within its territories of skins of fur seals taken in the area of the North Pacific Ocean mentioned in Article III, except only those taken by the Union of Soviet Socialist Republics or the United States of America on rookeries, those taken at sea for research purposes in accordance with Article II, paragraph 3, those taken under the provisions of Article VII, those confiscated under the provisions of Article IV, paragraph 5, and those inadvertently captured which are taken possession of by a Party; provided, however, that all such excepted skins shall be officially marked and duly certified by the authorities of the Party concerned.

Article IX

1.   The respective Parties agree that, of the total number of sealskins taken commercially each season on land, there shall at the end of the season be delivered a percentage of the gross in number and value thereof as follows:

By the Union of Soviet Socialist Republics
        to Canada   15 per cent
        to Japan   15 per cent

By the United States of America
    to Canada   15 per cent
    to Japan   15 per cent

2.   Each Party agrees to deliver such sealskins to an authorized agent of the recipient Party at the place of taking, or at some other place mutually agreed upon by such Parties.

3.   The respective Parties will seek to ensure the utilization of those methods for the capture and killing and marking of fur seals on land or at sea which will spare the fur seals pain and suffering to the greatest extent practicable.

Article X

1.   Each Party agrees to enact and enforce such legislation as may be necessary to guarantee the observance of this Convention and to make effective its provisions with appropriate penalties for violation thereof.

2.   The Parties further agree to co-operate with each other in taking such measures as may be appropriate to carry out the purposes of this Convention, including the prohibition of pelagic sealing as provided for by Article III.

Article XI

The Parties agree to meet in the twenty-sixth year after entry into force of the Convention to consider the recommendations in accordance with Article V, paragraph 2(e) and to determine what further agreements may be desirable in order to achieve the maximum sustainable productivity of the North Pacific fur seal herds.

Article XII

Should any Party consider that the obligations of Article II, paragraphs 3, 4, or 5 or any other obligation undertaken by the Parties is not being carried out and notify the other Parties to that effect, all the Parties shall, within three months of the receipt of such notification, meet to consult together on the need for and nature of remedial measures. In the event that such consultation shall not lead to agreement as to the need for and nature of remedial measures, any Party may give written notice to the other Parties of intention to terminate the Convention and, notwithstanding the provisions of Article XIII, paragraph 4, the Convention shall thereupon terminate as to all the Parties nine months from the date of such notice.

Article XIII

1.   This Convention shall be ratified and the instruments of ratification deposited with the Government of the United States of America as soon as practicable.

2.   The Government of the United States of America shall notify the other signatory Governments of ratifications deposited.

3.   The Convention shall enter into force on the date of the deposit of the fourth instrument of ratification.

4.   The Convention shall continue in force for twenty-six years and thereafter until the entry into force of a new or revised fur seal convention between the Parties, or until the expiration of one year after such period of twenty-six years, whichever may be the earlier; provided, however, that the Convention shall terminate one year from the day on which a Party gives written notice to the other Parties of an intention of terminating the Convention.

5.   At the request of any Party, representatives of the Parties will meet at a mutually convenient time within ninety days of such request to consider the desirability of modifications of the Convention.

6.   The original of this Convention shall be deposited with the Government of the United States of America, which shall communicate certified copies thereof to each of the Governments signatory to the Convention.

IN WITNESS WHEREOF the undersigned, being duly authorized by their respective Governments, have signed this Convention.

DONE in Washington this ninth day of February 1957, in the English, Japanese, and Russian languages, each text equally authentic.

AFRICAN CONVENTION ON THE CONSERVATION OF NATURE AND NATURAL RESOURCES, 1968

PREAMBLE:

We the Heads of State and Government of Independent African States,

FULLY CONSCIOUS that soil, water, flora and faunal resources constitute a capital of vital importance to mankind;

CONFIRMING, as we accepted upon declaring our adherence to the Charter of the Organization of African Unity, that we know that it is our duty "to harness the natural and human resources of our continent for the total advancement of our peoples in spheres of human endeavour";

FULLY CONSCIOUS of the ever-growing importance of natural resources from an economic, nutritional, scientific, educational, cultural and aesthetic point of view;

CONSCIOUS of the dangers which threaten some of these irreplaceable assets;

ACCEPTING that the utilization of the natural resources must aim at satisfying the needs of man according to the carrying capacity of the environment;

DESIROUS of undertaking individual and joint action for the conservation, utilization and development of these assets by establishing and maintaining their rational utilization for the present and future welfare of mankind;

CONVINCED that one of the most appropriate means of achieving this end is to bring into force a convention;

HAVE AGREED as follows:

Article I

The Contracting States hereby establish an African Convention on the Conservation of Nature and Natural Resources.

Article II

FUNDAMENTAL PRINCIPLE

The Contracting States shall undertake to adopt the measures to ensure conservation, utilization and development of soil, water, flora and faunal resources in accordance with scientific principles and with due regard to the best interests of the people.

Article III

DEFINITIONS

For purposes of the present Convention, the meaning of the following expressions shall be as defined below:

1.   "Natural Resources" means renewable resources, that is soil, water, flora and fauna.

2.   "Specimen" means an individual example of a species of wild animal or wild plant or part of a wild plant.

3.   "Trophy" means any dead animal specimen or part thereof whether included in a manufactured or processed object or otherwise dealt with, unless it has lost its original identity; also nests, eggs and eggshells.

4.   "Conservation area" means any protected natural resource area, whether it be a strict natural reserve, a national park or a special reserve;

   a)   "strict nature reserve" means an area:

      (i)   under State control and the boundaries of which may not be altered nor any portion alienated except by the competent legislative authority,

      (ii)   throughout which any form of hunting or fishing, any undertaking connected with forestry, agriculture or mining, any grazing, any excavation or prospecting, drilling, levelling of the ground or construction, any work tending to alter the configuration of the soil or the character of the vegetation, any water pollution and, generally, any act likely to harm or disturb the fauna or flora, including introduction of zoological or botanical species, whether indigenous or imported, wild or domesticated, are strictly forbidden.

(iii)   where it shall be forbidden to reside, enter, traverse or camp, and where it shall be forbidden to fly over at low altitude, without a special written permit from the competent authority, and in which scientific investigations (including removal of animals and plants in order to maintain an ecosystem) may only be undertaken by permission of the competent authority;

b)   "national park" means an area:

(i)   under State control and the boundaries of which may not be altered or any portion alienated except by the competent legislative authority,

(ii)   exclusively set aside for the propagation, protection, conservation and management of vegetation and wild animals as well as for the protection of sites, land-scapes or geological formations of particular scientific or aesthetic value, for the benefit and enjoyment of the general public, and

(iii)   in which the killing, hunting and capture of animals and the destruction or collection of plants are prohibited except for scientific and management purposes and on the condition that such measures are taken under the direction or control of the competent authority;

(iv)   covering any aquatic environment to which all of the provisions of section *(b)* (i-iii) above are applicable.

The activities prohibited in "strict nature reserve" under the provisions of section *(a)* (ii) of paragraph (4) of this article are equally prohibited in national parks except in so far as they are necessary to enable the park authorities to implement the provisions of section (ii) of this paragraph, by applying, for example, appropriate management practices, and to enable the public to visit these parks; however, sport fishing may be practised with the authorization and under the control of the competent authority;

c)   "special reserve" means other protected areas such as:

(i)   "game reserve" which shall denote an area

a)   set aside for the conservation, management and propagation of wild animal life and the protection and management of its habitat,

b)   within which the hunting, killing or capture of fauna shall be prohibited except by or under the direction or control of the reserve authorities, *c)* where settlement and other human activities shall be controlled or prohibited;

    (ii) "partial reserve" or "sanctuary" which shall denote an area

    a) set aside to protect characteristic wildlife and especially bird communities, or to protect particularly threatened animal or plant species and especially those listed in the Annex to this Convention, together with the biotopes essential for their survival,

    b) in which all other interests and activities shall be subordinated to this end;

    (iii) "soil", "water" or "forest" reserve shall denote areas set aside to protect such resources.

Article IV

SOIL

The Contracting States shall take effective measures for conservation and improvement of the soil and shall in particular combat erosion and misuse of the soil. To this end:

    a) they shall establish land-use plans based on scientific investigations (ecological, pedological, economic, and sociological) and, in particular, classification and land-use capability;

    b) they shall, when implementing agricultural practices and agrarian reforms,

    (i) improve soil conservation and introduce improved farming methods, which ensure long-term productivity of the land,

    (ii) control erosion caused by various forms of land-use which may lead to loss of vegetation cover.

Article V

WATER

1. The Contracting States shall establish policies for conservation, utilization and development of underground and surface water, and shall endeavour to guarantee for their populations a sufficient and continuous supply of suitable water, taking appropriate measures with due regard to:

(i)   the study of water cycles and the investigation of each catchment area,

(ii)   the co-ordination and planning of water resources development projects,

(iii)   the administration and control of all water utilization, and

(iv)   prevention and control of water pollution.

2.   Where surface or underground water resources are shared by two or more of the Contracting States, the latter shall act in consultation, and if the need arises, set up inter-State Commissions to study and resolve problems arising from the joint use of these resources, and for the joint development and conservation thereof.

Article VI

FLORA

1.   The Contracting States shall take all necessary measures for the protection of flora and to ensure its best utilization and development. To this end the Contracting States shall:

a)   adopt scientifically-based conservation, utilization and management plans of forests and ' rangeland, taking into account the social and economic needs of the States concerned, the importance of the vegetation cover for the maintenance of the water balance of an area, the productivity of soils and the habitat requirements of the fauna;

b)   observe section *(a)* above by paying particular attention to controlling bush fires, forest exploitation, land clearing for cultivation, and over-grazing by domestic and wild animals;

c)   set aside areas for forest reserves and carry out afforestation programmes where necessary;

d)   limitation of forest grazing to season and intensities that will not prevent forest regeneration; and

e)   establish botanical gardens to perpetuate plant species of particular interest.

2.   The Contracting States also shall undertake the conservation of plant species or communities, which are threatened and/or of special scientific or aesthetic value by ensuring that they are included in conservation areas.

Article VII

FAUNAL RESOURCES

1. The Contracting States shall ensure conservation, wise use and development of faunal resources and their environment, within the framework of land-use planning and of economic and social development. Management shall be carried out in accordance with plans based on scientific principles, and to that end the Contracting States shall:

> *a)* manage wildlife populations inside designated areas according to the objectives of such areas and also manage exploitable wildlife populations outside such areas for an optimum sustained yield, compatible with and complementary to other land uses; and

> *b)* manage aquatic environments, whether in fresh, brackish or coastal water, with a view to minimising deleterious effects of any water and land use practice which might adversely affect aquatic habitats.

2. The Contracting States shall adopt adequate legislation on hunting, capture and fishing, under which:

> *a)* the issue of permits is properly regulated;

> *b)* unauthorized methods are prohibited;

> *c)* the following methods of hunting, capture and fishing are prohibited:

>> (i) any method liable to cause a mass destruction of wild animals,

>> (ii) the use of drugs, poisons, poisoned weapons or poisoned baits,

>> (iii) the use of explosives;

>> (iv) the following methods of hunting and capture are particularly prohibited:

>>> (1) the use of mechanically propelled vehicles;

>>> (2) the use of fire;

>>> (3) the use of fire arms capable of firing more than one round at each pull of the trigger;

>>> (4) hunting or capture at night;

(5)   the use of missiles containing detonators;

d)   the following methods of hunting or capture are as far as possible prohibited:

(i)   the use of nets and stockades,

(ii)   the use of concealed traps, pits, snares, set-gun traps, deadfalls, and hunting from a blind or hide;

e)   with a view to as rational use as possible of game meat, the abandonment by hunters of carcasses of animals, which represent a food resource, is prohibited.

Capture of animals with the aid of drugs or mechanically propelled vehicles, or hunting or capture by night if carried out by, or under the control of, the competent authority shall nevertheless be exempted from the prohibitions under *(c)* above.

Article VIII

PROTECTED SPECIES

1.   The Contracting States recognize that it is important and urgent to accord a special protection to those animal and plant species that are threatened with extinction, or which may become so, and to the habitat necessary to their survival. Where such a species is represented only in the territory of one Contracting State, that State has a particular responsibility for its protection. These species which are, or may be, listed according to the degree of protection that shall be given to them are placed in Class A or B of the Annex to this Convention, and shall be protected by Contracting States as follows:

(i)   species in Class A shall be totally protected throughout the entire territory of the Contracting States; the hunting, killing, capture or collection of specimens shall be permitted only on the authorization in each case of the highest competent authority and only if required in the national interest or for scientific purposes; and

(ii)   species in Class B shall be totally protected, but may be hunted, killed, captured or collected under special authorization granted by the competent authority.

2.   The competent authority of each Contracting State shall examine the necessity of applying the provisions of this article to species not listed in the annex, in order to conserve the indigenous

flora and fauna of their respective countries. Such additional species shall be placed in Class A or B by the State concerned, according to its specific requirements.

Article IX

TRAFFIC IN SPECIMENS AND TROPHIES

1. In the case of animal species to which Article VIII does not apply the Contracting States shall:

   a)   regulate trade in and transport of specimens and trophies;

   b)   control the application of these regulations in such a way as to prevent trade in specimens and trophies which have been illegally captured or killed or obtained.

2. In the case of plant and animal species to which Article VIII paragraph (1) applies, the Contracting States shall:

   a)   take all measures similar to those in paragraph (1);

   b)   make the export of such specimens and trophies subject to an authorization-

      (i)   additional to that required for their capture, killing or collection by Article VIII,

      (ii)   which indicates their destination,

      (iii)   which shall not be given unless the specimens or trophies have been obtained legally,

      (iv)   which shall be examined prior to exportation,

      (v)   which shall be on a standard form, as may be arranged under Article XVI;

   c)   make the import and transit of such specimens and trophies subject to the presentation of the authorization required under section *(b)* above with due provision for the confiscation of specimens and trophies exported illegally, without prejudice to the application of other penalties.

Article X

CONSERVATION AREAS

1. The Contracting States shall maintain and extend where appropriate, within their territory and where applicable in their territorial waters, the Conservation areas existing at the time of entry

into force of the present Convention and, preferably within the framework of land-use planning programmes, assess the necessity of establishing additional conservation areas in order to:

(i)   protect those ecosystems which are most representative of and particularly those which are in any respect peculiar to their territories,

(ii)   ensure the conservation of all species and more particularly of those listed or which may be listed in the annex to this Convention;

2.   The Contracting States shall establish, where necessary, around the borders of conservation areas, zones within which the competent authorities shall control activities detrimental to the protected natural resources.

Article XI

CUSTOMARY RIGHTS

The Contracting States shall take all necessary legislative measures to reconcile customary rights with the provisions of this Convention.

Article XII

RESEARCH

The Contracting States shall encourage and promote research in conservation, utilization and management of natural resources and shall pay particular attention to ecological and sociological factors.

Article XIII

CONSERVATION EDUCATION

1.   *a)*   The Contracting States shall ensure that their peoples appreciate their close dependence on natural resources and that they understand the need, and rules for, the rational utilization of these resources.

b)   For this purpose they shall ensure that the principles indicated in paragraph (1):

(i)   are included in educational programmes at all levels,

(ii)   form the object of information campaigns capable of acquainting the public with, and winning it over to, the idea of conservation.

2. In order to put into effect paragraph (1) above, the Contracting States shall make maximum use of the educational value of conservation areas.

Article XIV

DEVELOPMENT PLANS

1. The Contracting States shall ensure that conservation and management of natural resources are treated as an integral part of national and/or regional development plans.

2. In the formulation of all development plans, full consideration shall be given to ecological, as well as to economic and social factors.

3. Where any development plan is likely to affect the natural resources of another State, the latter shall be consulted.

Article XV

ORGANIZATION OF NATIONAL CONSERVATION SERVICES

Each Contracting State shall establish, if it has not already done so, a single agency empowered to deal with all matters covered by the Convention, but, where this is not possible a co-ordinating machinery shall be established for this purpose.

Article XVI

INTERSTATE CO-OPERATION

1. The Contracting States shall co-operate:

   a) whenever such co-operation is necessary to give effect to the provisions of this Convention and

   b) whenever any national measure is likely to affect the natural resources of any other State.

2. The Contracting States shall supply the Organization of African Unity with:

   a) the text of laws, decrees, regulations and instructions in force in their territories, which are intended to ensure the implementation of this Convention,

   b) reports on the results achieved in applying the provisions of this Convention, and *c)* all the information necessary for the complete documentation of matters dealt with by this Convention if requested.

3. If so requested by Contracting States, the Organization of African Unity shall organize any meeting which may be necessary to dispose of any matters covered by this Convention. Requests for such meetings must be made by at least three of the Contracting States and be approved by two-thirds of the States which it is proposed should participate in such meetings.

4. Any expenditure arising from this Convention, which devolves upon the Organization of African Unity shall be included in its regular budget, unless shared by the Contracting States or otherwise defrayed.

Article XVII

PROVISION FOR EXCEPTIONS

1. The provisions of this Convention shall not affect the responsibilities of Contracting States concerning:

     (i)   the paramount interest of the State,

    (ii)   "force majeure",

   (iii)   defence of human life.

2. The provisions of this Convention shall not prevent Contracting States:

     (i)   in time of famine,

    (ii)   for the protection of public health,

   (iii)   in defence of property,

to enact measures contrary to the provions of the Convention, provided their application is precisely defined in respect of aim, time and place.

Article XVIII

SETTLEMENT OF DISPUTES

Any dispute between the Contracting States relating to the interpretation or application of this Convention which cannot be settled by negotiation, shall at the request of any party be submitted to the Commission of Mediation, Conciliation and Arbitration of the Organization of African Unity.

Article XIX

SIGNATURE AND RATIFICATION

1.   This Convention shall be open for signature immediately after being approved by the Assembly of Heads of State and Government of the Organization of African Unity.

2.   The Convention shall be ratified by each of the Contracting States. The instruments of ratification shall be deposited with the Administrative Secretary General of the Organization of African Unity.

Article XX

RESERVATIONS

1.   At the time of signature, ratification or accession, any State may declare its acceptance of this Convention in part only, provided that such reservation may not apply to the provisions of Articles II-XI.

2.   Reservations made in conformity with the preceding paragaph shall be deposited together with the instruments of ratification or accession.

3.   Any Contracting State which has formulated a reservation in conformity with the preceding paragraph may at any time withdraw it by notifying the Administrative Secretary General of the Organization of African Unity.

Article XXI

ENTRY INTO FORCE

1.   This Convention shall come into force on the thirtieth day following the date of deposit of the fourth instrument of ratification or accession with the Administrative Secretary General of the Organization of African Unity, who shall inform participating States accordingly.

2.   In the case of a State ratifying or acceding to the Convention after the depositing of the fourth instrument of ratification or accession, the Convention shall come into force on the thirtieth day

after the deposit by such State of its instrument of ratification or accession.

3. The London Convention of 1933 or any other Convention on the conservation of flora and fauna in their natural state shall cease to have effect in States in which this Convention has come into force.

Article XXII

ACCESSION

1. After the date of approval specified in Article XIX paragraph (1), this Convention shall be open to accession by any independent and sovereign African State.

2. The instruments of accession shall be deposited with the Administrative Secretary General of the Organization of African Unity.

Article XXIII

DENUNCIATION

1. Any Contracting State may denounce this Convention by notification in writing addressed to the Administrative Secretary General of the Organization of African Unity.

2. Such denunciation shall take effect, for such a State, one year after the date of receipt of its notification by the Administrative Secretary General of the Organization of African Unity.

3. No denunciation shall, however, be made before the expiry of a period of five years from the date at which for the State concerned this Convention comes into force.

Article XXIV

REVISION

1. After the expiry of a period of five years from the date of entry into force of this Convention, any Contracting State may at any time make a request for the revision of part or the whole of this Convention by notification in writing addressed to the Administrative Secretary General of the Organization of African Unity.

2. In the event of such a request the appropriate organ of the Organization of African Unity shall deal with the matter in accordance with the provisions of section 3 of Article XVI of this Convention.

3. (i) At the request of one or more Contracting States and notwithstanding the provisions of paragraph (1) and (2) of this Article, the annex to this Convention may be revised or added to by the appropriate organ of the Organization of African Unity.

(ii) Such revision or addition shall come into force three months after the approval by the appropriate organ of the Organization of African Unity.

Article XXV

FINAL PROVISIONS

The original of this Convention of which both the English and the French texts are authentic, shall be deposited with the Administrative Secretary General of the Organization of African Unity.

IN WITNESS WHEREOF we the Heads of State and Government of Independent African States, assembled at Algiers, Algeria, on 15 September 1968, have signed this Convention.

Author's note: The list of species included in Class A and B of the Annex, which is subject to periodic changes, is not reproduced here but may be obtained from the Organization of African Unity, PO Box 3243, Addis Ababa, Ethiopia.

CONVENTION ON WETLANDS OF INTERNATIONAL IMPORTANCE ESPECIALLY AS WATERFOWL HABITAT, 1971

The Contracting Parties,

RECOGNIZING the interdependence of man and his environment;

CONSIDERING the fundamental ecological functions of wetlands as regulators of water régimes and as habitats supporting a characteristic flora and fauna, especially waterfowl;

BEING convinced that wetlands constitute a resource of great economic, cultural, scientific and recreational value, the loss of which would be irreparable;

DESIRING to stem the progressive encroachment on and loss of wetlands now and in the future;

RECOGNIZING that waterfowl in their seasonal migrations may transcend frontiers and so should be regarded as an international resource;

BEING confident that the conservation of wetlands and their flora and fauna can be ensured by combining far-sighted national policies with coordinated international action;

HAVE AGREED as follows:

Article 1

1. For the purpose of this Convention wetlands are areas of marsh, fen, peatland or water, whether natural or artificial, permanent or temporary, with water that is static or flowing, fresh, brackish or salt, including areas of marine water the depth of which at low tide does not exceed six metres.

2. For the purpose of this Convention waterfowl are birds ecologically dependent on wetlands.

Article 2

1.   Each Contracting Party shall designate suitable wetlands within its territory for inclusion in a List of Wetlands of International Importance, hereinafter referred to as "the List" which is maintained by the bureau established under Article 8. The boundaries of each wetland shall be precisely described and also delimited on a map and they may incorporate riparian and coastal zones adjacent to the wetlands, and islands or bodies of marine water deeper than six metres at low tide lying within the wetlands, especially where these have importance as waterfowl habitat.

2.   Wetlands should be selected for the List on account of their international significance in terms of ecology, botany, zoology, limnology or hydrology. In the first instance wetlands of international importance to waterfowl at any season should be included.

3.   The inclusion of a wetland in the List does not prejudice the exclusive sovereign rights of the Contracting Party in whose territory the wetland is situated.

4.   Each Contracting Party shall designate at least one wetland to be included in the List when signing this Convention or when depositing its instrument of ratification or accession, as provided in Article 9.

5.   Any Contracting Party shall have the right to add to the List further wetlands situated within its territory, to extend the boundaries of those wetlands already included by it in the List, or, because of its urgent national interests, to delete or restrict the boundaries of wetlands already included by it in the List and shall, at the earliest possible time, inform the organization or government responsible for the continuing bureau duties specified in Article 8 of any such changes.

6.   Each Contracting Party shall consider its international responsibilities for the conservation, management and wise use of migratory stocks of waterfowl, both when designating entries for the List and when exercising its right to change entries in the List relating to wetlands within its territory.

Article 3

1. The Contracting Parties shall formulate and implement their planning so as to promote the conservation of the wetlands included in the List, and as far as possible the wise use of wetlands in their territory.

2. Each Contracting Party shall arrange to be informed at the earliest possible time if the ecological character of any wetland in its territory and included in the List has changed, is changing or is likely to change as the result of technological developments, pollution or other human interference. Information on such changes shall be passed without delay to the organization or government responsible for the continuing bureau duties specified in Article 8.

Article 4

1. Each Contracting Party shall promote the conservation of wetlands and waterfowl by establishing nature reserves on wetlands, whether they are included in the List or not, and provide adequately for their wardening.

2. Where a Contracting Party in its urgent national interest, deletes or restricts the boundaries of a wetland included in the List, it should as far as possible compensate for any loss of wetland resources, and in particular it should create additional nature reserves for waterfowl and for the protection, either in the same area or elsewhere, of an adequate portion of the original habitat.

3. The Contracting Parties shall encourage research and the exchange of data and publications regarding wetlands and their flora and fauna.

4. The Contracting Parties shall endeavour through management to increase waterfowl populations on appropriate wetlands.

5. The Contracting Parties shall promote the training of personnel competent in the fields of wetland research, management and wardening.

Article 5

The Contracting Parties shall consult with each other about implementing obligations arising from the Convention especially in the case of a wetland extending over the territories of more than one

Contracting Party or where a water system is shared by Contracting Parties.

They shall at the same time endeavour to coordinate and support present and future policies and regulations concerning the conservation of wetlands and their flora and fauna.

Article 6

1.   The Contracting Parties shall, as the necessity arises, convene Conferences on the Conservation of Wetlands and Waterfowl.

2.   These Conferences shall have an advisory character and shall be competent, *inter alia*:

    a)   to discuss the implementation of this Convention;

    b)   to discuss additions to and changes in the List;

    c)   to consider information regarding changes in the ecological character of wetlands included in the List provided in accordance with paragraph 2 of Article 3;

    d)   to make general or specific recommendations to the Contracting Parties regarding the conservation, management and wise use of wetlands and their flora and fauna;

    e)   to request relevant international bodies to prepare reports and statistics on matters which are essentially international in character affecting wetlands.

3.   The Contracting Parties shall ensure that those responsible at all levels for wetlands management shall be informed of, and take into consideration, recommendations of such Conferences concerning the conservation, management and wise use of wetlands and their flora and fauna.

Article 7

1.   The representatives of the Contracting Parties at such Conferences should include persons who are experts on wetlands or waterfowl by reason of knowledge and experience gained in scientific, administrative or other appropriate capacities.

2.   Each of the Contracting Parties represented at a Conference shall have one vote, recommendations being adopted by a simple majority of the votes cast, provided that not less than half the Contracting Parties cast votes.

Article 8

1.   The International Union for the Conservation of Nature and Natural Resources shall perform the continuing bureau duties under this Convention until such time as another organization or government is appointed by a majority of two-thirds of all Contracting Parties.

2.   The continuing bureau duties shall be, *inter alia*:

a)   to assist in the convening and organizing of Conferences specified in Article 6;

b)   to maintain the List of Wetlands of International Importance and to be informed by the Contracting Parties of any additions, extensions, deletions or restrictions concerning wetlands included in the List provided in accordance with paragraph 5 of Article 2;

c)   to be informed by the Contracting Parties of any changes in the ecological character of wetlands included in the List provided in accordance with paragraph 2 of Article 3;

d)   to forward notification of any alterations to the List, or changes in character of wetlands included therein, to all Contracting Parties and to arrange for these matters to be discussed at the next Conference;

e)   to make known to the Contracting Party concerned, the recommendations of the Conferences in respect of such alterations to the List or of changes in the character of wetlands included therein.

Article 9

1.   This Convention shall remain open for signature indefinitely.

2.   Any member of the United Nations or of one of the Specialized Agencies or of the International Atomic Energy Agency or Party to the Statute of the International Court of Justice may become a Party to this Convention by:

a)   signature without reservation as to ratification;

b)   signature subject to ratification followed by ratification;

c)   accession.

3.   Ratification or accession shall be effected by the deposit of an instrument of ratification or accession with the Director-General of the United Nations Educational, Scientific and Cultural Organization, (hereinafter referred to as "the Depository").

Article 10

1.   This Convention shall enter into force four months after seven States have become Parties to this Convention in accordance with paragraph 2 of Article 9.

2.   Thereafter this Convention shall enter into force for each Contracting Party four months after the day of its signature without reservation as to ratification, or its deposit of an instrument of ratification or accession.

Article 11

1.   This Convention shall continue in force for an indefinite period.

2.   Any Contracting Party may denounce this Convention after a period of five years from the date on which it entered into force for that Party by giving written notice thereof to the Depository. Denunciation shall take effect four months after the day on which notice thereof is received by the Depository.

Article 12

1.   The Depository shall inform all States that have signed and acceded to this Convention as soon as possible of:

   a)   signatures to the Convention;

   b)   deposits of instruments of ratification of this Convention;

   c)   deposits of instruments of accession to this Convention;

   d)   the date of entry into force of this Convention;

   e)   notifications of denunciation of this Convention.

2.   When this Convention has entered into force, the Depository shall have it registered with the Secretariat of the United Nations in accordance with Article 102 of the Charter.

IN WITNESS WHEREOF, the undersigned, being duly authorized to that effect, have signed this Convention.

DONE at Ramsar this 2nd day of February 1971, in a single original in the English, French, German and Russian languages, in any case of divergency the English text prevailing, which shall be deposited with the Depository which shall send true copies thereof to all Contracting Parties.

PROTOCOL OF AMENDMENT

A Protocol to amend the Convention on Wetlands of International Importance Especially as Waterfowl Habitat was adopted in Paris on 3 December 1982. The Protocol provides as follows:

The Contracting Parties,

CONSIDERING that for the effectiveness of the Convention on Wetlands of International Importance especially as Waterfowl Habitat, done at Ramsar on 2 February 1971 (hereinafter referred to as "the Convention"), it is indispensable to increase the number of Contracting Parties;

AWARE that the addition of authentic language versions would facilitate wider participation in the Convention;

CONSIDERING furthermore that the text of the Convention does not provide for an amendment procedure, which makes it difficult to amend the text as may be considered necessary;

HAVE AGREED as follows:

Article 1

The following Article shall be added between Article 10 and Article 11 of the Convention:

"Article 10 Bis"

1. This Convention may be amended at a meeting of the Contracting Parties convened for that purpose in accordance with this Article.

2. Proposals for amendment may be made by any Contracting Party.

3. The text of any proposed amendment and the reasons for it shall be communicated to the organization or government performing the

continuing bureau duties under the Convention (hereinafter referred to as "the Bureau") and shall promptly be communicated by the Bureau to all Contracting Parties. Any comments on the text by the Contracting Parties shall be communicated to the Bureau within three months of the date on which amendments were communicated to the Contracting Parties by the Bureau. The Bureau shall, immediately after the last day for submission of comments, communicate to the Contracting Parties all comments submitted by that day.

4. A meeting of Contacting Parties to consider an amendment communicated in accordance with paragraph 3 shall be convened by the Bureau upon the written request of one third of the Contracting Parties. The Bureau shall consult the Parties concerning the time and venue of the meeting.

5. Amendments shall be adopted by a two-thirds majority of the Contracting Parties present and voting.

6. An amendment adopted shall enter into force for the Contracting Parties which have accepted it on the first day of the fourth month following the date on which two-thirds of the Contracting Parties have deposited an instrument of acceptance with the Depository. For each Contracting Party which deposits an instrument of acceptance after the date on which two-thirds of the Contracting Parties have deposited an instrument of acceptance, the amendment shall enter into force on the first day of the fourth month following the date of the deposit of its instrument of acceptance.

Article 2

In the testimonium following Article 12 of the Convention, the words "in any case of divergency the English text prevailing" shall be deleted and replaced by the words "all texts being equally authentic".

Article 3

The revised text of the original French version of the Convention is reproduced in the Annex to this Protocol.

Article 4

This Protocol shall be open for signature at UNESCO headquarters in Paris from 3 December 1982.

Article 5

1. Any State referred to in Article 9, paragraph 2, of the Convention may become a Contracting Party to this Protocol by:

    a) signature without reservation as to ratification, acceptance or approval;

    b) signature subject to ratification, acceptance or approval, followed by ratification, acceptance or approval;

    c) accession.

2. Ratification, acceptance, approval or accession shall be effected by the deposit of an instrument of ratification, acceptance, approval or accession with the Director-General of the United Nations Educational, Scientific and Cultural Organization (hereinafter referred to as "the Depository").

3. Any State which becomes a Contracting Party to the Convention after the entry into force of this Protocol shall, failing an expression of a different intention at the time of signature or of the deposit of the instrument referred to in Article 9 of the Convention, be considered as a Party to the Convention as amended by this Protocol.

4. Any State which becomes a Contracting Party to this Protocol without being a Contracting Party to the Convention, shall be considered as a Party to the Convention as amended by this Protocol as of the date of entry into force of this Protocol for that State.

Article 6

1. This Protocol shall enter into force the first day of the fourth month following the date on which two-thirds of the States which are Contracting Parties to the Convention on the date on which this Protocol is opened for signature have signed it without reservation as to ratification, acceptance or approval, or have ratified, accepted, approved or acceded to it.

2. With regard to any State which becomes a Contracting Party to this Protocol in the manner described in paragraph 1 and 2 of Article 5 above, after the date of its entry into force, this Protocol shall enter into force on the date of its signature without reservation as to ratification, acceptance or approval, or of its ratification, acceptance, approval or accession.

3. With regard to any State which becomes a Contracting Party to this Protocol in the manner described in paragraph 1 and 2 of Article 5 above, during the period between the date on which this Protocol is opened for signature and its entry into force, this Protocol shall enter into force on the date determined in paragraph 1 above.

Article 7

1. The original of this Protocol, in the English and French languages, each version being equally authentic, shall be deposited with the Depository. The Depository shall transmit certified copies of each of these versions to all States that have signed this Protocol or deposited instruments of accession to it.

2. The Depository shall inform all Contracting Parties of the Convention and all States that have signed and acceded to this Protocol as soon as possible of:

a) signatures to this Protocol;

b) deposits of instruments of ratification, acceptance or approval of this Protocol;

c) deposits of instruments of accession to this Protocol;

d) the date of entry into force of this Protocol.

3. When this Protocol has entered into force, the Depository shall have it registered with the Secretariat of the United Nations in accordance with Article 102 of the Charter.

IN WITNESS WHEREOF, the undersigned, being duly authorized to that effect, have signed this Protocol.

DONE at Paris on 3 December 1982.

Author's note: The List of Wetlands of International Importance, which is continually being amended, is not reproduced here but may be obtained from IUCN, 1196 Gland, Switzerland.

CONVENTION FOR THE CONSERVATION OF ANTARCTIC SEALS, 1972

The Contracting Parties,

RECALLING the Agreed Measures for the Conservation of Antarctic Fauna and Flora, adopted under the Antarctic Treaty signed at Washington on 1 December 1959;

RECOGNIZING the general concern about the vulnerability of Antarctic seals to commercial exploitation and the consequent need for effective conservation measures;

RECOGNIZING that the stocks of Antarctic seals are an important living resource in the marine environment which requires an international agreement for its effective conservation;

RECOGNIZING that this resource should not be depleted by over-exploitation, and hence that any harvesting should be regulated so as not to exceed the levels of the optimum sustainable yield;

RECOGNIZING that in order to improve scientific knowledge and so place exploitation on a rational basis, every effort should be made both to encourage biological and other research on Antarctic seal populations and to gain information from such research and from the statistics of future sealing operations, so that further suitable regulations may be formulated;

NOTING that the Scientific Committee on Antarctic Research of the International Council of Scientific Unions (SCAR) is willing to carry out the tasks requested of it in this Convention;

DESIRING to promote and achieve the objectives of protection, scientific study and rational use of Antarctic seals, and to maintain a satisfactory balance within the ecological system,

HAVE AGREED as follows:

Article 1

SCOPE

1.   This Convention applies to the seas south of 60° South Latitude, in respect of which the Contracting Parties affirm the provisions of Article IV of the Antarctic Treaty.

2. This Convention may be applicable to any or all of the following species:

Southern elephant seal *Mirounga leonina,*

Leopard seal *Hydrurga leptonyx,*

Weddell seal *Leptonychotes weddelli,*

Crabeater seal *Lobodon carcinophagus,*

Ross seal *Ommatophoca rossi,*

Southern fur seals *Arctocephalus* sp.

3. The Annex to this Convention forms an integral part thereof.

Article 2

IMPLEMENTATION

1. The Contracting Parties agree that the species of seals enumerated in Article 1 shall not be killed or captured within the Convention area by their nationals or vessels under their respective flags except in accordance with the provisions of this Convention.

2. Each Contracting Party shall adopt for its nationals and for vessels under its flag such laws, regulations and other measures, including a permit system as appropriate, as may be necessary to implement this Convention.

Article 3

ANNEXED MEASURES

1. This Convention includes an Annex specifying measures which the Contracting Parties hereby adopt. Contracting Parties may from time to time in the future adopt other measures with respect to the conservation, scientific study and rational and humane use of seal resources, prescribing *inter alia:*

   a) permissible catch;

   b) protected and unprotected species;

   c) open and closed seasons;

   d) open and closed areas, including the designation of reserves;

e) the designation of special areas where there shall be no disturbance of seals;

f) limits relating to sex, size, or age for each species;

g) restrictions relating to time of day and duration, limitations of effort and methods of sealing;

h) types and specifications of gear and apparatus and appliances which may be used;

i) catch returns and other statistical and biological records;

j) procedures for facilitating the review and assessment of scientific information;

k) other regulatory measures including an effective system of inspection.

2. The measures adopted under paragraph (1) of this Article shall be based upon the best scientific and technical evidence available.

3. The Annex may from time to time be amended in accordance with the procedures provided for in Article 9.

Article 4

SPECIAL PERMITS

1. Notwithstanding the provisions of this Convention, any Contracting Party may issue permits to kill or capture seals in limited quantities and in conformity with the objectives and principles of this Convention for the following purposes:

a) to provide indispensable food for men or dogs;

b) to provide for scientific research; or

c) to provide specimens for museums, educational or cultural institutions.

2. Each Contracting Party shall, as soon as possible, inform the other Contracting Parties and SCAR of the purpose and content of all permits issued under paragraph (1) of this Article and subsequently of the numbers of seals killed or captured under these permits.

Article 5

EXCHANGE OF INFORMATION AND SCIENTIFIC ADVICE

1.   Each Contracting Party shall provide to the other Contracting Parties and to SCAR the information specified in the Annex within the period indicated therein.

2.   Each Contracting Party shall also provide to the other Contracting Parties and to SCAR before 31 October each year information on any steps it has taken in accordance with Article 2 of this Convention during the preceding period of 1 July to 30 June.

3.   Contracting Parties which have no information to report under the two preceding paragraphs shall indicate this formally before 31 October each year.

4.   SCAR is invited:

   a)   to assess information received pursuant to this Article; encourage exchange of scientific data and information among the Contracting Parties; recommend programmes for scientific research; recommend statistical and biological data to be collected by sealing expeditions within the Convention area; and suggest amendments to the Annex; and

   b)   to report on the basis of the statistical, biological and other evidence available when the harvest of any species of seal in the Convention area is having a significantly harmful effect on the total stocks of such species or on the ecological system in any particular locality.

5.   SCAR is invited to notify the Depositary which shall report to the Contracting Parties when SCAR estimates in any sealing season that the permissible catch limits for any species are likely to be exceeded and, in that case, to provide an estimate of the date upon which the permissible catch limits will be reached. Each Contracting Party shall then take appropriate measures to prevent its nationals and vessels under its flag from killing or capturing seals of that species after the estimated date until the Contracting Parties decide otherwise.

6.   SCAR may if necessary seek the technical assistance of the Food and Agriculture Organization of the United Nations in making its assessments.

7.   Notwithstanding the provisions of paragraph (1) of Article 1 the Contracting Parties shall, in accordance with their internal law, report to each other and to SCAR, for consideration, statistics relating to the Antarctic seals listed in paragraph (2) of Article 1 which have been killed or captured by their nationals and vessels under their respective flags in the area of floating sea ice north of 60° South Latitude.

Article 6

CONSULTATIONS BETWEEN CONTRACTING PARTIES

1.   At any time after commercial sealing has begun a Contracting Party may propose through the Depositary that a meeting of Contracting Parties be convened with a view to:

a)   establishing by a two-thirds majority of the Contracting Parties, including the concurring votes of all States signatory to this Convention present at the meeting, an effective system of control, including inspection, over the implementation of the provisions of this Convention;

b)   establishing a commission to perform such functions under this Convention as the Contracting Parties may deem necessary; or

c)   considering other proposals, including:

(i)   the provision of independent scientific advice;

(ii)   the establishment, by a two-thirds majority, of a scientific advisory committee which may be assigned some or all of the functions requested of SCAR under this Convention, if commercial sealing reaches significant proportions;

(iii)   the carrying out of scientific programmes with the participation of the Contracting Parties; and

(iv)   the provision of further regulatory measures, including moratoria.

2.   If one-third of the Contracting Parties indicate agreement the Depositary shall convene such a meeting, as soon as possible.

3.   A meeting shall be held at the request of any Contracting Party, if SCAR reports that the harvest of any species of Antarctic seal in the area to which this Convention applies is having a significantly harmful effect on the total stocks or the ecological system in any particular locality.

Article 7

REVIEW OF OPERATIONS

The Contracting Parties shall meet within five years after the entry into force of this Convention and at least every five years thereafter to review the operation of the Convention.

Article 8

AMENDMENTS TO THE CONVENTION

1.   This Convention may be amended at any time. The text of any amendment proposed by a Contracting Party shall be submitted to the Depositary, which shall transmit it to all the Contracting Parties.

2.   If one-third of the Contracting Parties request a meeting to discuss the proposed amendment the Depositary shall call such a meeting.

3.   An amendment shall enter into force when the Depositary has received instruments of ratification or acceptance thereof from all the Contracting Parties.

Article 9

AMENDMENTS TO THE ANNEX

1.   Any Contracting Party may propose amendments to the Annex to this Convention. The text of any such proposed amendment shall be submitted to the Depositary which shall transmit it to all Contracting Parties.

2.   Each such proposed amendment shall become effective for all Contracting Parties six months after the date appearing on the notification from the Depositary to the Contracting Parties, if within 120 days of the notification date, no objection has been received and two-thirds of the Contracting Parties have notified the Depositary in writing of their approval.

3.   If an objection is received from any Contracting Party within 120 days of the notification date, the matter shall be considered by the Contracting Parties at their next meeting. If unanimity on the matter is not reached at the meeting, the Contracting Parties shall notify the Depositary within 120 days from the date of the closure of the meeting of their approval or rejection of the original amendment or

of any new amendment proposed by the meeting. If, by the end of this period, two-thirds of the Contracting Parties have approved such amendment, it shall become effective six months from the date of the closure of the meeting for those Contracting Parties which have by then notified their approval.

4. Any Contracting Party which has objected to a proposed amendment may at any time withdraw that objection, and the proposed amendment shall become effective with respect to such Party immediately if the amendment is already in effect, or at such time as it becomes effective under the terms of this Article.

5. The Depositary shall notify each Contracting Party immediately upon receipt of each approval or objection, of each withdrawal of objection, and of the entry into force of any amendment.

6. Any State which becomes a party to this Convention after an amendment to the Annex has entered into force shall be bound by the Annex as so amended. Any State which becomes a Party to this Convention during the period when a proposed amendment is pending may approve or object to such an amendment within the time limits applicable to other Contracting Parties.

Article 10

SIGNATURE

This Convention shall be open for signature at London from 1 June to 31 December 1972 by States participating in the Conference on the Conservation of Antarctic Seals held at London from 3 to 11 February 1972.

Article 11

RATIFICATION

This Convention is subject to ratification or acceptance. Instruments of ratification or acceptance shall be deposited with the Government of the United Kingdom of Great Britain and Northern Ireland, hereby designated as the Depositary.

Article 12

ACCESSION

This Convention shall be open for accession by any State which may be invited to accede to this Convention with the consent of all the Contracting Parties.

Article 13

ENTRY INTO FORCE

1.   This Convention shall enter into force on the thirtieth day following the date of deposit of the seventh instrument of ratification or acceptance.

2.   Thereafter this Convention shall enter into force for each ratifying, accepting or acceding State on the thirtieth day after deposit by such State of its instrument of ratification, acceptance or accession.

Article 14

WITHDRAWAL

Any Contracting Party may withdraw from this Convention on 30 June of any year by giving notice on or before 1 January of the same year to the Depositary, which upon receipt of such a notice shall at once communicate it to the other Contracting Parties. Any other Contracting Party may, in like manner, within one month of the receipt of a copy of such a notice from the Depositary, give notice of withdrawal, so that the Convention shall cease to be in force on 30 June of the same year with respect to the Contracting Party giving such notice.

Article 15

NOTIFICATION BY THE DEPOSITARY

The Depositary shall notify all signatory and acceding States of the following:

> *a)*   signatures of this Convention, the deposit of instruments of ratification, acceptance or accession and notices of withdrawal;

> *b)*   the date of entry into force of this Convention and of any amendments to it or its Annex.

Article 16

CERTIFIED COPIES AND REGISTRATION

1.   This Convention, done in the English, French, Russian and Spanish languages, each version being equally authentic, shall be deposited in the archives of the Government of the United Kingdom of Great Britain and Northern Ireland, which shall transmit duly certified copies thereof to all signatory and acceding States.

2.   This Convention shall be registered by the Depositary pursuant to Article 102 of the Charter of the United Nations.

IN WITNESS WHEREOF, the undersigned, duly authorized, have signed this Convention.

DONE at London, this 1st day of June 1972.

ANNEX

1.   *Permissible Catch*

The Contracting Parties shall in any one year, which shall run from 1 July to 30 June inclusive, restrict the total number of seals of each species killed or captured to the numbers specified below. These numbers are subject to review in the light of scientific assessments:

   a)   in the case of Crabeater seals *Lobodon carcinophagus,* 175,000;

   b)   in the case of Leopard seals *Hydrurga leptonyx,* 12,000;

   c)   in the case of Weddell seals *Leptonychotes weddelli,* 5,000.

2.   *Protected Species*

   a)   It is forbidden to kill or capture Ross seals *Ommatophoca rossi,* Southern elephant seals *Mirounga leonina,* or fur seals of the genus *Arctocephalus.*

   b)   In order to protect the adult breeding stock when it it is most concentrated and vulnerable, it is forbidden to kill or capture any Weddell seal *Leptonychotes weddelli* one year old or older between 1 September and 31 January inclusive.

3.   *Closed Season and Sealing Season*

The period between 1 March and 31 August inclusive is a Closed Season, during which the killing or capturing of seals is forbidden. The period 1 September to the last day in February constitutes a Sealing Season.

4.   *Sealing Zones*

Each of the sealing zones listed in this paragraph shall be closed in numerical sequence to all sealing operations for the seal species listed in paragraph 1 of this Annex for the period 1 September to the last day of February inclusive. Such closures shall begin with the same zone as is closed under paragraph 2 of Annex B to Annex 1 of the Report of the Fifth Antarctic Treaty Consultative Meeting at the moment the Convention enters into force. Upon the expiration of each closed period, the affected zone shall reopen:

Zone 1 —— between 60° and 120° West Longitude

Zone 2 —— between 0° and 60° West Longitude, together with that part of the Weddell Sea lying westward of 60° West Longitude

Zone 3 —— between 0° and 70° East Longitude

Zone 4 —— between 70° and 130° East Longitude

Zone 5 —— between 130° East Longitude and 170° West Longitude

Zone 6 —— between 120° and 170° West Longitude.

5. *Seal Reserves*

It is forbidden to kill or capture seals in the following reserves, which are seal breeding areas or the site of long-term scientific research:

a) The area around the South Orkney Islands between 60° 20′ and 60° 56′ South Latitude and 44° 05′ and 46° 25′ West Longitude.

b) The area of the southwestern Ross Sea south of 76° South Latitude and west of 170° East Longitude.

c) The area of Edisto Inlet south and west of a line drawn between Cape Hallett at 72° 19′ South Latitude, 170° 18′ East Longitude and Helm Point at 72° 11′ South Latitude, 170° 00′ East Longitude.

6. *Exchange of Information*

a) Contracting Parties shall provide before 31 October each year to other Contracting Parties and to SCAR a summary of statistical information on all seals killed or captured by their nationals and vessels under their respective flags in the Convention area, in respect of the preceding period 1 July to 30 June. This information shall include by zones and months:

(i) The gross and net tonnage, brake horse-power, number of crew, and number of days' operation of vessels under the flag of the Contracting Party;

(ii) The number of adult individuals and pups of each species taken. When specially requested, this information shall be provided in respect of each ship, together with its daily position at noon each operating day and the catch on that day.

b) When an industry has started, reports of the number of seals of each species killed or captured in each zone shall be made to SCAR in the form and at the intervals (not shorter than one week) requested by that body.

c) Contracting Parties shall provide to SCAR biological information concerning, in particular:

(i) Sex

(ii) Reproductive condition

(iii) Age

SCAR may request additional information or material with the approval of the Contracting Parties.

d) Contracting Parties shall provide to other Contracting Parties and to SCAR at least 30 days in advance of departure from their home ports, information on proposed sealing expeditions.

7. *Sealing Methods*

a) SCAR is invited to report on methods of sealing and to make recommendations with a view to ensuring that the killing or capturing of seals is quick, painless and efficient. Contracting Parties, as appropriate, shall adopt rules for their nationals and vessels under their respective flags engaged in the killing and capturing of seals, giving due consideration to the views of SCAR.

b) In the light of the available scientific and technical data, Contracting Parties agree to take appropriate steps to ensure that their nationals and vessels under their respective flags refrain from killing or capturing seals in the water, except in limited quantities to provide for scientific research in conformity with the objectives and principles of this Convention. Such research shall include studies as to the effectiveness of methods of sealing from the viewpoint of the management and humane and rational utilization of the Antarctic seal resources for conservation purposes. The undertaking and the results of any such scientific research programme shall be communicated to SCAR and the Depositary which shall transmit them to the Contracting Parties.

ADDENDUM

At the signature of the Antarctic Seals Convention, the following statement was made by the Representative of Chile:

"The Delegation of Chile states that the reference to Article IV of the Antarctic Treaty contained in Article 1 of the present Convention signifies that nothing specified therein shall confirm, deny or impair the rights of the Contracting Parties as regards their maritime jurisdictions and their declared juridical position on this matter."

The following statement was made by the Representative of the United States of America:

"The Delegation of the United States of America believes that the Convention should contain stronger provisions for the observation of operations and enforcement of regulations, especially with regard to the use of observers of the Contracting Parties with each others' sealing expeditions. Opposition to stronger provisions has chiefly arisen not from commercial but from juridical interests.

"Nevertheless, the Convention is a new and valuable International Agreement, achieved in advance of the development of commercial sealing in the Antarctic, that contains many provisions important to the conservation of seals and their protection against over-exploitation. We understand exploratory commercial sealing ventures may be imminent.

"In order not to diminish the progress achieved by this Conference in international co-operation for effective conservation in the Antarctic, the delegation of the United States of America has decided to sign the Final Act and will submit the Convention for its Government's consideration."

CONVENTION FOR THE PROTECTION OF THE WORLD CULTURAL AND NATURAL HERITAGE, 1972

The General Conference of the United Nations Educational, Scientific and Cultural Organization meeting in Paris from 17 October to 21 November 1972, at its seventeenth session,

NOTING that the cultural heritage and the natural heritage are increasingly threatened with destruction not only by the traditional causes of decay, but also by changing social and economic conditions which aggravate the situation with even more formidable phenomena of damage or destruction,

CONSIDERING that deterioration or disappearance of any item of the cultural or natural heritage constitutes a harmful impoverishment of the heritage of all the nations of the world,

CONSIDERING that protection of this heritage at the national level often remains incomplete because of the scale of the resources which it requires and of the insufficient economic, scientific and technical resources of the country where the property to be protected is situated,

RECALLING that the Constitution of the Organization provides that it will maintain, increase and diffuse knowledge, by assuring the conservation and protection of the world's heritage, and recommending to the nations concerned the necessary international conventions,

CONSIDERING that the existing international conventions, recommendations and resolutions concerning cultural and natural property demonstrate the importance, for all the peoples of the world, of safeguarding this unique and irreplaceable property, to whatever people it may belong,

CONSIDERING that parts of the cultural or natural heritage are of outstanding interest and therefore need to be preserved as part of the world heritage of mankind as a whole,

CONSIDERING that, in view of the magnitude and gravity of the new dangers threatening them, it is incumbent on the international community as a whole to participate in the protection of the cultural and natural heritage of outstanding universal value, by the granting of collective assistance which, although not taking the place of action by the State concerned, will serve as an effective complement thereto,

CONSIDERING that it is essential for this purpose to adopt new provisions in the form of a convention establishing an effective system of collective protection of the cultural and natural heritage of outstanding universal value, organized on a permanent basis and in accordance with modern scientific methods,

HAVING DECIDED, at its sixteenth session, that this question should be made the subject of an international convention,

ADOPTS this sixteenth day of November 1972 this Convention.

I.   DEFINITIONS OF THE CULTURAL AND THE NATURAL HERITAGE

Article 1

For the purposes of this Convention, the following shall be considered as "cultural heritage":

monuments: architectural works, works of monumental sculpture and painting, elements or structures of an archaeological nature, inscriptions, cave dwellings and combinations of features, which are of outstanding universal value from the point of view of history, art or science;

groups of buildings: groups of separate or connected buildings which, because of their architecture, their homogeneity or their place in the landscape, are of outstanding universal value from the point of view of history, art or science;

sites: works of man or the combined works of nature and of man, and areas including archeological sites which are of outstanding universal value from the historical, aesthetic, ethnological or anthropological points of view.

Article 2

For the purposes of this Convention, the following shall be considered as "natural heritage":

natural features consisting of physical and biological formations or groups of such formations, which are of outstanding universal value from the aesthetic or scientific point of view;

geological and physiographical formations and precisely delineated areas which constitute the habitat of threatened species of animals and plants of outstanding universal value from the point of view of science or conservation;

natural sites or precisely delineated areas of outstanding universal value from the point of view of science, conservation or natural beauty.

Article 3

It is for each State Party to this Convention to identify and delineate the different properties situated on its territory mentioned in Articles 1 and 2 above.

II. NATIONAL PROTECTION AND INTERNATIONAL PROTECTION OF THE CULTURAL AND NATURAL HERITAGE

Article 4

Each State Party to this Convention recognizes that the duty of ensuring the identification, protection, conservation, presentation and transmission to future generations of the cultural and natural heritage referred to in Articles 1 and 2 and situated on its territory, belongs primarily to that State. It will do all it can to this end, to the utmost of its own resources and, where appropriate, with any international assistance and co-operation, in particular, financial, artistic, scientific and technical, which it may be able to obtain.

Article 5

To ensure that effective and active measures are taken for the protection, conservation and presentation of the cultural and natural heritage situated on its territory, each State Party to this Convention shall endeavour, in so far as possible, and as appropriate for each country:

a) to adopt a general policy which aims to give the cultural and natural heritage a function in the life of the community and to integrate the protection of that heritage into comprehensive planning programmes;

b) to set up within its territories, where such services do not exist, one or more services for the protection, conservation and presentation of the cultural and natural heritage with an appropriate staff and possessing the means to discharge their functions;

c) to develop scientific and technical studies and research and to work out such operating methods as will make the State capable of counteracting the dangers that threaten its cultural or natural heritage;

d) to take the appropriate legal, scientific, technical, administrative and financial measures necessary for the identification, protection, conservation, presentation and rehabilitation of this heritage; and

e) to foster the establishment or development of national or regional centres for training in the protection, conservation and presentation of the cultural and natural heritage and to encourage scientific research in this field.

Article 6

1. Whilst fully respecting the sovereignty of the States on whose territory the cultural and natural heritage mentioned in Articles 1 and 2 is situated, and without prejudice to property rights provided by national legislation, the States Parties to this Convention recognize that such heritage constitutes a world heritage for whose protection it is the duty of the international community as a whole to co-operate.

2. The States Parties undertake, in accordance with the provisions of this Convention, to give their help in the identification, protection, conservation and preservation of the cultural and natural heritage referred to in paragraphs 2 and 4 of Article 11 if the States on whose territory it is situated so request.

3. Each State Party to this Convention undertakes not to take any deliberate measures which might damage directly or indirectly the cultural and natural heritage referred to in Articles 1 and 2 situated on the territory of other States Parties to this Convention.

Article 7

For the purpose of this Convention, international protection of the world cultural and natural heritage shall be understood to mean the establishment of a system of international co-operation and assistance designed to support States Parties to the Convention in their efforts to conserve and identify that heritage.

III. INTERGOVERNMENTAL COMMITTEE FOR THE PROTECTION OF THE WORLD CULTURAL AND NATURAL HERITAGE

Article 8

1.   An Intergovermental Committee for the Protection of the Cultural and Natural Heritage of Outstanding Universal Value, called "the World Heritage Committee", is hereby established within the United Nations Educational, Scientific and Cultural Organization. It shall be composed of 15 States Parties to the Convention, elected by States Parties to the Convention meeting in general assembly during the ordinary session of the General Conference of the United Nations Educational, Scientific and Cultural Organization. The number of States members of the Committee shall be increased to 21 as from the date of the ordinary session of the General Conference following the entry into force of this Convention for at least 40 States.

2.   Election of members of the Committee shall ensure an equitable representation of the different regions and cultures of the world.

3.   A representative of the International Centre for the Study of the Preservation and Restoration of Cultural Property (Rome Centre), a representative of the International Council of Monuments and Sites (ICOMOS) and a representative of the International Union for Conservation of Nature and Natural Resources (IUCN), to whom may be added, at the request of States Parties to the Convention meeting in general assembly during the ordinary sessions of the General Conference of the United Nations Educational, Scientific and Cultural Organization, representatives of other inter-governmental or non-governmental organizations, with similar objectives, may attend the meetings of the Committee in an advisory capacity.

Article 9

1.   The term of office of States members of the World Heritage Committee shall extend from the end of the ordinary session of the General Conference during which they are elected until the end of its third subsequent ordinary session.

2.   The term of office of one-third of the members designated at the time of the first election shall, however, cease at the end of the first ordinary session of the General Conference following that at which

they were elected; and the term of office of a further third of the members designated at the same time shall cease at the end of the second ordinary session of the General Conference following that at which they were elected. The names of these members shall be chosen by lot by the President of the General Conference of the United Nations Educational, Scientific and Cultural Organization after the first election.

3. States members of the Committee shall choose as their representatives persons qualified in the field of the cultural or natural heritage.

Article 10

1. The World Heritage Committee shall adopt its Rules of Procedure.

2. The Committee may at any time invite public or private organizations or individuals to participate in its meetings for consultation on particular problems.

3. The Committee may create such consultative bodies as it deems necessary for the performance of its functions.

Article 11

1. Every State Party to this Convention shall, in so far as possible, submit to the World Heritage Committee an inventory of property forming part of the cultural and natural heritage, situated in its territory and suitable for inclusion in the list provided for in paragraph 2 of this Article. This inventory, which shall not be considered exhaustive, shall include documentation about the location of the property in question and its significance.

2. On the basis of the inventories submitted by States in accordance with paragraph 1, the Committee shall establish, keep up to date and publish, under the title of "World Heritage List", a list of properties forming part of the cultural heritage and natural heritage, as defined in Articles 1 and 2 of this Convention, which it considers as having outstanding universal value in terms of such criteria as it shall have established. An updated list shall be distributed at least every two years.

3.   The inclusion of a property in the World Heritage List requires the consent of the State concerned. The inclusion of a property situated in a territory, sovereignty or jurisdiction over which is claimed by more than one State shall in no way prejudice the rights of the parties to the dispute.

4.   The Committee shall establish, keep up to date and publish, whenever circumstances shall so require, under the title of "List of World Heritage in Danger", a list of the property appearing in the World Heritage List for the conservation of which major operations are necessary and for which assistance has been requested under this Convention. This list shall contain an estimate of the cost of such operations. The list may include only such property forming part of the cultural and natural heritage as is threatened by serious and specific dangers, such as the threat of disappearance caused by accelerated deterioration, large-scale public or private projects or rapid urban or tourist development projects; destruction caused by changes in the use or ownership of the land; major alterations due to unknown causes; abandonment for any reason whatsoever; the outbreak or the threat of an armed conflict; calamities and cataclysms; serious fires, earthquakes, landslides; volcanic erupt-ions; changes in water level, floods, and tidal waves. The Committee may at any time, in case of urgent need, make a new entry in the List of World Heritage in Danger and publicize such entry immediately.

5.   The Committee shall define the criteria on the basis of which a property belonging to the cultural or natural heritage may be included in either of the lists mentioned in paragraphs 2 and 4 of this Article.

6.   Before refusing a request for inclusion in one of the two lists mentioned in paragraphs 2 and 4 of this Article, the Committee shall consult the State Party in whose territory the cultural or natural property in question is situated.

7.   The Committee shall, with the agreement of the States con-cerned, co-ordinate and encourage the studies and research needed for the drawing up of the lists referred to in paragraphs 2 and 4 of this Article.

Article 12

The fact that a property belonging to the cultural or natural heritage has not been included in either of the two lists mentioned in paragraphs 2 and 4 of Article 11 shall in no way be construed to mean that it does not have an outstanding universal value for purposes other than those resulting from inclusion in these lists.

Article 13

1. The World Heritage Committee shall receive and study requests for international assistance formulated by States Parties to this Convention with respect to property forming part of the cultural or natural heritage, situated in their territories, and included or potentially suitable for inclusion in the lists referred to in paragraphs 2 and 4 of Article 11. The purpose of such requests may be to secure the protection, conservation, presentation or rehabilitation of such property.

2. Requests for internal assistance under paragraph 1 of this Article may also be concerned with identification of cultural or natural property defined in Articles 1 and 2, when preliminary investigations have shown that further inquiries would be justified.

3. The Committee shall decide on the action to be taken with regard to these requests, determine where appropriate, the nature and extent of its assistance, and authorize the conclusion, on its behalf, of the necessary arrangements with the government concerned.

4. The Committee shall determine an order of priorities for its operations. It shall in so doing bear in mind the respective importance for the world cultural and natural heritage of the property requiring protection, the need to give international assistance to the property most representative of a natural environment or of the genius and the history of the peoples of the world, the urgency of the work to be done, the resources available to the States on whose territory the threatened property is situated and in particular the extent to which they are able to safeguard such property by their own means.

5. The Committee shall draw up, keep up to date and publicize a list of property for which international assistance has been granted.

6. The Committee shall decide on the use of the resources of the Fund established under Article 15 of this Convention. It shall seek ways of increasing these resources and shall take all useful steps to this end.

7. The Committee shall co-operate with international and national governmental and non-governmental organizations having objectives similar to those of this Convention. For the implementation of its programmes and projects, the Committee may call on such organizations, particularly the International Centre for the Study of the Preservation and Restoration of Cultural Property (the Rome Centre), the International Council of Monuments and Sites (ICOMOS) and the International Union for Conservation of Nature and Natural Resources (IUCN), as well as on public and private bodies and individuals.

8. Decisions of the Committee shall be taken by a majority of two-thirds of its members present and voting. A majority of the members of the Committee shall constitute a quorum.

Article 14

1. The World Heritage Committee shall be assisted by a Secretariat appointed by the Director-General of the United Nations Educational, Scientific and Cultural Organization.

2. The Director-General of the United Nations Educational, Scientific and Cultural Organization, utilizing to the fullest extent possible the service of the International Centre for the Study of the Preservation and the Restoration of Cultural Property (the Rome Centre), the International Council of Monuments and Sites (ICOMOS) and the International Union for Conservation of Nature and Natural Resources (IUCN) in their respective areas of competence and capability, shall prepare the Committee's documentation and the agenda of its meetings and shall have the responsibility for the implementation of its decisions.

IV. FUND FOR THE PROTECTION OF THE WORLD CULTURAL AND NATURAL HERITAGE

Article 15

1. A Fund for the Protection of the World Cultural and Natural Heritage of Outstanding Universal Value, called "the World Heritage Fund", is hereby established.

2. The Fund shall constitute a trust fund, in conformity with the provisions of the Financial Regulations of the United Nations Educational, Scientific and Cultural Organization.

3. The resources of the Fund shall consist of:

a) compulsory and voluntary contributions made by the States Parties to this Convention,

b) contributions, gifts or bequests which may be made by:

(i)   other States;

(ii) the United Nations Educational, Scientific and Cultural Organization, other organizations of the United Nations system, particularly the United Nations Development Programme or other intergovernmental organizations;

(iii) public or private bodies or individuals;

c) any interest due on the resources of the Fund;

d) funds raised by collections and receipts from events organized for the benefit of the Fund; and

e) all other resources authorized by the Fund's regulations, as drawn up by the World Heritage Committee.

4. Contributions to the Fund and other forms of assistance made available to the Committee may be used only for such purposes as the Committee shall define. The Committee may accept contributions to be used only for a certain programme or project, provided that the Committee shall have decided on the implementation of such programme or project. No political conditions may be attached to contributions made to the Fund.

Article 16

1. Without prejudice to any supplementary voluntary contribution, the States Parties to this Convention undertake to pay regularly, every two years, to the World Heritage Fund, contributions, the amount of which, in the form of a uniform percentage applicable to all States, shall be determined by the General Assembly of States Parties to the Convention, meeting during the sessions of the General Conference of the United Nations Educational, Scientific and Cultural Organization. This decision of the General Assembly requires the majority of the States Parties

present and voting, which have not made the declaration referred to in paragraph 2 of this Article. In no case shall the compulsory contribution of States Parties to the Convention exceed 1% of the contribution to the Regular Budget of the United Nations Educational, Scientific and Cultural Organization.

2.   However, each State referred to in Article 31 or in Article 32 of this Convention may declare, at the time of the deposit of its instruments of ratification, acceptance or accession, that it shall not be bound by the provisions of paragraph 1 of this Article.

3.   A State Party to the Convention which has made the declaration referred to in paragraph 2 of this Article may at any time withdraw the said declaration by notifying the Director-General of the United Nations Educational, Scientific and Cultural Organization. However, the withdrawal of the declaration shall not take effect in regard to the compulsory contribution due by the State until the date of the subsequent General Assembly of States Parties to the Convention.

4.   In order that the Committee may be able to plan its operations effectively, the contributions of States Parties to this Convention which have made the declaration referred to in paragraph 2 of this Article, shall be paid on a regular basis, at least every two years, and should not be less than the contributions which they should have paid if they had been bound by the provisions of paragraph 1 of this Article.

5.   Any State Party to the Convention which is in arrears with the payment of its compulsory or voluntary contribution for the current year and the calendar year immediately preceding it shall not be eligible as a Member of the World Heritage Committee, although this provision shall not apply to the first election. The terms of office of any such State which is already a member of the Committee shall terminate at the time of the elections provided for in Article 8, paragraph 1 of this Convention.

Article 17

The States Parties to this Convention shall consider or encourage the establishment of national, public and private foundations or associations whose purpose is to invite donations for the protection of the cultural and natural heritage as defined in Articles 1 and 2 of this Convention.

Article 18

The States Parties to this Convention shall give their assistance to international fund-raising campaigns organized for the World Heritage Fund under the auspices of the United Nations Educational, Scientific and Cultural Organization. They shall facilitate collections made by the bodies mentioned in paragraph 3 of Article 15 for this purpose.

V.   CONDITIONS AND ARRANGEMENTS FOR INTERNATIONAL ASSISTANCE

Article 19

Any State Party to this Convention may request international assistance for property forming part of the cultural or natural heritage of outstanding universal value situated within its territory. It shall submit with its request such information and documentation provided for in Article 21 as it has in its possession and as will enable the Committee to come to a decision.

Article 20

Subject to the provisions of paragraph 2 of Article 13, subparagraph *(c)* of Article 22 and Article 23, international assistance provided for by this Convention may be granted only to property forming part of the cultural and natural heritage which the World Heritage Committee has decided, or may decide, to enter in one of the lists mentioned in paragraphs 2 and 4 of Article 11.

Article 21

1.   The World Heritage Committee shall define the procedure by which requests to it for international assistance shall be considered and shall specify the content of the request, which should define the operation contemplated, the work that is necessary, the expected cost thereof, the degree of urgency and the reasons why the resources of the State requesting assistance do not allow it to meet all the expenses. Such requests must be supported by experts' reports whenever possible.

2.   Requests based upon disasters or natural calamities should, by reasons of the urgent work which they may involve, be given immediate priority consideration by the Committee, which should have a reserve fund at its disposal against such contingencies.

3. Before coming to a decision, the Committee shall carry out such studies and consultations as it deems necessary.

Article 22

Assistance granted by the World Heritage Committee may take the following forms:

a) studies concerning the artistic, scientific and technical problems raised by the protection, conservation, presentation and rehabilitation of the cultural and natural heritage, as defined in paragraph 2 and 4 of Article 11 of this Convention;

b) provision of experts, technicians and skilled labour to ensure that the approved work is correctly carried out;

c) training of staff and specialists at all levels in the field of identification, protection, conservation, presentation and rehabilitation of the cultural and natural heritage;

d) supply of equipment which the State concerned does not possess or is not in a position to acquire;

e) low-interest or interest-free loans which might be repayable on a longer-term basis;

f) the granting, in exceptional cases and for special reasons, of non-repayable subsidies.

Article 23

The World Heritage Committee may also provide international assistance to national or regional centres for the training of staff and specialists at all levels in the field of identification, protection, conservation, presentation and rehabilitation of the cultural and natural heritage.

Article 24

International assistance on a large scale shall be preceded by detailed scientific, economic and technical studies. These studies shall draw upon the most advanced techniques for the protection, conservation, presentation and rehabilitation of the natural and cultural heritage and shall be consistent with the objectives of this Convention. The studies shall also seek means of making rational use of the resources available in the State concerned.

Article 25

As a general rule, only part of the cost of work necessary shall be borne by the international community. The contribution of the State benefiting from international assistance shall constitute a substantial share of the resources devoted to each programme or project, unless its resources do not permit this.

Article 26

The World Heritage Committee and the recipient State shall define in the agreement they conclude the conditions in which a programme or project for which international assistance under the terms of this Convention is provided, shall be carried out. It shall be the responsibility of the State receiving such international assistance to continue to protect, conserve and present the property so safeguarded, in observance of the conditions laid down by the agreement.

VI.   EDUCATIONAL PROGRAMMES

Article 27

1.   The States Parties to this Convention shall endeavour by all appropriate means, and in particular by educational and information programmes, to strengthen appreciation and respect by their peoples of the cultural and natural heritage defined in Articles 1 and 2 of the Convention.

2.   They shall undertake to keep the public broadly informed of the dangers threatening this heritage and of activities carried on in pursuance of this Convention.

Article 28

States Parties to this Convention which receive international assistance under the Convention shall take appropriate measures to make known the importance of the property for which assistance has been received and the role played by such assistance.

VII.   REPORTS

Article 29

1.   The States Parties to this Convention shall, in the reports which they submit to the General Conference of the United Nations Educational, Scientific and Cultural Organization on dates and in a

manner to be determined by it, give information on the legislative and administrative provisions which they have adopted and other action which they have taken for the application of this Convention, together with details of the experience acquired in this field.

2.   These reports shall be brought to the attention of the World Heritage Committee.

3.   The Committee shall submit a report on its activities at each of the ordinary sessions of the General Conference of the United Nations Educational, Scientific and Cultural Organization.

VIII.   FINAL CLAUSES

Article 30

This Convention is drawn up in Arabic, English, French, Russian and Spanish, the five texts being equally authoritative.

Article 31

1.   This Convention shall be subject to ratification or acceptance by States members of the United Nations Educational, Scientific and Cultural Organization in accordance with their respective con-stitutional procedures.

2.   The instruments of ratification or acceptance shall be deposited with the Director-General of the United Nations Educational, Scientific and Cultural Organization.

Article 32

1.   This Convention shall be open to accession by all States not members of the United Nations Educational, Scientific and Cultural Organization which are invited by the General Conference of the Organization to accede to it.

2.   Accession shall be effected by the deposit of an instrument of accession with the Director-General of the United Nations Edu-cational, Scientific and Cultural Organization.

Article 33

This Convention shall enter into force three months after the date of the deposit of the twentieth instrument of ratification, acceptance or accession, but only with respect to those States which have deposited their respective instruments of ratification, acceptance or accession on or before that date. It shall enter into force with respect to any other State three months after the deposit of its instrument of ratification, acceptance or accession.

Article 34

The following provisions shall apply to those States Parties to this Convention which have a federal or non-unitary constitutional system:

> *a)* with regard to the provisions of this Convention, the implementation of which comes under the legal jurisdiction of the federal or central legislative power, the obligations of the federal or central government shall be the same as for those States Parties which are not federal States;

> *b)* with regard to the provisions of this Convention, the implementation of which comes under the legal jurisdiction of individual constituent States, countries, provinces or cantons that are not obliged by the constitutional system of the federation to take legislative measures, the federal government shall inform the competent authorities of such States, countries, provinces or cantons of the said provisions, with its recommendation for their adoption.

Article 35

1.   Each State Party to this Convention may denounce the Convention.

2.   The denunciation shall be notified by an instrument in writing, deposited with the Director-General of the United Nations Educational, Scientific and Cultural Organization.

3.   The denunciation shall take effect twelve months after the receipt of the instrument of denunciation. It shall not affect the financial obligations of the denouncing State until the date on which the withdrawal takes effect.

Article 36

The Director-General of the United Nations Educational, Scientific and Cultural Organization shall inform the States members of the Organization, the States not members of the Organization which are referred to in Article 32, as well as the United Nations, of the deposit of all the instruments of ratification, acceptance, or accession provided for in Articles 31 and 32, and of the denunciations provided for in Article 35.

Article 37

1. This Convention may be revised by the General Conference of the United Nations Educational, Scientific and Cultural Organization. Any such revision shall, however, bind only the States which shall become Parties to the revising convention.

2. If the General Conference should adopt a new convention revising this Convention in whole or in part, then, unless the new convention otherwise provides, this Convention shall cease to be open to ratification, acceptance or accession, as from the date on which the new revising convention enters into force.

Article 38

In conformity with Article 102 of the Charter of the United Nations, this Convention shall be registered with the Secretariat of the United Nations at the request of the Director-General of the United Nations Educational, Scientific and Cultural Organization.

DONE at Paris, this twenty-third day of November 1972, in two authentic copies bearing the signature of the President of the seventeenth session of the General Conference and of the Director-General of the United Nations Educational, Scientific and Cultural Organization, which shall be deposited in the archives of the United Nations Educational, Scientific and Cultural Organization, and certified true copies of which shall be delivered to all the States referred to in Articles 31 and 32 as well as to the United Nations.

CONVENTION ON INTERNATIONAL TRADE IN ENDANGERED SPECIES OF WILD FAUNA AND FLORA, 1973

The Contracting States,

RECOGNIZING that wild fauna and flora in their many beautiful and varied forms are an irreplaceable part of the natural systems of the earth which must be protected for this and the generations to come;

CONSCIOUS of the ever-growing value of wild fauna and flora from aesthetic, scientific, cultural, recreational and economic points of view;

RECOGNIZING that peoples and States are and should be the best protectors of their own wild fauna and flora;

RECOGNIZING, in addition, that international cooperation is essential for the protection of certain species of wild fauna and flora against overexploitation through international trade;

CONVINCED of the urgency of taking appropriate measures to this end;

HAVE AGREED as follows:

Article I

DEFINITIONS

For the purpose of the present Convention, unless the context otherwise requires:

a) "Species" means any species, sub-species, or geographically separate population thereof;

b) "Specimen" means:

(i) an animal or plant, whether alive or dead;

(ii) in the case of an animal: for species included in Appendices I and II, any readily recognizable part or derivative thereof; and for species included in Appendix III, any readily recognizable part or derivative thereof specified in Appendix III in relation to the species; and

(iii) in the case of a plant: for species included in Appendix I, any readily recognizable part or derivative thereof; and for species included in Appendices II and III, any readily recognizable part or derivative thereof specified in Appendices II and III in relation to the species;

c) "Trade" means export, re-export, import and introduction from the sea;

d) "Re-export" means export of any specimen that has previously been imported;

e) "Introduction from the sea" means transportation into a State of specimens of any species which were taken in the marine environment not under the jurisdiction of any State;

f) "Scientific Authority" means a national scientific authority designated in accordance with Article IX;

g) "Management Authority" means a national management authority designated in accordance with Article IX;

h) "Party" means a State for which the present Convention has entered into force.

Article II

FUNDAMENTAL PRINCIPLES

1. Appendix I shall include all species threatened with extinction which are or may be affected by trade. Trade in specimens of these species must be subject to particularly strict regulation in order not to endanger further their survival and must only be authorized in exceptional circumstances.

2. Appendix II shall include:

a) all species which although not necessarily now threatened with extinction may become so unless trade in specimens of such species is subject to strict regulation in order to avoid utilization incompatible with their survival; and

b) other species which must be subject to regulation in order that trade in specimens of certain species referred to in sub-paragraph *(a)* of this paragraph may be brought under effective control.

3.   Appendix III shall include all species which any Party identifies as being subject to regulation within its jurisdiction for the purposes of preventing or restricting exploitation, and as needing the co-operation of other parties in the control of trade.

4.   The Parties shall not allow trade in specimens of species included in Appendices I, II and III except in accordance with the provisions of the present Convention.

Article III

REGULATION OF TRADE IN SPECIMENS OF SPECIES INCLUDED IN APPENDIX I

1.   All trade in specimens of species included in Appendix I shall be in accordance with the provisions of this Article.

2.   The export of any specimen of a species included in Appendix I shall require the prior grant and presentation of an export permit. An export permit shall only be granted when the following conditions have been met:

a)   a Scientific Authority of the State of export has advised that such export will not be detrimental to the survival of that species;

b)   a Management Authority of the State of export is satisfied that the specimen was not obtained in contravention of the laws of that State for the protection of fauna and flora;

c)   a Management Authority of the State of export is satisfied that any living specimen will be so prepared and shipped as to minimize the risk of injury, damage to health or cruel treatment; and

d)   a Management Authority of the State of export is satisfied that an import permit has been granted for the specimen.

3.   The import of any specimen of a species included in Appendix I shall require the prior grant and presentation of an import permit and either an export permit or a re-export certificate. An import permit shall only be granted when the following conditions have been met:

a)   a Scientific Authority of the State of import has advised that the import will be for purposes which are not detrimental to the survival of the species involved;

b) a Scientific Authority of the State of import is satisfied that the proposed recipient of a living specimen is suitably equipped to house and care for it; and

c) a Management Authority of the State of import is satisfied that the specimen is not to be used for primarily commercial purposes.

4. The re-export of any specimen of a species included in Appendix I shall require the prior grant and presentation of a re-export certificate. A re-export certificate shall only be granted when the following conditions have been met:

a) a Management Authority of the State of re-export is satisfied that the specimen was imported into that State in accordance with the provisions of the present Convention;

b) a Management Authority of the State of re-export is satisfied that any living specimen will be so prepared and shipped as to minimize the risk of injury, damage to health or cruel treatment; and

c) a Management Authority of the State of re-export is satisfied that an import permit has been granted for any living specimen.

5. The introduction from the sea of any specimen of a species included in Appendix I shall require the prior grant of a certificate from a Management Authority of the State of introduction. A certificate shall only be granted when the following conditions have been met:

a) a Scientific Authority of the State of introduction advises that the introduction will not be detrimental to the survival of the species involved;

b) a Management Authority of the State of introduction is satisfied that the proposed recipient of a living specimen is suitably equipped to house and care for it; and

c) a Management Authority of the State of introduction is satisfied that the specimen is not to be used for primarily commercial purposes.

Article IV

REGULATION OF TRADE IN SPECIMENS OF SPECIES INCLUDED IN APPENDIX II

1.   All trade in specimens of species included in Appendix II shall be in accordance with the provisions of this Article.

2.   The export of any specimen of a species included in Appendix II shall require the prior grant and presentation of an export permit. An export permit shall only be granted when the following conditions have been met:

> *a)*   a Scientific Authority of the State of export has advised that such export will not be detrimental to the survival of that species;
>
> *b)*   a Management Authority of the State of export is satisfied that the specimen was not obtained in contravention of the laws of that State for the protection of fauna and flora; and
>
> *c)*   a Management Authority of the State of export is satisfied that any living specimen will be so prepared and shipped as to minimize the risk of injury, damage to health or cruel treatment.

3.   A Scientific Authority in each Party shall monitor both the export permits granted by that State for specimens of species included in Appendix II and the actual exports of such specimens. Whenever a Scientific Authority determines that the export of specimens of any such species should be limited in order to maintain that species throughout its range at a level consistent with its role in the ecosystems in which it occurs and well above the level at which that species might become eligible for inclusion in Appendix I, the Scientific Authority shall advise the appropriate Management Authority of suitable measures to be taken to limit the grant of export permits for specimens of that species.

4.   The import of any specimen of a species included in Appendix II shall require the prior presentation of either an export permit or a re-export certificate.

5.   The re-export of any specimen of a species included in Appendix II shall require the prior grant and presentation of a re-export certificate. A re-export certificate shall only be granted when the following conditions have been met:

a) a Management Authority of the State of re-export is satisfied that the specimen was imported into that State in accordance with the provisions of the present Convention; and

b) a Management Authority of the State of re-export is satisfied that any living specimen will be so prepared and shipped as to minimize the risk of injury, damage to health or cruel treatment.

6. The introduction from the sea of any specimen of a species included in Appendix II shall require the prior grant of a certificate from a Management Authority of the State of introduction. A certificate shall only be granted when the following conditions have been met:

a) a Scientific Authority of the State of introduction advises that the introduction will not be detrimental to the survival of the species involved; and

b) a Management Authority of the State of introduction is satisfied that any living specimen will be so handled as to minimize the risk of injury, damage to health or cruel treatment.

7. Certificates referred to in paragraph 6 of this Article may be granted on the advice of a Scientific Authority, in consultation with other national scientific authorities or, when appropriate, international scientific authorities, in respect of periods not exceeding one year for total numbers of specimens to be introduced in such periods.

Article V

REGULATION OF TRADE IN SPECIMENS OF SPECIES INCLUDED IN APPENDIX III

1. All trade in specimens of species included in Appendix III shall be in accordance with the provisions of this Article.

2. The export of any specimen of a species included in Appendix III from any State which has included that species in Appendix III shall require the prior grant and presentation of an export permit. An export permit shall only be granted when the following conditions have been met:

a) a Management Authority of the State of export is satisfied that the specimen was not obtained in contravention of the laws of that State for the protection of fauna and flora; and

b) a Management Authority of the State of export is satisfied that any living specimen will be so prepared and shipped as to minimize the risk of injury, damage to health or cruel treatment.

3. The import of any specimen of a species included in Appendix III shall require, except in circumstances to which paragraph 4 of this Article applies, the prior presentation of a certificate of origin and, where the import is from a State which has included that species in Appendix III, an export permit.

4. In the case of re-export, a certificate granted by the Management Authority of the State of re-export that the specimen was processed in that State or is being re-exported shall be accepted by the State of import as evidence that the provisions of the present Convention have been complied with in respect of the specimen concerned.

Article VI

PERMITS AND CERTIFICATES

1. Permits and certificates granted under the provisions of Articles III, IV and V shall be in accordance with the provisions of this Article.

2. An export permit shall contain the information specified in the model set forth in Appendix IV, and may only be used for export within a period of six months from the date on which it was granted.

3. Each permit or certificate shall contain the title of the present Convention, the name and any identifying stamp of the Management Authority granting it and a control number assigned by the Management Authority.

4. Any copies of a permit or certificates issued by a Management Authority shall be clearly marked as copies only and no such copy may be used in place of the original, except to the extent endorsed thereon.

5. A separate permit or certificate shall be required for each consignment of specimens.

6. A Management Authority of the State of import of any specimen shall cancel and retain the export permit or re-export certificate and any corresponding import permit presented in respect of the import of that specimen.

7. Where appropriate and feasible a Management Authority may affix a mark upon any specimen to assist in identifying the specimen. For these purposes "mark" means any indelible imprint, lead seal or other suitable means of identifying a specimen, designed in such a way as to render its imitation by unauthorized persons as difficult as possible.

Article VII

EXEMPTIONS AND OTHER SPECIAL PROVISIONS RELATING TO TRADE

1. The provisions of Articles III, IV and V shall not apply to the transit or trans-shipment of specimens through or in the territory of a Party while the specimens remain in Customs control.

2. Where a Management Authority of the State of export or re-export is satisfied that a specimen was acquired before the provisions of the present Convention applied to that specimen, the provisions of Articles III, IV and V shall not apply to that specimen where the Management Authority issues a certificate to that effect.

3. The provisions of Articles III, IV and V shall not apply to specimens that are personal or household effects. This exemption shall not apply where:

  a) in the case of specimens of a species included in Appendix I, they were acquired by the owner outside his State of usual residence, and are being imported into that State; or

  b) in the case of specimens of species included in Appendix II:

    (i) they were acquired by the owner outside his State of usual residence and in a State where removal from the wild occurred;

(ii)   they are being imported into the owner's State of usual residence; and

(iii)   the State where removal from the wild occurred requires the prior grant of export permits before any export of such specimens; unless a Management Authority is satisfied that the specimens were acquired before the provisions of the present Convention applied to such specimens.

4.   Specimens of an animal species included in Appendix I bred in captivity for commercial purposes, or of a plant species included in Appendix I artificially propagated for commercial purposes, shall be deemed to be specimens of species included in Appendix II.

5.   Where a Management Authority of the State of export is satisfied that any specimen of an animal species was bred in captivity or any specimen of a plant species was artificially propagated, or is a part of such an animal or plant or was derived therefrom, a certificate by that Management Authority to that effect shall be accepted in lieu of any of the permits or certificates required under the provisions of Articles III, IV or V.

6.   The provisions of Articles III, IV and V shall not apply to the non-commercial loan, donation or exchange between scientists or scientific institutions registered by a Management Authority of their State, of herbarium specimens, other preserved, dried or embedded museum specimens, and live plant material which carry a label issued or approved by a Management Authority.

7.   A Management Authority of any State may waive the requirements of Articles III, IV and V and allow the movement without permits or certificates of specimens which form part of a travelling zoo, circus, menagerie, plant exhibition or other travelling exhibition provided that:

a)   the exporter or importer registers full details of such specimens with that Management Authority;

b)   the specimens are in either of the categories specified in paragraphs 2 and 5 of this Article; and

c)   the Management Authority is satisfied that any living specimen will be so transported and cared for as to minimize the risk of injury, damage to health or cruel treatment.

Article VIII

MEASURES TO BE TAKEN BY THE PARTIES

1.   The Parties shall take appropriate measures to enforce the provisions of the present Convention and to prohibit trade in specimens in violation thereof. These shall include measures:

a)   to penalize trade in, or possession of, such specimens, or both; and

b)   to provide for the confiscation or return to the State of export of such specimens.

2.   In addition to the measures taken under paragraph 1 of this Article a Party may, when it deems it necessary, provide for any method of internal reimbursement for expenses incurred as a result of the confiscation of a specimen traded in violation of the measures taken in the application of the provisions of the present Convention.

3.   As far as possible, the Parties shall ensure that specimens shall pass through any formalities required for trade with a minimum of delay. To facilitate such passage, a Party may designate ports of exit and ports of entry at which specimens must be presented for clearance. The Parties shall ensure further that all living specimens, during any period of transit, holding or shipment, are properly cared for so as to minimize the risk of injury, damage to health or cruel treatment.

4.   Where a living specimen is confiscated as a result of measures referred to in paragraph 1 of this Article:

a)   the specimen shall be entrusted to a Management Authority of the State of confiscation;

b)   the Management Authority shall, after consultation with the State of export, return the specimen to that State at the expense of that State, or to a rescue centre or such other place as the Management Authority deems appropriate and consistent with the purposes of the present Convention; and

c)   the Management Authority may obtain the advice of a Scientific Authority, or may, wherever it considers it desirable, consult the Secretariat in order to facilitate the decision under sub-paragraph *(b)* of this paragraph, including the choice of a rescue centre or other place.

5.   A rescue centre as referred to in paragraph 4 of this Article means an institution designated by a Management Authority to look after the welfare of living specimens, particularly those that have been confiscated.

6.   Each Party shall maintain records of trade in specimens of species included in Appendices I, II and III which shall cover:

   a)   the names and addresses of exporters and importers; and

   b)   the number and type of permits and certificates granted; the States with which such trade occurred; the numbers or quantities and types of specimens, names of species as included in Appendices I, II and III and, where applicable, the size and sex of the specimens in question.

7.   Each Party shall prepare periodic reports on its implementation of the present Convention and shall transmit to the Secretariat:

   a)   an annual report containing a summary of the information specified in sub-paragraph *(b)* of paragraph 6 of this Article; and

   b)   a biennial report on legislative, regulatory and administrative measures taken to enforce the provisions of the present Convention.

8.   The information referred to in paragraph 7 of this Article shall be available to the public where this is not inconsistent with the law of the Party concerned.

Article IX

MANAGEMENT AND SCIENTIFIC AUTHORITIES

1.   Each Party shall designate for the purposes of the present Convention:

   a)   one or more Management Authorities competent to grant permits or certificates on behalf of that Party; and

   b)   one or more Scientific Authorities.

2.   A State depositing an instrument of ratification, acceptance, approval or accession shall at that time inform the Depositary Government of the name and address of the Management Authority authorized to communicate with other Parties and with the Secretariat.

3. Any changes in the designations or authorizations under the provisions of this Article shall be communicated by the Party concerned to the Secretariat for transmission to all other Parties.

4. Any Management Authority referred to in paragraph 2 of this Article shall if so requested by the Secretariat or the Management Authority of another Party, communicate to it impression of stamps, seals or other devices used to authenticate permits or certificates.

Article X

TRADE WITH STATES NOT PARTY TO THE CONVENTION

Where export or re-export is to, or import is from, a State not a Party to the present Convention, comparable documentation issued by the competent authorities in that State which substantially conforms with the requirements of the present Convention for permits and certificates may be accepted in lieu thereof by any Party.

Article XI

CONFERENCE OF THE PARTIES

1. The Secretariat shall call a meeting of the Conference of the Parties not later than two years after the entry into force of the present Convention.

2. Thereafter the Secretariat shall convene regular meetings at least once every two years, unless the Conference decides otherwise, and extraordinary meetings at any time on the written request of a least one-third of the Parties.

3. At meetings, whether regular or extraordinary, the Parties shall review the implementation of the present Convention and may:

   a) make such provision as may be necessary to enable the Secretariat to carry out its duties[, and adopt financial provisions]*;

* The words in square brackets are an amendment to the Convention which was adopted at an extraordinary meeting of the Conference of the Parties in Bonn (Federal Republic of Germany) on 22 June 1979. The amendment is not yet in force. It will enter into force when it has been formally accepted by 34 of the 51 States which were Parties to the Convention on that date. By 31 December 1984 it had been accepted by 26 of those States.

b) consider and adopt amendments to Appendices I and II in accordance with Article XV;

c) review the progress made towards the restoration and conservation of the species included in Appendices I, II and III;

d) receive and consider any reports presented by the Secretariat or by any Party; and

e) where appropriate, make recommendations for improving the effectiveness of the present Convention.

4. At each regular meeting, the Parties may determine the time and venue of the next regular meeting to be held in accordance with the provisions of paragraph 2 of this Article.

5. At any meeting, the Parties may determine and adopt rules of procedure for the meeting.

6. The United Nations, its Specialized Agencies and the International Atomic Energy Agency, as well as any State not a Party to the present Convention, may be represented at meetings of the Conference by observers, who shall have the right to participate but not to vote.

7. Any body or agency technically qualified in protection, conservation or management of wild fauna and flora, in the following categories, which has informed the Secretariat of its desire to be represented at meetings of the Conference by observers, shall be admitted unless at least one-third of the Parties present object:

a) international agencies or bodies, either governmental or non-governmental, and national governmental agencies and bodies; and

b) national non-governmental agencies or bodies which have been approved for this purpose by the State in which they are located.

Once admitted, these observers shall have the right to participate but not to vote.

Article XII

THE SECRETARIAT

1. Upon entry into force of the present Convention, a Secretariat shall be provided by the Executive Director of the United Nations Environment Programme. To the extent and in the manner he

considers appropriate, he may be assisted by suitable inter-governmental or non-governmental international or national agencies and bodies technically qualified in protection, conservation and management of wild fauna and flora.

2.   The functions of the Secretariat shall be:

a)   to arrange for and service meetings of the Parties;

b)   to perform the functions entrusted to it under the provisions of Articles XV and XVI of the present Convention;

c)   to undertake scientific and technical studies in accordance with programmes authorized by the Conference of the Parties as will contribute to the implementation of the present Convention, including studies concerning standards for appropriate preparation and shipment of living specimens and the means of identifying specimens;

d)   to study the reports of Parties and to request from Parties such further information with respect thereto as it deems necessary to ensure implementation of the present Convention;

e)   to invite the attention of the Parties to any matter pertaining to the aims of the present Convention;

f)   to publish periodically and distribute to the Parties current editions of Appendices I, II and III together with any information which will facilitate identification of specimens of species included in those Appendices.

g)   to prepare annual reports to the Parties on its work and on the implementation of the present Convention and such other reports as meetings of the Parties may request;

h)   to make recommendations for the implementation of the aims and provisions of the present Convention, including the exchange of information of a scientific or technical nature;

i)   to perform any other function as may be entrusted to it by the Parties.

Article XIII

INTERNATIONAL MEASURES

1.   When the Secretariat in the light of information received is satisfied that any species included in Appendices I or II is being affected adversely by trade in specimens of that species or that the

provisions of the present Convention are not being effectively implemented, it shall communicate such information to the authorized Management Authority of the Party or Parties concerned.

2.   When any Party receives a communication as indicated in paragraph 1 of this Article, it shall, as soon as possible, inform the Secretariat of any relevant facts insofar as its laws permit and, where appropriate, propose remedial action. Where the Party considers that an inquiry is desirable, such inquiry may be carried out by one or more persons expressly authorized by the Party.

3.   The information provided by the Party or resulting from any inquiry as specified in paragraph 2 of this Article shall be reviewed by the next Conference of the Parties which may make whatever recommendations it deems appropriate.

Article XIV

EFFECT ON DOMESTIC LEGISLATION AND INTERNATIONAL CONVENTIONS

1.   The provisions of the present Convention shall in no way affect the right of Parties to adopt:

> *a)*   stricter domestic measures regarding the conditions for trade, taking, possession or transport of specimens of species included in Appendices I, II and III, or the complete prohibition thereof; or
>
> *b)*   domestic measures restricting or prohibiting trade, taking possession, or transport of species not included in Appendices I, II or III.

2.   The provisions of the present Convention shall in no way affect the provisions of any domestic measures or the obligations of Parties deriving from any treaty, convention, or international agreement relating to other aspects of trade, taking, possession, or transport of specimens which is in force or subsequently may enter into force for any Party including any measure pertaining to the Customs, public health, veterinary or plant quarantine fields.

3.   The provisions of the present Convention shall in no way affect the provisions of, or the obligations deriving from, any treaty, convention or international agreement concluded or which may be

concluded between States creating a union or regional trade agreement establishing or maintaining a common external customs control and removing customs controls between the parties thereto insofar as they relate to trade among the States members of that union or agreement.

4.   A State Party to the present Convention, which is also a Party to any other treaty, convention or international agreement which is in force at the time of the coming into force of the present Convention and under the provisions of which protection is afforded to marine species included in Appendix II, shall be relieved of the obligations imposed on it under the provisions of the present Convention with respect to trade in specimens of species included in Appendix II that are taken by ships registered in that State and in accordance with the provisions of such other treaty, convention or international agreement.

5.   Notwithstanding the provisions of Articles III, IV and V, any export of a specimen taken in accordance with paragraph 4 of this Article shall only require a certificate from a Management Authority of the State of introduction to the effect that the specimen was taken in accordance with the provisions of the other treaty, convention or international agreement in question.

6.   Nothing in the present Convention shall prejudice the codification and development of the law of the sea by the United Nations Conference on the Law of the Sea convened pursuant to Resolution 2750 C (XXV) of the General Assembly of the United Nations nor the present or future claims and legal views of any State concerning the law of the sea and the nature and extent of coastal and flag State jurisdiction.

Article XV

AMENDMENTS TO APPENDICES I AND II

1.   The following provisions shall apply in relation to amendments to Appendices I and II at meetings of the Conference of the Parties:

  a)   Any Party may propose an amendment to Appendix I or II for consideration at the next meeting. The text of the proposed amendment shall be communicated to the Secretariat at least 150 days before the meeting. The Secretariat shall consult the other Parties and interested bodies on the amendment in accordance with the provisions of sub-paragraphs *(b)* and *(c)* of paragraph 2 of this Article and shall communicate the response to all Parties not later than 30 days before the meeting.

b)   Amendments shall be adopted by a two-thirds majority of Parties present and voting. For these purposes "Parties present and voting" means Parties present and casting an affirmative or negative vote. Parties abstaining from voting shall not be counted among the two-thirds required for adopting an amendment.

c)   Amendments adopted at a meeting shall enter into force 90 days after that meeting for all Parties except those which make a reservation in accordance with paragraph 3 of this Article.

2.   The following provisions shall apply in relation to amendments to Appendices I and II between meetings of the Conference of the Parties:

a)   Any Party may propose an amendment to Appendix I and II for consideration between meetings by the postal procedures set forth in this paragraph.

b)   For marine species, the Secretariat shall, upon receiving the text of the proposed amendment, immediately communicate it to the Parties. It shall also consult inter-governmental bodies having a function in relation to those species especially with a view to obtaining scientific data these bodies may be able to provide and to ensuring co-ordination with any conservation measures enforced by such bodies. The Secretariat shall communicate the views expressed and data provided by these bodies and its own findings and recommendations to the Parties as soon as possible.

c)   For species other than marine species, the Secretariat shall, upon receiving the text of the proposed amendments, immediately communicate it to the Parties, and, as soon as possible thereafter, its own recommendations.

d)   Any Party may, within 60 days of the date on which the Secretariat communicated its recommendations to the Parties under sub-paragraphs *(b)* or *(c)* of this paragraph, transmit to the Secretariat any comments on the proposed amendment together with any relevant scientific data and information.

e)   The Secretariat shall communicate the replies received together with its own recommendations to the Parties as soon as possible.

f) If no objection to the proposed amendment is received by the Secretariat within 30 days of the date the replies and recommendations were communicated under the provisions of sub-paragraph *(e)* of this paragraph, the amendment shall enter into force 90 days later for all Parties except those which make a reservation in accordance with paragraph 3 of this Article.

g) If an objection by any Party is received by the Secretariat the proposed amendment shall be submitted to a postal vote in accordance with the provisions of sub-paragraphs *(h)*, *(i)* and *(j)* of this paragraph.

h) The Secretariat shall notify the Parties that notification of objection has been received.

i) Unless the Secretariat receives the votes for, against or in abstention from at least one-half of the Parties within 60 days of the date of notification under sub-paragraph *(h)* of this paragraph, the proposed amendment shall be referred to the next meeting of the Conference for further consideration.

j) Provided that votes are received from one-half of the Parties, the amendment shall be adopted by a two-thirds majority of Parties casting an affirmative or negative vote.

k) The Secretariat shall notify all Parties of the result of the vote.

l) If the proposed amendment is adopted it shall enter into force 90 days after the date of the notification by the Secretariat of its acceptance for all Parties except those which make a reservation in accordance with paragraph 3 of this Article.

3. During the period of 90 days provided for by sub-paragraph *(c)* of paragraph 1 or sub-paragraph *(l)* of paragraph 2 of this Article any Party may by notification in writing to the Depositary Government make a reservation with respect to the amendment. Until such reservation is withdrawn the Party shall be treated as a State not a Party to the present Convention with respect to trade in the species concerned.

Article XVI

APPENDIX III AND AMENDMENTS THERETO

1. Any Party may at any time submit to the Secretariat a list of species which it identifies as being subject to regulation within its jurisdiction for the purpose mentioned in paragraph 3 of Article II.

Appendix III shall include the names of the Parties submitting the species for inclusion therein, the scientific names of the species so submitted, and any parts or derivatives of the animals or plants concerned that are specified in relation to the species for the purposes of sub-paragraph *(b)* of Article I.

2.　Each list submitted under the provisions of paragraph 1 of this Article shall be communicated to the Parties by the Secretariat as soon as possible after receiving it. The list shall take effect as part of Appendix III 90 days after the date of such communication. At any time after the communication of such list, any Party may by notification in writing to the Depositary Government enter a reservation with respect to any species or any parts or derivatives, and until such reservation is withdrawn, the State shall be treated as a State not a Party to the present Convention with respect to trade in the species or part or derivative concerned.

3.　A Party which has submitted a species for inclusion in Appendix III may withdraw it at any time by notification to the Secretariat which shall communicate the withdrawal to all Parties. The withdrawal shall take effect 30 days after the date of such communication.

4.　Any Party submitting a list under the provisions of paragraph 1 of this Article shall submit to the Secretariat a copy of all domestic laws and regulations applicable to the protection of such species, together with any interpretations which the Party may deem appropriate or the Secretariat may request. The Party shall, for as long as the species in question is included in Appendix III, submit any amendments of such laws and regulations or any new interpretations as they are adopted.

Article XVII

AMENDMENT OF THE CONVENTION

1.　An extraordinary meeting of the Conference of the Parties shall be convened by the Secretariat on the written request of at least one-third of the Parties to consider and adopt amendments to the present Convention. Such amendments shall be adopted by a two-thirds majority of Parties present and voting. For these purposes "Parties present and voting" means Parties present and casting an affirmative or negative vote. Parties abstaining from voting shall not be counted among the two-thirds required for adopting an amendment.

2.   The text of any proposed amendment shall be communicated by the Secretariat to all Parties at least 90 days before the meeting.

3.   An amendment shall enter into force for the Parties which have accepted it 60 days after two-thirds of the Parties have deposited an instrument of acceptance of the amendment with the Depositary Government. Thereafter, the amendment shall enter into force for any other Party 60 days after that Party deposits its instrument of acceptance of the amendment.

Article XVIII

RESOLUTION OF DISPUTES

1.   Any dispute which may arise between two or more Parties with respect to the interpretation or application of the provisions of the present Convention shall be subject to negotiation between the Parties involved in the dispute.

2.   If the dispute cannot be resolved in accordance with paragraph 1 of this Article, the Parties may, by mutual consent, submit the dispute to arbitration, in particular that of the Permanent Court of Arbitration at The Hague, and the Parties submitting the dispute shall be bound by the arbitral decision.

Article XIX

SIGNATURE

The present Convention shall be open for signature at Washington until 30 April 1973 and thereafter at Berne until 31 December 1974.

Article XX

RATIFICATION, ACCEPTANCE, APPROVAL

The present Convention shall be subject to ratification, acceptance or approval. Instruments of ratification, acceptance or approval shall be deposited with the Government of the Swiss Confederation which shall be the Depositary Government.

Article XXI

ACCESSION

The present Convention shall be open indefinitely for accession. Instruments of accession shall be deposited with the Depositary Government.

[1. This Convention shall be open for accession by regional economic integration organizations constituted by sovereign States which have competence in respect of the negotiation, conclusion and implementation of international agreements in matters transferred to them by their Member States and covered by this Convention.

2. In their instruments of accession, such organizations shall declare the extent of their competence with respect to the matters governed by the Convention. These organizations shall also inform the Depositary Government of any substantial modification in the extent of their competence. Notifications by regional economic integration organizations concerning their competence with respect to matters governed by this Convention and modifications thereto shall be distributed to the Parties by the Depositary Government.

3. In matters within their competence, such regional integration organizations shall exercise the rights and fulfill the obligations which this Convention attributes to their Member States, which are Parties to the Convention. In such cases the Member States of the organizations shall not be entitled to exercise such rights individually.

4. In the fields of their competence, regional economic integration organizations shall exercise their right to vote with a number of votes equal to the number of their Member States which are Parties to the Convention. Such organizations shall not exercise their right to vote if their Member States exercise theirs, and *vice versa.*

5. Any reference to "Party" in the sense used in Article 1(h) of this Convention to "State"/"States" or to "State Party"/"States Parties" to the Convention shall be construed as including a reference to any regional economic integration organization having competence in respect of the negotiation, conclusion and application of international agreements in matters covered by this Convention.]**

** The paragraphs in square brackets are an amendment to the Convention which was adopted at an extraordinary meeting of the Conference of the Parties in Gaborone (Botswana) on 30 April 1983. The amendment is not yet in force. It will enter into force when it has been formally accepted by 54 of the 80 States which were Parties to the Convention on that date. By 31 December 1984 it had been accepted by 4 of those States.

Article XXII

ENTRY INTO FORCE

1.   The present Convention shall enter into force 90 days after the date of deposit of the tenth instrument of ratification, acceptance, approval or accession, with the Depositary Government.

2.   For each State which ratifies, accepts or approves the present Convention or accedes thereto after the deposit of the tenth instrument of ratification, acceptance, approval or accession, the present Convention shall enter into force 90 days after the deposit by such State of its instrument of ratification, acceptance, approval or accession.

Article XXIII

RESERVATIONS

1.   The provisions of the present Convention shall not be subject to general reservations. Specific reservations may be entered in accordance with the provisions of this Article and Articles XV and XVI.

2.   Any State may, on depositing its instrument of ratification, acceptance, approval or accession, enter a specific reservation with regard to:

   a)   any species included in Appendix I, II, III; or

   b)   any parts or derivatives specified in relation to a species included in Appendix III.

3.   Until a Party withdraws its reservation entered under the provisions of this Article, it shall be treated as a State not a Party to the present Convention with respect to trade in the particular species or parts or derivatives specifed in such reservation.

Article XXIV

DENUNCIATION

   Any Party may denounce the present Convention by written notification to the Depositary Government at any time. The denunciation shall take effect twelve months after the Depositary Government has received the notification.

Article XXV

DEPOSITARY

1. The original of the present Convention, in the Chinese, English, French, Russian and Spanish languages, each version being equally authentic, shall be deposited with the Depositary Government, which shall transmit certified copies thereof to all States that have signed it or deposited instruments of accession to it.

2. The Depositary Government shall inform all signatory and acceding States and the Secretariat of signatures, deposit of instruments of ratification, acceptance, approval or accession, entry into force of the present Convention, amendments thereto, entry and withdrawal of reservations and notifications of denunciation.

3. As soon as the present Convention enters into force, a certified copy thereof shall be transmitted by the Depositary Government to the Secretariat of the United Nations for registration and publication in accordance with Article 102 of the Charter of the United Nations.

IN WITNESS WHEREOF the undersigned Plenipotentiaries, being duly authorized to that effect, have signed the present Convention.

DONE at Washington this third day of March, One Thousand Nine Hundred and Seventy-three.

Author's note: The Appendices I, II, and III, which are subject to periodic changes, are not reproduced here but may be obtained from the CITES Secretariat, PO Box 78, 1000 Lausanne, Switzerland.

AGREEMENT ON THE CONSERVATION OF POLAR BEARS, 1973

THE GOVERNMENTS of Canada, Denmark, Norway, the Union of Soviet Socialist Republics, and the United States of America,

RECOGNIZING the special responsibilities and special interests of the States of the Arctic Region in relation to the protection of the fauna and flora of the Arctic Region;

RECOGNIZING that the polar bear is a significant resource of the Arctic Region which requires additional protection;

HAVING DECIDED that such protection should be achieved through co-ordinated national measures taken by the States of the Arctic Region;

DESIRING to take immediate action to bring further conservation and management measures into effect;

HAVE AGREED as follows:

Article I

1.   The taking of polar bears shall be prohibited except as provided in Article III.

2.   For the purposes of this Agreement, the term "taking" includes hunting, killing and capturing.

Article II

Each Contracting Party shall take appropriate action to protect the ecosystems of which polar bears are a part, with special attention to habitat components such as denning and feeding sites and migration patterns, and shall manage polar bear populations in accordance with sound conservation practices based on the best available scientific data.

Article III

1. Subject to the provisions of Articles II and IV, any Contracting Party may allow the taking of polar bears when such taking is carried out:

    a)   for *bona fide* scientific purposes; or

    b)   by that Party for conservation purposes; or

    c)   to prevent serious disturbance of the management of other living resources, subject to forfeiture to that Party of the skins and other items of value resulting from such taking; or

    d)   by local people using traditional methods in the exercise of their traditional rights and in accordance with the laws of that Party; or

    e)   wherever polar bears have or might have been subject to taking by traditional means by its nationals.

2. The skins and other items of value resulting from taking under sub-paragraphs *(b)* and *(c)* of paragraph 1 of this Article shall not be available for commercial purposes.

Article IV

The use of aircraft and large motorized vessels for the purpose of taking polar bears shall be prohibited, except where the application of such prohibition would be inconsistent with domestic laws.

Article V

A Contracting Party shall prohibit the exportation from, the importation and delivery into, and traffic within, its territory of polar bears or any part or product thereof taken in violation of this Agreement.

Article VI

1. Each Contracting Party shall enact and enforce such legislation and other measures as may be necessary for the purpose of giving effect to this Agreement.

2. Nothing in this Agreement shall prevent a Contracting Party from maintaining or amending existing legislation or other measures or establishing new measures on the taking of polar bears so as to provide more stringent controls than those required under the provisions of this Agreement.

Article VII

The Contracting Parties shall conduct national research programmes on polar bears, particularly research relating to the conservation and management of the species. They shall as appropriate co-ordinate such research with research carried out by other Parties, consult with other Parties on the management of migrating polar bear populations, and exchange information on research and management programmes, research results and data on bears taken.

Article VIII

Each Contracting Party shall take action as appropriate to promote compliance with the provisions of this Agreement by nationals of States not party to this Agreement.

Article IX

The Contracting Parties shall continue to consult with one another with the object of giving further protection to polar bears.

Article X

1. This Agreement shall be open for signature at Oslo by the Governments of Canada, Denmark, Norway, the Union of Soviet Socialist Republics and the United States of America until 31 March 1974.

2. This Agreement shall be subject to ratification or approval by the signatory Governments. Instruments of ratification or approval shall be deposited with the Government of Norway as soon as possible.

3. This Agreement shall be open for accession by the Governments referred to in paragraph 1 of this Article. Instruments of accession shall be deposited with the Depositary Government.

4. This Agreement shall enter into force ninety days after the deposit of the third instrument of ratification, approval or accession. Thereafter, it shall enter into force for a signatory or acceding Government on the date of deposit of its instrument of ratification, approval or accession.

5. This Agreement shall remain in force initially for a period of five years from its date of entry into force, and unless any Contracting Party during that period requests the termination of the Agreement at the end of that period, it shall continue in force thereafter.

6. On the request addressed to the Depositary Government by any of the Governments referred to in paragraph 1 of this Article, consultations shall be conducted with a view to convening a meeting of representatives of the five Governments to consider the revision or amendment of this Agreement.

7. Any Party may denounce this Agreement by written notification to the Depositary Government at any time after five years from the date of entry into force of this Agreement. The denunciation shall take effect twelve months after the Depositary Government has received the notification.

8. The Depositary Government shall notify the Governments referred to in paragraph 1 of this Article of the deposit of instruments of ratification, approval or accession, of the entry into force of this Agreement and of the receipt of notifications of denunciation and any other communications from a Contracting Party specifically provided for in this Agreement.

9. The original of this Agreement shall be deposited with the Government of Norway which shall deliver certified copies thereof to each of the Governments referred to in paragraph 1 of this Article.

10. The Depositary Government shall transmit certified copies of this Agreement to the Secretary-General of the United Nations for registration and publication in accordance with Article 102 of the Charter of the United Nations.

IN WITNESS WHEREOF the undersigned, being duly authorized by their Governments, have signed this Agreement.

DONE at Oslo, in the English and Russian languages, each text being equally authentic, this fifteenth day of November, 1973.

CONVENTION ON THE CONSERVATION OF MIGRATORY SPECIES OF WILD ANIMALS, 1979

The Contracting Parties,

RECOGNIZING that wild animals in their innumerable forms are an irreplaceable part of the earth's natural system which must be conserved for the good of mankind;

AWARE that each generation of man holds the resources of the earth for future generations and has an obligation to ensure that this legacy is conserved and, where utilized, is used wisely;

CONSCIOUS of the ever-growing value of wild animals from environmental, ecological, genetic, scientific, aesthetic, recreational, cultural, educational, social and economic points of view;

CONCERNED particularly with those species of wild animals that migrate across or outside national jurisdictional boundaries;

RECOGNIZING that the States are and must be the protectors of the migratory species of wild animals that live within or pass through their national jurisdictional boundaries;

CONVINCED that conservation and effective management of migratory species of wild animals require the concerted action of all States within the national jurisdictional boundaries of which such species spend any part of their life cycles;

RECALLING Recommendation 32 of the Action Plan adopted by the United Nations Conference on the Human Environment (Stockholm, 1972) and noted with satisfaction at the Twenty-seventh Session of the General Assembly of the United Nations;

HAVE AGREED as follows:

Article I

INTERPRETATION

1. For the purpose of this Convention:

    a) "Migratory species" means the entire population or any geographically separate part of the population of any species or lower taxon of wild animals, a significant proportion of whose members cyclically and predictably cross one or more national jurisdictional boundaries;

b) "Conservation status of a migratory species" means the sum of the influences acting on the migratory species that may affect its long-term distribution and abundance;

c) "Conservation status" will be taken as "favourable" when:

(1) population dynamics data indicate that the migratory species is maintaining itself on a long-term basis as a viable component of its ecosystems;

(2) the range of the migratory species is neither currently being reduced, nor is likely to be reduced, on a long-term basis;

(3) there is, and will be in the foreseeable future, sufficient habitat to maintain the population of the migratory species on a long-term basis; and

(4) the distribution and abundance of the migratory species approach historic coverage and levels to the extent that potentially suitable ecosystems exist and to the extent consistent with wise wildlife management;

d) "Conservation status" will be taken as "unfavourable" if any of the conditions set out in sub-paragraph (c) of this paragraph is not met;

e) "Endangered" in relation to a particular migratory species means that the migratory species is in danger of extinction throughout all or a significant portion of its range;

f) "Range" means all the areas of land or water that a migratory species inhabits, stays in temporarily, crosses or overflies at any time on its normal migration route;

g) "Habitat" means any area in the range of a migratory species which contains suitable living conditions for that species;

h) "Range State" in relation to a particular migratory species means any State (and where appropriate any other Party referred to under sub-paragraph (k) of this paragraph) that exercises jurisdiction over any part of the range of that migratory species, or a State, flag vessels of which are engaged outside national jurisdictional limits in taking that migratory species;

i) "Taking" means taking, hunting, fishing, capturing, harassing, deliberate killing, or attempting to engage in any such conduct;

j) "AGREEMENT" means an international agreement relating to the conservation of one or more migratory species as provided for in Articles IV and V of this Convention; and

k) "Party" means a State or any regional economic integration organization constituted by sovereign States which has competence in respect of the negotiation, conclusion and application of international agreements in matters covered by this Convention for which this Convention is in force.

2. In matters within their competence, the regional economic integration organizations which are Parties to this Convention shall in their own name exercise the rights and fulfil the responsibilities which this Convention attributes to their member States. In such cases the member States of these organizations shall not be entitled to exercise such rights individually.

3. Where this Convention provides for a decision to be taken by either a two-thirds majority or a unanimous decision of "the Parties present and voting" this shall mean "the Parties present and casting an affirmative or negative vote". Those abstaining from voting shall not be counted amongst "the Parties present and voting" in determining the majority.

Article II

FUNDAMENTAL PRINCIPLES

1. The Parties acknowledge the importance of migratory species being conserved and of Range States agreeing to take action to this end whenever possible and appropriate, paying special attention to migratory species the conservation status of which is unfavourable, and taking individually or in co-operation appropriate and necessary steps to conserve such species and their habitat.

2. The Parties acknowledge the need to take action to avoid any migratory species becoming endangered.

3. In particular, the Parties:

a) should promote, co-operate in and support research relating to migratory species;

b) shall endeavour to provide immediate protection for migratory species included in Appendix I; and

c) shall endeavour to conclude AGREEMENTS covering the conservation and management of migratory species included in Appendix II.

Article III

ENDANGERED MIGRATORY SPECIES: APPENDIX I

1.   Appendix I shall list migratory species which are endangered.

2.   A migratory species may be listed in Appendix I provided that reliable evidence, including the best scientific evidence available, indicates that the species is endangered.

3.   A migratory species may be removed from Appendix I when the Conference of the Parties determines that:

a) reliable evidence, including the best scientific evidence available, indicates that the species is no longer endangered, and

b) the species is not likely to become endangered again because of loss of protection due to its removal from Appendix I.

4.   Parties that are Range States of a migratory species listed in Appendix I shall endeavour:

a) to conserve and, where feasible and appropriate, restore those habitats of the species which are of importance in removing the species from danger of extinction;

b) to prevent, remove, compensate for or minimize, as appropriate, the adverse effects of activities or obstacles that seriously impede or prevent the migration of the species; and

c) to the extent feasible and appropriate, to prevent, reduce or control factors that are endangering or are likely to further endanger the species, including strictly controlling the introduction of, or controlling or eliminating, already introduced exotic species.

5.   Parties that are Range States of a migratory species listed in Appendix I shall prohibit the taking of animals belonging to such species. Exceptions may be made to this prohibition only if:

a) the taking is for scientific purposes;

b) the taking is for the purpose of enhancing the propagation or survival of the affected species;

c) the taking is to accommodate the needs of traditional subsistence users of such species; or

d) extraordinary circumstances so require;

provided that such exceptions are precise as to content and limited in space and time. Such taking should not operate to the disadvantage of the species.

6. The Conferences of the Parties may recommend to the Parties that are Range States of a migratory species listed in Appendix I that they take further measures considered appropriate to benefit the species.

7. The Parties shall as soon as possible inform the Secretariat of any exceptions made pursuant to paragraph 5 of this Article.

Article IV

MIGRATORY SPECIES TO BE THE SUBJECT TO AGREEMENTS: APPENDIX II

1. Appendix II shall list migratory species which have an unfavourable conservation status and which require international agreements for their conservation and management, as well as those which have a conservation status which would significantly benefit from the international co-operation that could be achieved by an international agreement.

2. If the circumstances so warrant, a migratory species may be listed both in Appendix I and Appendix II.

3. Parties that are Range States of migratory species listed in Appendix II shall endeavour to conclude AGREEMENTS where these would benefit the species and should give priority to those species in an unfavourable conservation status.

4. Parties are encouraged to take action with a view to concluding AGREEMENTS for any population or any geographically separate part of the population of any species or lower taxon of wild animals,

members of which periodically cross one or more national jurisdictional boundaries.

5. The Secretariat shall be provided with a copy of each AGREEMENT concluded pursuant to the provisions of this Article.

Article V

GUIDELINES FOR AGREEMENTS

1. The object of each AGREEMENT shall be to restore the migratory species concerned to a favourable conservation status or to maintain it in such a status. Each AGREEMENT should deal with those aspects of the conservation and management of the migratory species concerned which serve to achieve that object.

2. Each AGREEMENT should cover the whole of the range of the migratory species concerned and should be open to accession by all Range States of that species, whether or not they are Parties to this Convention.

3. An AGREEMENT should, wherever possible, deal with more than one migratory species.

4. Each AGREEMENT should:

    a) identify the migratory species covered;

    b) describe the range and migration route of the migratory species;

    c) provide for each Party to designate its national authority concerned with the implementation of the AGREEMENT;

    d) establish, if necessary, appropriate machinery to assist in carrying out the aims of the AGREEMENT, to monitor its effectiveness, and to prepare reports for the Conference of the Parties;

    e) provide for procedures for the settlement of disputes between Parties to the AGREEMENT; and

    f) at a minimum, prohibit, in relation to a migratory species of the Order Cetacea, any taking that is not permitted for that migratory species under any other multilateral agreement and provide for accession to the AGREEMENT by States that are not Range States of that migratory species.

5.   Where appropriate and feasible, each AGREEMENT should provide for but not be limited to:

a)   periodic review of the conservation status of the migratory species concerned and the identification of the factors which may be harmful to that status;

b)   co-ordinated conservation and management plans;

c)   research into the ecology and population dynamics of the migratory species concerned, with special regard to migration;

d)   the exchange of information on the migratory species concerned, special regard being paid to the exchange of the results of research and of relevant statistics;

e)   conservation and, where required and feasible, restoration of the habitats of importance in maintaining a favourable conservation status, and protection of such habitats from disturbances, including strict control of the introduction of, or control of already introduced, exotic species detrimental to the migratory species;

f) maintenance   of   a   network   of   suitable   habitats appropriately disposed in relation to the migration routes;

g)   where it appears desirable, the provision of new habitats favourable to the migratory species or reintroduction of the migratory species into favourable habitats;

h)   elimination of, to the maximum extent possible, or compensation for activities and obstacles which hinder or impede migration;

i)   prevention, reduction or control of the release into the habitat of the migratory species of substances harmful to that migratory species;

j)   measures based on sound ecological principles to control and manage the taking of the migratory species;

k)   procedures for co-ordinating action to suppress illegal taking;

l)   exchange of information on substantial threats to the migratory species;

m)   emergency procedures whereby conservation action would be considerably and rapidly strengthened when the conservation status of the migratory species is seriously affected; and

n) making the general public aware of the contents and aims of the AGREEMENT.

Article VI

RANGE STATES

1. A list of the Range States of migratory species listed in Appendices I and II shall be kept up to date by the Secretariat using information it has received from the Parties.

2. The Parties shall keep the Secretariat informed as to which of the migratory species listed in Appendices I and II they consider they are Range States, including provision of information on their flag vessels engaged outside national jurisdictional limits in taking the migratory species concerned and, where possible, future plans in respect of such taking.

3. The Parties which are Range States for migratory species listed in Appendix I or Appendix II should inform the Conference of the Parties through the Secretariat, at least six months prior to each ordinary meeting of the Conference, on measures that they are taking to implement the provisions of this Convention for these species.

Article VII

THE CONFERENCE OF THE PARTIES

1. The Conference of the Parties shall be the decision-making organ of this Convention.

2. The Secretariat shall call a meeting of the Conference of the Parties not later than two years after the entry into force of this Convention.

3. Thereafter the Secretariat shall convene ordinary meetings of the Conference of the Parties at intervals of not more than three years, unless the Conference decides otherwise, and extraordinary meetings at any time on the written request of at least one-third of the Parties.

4. The Conference of the Parties shall establish and keep under review the financial regulations of this Convention. The Conference of the Parties shall, at each of its ordinary meetings, adopt the budget for the next financial period. Each Party shall contribute to this budget according to a scale to be agreed upon by the Conference. Financial regulations, including the provisions on the budget and the scale of contributions as well as their modifications, shall be adopted by unanimous vote of the Parties present and voting.

5. At each of its meetings the Conference of the Parties shall review the implementation of this Convention and may in particular:

a) review and assess the conservation status of migratory species;

b) review the progress made towards the conservation of migratory species, especially those listed in Appendices I and II;

c) make such provision and provide such guidance as may be necessary to enable the Scientific Council and the Secretariat to carry out their duties;

d) receive and consider any reports presented by the Scientific Council, the Secretariat, any Party or any standing body established pursuant to an AGREEMENT;

e) make recommendations to the Parties for improving the conservation status of migratory species and review the progress being made under AGREEMENTS;

f) in those cases where an AGREEMENT has not been concluded, make recommendations for the convening of meetings of the Parties that are Range States of a migratory species or group of migratory species to discuss measures to improve the conservation status of the species;

g) make recommendations to the Parties for improving the effectiveness of this Convention; and

h) decide on any additional measure that should be taken to implement the objectives of this Convention.

6. Each meeting of the Conference of the Parties should determine the time and venue of the next meeting.

7.   Any meeting of the Conference of the Parties shall determine and adopt rules of procedure for that meeting. Decisions at a meeting of the Conference of the Parties shall require a two-thirds majority of the Parties present and voting, except where otherwise provided for by this Convention.

8.   The United Nations, its Specialized Agencies, the International Atomic Energy Agency, as well as any State not a party to this Convention and, for each AGREEMENT, the body designated by the parties to that AGREEMENT, may be represented by observers at meetings of the Conference of the Parties.

9.   Any agency or body technically qualified in protection, conservation and management of migratory species, in the following categories, which has informed the Secretariat of its desire to be represented at meetings of the Conference of the Parties by observers, shall be admitted unless at least one-third of the Parties present object:

> *a)*   international agencies or bodies, either governmental or non-governmental, and national governmental agencies and bodies; and
>
> *b)*   national non-governmental agencies or bodies which have been approved for this purpose by the State in which they are located.

Once admitted, these observers shall have the right to participate but not to vote.

Article VIII

THE SCIENTIFIC COUNCIL

1.   At its first meeting, the Conference of the Parties shall establish a Scientific Council to provide advice on scientific matters.

2.   Any Party may appoint a qualified expert as a member of the Scientific Council. In addition, the Scientific Council shall include as members qualified experts selected and appointed by the Conference of the Parties; the number of these experts, the criteria for their selection and the terms of their appointments shall be as determined by the Conference of the Parties.

3.   The Scientific Council shall meet at the request of the Secretariat as required by the Conference of the Parties.

4. Subject to the approval of the Conference of the Parties, the Scientific Council shall establish its own rules of procedure.

5. The Conference of the Parties shall determine the functions of the Scientific Council, which may include:

a) providing scientific advice to the Conference of the Parties, to the Secretariat, and, if approved by the Conference of the Parties, to any body set up under this Convention or an AGREEMENT or to any Party;

b) recommending research and the co-ordination of research on migratory species, evaluating the results of such research in order to ascertain the conservation status of migratory species and reporting to the Conference of the Parties on such status and measures for its improvement;

c) making recommendations to the Conference of the Parties as to the migratory species to be included in Appendices I or II, together with an indication of the range of such migratory species;

d) making recommendations to the Conference of the Parties as to specific conservation and management measures to be included in AGREEMENTS on migratory species; and

e) recommending to the Conference of the Parties solutions to problems relating to the scientific aspects of the implementation of this Convention, in particular with regard to the habitats of migratory species.

Article IX

THE SECRETARIAT

1. For the purposes of this Convention a Secretariat shall be established.

2. Upon entry into force of this Convention, the Secretariat is provided by the Executive Director of the United Nations Environment Programme. To the extent and in the manner he considers appropriate, he may be assisted by suitable inter-governmental and non-governmental, international or national agencies and bodies technically qualified in protection, conservation and management of wild animals.

3. If the United Nations Environment Programme is no longer able to provide the Secretariat, the Conference of the Parties shall make alternative arrangements for the Secretariat.

4. The functions of the Secretariat shall be:

   a) to arrange for and service meetings:

   (i)   of the Conference of the Parties, and

   (ii) of the Scientific Council;

   b) to maintain liaison with and promote liaison between the Parties, the standing bodies set up under AGREEMENTS and other international organizations concerned with migratory species;

   c) to obtain from any appropriate source reports and other information which will further the objectives and implementation of this Convention and to arrange for the appropriate dissemination of such information;

   d) to invite the attention of the Conference of the Parties to any matter pertaining to the objectives of this Convention;

   e) to prepare for the Conference of the Parties reports on the work of the Secretariat and on the implementation of this Convention;

   f) to maintain and publish a list of Range States of all migratory species included in Appendices I and II;

   g) to promote, under the direction of the Conference of the Parties, the conclusion of AGREEMENTS,

   h) to maintain and make available to the Parties a list of AGREEMENTS and, if so required by the Conference of the Parties, to provide any information on such AGREEMENTS;

   i) to maintain and publish a list of the recommendations made by the Conference of the Parties pursuant to sub-paragraphs (e), (f) and (g) of paragraph 5 of Article VII or of decisions made pursuant to sub-paragraph (h) of that paragraph;

   j) to provide for the general public information concerning this Convention and its objectives; and

   k) to perform any other function entrusted to it under this Convention or by the Conference of the Parties.

Article X

AMENDMENT OF THE CONVENTION

1. This Convention may be amended at any ordinary or extraordinary meeting of the Conference of the Parties.

2. Proposals for amendment may be made by any Party.

3. The text of any proposed amendment and the reasons for it shall be communicated to the Secretary at least one hundred and fifty days before the meeting at which it is to be considered and shall promptly be communicated by the Secretary to all Parties. Any comments on the text by the Parties shall be communicated to the Secretariat not less than sixty days before the meeting begins. The Secretariat shall, immediately after the last day for submission of comments, communicate to the Parties all comments submitted by that day.

4. Amendments shall be adopted by a two-thirds majority of Parties present and voting.

5. An amendment adopted shall enter into force for all Parties which have accepted it on the first day of the third month following the date on which two-thirds of the Parties have deposited an instrument of acceptance with the Depositary. For each Party which deposits an instrument of acceptance after the date on which two-thirds of the Parties have deposited an instrument of acceptance, the amendment shall enter into force for that Party on the first day of the third month following the deposit of its instrument of acceptance.

Article XI

AMENDMENT OF THE APPENDICES

1. Appendices I and II may be amended at any ordinary or extraordinary meeting of the Conference of the Parties.

2. Proposals for amendment may be made by any Party.

3. The text of any proposed amendment and the reasons for it, based on the best scientific evidence available, shall be communicated to the Secretariat at least 150 days before the meeting and shall promptly be communicated by the Secretariat to all Parties. Any comments on the text by the Parties shall be

communicated to the Secretariat not less than 60 days before the meeting begins. The Secretariat shall, immediately after the last day for submission of comments, communicate to the Parties all comments submitted by that day.

4.   Amendments shall be adopted by a two-thirds majority of Parties present and voting.

5.   An amendment to the Appendices shall enter into force for all Parties 90 days after the meeting of the Conference of the Parties at which it was adopted, except for those Parties which make a reservation in accordance with paragraph 6 of this Article.

6.   During the period of 90 days provided for in paragraph 5 of this Article, any Party may by notification in writing to the Depositary make a reservation with respect to the amendment. A reservation to an amendment may be withdrawn by written notification to the Depositary and thereupon the amendment shall enter into force for that Party 90 days after the reservation is withdrawn.

Article XII

EFFECT ON INTERNATIONAL CONVENTIONS AND OTHER LEGISLATION

1.   Nothing in this Convention shall prejudice the codification and development of the law of the sea by the United Nations Conference on the Law of the Sea convened pursuant to Resolution 2750 C (XXV) of the General Assembly of the United Nations nor the present or future claims and legal views of any State concerning the law of the sea and the nature and extent of coastal and flag State jurisdiction.

2.   The provisions of this Convention shall in no way affect the rights or obligations of any Party deriving from any existing treaty convention or agreement.

3.   The provisions of this Convention shall in no way affect the right of Parties to adopt stricter domestic measures concerning the conservation of migratory species listed in Appendices I and II or to adopt domestic measures concerning the conservation of species not listed in Appendices I and II.

Article XIII

SETTLEMENT OF DISPUTES

1.   Any dispute which may arise between two or more Parties with respect to the interpretation or application of the provisions of this Convention shall be subject to negotiation between the Parties involved in the dispute.

2.   If the dispute cannot be resolved in accordance with paragraph 1 of this Article, the Parties may, by mutual consent, submit the dispute to arbitration, in particular that of the Permanent Court of Arbitration at The Hague, and the Parties submitting the dispute shall be bound by the arbitral decision.

Article XIV

RESERVATIONS

1.   The provisions of this Convention shall not be subject to general reservations. Specific reservations may be entered in accordance with the provisions of this Article and Article XI.

2.   Any State or any regional economic integration organization may, on depositing its instrument of ratification, acceptance, approval or accession, enter a specific reservation with regard to the presence on either Appendix I or Appendix II or both, of any migratory species and shall then not be regarded as a Party in regard to the subject of that reservation until ninety days after the Depositary has transmitted to the Parties notification that such reservation has been withdrawn.

Article XV

SIGNATURE

This Convention shall be open for signature at Bonn for all States and any regional economic integration organization until the twenty-second day of June 1980.

Article XVI

RATIFICATION, ACCEPTANCE, APPROVAL

This Convention shall be subject to ratification, acceptance or approval. Instruments of ratification, acceptance or approval shall be deposited with the Government of the Federal Republic of Germany, which shall be the Depositary.

Article XVII

ACCESSION

After the twenty-second day of June 1980 this Convention shall be open for accession by all non-signatory States and any regional economic integration organization. Instruments of accession shall be deposited with the Depositary.

Article XVIII

ENTRY INTO FORCE

1.   This Convention shall enter into force on the first day of the third month following the date of deposit of the fifteenth instrument of ratification, acceptance, approval or accession with the Depositary.

2.   For each State or each regional economic intergration organization which ratifies, accepts or approves this Convention or accedes thereto after the deposit of the fifteenth instrument of ratification, acceptance, approval or accession, this Convention shall enter into force on the first day of the third month following the deposit by such State or such organization of its instrument of ratification, acceptance, approval or accession.

Article XIX

DENUNCIATION

Any Party may denounce this Convention by written notification to the Depositary at any time. The denunciation shall take effect twelve months after the Depositary has received the notification.

Article XX

DEPOSITARY

1.   The original of this Convention, in the English, French, German, Russian and Spanish languages, each version being equally authentic, shall be deposited with the Depositary. The Depositary shall transmit certified copies of each of these versions to all States and all regional economic integration organizations that have signed the Convention or deposited instruments of accession to it.

2. The Depositary shall, after consultation with the Governments concerned, prepare official versions of the text of this Convention in the Arabic and Chinese languages.

3. The Depositary shall inform all signatory and acceding States and all signatory and acceding regional economic integration organizations and the Secretariat of signatures, deposit of instruments of ratification, acceptance, approval or accession, entry into force of this Convention, amendments thereto, specific reservations and notifications of denunciation.

4. As soon as this Convention enters into force, a certified copy thereof shall be transmitted by the Depositary to the Secretariat of the United Nations for registration and publication in accordance with Article 102 of the Charter of the United Nations.

IN WITNESS WHEREOF the undersigned, being duly authorized to the effect, have signed the present Convention.

DONE at Bonn, this 23rd day of June 1979.

Author's note: The Appendices I and II, which are subject to periodic changes, are not reproduced here but may be obtained from the Federal Ministry of Food, Agriculture and Forestry, Bonn, Federal Republic of Germany.

CONVENTION ON THE CONSERVATION OF EUROPEAN WILDLIFE AND NATURAL HABITATS, 1979

PREAMBLE

The Member States of the Council of Europe and the other signatories hereto,

CONSIDERING that the aim of the Council of Europe is to achieve a greater unity between its members;

CONSIDERING the wish of the Council of Europe to co-operate with other States in the field of nature conservation;

RECOGNIZING that wild flora and fauna constitute a natural heritage of aesthetic, scientific, cultural, recreational, economic and intrinsic value that needs to be preserved and handed on to future generations;

RECOGNIZING the essential role played by wild flora and fauna in maintaining biological balances;

NOTING that numerous species of wild flora and fauna are being seriously depleted and that some of them are threatened with extinction;

AWARE that the conservation of natural habitats is a vital component of the protection and conservation of wild flora and fauna;

RECOGNIZING that the conservation of wild flora and fauna should be taken into consideration by the governments in their national goals and programmes, and that international co-operation should be established to protect migratory species in particular;

BEARING in mind the widespread requests for common action made by governments or by international bodies, in particular the requests expressed by the United Nations Conference on the Human Environment 1972 and the Consultative Assembly of the Council of Europe;

DESIRING particularly to follow, in the field of wildlife conservation, the recommendations of Resolution No. 2 of the Second

European Ministerial Conference on the Environment;

HAVE AGREED as follows:

Chapter I
GENERAL PROVISIONS

Article 1

1.   The aims of this Convention are to conserve wild flora and fauna and their natural habitats, especially those species and habitats whose conservation requires the co-operation of several States, and to promote such co-operation.

2.   Particular emphasis is given to endangered and vulnerable species, including endangered and vulnerable migratory species.

Article 2

The Contracting Parties shall take requisite measures to maintain the population of wild flora and fauna at, or adapt it to, a level which corresponds in particular to ecological, scientific and cultural requirements, while taking account of economic and recreational requirements and the needs of sub-species, varieties or forms at risk locally.

Article 3

1.   Each Contracting Party shall take steps to promote national policies for the conservation of wild flora, wild fauna and natural habitats, with particular attention to endangered and vulnerable species, especially endemic ones, and endangered habitats, in accordance with the provisions of this Convention.

2.   Each Contracting Party undertakes, in its planning and development policies and in its measures against pollution, to have regard to the conservation of wild flora and fauna.

3.   Each Contracting Party shall promote education and disseminate general information on the need to conserve species of wild flora and fauna and their habitats.

Chapter II

PROTECTION OF HABITATS

Article 4

1. Each Contracting Party shall take appropriate and necessary legislative and administrative measures to ensure the conservation of the habitats of the wild flora and fauna species, especially those specified in the Appendices I and II, and the conservation of endangered natural habitats.

2. The Contracting Parties in their planning and development policies shall have regard to the conservation requirements of the areas protected under the preceding paragraph, so as to avoid or minimise as far as possible any deterioration of such areas.

3. The Contracting Parties undertake to give special attention to the protection of areas that are of importance for the migratory species specified in Appendices II and III and which are appropriately situated in relation to migration routes, as wintering, staging, feeding, breeding or moulting areas.

4. The Contracting Parties undertake to co-ordinate as appropriate their efforts for the protection of the natural habitats referred to in this Article when these are situated in frontier areas.

Chapter III

PROTECTION OF SPECIES

Article 5

Each Contracting Party shall take appropriate and necessary legislative and administrative measures to ensure the special protection of the wild flora species specified in Appendix I. Deliberate picking, collecting, cutting or uprooting of such plants shall be prohibited. Each Contracting Party shall, as apropriate, prohibit the possession or sale of these species.

Article 6

Each Contracting Party shall take appropriate and necessary legislative and administrative measures to ensure the special protection of the wild fauna species specified in Appendix II. The following will in particular be prohibited for these species:

a) all forms of deliberate capture and keeping and deliberate killing;

b) the deliberate damage to or destruction of breeding or resting sites;

c) the deliberate disturbance of wild fauna, particularly during the period of breeding, rearing and hibernation, insofar as disturbance would be significant in relation to the objectives of this Convention;

d) the deliberate destruction or taking of eggs from the wild or keeping these eggs even if empty;

e) the possession of and internal trade in these animals, alive or dead, including stuffed animals and any readily recognizable part or derivative thereof, where this would contribute to the effectiveness of the provisions of this Article.

Article 7

1. Each Contracting Party shall take appropriate and necessary legislative and administrative measures to ensure the protection of the wild fauna species specified in Appendix III.

2. Any exploitation of wild fauna specified in Appendix III shall be regulated in order to keep the populations out of danger, taking into account the requirements of Article 2.

3. Measures to be taken shall include:

a) closed seasons and/or other procedures regulating the exploitation;

b) the temporary or local prohibition of exploitation, as appropriate, in order to restore satisfactory population levels;

c) the regulation as appropriate of sale, keeping for sale, transport for sale or offering for sale of live and dead wild animals.

Article 8

In respect of the capture or killing of wild fauna species specified in Appendix III and in cases where, in accordance with Article 9, exceptions are applied to species specified in Appendix II, Contracting Parties shall prohibit the use of all indiscriminate means of capture and killing and the use of all means capable of causing local disappearance of, or serious disturbance to, populations of a species, and in particular, the means specified in Appendix IV.

Article 9

1. Each Contracting Party may make exceptions from the provisions of Articles 4, 5, 6, 7 and from the prohibition of the use of the means mentioned in Article 8 provided that there is no other satisfactory solution and that the exception will not be detrimental to the survival of the population concerned:

—— for the protection of flora and fauna;

—— to prevent serious damage to crops, livestock, forests, fisheries, water and other forms of property;

-    in the interests of public health and safety, air safety or other overriding public interests;

—— for the purposes of research and education, of repopulation, of reintroduction and for the necessary breeding;

—— to permit, under strictly supervised conditions, on a selective basis and to a limited extent, the taking, keeping or other judicious exploitation of certain wild animals and plants in small numbers.

2. The Contracting Parties shall report every two years to the Standing Committee on the exceptions made under the preceding paragraph. These reports must specify:

—— the populations which are or have been subject to the exceptions and, when practical, the number of specimens involved;

—— the means authorised for the killing or capture;

—— the conditions of risk and the circumstances of time and place under which such exceptions were granted;

—— the authority empowered to declare that these conditions have been fulfilled, and to take decisions in respect of the means that may be used, their limits and the persons instructed to carry them out;

—— the controls involved.

Chapter IV

SPECIAL PROVISIONS FOR MIGRATORY SPECIES

Article 10

1. The Contracting Parties undertake, in addition to the measures specified in Articles 4, 6, 7 and 8, to co-ordinate their efforts for the protection of the migratory species specified in Appendices II and III whose range extends into their territories.

2. The Contracting Parties shall take measures to seek to ensure that the closed seasons and/or other procedures regulating the exploitation established under paragraph 3.*a* of Article 7 are adequate and approximately disposed to meet the requirements of the migratory species specified in Appendix III.

Chapter V

SUPPLEMENTARY PROVISIONS

Article 11

1. In carrying out the provisions of the Convention, the Contracting Parties undertake:

> *a)* to co-operate whenever appropriate and in particular where this would enhance the effectiveness of measures taken under other articles of this Convention;
>
> *b)* to encourage and co-ordinate research related to the purposes of this Convention.

2. Each Contracting Party undertakes:

> *a)* to encourage the reintroduction of native species of wild flora and fauna when this would contribute to the conservation of an endangered species, provided that a study is first made in the light of the experiences of other Contracting Parties to establish that such reintroduction would be effective and acceptable;
>
> *b)* to strictly control the introduction of non-native species.

3. Each Contracting Party shall inform the Standing Committee of the species receiving complete protection on its territory and not included in Appendices I and II.

Article 12

The Contracting Parties may adopt stricter measures for the conservation of wild flora and fauna and their natural habitats than those provided under this Convention.

Chapter VI

STANDING COMMITTEE

Article 13

1. For the purposes of this Convention, a Standing Committee shall be set up.

2. Any Contracting Party may be represented on the Standing Committee by one or more delegates. Each delegation shall have one vote. Within the areas of its competence, the European Economic Community shall exercise its right to vote with a number of votes equal to the number of its member States which are Contracting Parties to this Convention; the European Economic Community shall not exercise its right to vote in cases where the member States concerned exercise theirs, and conversely.

3. Any member State of the Council of Europe which is not a Contracting Party to the Convention may be represented on the Committee as an observer.

The Standing Committee may, by unanimous decision, invite any non-member State of the Council of Europe which is not a Contracting Party to the Convention to be represented by an observer at one of its meetings.

Any body or agency technically qualified in the protection, conservation or management of wild fauna and flora and their habitats, and belonging to one of the following categories:

> *a)* international agencies or bodies, either governmental or non-governmental, and national governmental agencies or bodies;

> *b)* national non-governmental agencies or bodies which have been approved for this purpose by the State in which they are located,

may inform the Secretary-General of the Council of Europe, at least three months before the meeting of the Committee, of its wish to be represented at that meeting by observers. They shall be admitted unless, at least one month before the meeting, one-third of the Contracting Parties have informed the Secretary General of their objection.

4.   The Standing Committee shall be convened by the Secretary General of the Council of Europe. Its first meeting shall be held within one year of the date of the entry into force of the Convention. It shall subsequently meet at least every two years and whenever a majority of the Contracting Parties so request.

5.   A majority of the Contracting Parties shall constitute a quorum for holding a meeting of the Standing Committee.

6.   Subject to the provisions of the Convention, the Standing Committee shall draw up its own Rules of Procedure.

Article 14

1.   The Standing Committee shall be responsible for following the application of this Convention. It may in particular:

—— keep under review the provisions of this Convention, including its Appendices, and examine any modifications necessary;

—— make recommendations to the Contracting Parties concerning measures to be taken for the purposes of this Convention;

—— recommend the appropriate measures to keep the public informed about the activities undertaken within the framework of this Convention;

—— make recommendations to the Committee of Ministers concerning non-member States of the Council of Europe to be invited to accede to this Convention;

—— make any proposal for improving the effectiveness of this Convention, including proposals for the conclusion, with the States which are not Contracting Parties to the Convention, of agreements that would enhance the effective conservation of species or groups of species.

2.   In order to discharge its functions, the Standing Committee may, on its own initiative, arrange for meetings of groups of experts.

Article 15

After each meeting, the Standing Committee shall forward to the Committee of Ministers of the Council of Europe a report on its work and on the functioning of the Convention.

Chapter VII

AMENDMENTS

Article 16

1.   Any amendment to the articles of this Convention proposed by a Contracting Party or the Committee of Ministers shall be communicated to the Secretary General of the Council of Europe and forwarded by him at least two months before the meeting of the Standing Committee to the member States of the Council of Europe, to any signatory, to any Contracting Party, to any State invited to sign this Convention in accordance with the provisions of Article 19 and to any State invited to accede to it in accordance with the provisions of Article 20.

2.   Any amendment proposed in accordance with the provisions of the preceding paragraph shall be examined by the Standing Committee which:

   a) for amendments to Articles 1 to 12, shall submit the text adopted by a three-quarters majority of the votes cast of the Contracting Parties for acceptance;

   b) for amendments to Articles 13 to 24, shall submit the text adopted by a three-quarters majority of the votes cast to the Committee of Ministers for approval. After its approval, this text shall be forwarded to the Contracting Parties for acceptance.

3.   Any amendment shall enter into force on the thirtieth day after all the Contracting Parties have informed the Secretary General that they have accepted it.

4.   The provisions of paragraphs 1, 2.*a* and 3 of this Article shall apply to the adoption of new Appendices to this Convention.

Article 17

1.   Any amendment to the Appendices of this Convention proposed by a Contracting Party or the Committee of Ministers shall be communicated to the Secretary General of the Council of Europe and forwarded by him at least two months before the meeting of the Standing Committee to the member States of the Council of Europe, to any signatory, to any Contracting Party, to any State invited to sign this Convention in accordance with the provisions of Article 19 and to any State invited to accede to it in accordance with the provisions of Article 20.

2.   Any amendment proposed in accordance with the provisions of the preceding paragraph shall be examined by the Standing Committee, which may adopt it by a two-thirds majority of the Contracting Parties. The text adopted shall be forwarded to the Contracting Parties.

3.   Three months after its adoption by the Standing Committee and unless one-third of the Contracting Parties have notified objections, any amendment shall enter into force for those Contracting Parties which have not notified objections.

Chapter VIII

SETTLEMENT OF DISPUTES

Article 18

1.   The Standing Committee shall use its best endeavours to facilitate a friendly settlement of any difficulty to which the execution of this Convention may give rise.

2.   Any dispute between Contracting Parties concerning the interpretation or application of this Convention which has not been settled on the basis of the provisions of the preceding paragraph or by negotiation between the parties concerned shall, unless the said parties agree otherwise, be submitted, at the request of one of them, to arbitration. Each party shall designate an arbitrator and the two arbitrators shall designate a third arbitrator. Subject to the provisions of paragraph 3 of this Article, if one of the parties has not designated its arbitrator within the three months following the request for arbitration, he shall be designated at the request of the other party by the President of the European Court of Human

Rights within a further three months period. The same procedure shall be observed if the arbitrators cannot agree on the choice of the third arbitrator within the three months following the designation of the two first arbitrators.

3.   In the event of a dispute between two Contracting Parties one of which is a member State of the European Economic Community, the latter itself being a Contracting Party, the other Contracting Party shall address the request for arbitration both to the member State and to the Community, which jointly, shall notify it, within two months of receipt of the request, whether the member State or the Community, or the member and the Community jointly, shall be party to the dispute. In the absence of such notification within the said time limit, the member State and the Community shall be considered as being one and the same party to the dispute for the purposes of the application of the provisions governing the constitution and procedure of the arbitration tribunal. The same shall apply when the member State and the Community jointly present themselves as party to the dispute.

4.   The arbitration tribunal shall draw up its own Rule of Procedure. Its decisions shall be taken by majority vote. Its award shall be final and binding.

5.   Each party to the dispute shall bear the expenses of the arbitrator designated by it and the parties shall share equally the expenses of the third arbitrator, as well as other costs entailed by the arbitration.

Chapter IX

FINAL PROVISIONS

Article 19

1.   This Convention shall be open for signature by the member States of the Council of Europe and non-member States which have participated in its elaboration and by the European Economic Community.

Up until the date when the Convention enters into force, it shall also be open for signature by any other State so invited by the Committee of Ministers.

The Convention is subject to ratification, acceptance or approval. Instruments of ratification, acceptance or approval shall be deposited with the Secretary General of the Council of Europe.

2.   The Convention shall enter into force on the first day of the month following the expiry of a period of three months after the date on which five States, including at least four member States of the Council of Europe, have expressed their consent to be bound by the Convention in accordance with the provisions of the preceding paragraph.

3.   In respect of any signatory State or the European Economic Community which subsequently express their consent to be bound by it, the Convention shall enter into force on the first day of the month following the expiry of a period of three months after the date of the deposit of the instrument of ratification, acceptance or approval.

Article 20

1.   After the entry into force of this Convention, the Committee of Ministers of the Council of Europe, after consulting the Contracting Parties, may invite to accede to the Convention any non-member State of the Council which, invited to sign in accordance with the provisions of Article 19, has not yet done so, and any other non-member State.

2.   In respect of any acceding State, the Convention shall enter into force on the first day of the month following the expiry of a period of three months after the date of the deposit of the instrument of accession with the Secretary General of the Council of Europe.

Article 21

1.   Any State may, at the time of signature or when depositing its instrument of ratification, acceptance, approval or accession, specify the territory or territories to which this Convention shall apply.

2.   Any Contracting Party may, when depositing its instrument of ratification, acceptance, approval or accession or at any later date, by declaration addressed to the Secretary General of the Council of Europe, extend the application of this Convention to any other territory specified in the declaration and for whose international relations it is responsible or on whose behalf it is authorized to give undertakings.

3.   Any declaration made under the preceding paragraph may, in respect of any territory mentioned in such declaration, be withdrawn by notification addressed to the Secretary General. Such withdrawal shall become effective on the first day of the month following the expiry of a period of six months after the date of receipt of the notification by the Secretary General.

Article 22

1.   Any State may, at the time of signature or when depositing its instrument of ratification, acceptance, approval or accession, make one or more reservations regarding certain species specified in Appendices I to III and/or, for certain species mentioned in the reservation or reservations, regarding certain means or methods of killing, capture and other exploitation listed in Appendix IV. No reservations of a general nature may be made.

2.   Any Contracting Party which extends the application of this Convention to a territory mentioned in the declaration referred to in paragraph 2 of Article 21 may, in respect of the territory concerned, make one or more reservations in accordance with the provisions of the preceding paragraph.

3.   No other reservation may be made.

4.   Any Contracting Party which has made a reservation under paragraph 1 and 2 of this Article may wholly or partly withdraw it by means of a notification addressed to the Secretary General or the Council of Europe. Such withdrawal shall take effect as from the date of receipt of the notification by the Secretary General.

Article 23

1.   Any Contracting Party may, at any time, denounce this Convention by means of a notification addressed to the Secretary General of the Council of Europe.

2.   Such denunciation shall become effective on the first day of the month following the expiry of a period of six months after the date of receipt of the notification by the Secretary General.

Article 24

The Secretary General of the Council of Europe shall notify the member States of the Council of Europe, any signatory State, the

European Economic Community if a signatory of this Convention and any Contracting Party of:

a)   any signature;

b)   the deposit of any instrument of ratification, acceptance, approval or accession;

c)   any date of entry into force of this Convention in accordance with Articles 19 and 20;

d)   any information forwarded under the provisions of paragraph 3 of Article 13;

e)   any report established in pursuance of the provisions of Article 15;

f)   any amendment or any new Appendix adopted in accordance with Articles 16 and 17 and the date on which the amendment or new Appendix comes into force;

g)   any declaration made under the provisions of paragraphs 2 and 3 of Article 21;

h)   any reservation made under the provisions of paragraphs 1 and 2 of Article 22;

i)   the withdrawal of any reservation carried out under the provisions of paragaph 4 of Article 22;

j)   any notification made under the provisions of Article 23 and the date on which the denunciation takes effect.

IN WITNESS WHEREOF the undersigned, being duly authorised thereto, have signed this Convention.

DONE at Bern, this 19th day of September 1979, in English and French, both texts being equally authentic, in a single copy which shall be deposited in the archives of the Council of Europe. The Secretary General of the Council of Europe shall transmit certified copies to each member State of the Council of Europe, to any signatory State, to the European Economic Community if a signatory and to any State invited to sign this Convention or to accede thereto.

Author's note: The Appendices I, II, III and IV, which are subject to periodic changes, are not reproduced here but may be obtained from the Council of Europe, Strasbourg, France.

CONVENTION ON THE CONSERVATION OF ANTARCTIC MARINE LIVING RESOURCES, 1980

The Contracting Parties,

RECOGNISING the importance of safeguarding the environment and protecting the integrity of the ecosystem of the seas surrounding Antarctica;

NOTING the concentration of marine living resources found in Antarctic waters and the increased interest in the possibilities offered by the utilization of these resources as a source of protein;

CONSCIOUS of the urgency of ensuring the conservation of Antarctic marine living resources;

CONSIDERING that it is essential to increase knowledge of the Antarctic marine ecosystem and its components so as to be able to base decisions on harvesting on sound scientific information;

BELIEVING that the conservation of Antarctic marine living resources calls for international co-operation with due regard for the provisions of the Antarctic Treaty and with the active involvement of all States engaged in research or harvesting activities in Antarctic waters;

RECOGNISING the prime responsibilities of the Antarctic Treaty Consultative Parties for the protection and preservation of the Antarctic environment and, in particular, their responsibilities under Article IX, paragraph l(f) of the Antarctic Treaty in respect of the preservation and conservation of living resources in Antarctica;

RECALLING the action already taken by the Antarctic Treaty Consultative Parties including in particular the Agreed Measures for the Conservation of Antarctic Fauna and Flora, as well as the provisions of the Convention for the Conservation of Antarctic Seals;

BEARING in mind the concern regarding the conservation of Antarctic marine living resources expressed by the Consultative Parties at the Ninth Consultative Meeting of the Antarctic Treaty and the importance of the provisions of Recommendation IX-2 which led to the establishment of the present Convention;

BELIEVING that it is in the interest of all mankind to preserve the waters surrounding the Antarctic continent for peaceful purposes only and to prevent their becoming the scene or object of international discord;

RECOGNISING, in the light of the foregoing, that it is desirable to establish suitable machinery for recommending, promoting, deciding upon and coordinating the measures and scientific studies needed to ensure the conservation of Antarctic marine living organisms;

HAVE AGREED as follows:

Article I

1.   This Convention applies to the Antarctic marine living resources of the area south of 60° South latitude and to the Antarctic marine living resources of the area between that latitude and the Antarctic Convergence which form part of the Antarctic marine ecosystem.

2.   Antarctic marine living resources means the populations of fin fish, molluscs, crustaceans and all other species of living organisms, including birds, found south of the Antarctic Convergence.

3.   The Antarctic marine ecosystem means the complex of relationships of Antarctic marine living resources with each other and with their physical environment.

4.   The Antarctic Convergence shall be deemed to be a line joining the following points along parallels of latitude and meridians of longitude: 50°S, 0°; 50°S, 30°E; 45°S, 30°E; 45°S, 80°E; 55°S, 80°E; 55°S, 150°E; 60°S, 150°E; 60°S, 50°W; 50°S, 50°W; 50°S, 0°.

Article II

1.   The objective of this Convention is the conservation of Antarctic marine living resources.

2.   For the purposes of this Convention, the term "conservation" includes rational use.

3.   Any harvesting and associated activities in the area to which this Convention applies shall be conducted in accordance with the provisions of this Convention and with the following principles of conservation:

    a)   prevention of decrease in the size of any harvested population to levels below those which ensure its stable recruitment. For this purpose its size should not be allowed to fall below a level close to that which ensures the greatest net annual increment;

b) maintenance of the ecological relationships between harvested, dependent and related populations of Antarctic marine living resources and the restoration of depleted populations to the levels defined in sub-paragraph *a)* above;

and

c) prevention of changes or minimization of the risk of changes in the marine ecosystem which are not potentially reversible over two or three decades, taking into account the state of available knowledge of the direct and indirect impact of harvesting, the effect of the introduction of alien species, the effects of associated activities on the marine ecosystem and of the effects of environmental changes, with the aim of making possible the sustained conservation of Antarctic marine living resources.

Article III

The Contracting Parties, whether or not they are Parties to the Antarctic Treaty, agree that they will not engage in any activities in the Antarctic Treaty area contrary to the principles and purposes of that Treaty and that, in their relations with each other, they are bound by the obligations contained in Articles I and V of the Antarctic Treaty.

Article IV

1.   With respect to the Antarctic Treaty area, all Contracting Parties, whether or not they are Parties to the Antarctic Treaty, are bound by Articles IV and VI of the Antarctic Treaty in their relations with each other.

2.   Nothing in this Convention and no acts or activities taking place while the present Convention is in force shall:

a)   constitute a basis for asserting, supporting or denying a claim to territorial sovereignty in the Antarctic Treaty area or create any rights of sovereignty in the Antarctic Treaty area;

b)   be interpreted as a renunciation or diminution by any Contracting Party of, or as prejudicing, any right or claim or basis of claim to exercise coastal state jurisdiction under international law within the area to which this Convention applies;

c) be interpreted as prejudicing the position of any Contracting Party as regards its recognition or non-recognition of any such right, claim or basis of claim;

d) affect the provision of Article IV, paragraph 2, of the Antarctic Treaty that no new claim, or enlargement of an existing claim, to territorial sovereignty in Antarctica shall be asserted while the Antarctic Treaty is in force.

Article V

1. The Contracting Parties which are not Parties to the Antarctic Treaty acknowledge the special obligations and responsibilities of the Antarctic Treaty Consultative Parties for the protection and preservation of the environment of the Antarctic Treaty area.

2. The Contracting Parties which are not Parties to the Antarctic Treaty agree that, in their activities in the Antarctic Treaty area, they will observe as and when appropriate the Agreed Measures for the Conservation of Antarctic Fauna and Flora and such other measures as have been recommended by the Antarctic Treaty Consultative Parties in fulfilment of their responsibility for the protection of the Antarctic environment from all forms of harmful human interference.

3. For the purposes of this Convention, "Antarctic Treaty Consultative Parties" means the Contracting Parties to the Antarctic Treaty whose Representatives participate in meetings under Article IX of the Antarctic Treaty.

Article VI

Nothing in this Convention shall derogate from the rights and obligations of Contracting Parties under the International Convention for the Regulation of Whaling and the Convention for the Conservation of Antarctic Seals.

Article VII

1. The Contracting Parties hereby establish and agree to maintain the Commission for the Conservation of Antarctic Marine Living Resources (hereinafter referred to as "the Commission").

2.   Membership in the Commission shall be as follows:

a)   each Contracting Party which participated in the meeting at which this Convention was adopted shall be a Member of the Commission;

b)   each State Party which has acceded to this Convention pursuant to Article XXIX shall be entitled to be a Member of the Commission during such time as that acceding party is engaged in research or harvesting activities in relation to the marine living resources to which this Convention applies;

c)   each regional economic integration organization which has acceded to this Convention pursuant to Article XXIX shall be entitled to be a Member of the Commission during such time as its States members are so entitled;

d)   a Contracting Party seeking to participate in the work of the Commission pursuant to sub-paragraphs *b)* and *c)* above shall notify the Depositary of the basis upon which it seeks to become a Member of the Commission and of its willingness to accept conservation measures in force. The Depositary shall communicate to each Member of the Commission such notification and accompanying information. Within two months of receipt of such communication from the Depositary, any Member of the Commission may request that a special meeting of the Commission be held to consider the matter. Upon receipt of such request, the Depositary shall call such a meeting. If there is no request for a meeting, the Contracting Party submitting the notification shall be deemed to have satisfied the requirements for Commission Membership.

3.   Each Member of the Commission shall be represented by one representative who may be accompanied by alternate representatives and advisers.

Article VIII

The Commission shall have legal personality and shall enjoy in the territory of each of the States Parties such legal capacity as may be necessary to perform its function and achieve the purposes of this Convention. The privileges and immunities to be enjoyed by the Commission and its staff in the territory of a State Party shall be determined by agreement between the Commission and the State Party concerned.

Article IX

1.   The function of the Commission shall be to give effect to the objective and principles set out in Article II of this Convention. To this end, it shall:

a)   facilitate research into and comprehensive studies of Antarctic marine living resources and of the Antarctic marine ecosystem;

b)   compile data on the status of and changes in population of Antarctic marine living resources and on factors affecting the distribution, abundance and productivity of harvested species and dependent or related species or populations;

c)   ensure the acquisition of catch and effort statistics on harvested populations;

d)   analyse, disseminate and publish the information referred to in sub-paragraphs b) and c) above and the reports of the Scientific Committee;

e)   identify conservation needs and analyse the effectiveness of conservation measures;

f)   formulate, adopt and revise conservation measures on the basis of the best scientific evidence available, subject to the provisions of paragraph 5 of this Article;

g)   implement the system of observation and inspection established under Article XXIV of this Convention;

h)   carry out such other activities as are necessary to fulfil the objective of this Convention.

2.   The conservation measures referred to in paragraph f) above include the following:

a)   the designation of the quantity of any species which may be harvested in the area to which this Convention applies;

b)   the designation of regions and sub-regions based on the distribution of populations of Antarctic marine living resources;

c)   the designation of the quantity which may be harvested from the populations of regions and sub-regions;

d)   the designation of protected species;

e)   the designation of the size, age and, as appropriate, sex of species which may be harvested;

f)   the designation of open and closed seasons for harvesting;

g)   the designation of the opening and closing of areas, regions or sub-regions for purposes of scientific study or conservation, including special areas for protection and scientific study;

h)   regulation of the effort employed and methods of harvesting, including fishing gear, with a view, *inter alia*, to avoiding undue concentration of harvesting in any region or sub-region;

i)   the taking of such other conservation measures as the Commission considers necessary for the fulfilment of the objective of this Convention, including measures concerning the effects of harvesting and associated activities on components of the marine ecosystem other than the harvested populations.

3.   The Commission shall publish and maintain a record of all conservation measures in force.

4.   In exercising its functions under paragraph 1 above, the Commission shall take full account of the recommendations and advice of the Scientific Committee.

5.   The Commission shall take full account of any relevant measures or regulations established or recommended by the Consultative Meetings pursuant to Article IX of the Antarctic Treaty or by existing fisheries commissions responsible for species which may enter the area to which this Convention applies, in order that there shall be no inconsistency between the rights and obligations of a Contracting Party under such regulations or measures and conservation measures which may be adopted by the Commission.

6.   Conservation measures adopted by the Commission in accordance with this Convention shall be implemented by Members of the Commission in the following manner:

a)   the Commission shall notify conservation measures to all Members of the Commission;

b) conservation measures shall become binding upon all Members of the Commission 180 days after such notification, except as provided in sub-paragraphs *c)* and *d)* below;

c) if a Member of the Commission, within ninety days following the notification specified in sub-paragraph *a)*, notifies the Commission that it is unable to accept the conservation measure, in whole or in part, the measure shall not, to the extent stated, be binding upon that Member of the Commission;

d) in the event that any Member of the Commission invokes the procedure set forth in sub-paragraph *c)* above, the Commission shall meet at the request of any Member of the Commission to review the conservation measure. At the time of such meeting and within thirty days following the meeting, any Member of the Commission shall have the right to declare that it is no longer able to accept the conservation measure, in which case the Member shall no longer be bound by such measure.

Article X

1. The Commission shall draw the attention of any State which is not a Party to this Convention to any activity undertaken by its nationals or vessels which, in the opinion of the Commission, affects the implementation of the objective of this Convention.

2. The Commission shall draw the attention of all Contracting Parties to any activity which, in the opinion of the Commission, affects the implementation by a Contracting Party of the objective of this Convention or the compliance by that Contracting Party with its obligations under this Convention.

Article XI

The Commission shall seek to cooperate with Contracting Parties which may exercise jurisdiction in marine areas adjacent to the area to which this Convention applies in respect of the conservation of any stock or stocks of associated species which occur both within those areas and the area to which this Convention applies, with a view to harmonizing the conservation measures adopted in respect of such stocks.

Article XII

1.   Decisions of the Commission on matters of substance shall be taken by consensus. The question of whether a matter is one of substance shall be treated as a matter of substance.

2.   Decisions on matters other than those referred to in paragraph 1 above shall be taken by a simple majority of the Members of the Commission present and voting.

3.   In Commission consideration of any item requiring a decision, it shall be made clear whether a regional economic integration organization will participate in the taking of the decision and, if so, whether any of its member States will also participate. The number of Contracting Parties so participating shall not exceed the number of member States of the regional economic integration organization which are members of the Commission.

4.   In the taking of decisions pursuant to this Article, a regional economic integration organization shall have only one vote.

Article XIII

1.   The headquarters of the Commission shall be established at Hobart, Tasmania, Australia.

2.   The Commission shall hold a regular annual meeting. Other meetings shall also be held at the request of one-third of its members and as otherwise provided in this Convention. The first meeting of the Commission shall be held within three months of the entry into force of this Convention, provided that among the Contracting Parties there are at least two States conducting harvesting activities within the area to which this Convention applies. The first meeting shall, in any event, be held within one year of the entry into force of this Convention. The Depositary shall consult with the signatory States regarding the first Commission meeting, taking into account that a broad representation of such States is necessary for the effective operation of the Commission.

3.   The Depositary shall convene the first meeting of the Commission at the headquarters of the Commission. Thereafter, meetings of the Commission shall be held at its headquarters, unless it decides otherwise.

4. The Commission shall elect from among its members a Chairman and Vice-Chairman, each of whom shall serve for a term of two years and shall be eligible for re-election for one additional term. The first Chairman shall, however, be elected for an initial term of three years. The Chairman and Vice-Chairman shall not be representatives of the same Contracting Party.

5. The Commission shall adopt and amend as necessary the rules of procedure for the conduct of its meetings, except with respect to the matters dealt with in Article XII of this Convention.

6. The Commission may establish such subsidiary bodies as are necessary for the performance of its functions.

Article XIV

1. The Contracting Parties hereby establish the Scientific Committee for the Conservation of Antarctic Marine Living Resources (hereinafter referred to as "the Scientific Committee") which shall be a consultative body to the Commission. The Scientific Committee shall normally meet at the headquarters of the Commission unless the Scientific Committee decides otherwise.

2. Each Member of the Commission shall be a member of the Scientific Committee and shall appoint a representative with suitable scientific qualifications who may be accompanied by other experts and advisers.

3. The Scientific Committee may seek the advice of other scientists and experts as may be required on an *ad hoc* basis.

Article XV

1. The Scientific Committee shall provide a forum for consultation and cooperation concerning the collection, study and exchange of information with respect to the marine living resources to which this Convention applies. It shall encourage and promote cooperation in the field of scientific research in order to extend knowledge of the marine living resources of the Antarctic marine ecosystem.

2. The Scientific Committee shall conduct such activities as the Commission may direct in pursuance of the objective of this Convention and shall:

a) establish criteria and methods to be used for determinations concerning the conservation measures referred to in Article IX of this Convention;

b) regularly assess the status and trends of the populations of Antarctic marine living resources;

c) analyse data concerning the direct and indirect effects of harvesting on the populations of Antarctic marine living resources;

d) assess the effects of proposed changes in the methods or levels of harvesting and proposed conservation measures;

e) transmit assessments, analyses, reports and recommendations to the Commission as requested or on its own initiative regarding measures and research to implement the objective of this Convention;

f) formulate proposals for the conduct of international and national programs of research into Antarctic marine living resources.

3. In carrying out its functions, the Scientific Committee shall have regard to the work of other relevant technical and scientific organizations and to the scientific activities conducted within the framework of the Antarctic Treaty.

Article XVI

1. The first meeting of the Scientific Committee shall be held within three months of the first meeting of the Commission. The Scientific Committee shall meet thereafter as often as may be necessary to fulfil its functions.

2. The Scientific Committee shall adopt and amend as necessary its rules of procedure. The rules and any amendments thereto shall be approved by the Commission. The rules shall include procedures for the presentation of minority reports.

3. The Scientific Committee may establish, with the approval of the Commission, such subsidiary bodies as are necessary for the performance of its functions.

Article XVII

1.   The Commission shall appoint an Executive Secretary to serve the Commission and Scientific Committee according to such procedures and on such terms and conditions as the Commission may determine. His term of office shall be for four years and he shall be eligible for re-appointment.

2.   The Commission shall authorize such staff establishment for the Secretariat as may be necessary and the Executive Secretary shall appoint, direct and supervise such staff according to such rules and procedures and on such terms and conditions as the Commission may determine.

3.   The Executive Secretary and Secretariat shall perform the functions entrusted to them by the Commission.

Article XVIII

The official languages of the Commission and of the Scientific Committee shall be English, French, Russian and Spanish.

Article XIX

1.   At each annual meeting, the Commission shall adopt by consensus its budget and the budget of the Scientific Committee.

2.   A draft budget for the Commission and the Scientific Committee and any subsidiary bodies shall be prepared by the Executive Secretary and submitted to the Members of the Commission at least sixty days before the annual meeting of the Commission.

3.   Each Member of the Commission shall contribute to the budget. Until the expiration of five years after the entry into force of this Convention, the contribution of each Member of the Commission shall be equal. Thereafter the contribution shall be determined in accordance with two criteria: the amount harvested and an equal sharing among all Members of the Commission. The Commission shall determine by consensus the proportion in which these two criteria shall apply.

4.   The financial activities of the Commission and Scientific Committee shall be conducted in accordance with financial

regulations adopted by the Commission and shall be subject to an annual audit by external auditors selected by the Commission.

5.   Each Member of the Commission shall meet its own expenses arising from attendance at meetings of the Commission and of the Scientific Committee.

6.   A Member of the Commission that fails to pay its contributions for two consecutive years shall not, during the period of its default, have the right to participate in the taking of decisions in the Commission.

Article XX

1.   The Members of the Commission shall, to the greatest extent possible, provide annually to the Commission and to the Scientific Committee such statistical, biological and other data and information as the Commission and Scientific Committee may require in the exercise of their functions.

2.   The Members of the Commission shall provide, in the manner and at such intervals as may be prescribed, information about their harvesting activities, including fishing areas and vessels, so as to enable reliable catch and effort statistics to be compiled.

3.   The Members of the Commission shall provide to the Commission at such intervals as may be prescribed information on steps taken to implement the conservation measures adopted by the Commission.

4.   The Members of the Commission agree that in any of their harvesting activities, advantage shall be taken of opportunities to collect data needed to assess the impact of harvesting.

Article XXI

1.   Each Contracting Party shall take appropriate measures within its competence to ensure compliance with the provisions of this Convention and with conservation measures adopted by the Commission to which the Party is bound in accordance with Article IX of this Convention.

2.   Each Contracting Party shall transmit to the Commission information on measures taken pursuant to paragraph 1 above, including the imposition of sanctions for any violation.

Article XXII

1.   Each Contracting Party undertakes to exert appropriate efforts, consistent with the Charter of the United Nations, to the end that no one engages in any activity contrary to the objective of this Convention.

2.   Each Contracting Party shall notify the Commission of any such activity which comes to its attention.

Article XXIII

1.   The Commission and the Scientific Committee shall co-operate with the Antarctic Treaty Consultative Parties on matters falling within the competence of the latter.

2.   The Commission and the Scientific Committee shall co-operate, as appropriate, with the Food and Agriculture Organisation of the United Nations and with other Specialised Agencies.

3.   The Commission and the Scientific Committee shall seek to develop cooperative working relationships, as appropriate, with inter-governmental and non-governmental organizations which could contribute to their work, including the Scientific Committee on Antarctic Research, the Scientific Committee on Oceanic Research and the International Whaling Commission.

4.   The Commission may enter into agreements with the organizations referred to in this Article and with other organizations as may be appropriate. The Commission and the Scientific Committee may invite such organizations to send observers to their meetings and to meetings of their subsidiary bodies.

Article XXIV

1.   In order to promote the objective and ensure observance of the provisions of this Convention, the Contracting Parties agree that a system of observation and inspection shall be established.

2.   The system of observation and inspection shall be elaborated by the Commission on the basis of the following principles:

   a) Contracting Parties shall cooperate with each other to ensure the effective implementation of the system of observation and inspection, taking account of the existing international practice. This system shall include, *inter alia,* procedures for boarding and inspection by observers and inspectors designated by the Members of the Commission and procedures for flag state prosecution and sanctions on the basis of evidence resulting from such boarding and inspections. A report of such prosecutions and sanctions imposed shall be included in the information referred to in Article XXI of this Convention;

b) in order to verify compliance with measures adopted under this Convention, observation and inspection shall be carried out on board vessels engaged in scientific research or harvesting of marine living resources in the area to which this Convention applies, through observers and inspectors designated by the Members of the Commission and operating under terms and conditions to be established by the Commission;

c) designated observers and inspectors shall remain subject to the jurisdiction of the Contracting Party of which they are nationals. They shall report to the Member of the Commission by which they have been designated which in turn shall report to the Commission.

3. Pending the establishment of the system of observation and inspection, the Members of the Commission shall seek to establish interim arrangements to designate observers and inspectors and such designated observers and inspectors shall be entitled to carry out inspections in accordance with the principles set out in paragraph 2 above.

Article XXV

1. If any dispute arises between two or more of the Contracting Parties concerning the interpretation or application of this Convention, those Contracting Parties shall consult among themselves with a view to having the dispute resolved by negotiation, inquiry, mediation, conciliation, arbitration, judicial settlement or other peaceful means of their own choice.

2. Any dispute of this character not so resolved shall, with the consent in each case of all Parties to the dispute, be referred for settlement to the International Court of Justice or to arbitration; but failure to reach agreement on reference to the International Court or to arbitration shall not absolve Parties to the dispute from the responsibility of continuing to seek to resolve it by any of the various peaceful means referred to in paragraph 1 above.

3.   In cases where the dispute is referred to arbitration, the arbitral tribunal shall be constituted as provided in the Annex to this Convention.

Article XXVI

1.   This Convention shall be open for signature at Canberra from 1 August to 31 December 1980 by the States participating in the Conference on the Conservation of Antarctic Marine Living Resources held at Canberra from 7 to 20 May 1980.

2.   The States which so sign will be the original signatory States of the Convention.

Article XXVII

1.   This Convention is subject to ratification, acceptance or approval by signatory States.

2.   Instruments of ratification, acceptance or approval shall be deposited with the Government of Australia, hereby designated as the Depositary.

Article XXVIII

1.   This Convention shall enter into force on the thirtieth day following the date of deposit of the eighth instrument of ratification, acceptance or approval by States referred to in paragraph 1 of Article XXVI of this Convention.

2.   With respect to each State or regional economic integration organization which subsequent to the date of entry into force of this Convention deposits an instrument of ratification, acceptance, approval or accession, the Convention shall enter into force on the thirtieth day following such deposit.

Article XXIX

1.   This Convention shall be open for accession by any State interested in research or harvesting activities in relation to the marine living resources to which this Convention applies.

2.   This Convention shall be open for accession by regional economic integration organizations constituted by sovereign States which include among their members one or more States Members

of the Commission and to which the States members of the organization have transferred, in whole or in part, competences with regard to the matters covered by this Convention. The accession of such regional economic integration organizations shall be the subject of consultations among Members of the Commission.

Article XXX

1.   This Convention may be amended at any time.

2.   If one-third of the Members of the Commission request a meeting to discuss a proposed amendment the Depositary shall call such a meeting.

3.   An amendment shall enter into force when the Depositary has received instruments of ratification, acceptance or approval thereof from all the Members of the Commission.

4.   Such amendment shall thereafter enter into force as to any other Contracting Party when notice of ratification, acceptance or approval by it has been received by the Depositary. Any such Contracting Party from which no such notice has been received within a period of one year from the date of entry into force of the amendment in accordance with paragraph 3 above shall be deemed to have withdrawn from this Convention.

Article XXXI

1.   Any Contracting Party may withdraw from this Convention on 30 June of any year, by giving written notice not later than 1 January of the same year to the Depositary, which, upon receipt of such a notice, shall communicate it forthwith to the other Contracting Parties.

2.   Any other Contracting Party may, within sixty days of the receipt of a copy of such a notice from the Depositary, give written notice of withdrawal to the Depositary in which case the Convention shall cease to be in force on 30 June of the same year with respect to the Contracting Party giving such notice.

3.   Withdrawal from this Convention by any Member of the Commission shall not affect its financial obligations under this Convention.

Article XXXII

The Depositary shall notify all Contracting Parties of the following:

> *a)* signatures of this Convention and the deposit of instruments of ratification, acceptance, approval or accession;
>
> *b)* the date of entry into force of this Convention and of any amendment thereto.

Article XXXIII

1. This Convention, of which the English, French, Russian and Spanish texts are equally authentic, shall be deposited with the Government of Australia which shall transmit duly certified copies thereof to all signatory and acceding Parties.

2. This Convention shall be registered by the Depositary pursuant to Article 102 of the Charter of the United Nations.

Drawn up at Canberra this twentieth day of May 1980.

IN WITNESS WHEREOF the undersigned, being duly authorized, have signed this Convention.

ANNEX FOR AN ARBITRAL TRIBUNAL

The arbitral tribunal referred to in paragraph 3 of Article XXV shall be composed of three arbitrators who shall be appointed as follows: The Party commencing proceedings shall communicate the name of an arbitrator to the other Party which, in turn, within a period of forty days following such notification, shall communicate the name of the second arbitrator. The Parties shall, within a period of sixty days following the appointment of the second arbitrator, appoint the third arbitrator, who shall not be a national of either Party and shall not be of the same nationality as either of the first two arbitrators. The third arbitrator shall preside over the tribunal.

If the second arbitrator has not been appointed within the prescribed period, or if the Parties have not reached agreement within the prescribed period on the appointment of the third arbitrator, that arbitrator shall be appointed, at the request of either Party, by the Secretary-General of the Permanent Court of Arbitration, from among persons of international standing not having the nationality of a State which is a Party to this Convention.

The arbitral tribunal shall decide where its headquarters will be located and shall adopt its own rules of procedure. The award of the arbitral tribunal shall be made by a majority of its members, who may not abstain from voting. Any Contracting Party which is not a Party to the dispute may intervene in the proceedings with the consent of the arbitral tribunal. The award of the arbitral tribunal shall be final and binding on all Parties to the dispute and on any Party which intervenes in the proceedings and shall be complied with without delay. The arbitral tribunal shall interpret the award at the request of one of the Parties to the dispute or of any intervening Party. Unless the arbitral tribunal determines otherwise because of the particular circumstances of the case, the expenses of the tribunal, including the remuneration of its members, shall be borne by the Parties to the dispute in equal shares.

DECLARATION INCLUDED IN THE FINAL ACT

The Conference at which the Convention on the Conservation of Antarctic Marine Living Resources was adopted decided to include in the Final Act the following declaration by France concerning the application of the Convention to waters adjacent to Kerguelen and Crozet over which France exercises jurisdiction and to waters adjacent to other islands situated within the field of application of the Convention over which the exercise of State sovereignty is recognised by all of the Parties:

"1.   Measures for the conservation of Antarctic marine living resources of the waters adjacent to Kerguelen and Crozet, over which France has jurisdiction, adopted by France prior to the entry into force of the Convention, would remain in force after the entry into force of the Convention until modified by France acting within the framework of the Commission or otherwise.

2.   After the Convention has come into force, each time the Commission should undertake examination of the conservation needs of the marine living resources of the general area in which the waters adjacent to Kerguelen and Crozet are to be found, it would be open to France either to agree that the waters in question should be included in the area of application of any specific conservation measure under consideration or to indicate that they should be excluded. In the latter event, the Commission would not proceed to

the adoption of the specific conservation measure in a form applicable to the waters in question unless France removed its objection to it. France could also adopt such national measures as it might deem appropriate for the waters in question.

3. Accordingly, when specific conservation measures are considered within the framework of the Commission and with the participation of France, then:

    (a) France would be bound by any conservation measures adopted by consensus with its participation for the duration of those measures. This would not prevent France from promulgating national measures that were more strict than the Commission's measures or which dealt with other matters;

    b) In the absence of consensus, France could promulgate any national measures which it might deem appropriate.

4. Conservation measures, whether national measures or measures adopted by the Commission, in respect of the waters adjacent to Kerguelen and Crozet, would be enforced by France. The system of observation and inspection foreseen by the Convention would not be implemented in the waters adjacent to Kerguelen and Crozet except as agreed by France and in the manner so agreed.

5. The understandings, set forth in paragraphs 1-4 above, regarding the application of the Convention to waters adjacent to the Islands of Kerguelen and Crozet, also apply to waters adjacent to the islands within the area to which this Convention applies over which the existence of State sovereignty is recognized by all Contracting Parties."

No objection to the statement was made.

INDEX